THE SUPREME COURT

AND

Patents and Monopolies

THE SUPREME COURT

AND

Patents and Monopolies

Edited by

PHILIP B. KURLAND

THE UNIVERSITY OF CHICAGO PRESS

CHICAGO AND LONDON

THE UNIVERSITY OF CHICAGO PRESS, CHICAGO 60637
THE UNIVERSITY OF CHICAGO PRESS, LTD., LONDON

ISBN: 0-226-46404-0

TO

MARY AND PHIL

for three decades
of friendship

CONTENTS

PREFACE

Problems of monopoly pervade the history of American law. They have played an important, if often sublimated, role in the decisions of the Supreme Court almost from the beginning. For certainly it was not only the Commerce Clause that was involved in the resolution of the famous *Gibbons* v. *Ogden,* 9 Wheat. 1 (1824), nor only the Fourteenth Amendment that was in issue in *The Slaughter House Cases,* 16 Wall. 36 (1872). The legal monopoly that is conferred by patents and the illegal monopoly that is condemned by the national antitrust laws have provided the Supreme Court with the subject of some of its most noted opinions.

Since the passage of the Sherman Law in 1890, antitrust cases have been treated by the Court as almost on a par in importance with the major constitutional controversies that come before it for resolution. Indeed, antitrust law, like the law of the Constitution, has largely been made by the Court, with the congressional legislation, like the Constitution, affording an excuse for, rather than a guide to, decision. As Mr. Justice Frankfurter once said: "The vagueness of the Sherman Law was saved by imparting to it the gloss of history." *F.T.C.* v. *Motion Picture Advertising Service Co.,* 344 U.S. 392, 405 (1953). The difficulty is that each Justice has read that gloss of history in his own subjective terms.

As Frankfurter saw it: "The concentration of wealth consequent upon the industrial expansion in the post–Civil War era had profound implications for American life. The impact of the abuses resulting from this concentration gradually made itself felt by a rising tide of reform protest in the last decade of the nineteenth century. The Sherman Law was a response to the felt threat to economic freedom created by enormous industrial combines." *United States* v. *U.A.W.,* 352 U.S. 567, 572 (1957). The country, the Congress, and the President may have all shared the Frankfurter reading. But, at least at the beginning, the Supreme Court did not. As Robert Jackson wrote shortly before he became a Justice: "There was judicial supremacy at work subduing the self-preservation impulses of democracy. Regulation or destruction of monopoly was an issue going to the very foundation of our economic system. Popular government demanded a curb on the growing financial and industrial giants. The courts put a curb on the popular will instead." JACKSON, THE STRUGGLE FOR JUDICIAL SUPREMACY 59–60 (1941).

Thurman Arnold once suggested that the American people wanted the façade of trust-busting only to satisfy its conscience, while in fact condoning and fostering the immorality of concentration of economic power. In *The Folklore of Capitalism* 207–08 (1937), he wrote:

> In order to reconcile the ideal with the practical necessity, it became necessary to develop a procedure which constantly attacked bigness on rational legal and economic grounds, and at the same time never really interfered with combinations. Such pressures gave rise to the antitrust laws which appeared to be a complete prohibition of large combinations. The same pressures made the enforcement of the antitrust laws a pure ritual. The effect of this statement of the ideal and its lack of actual enforcement was to convince reformers either that large combinations did not actually exist, or else that if they did exist, they were about to be done away with just as soon as right-thinking men were elected to office. Trust busting therefore became one of the great moral issues of the day, while at the same time great combinations thrived and escaped regulation.

The Court has been the great writer and performer of the ritual. And even when its attitude changed from that which produced the original stultification of the antitrust laws, it could operate only at the molecular and not the molar level. The morality play goes on. And, while any particular defendant may feel the real lash of the Court, judicial decisions are too little and too late to inhibit the gross concentration of American economic power.

Economists have adequately shown that the Court doesn't understand the economic problems brought to it in the antitrust cases that it decides. But then the economists themselves have proved equally ignorant that antitrust principles are not limited to economics, that the claims of society go beyond the monetary measures of efficiency that are the foundations of the economists' conception of a bloodless, inhumane model of the proper nature of the human condition. Nor has the law or any other discipline done better.

Antitrust cases still loom large, if less frequent, on the Supreme Court docket. What Brandeis called the "curse of bigness" is not likely to be diminished much, if at all, through the judicial processes. But the Court has never acknowledged that the problem is "bigness" rather than evil motive, design, or effect. It is not only American business that is elephantoid. It is not only economic power that has been concentrated in the hands of a few. Even if the Court were prepared to play David to Big Business's Goliath, it lacks a slingshot with which to perform its duty. The jawbone of an ass must be wielded by a Samson not a David and the Court is no unshorn Samson. Holmes's analysis has proved stronger than Brandeis's ideal. For it was as long ago as *Vegelahn* v. *Gunther*, 167 Mass. 92, 108 (1896), that Holmes pronounced:

> [I]t is plain from the slightest consideration of practical affairs, or the most superficial reading of industrial history, that free competition means combination, and that the organization of the world, now going on so fast, means an ever increasing might and scope of combination. It seems to me futile to set our faces against this tendency. Whether beneficial on the whole, as I think it, or detrimental, it is inevitable, unless the fundamental axioms of society, and even the fundamental conditions of life, are to be changed.

But it should be remembered that, according to Holmes, the inevitable comes to pass only through effort.

The other side of the monopoly coin is to be found in the patent laws which validate rather than strike down monopoly power. The legality of the patent monopoly has been dependent on proof of both novelty and usefulness. This is not the command of the Constitution, which speaks to patents if not to other monopolies. Article I, § 8, cl. 8 provides only that "Congress shall have Power . . . To promote the Progress of Science and useful Arts, by securing for limited Times to Authors and Inventors the exclusive Rights to their respective Writings and Discoveries." Here, as elsewhere, then, the explanation of the constitutional text has fallen first to Congress and then to the courts, with the Supreme Court as the ultimate arbiter. Here, as elsewhere, it is probably true that the real power rests less with the legislature and the judiciary than with the bureaucracy charged with administering the law.

The subjects of the Court's opinions in this field cover a very wide range from the wireless and the telephone to such mundane matters as the three-sided bar that moves groceries along a checkout counter in a supermarket. It was with regard to the last that Mr. Justice Douglas charged that the power of monopoly granted by the Constitution had been grossly abused. "It is not enough that an article is new and useful. The Constitution never sanctioned the patenting of gadgets. Patents serve a higher end in the advancement of science. An invention need not be as startling as an atomic bomb to be patentable. But it has to be of such quality and distinction that masters of the scientific field in which it falls will regard it as an advance." *A. & P. Tea Co.* v. *Supermarket Equipment Corp.*, 340 U.S. 147, 154–55 (1950).

This was a statement of an ideal that could find no support in the debates of the Federal Convention of 1787 or *The Federalist Papers*. And so, if the "Constitution never sanctioned the patenting of gadgets," neither did it forbid it. With the result that, throughout our history, the courts have not been concerned with the magnitude of the "Discoveries," to use the Constitution's word, but only with even more abstruse standards of invention, such as, *e.g.*, the requirement of a "flash of genius." The law of patents became a highly technical specialty, not confined to lawyers, for members of the patent bar are not required to be admitted to the general practice of law.

The technical facts of the cases have often obscured the fundamental principles in issue. In any event, they have made patent litigation among the least popular of cases among federal judges. Cases have come to be resolved on an ad hoc basis; rationalization has been less important than resolution. The recondite subject matter has resulted in shadowy opinions, the explanation of which has been the function of professional commentators even more than judges.

Patents do not bulk large in the present business of the Supreme Court. It has, for the most part, relegated the resolution of patent controversies to the lower levels of the federal judiciary. There is a respected suggestion that the subject matter be turned over entirely to a specialized court with an expertise in reading diagrams and understanding formulas. And yet the absence of oversight by a court of general jurisdiction might exacerbate rather than relieve the problem that patent claims afford: an excessive amount of litigation and consequent uncertainty in a society that already suffers from too much litigation. And the economic consequences of sustaining the validity of a patent can be enormous.

The articles in this volume are concerned with both facets of the monopoly problem: the antitrust laws and the patent laws. They turn a searchlight on the ratiocinations of the Supreme Court in these areas. The criticism is strong but not harsh. Both the Court and those who are concerned with its work can learn appropriate lessons from the texts that follow.

PHILIP B. KURLAND

EDWARD H. LEVI

THE PARKE, DAVIS-COLGATE

DOCTRINE: THE BAN ON RESALE

PRICE MAINTENANCE

For the last fifty years, the prohibition against resale price maintenance, except when authorized through a combination of federal
and state statutes, has been in conflict with the principle that a seller
may select his own customers, and thus has a right to refuse to deal
with a customer, or to deal with him only on the basis of conditions
specified by the seller. The history of the conflict is found in the
series of cases beginning in 1911 with *Dr. Miles*,[1] and including *Colgate*,[2]
Schrader's Son,[3] *Cudahy*,[4] *Beech-Nut*,[5] and *Bausch & Lomb*.[6] To this
series must now be added *United States v. Parke, Davis & Co.*,[7] in
which the Supreme Court, speaking through Mr. Justice Brennan,
made or accepted a change in the balance between the two competing
principles.

Edward H. Levi is Dean of The Law School and Professor of Law, The University of
Chicago.

[1] Dr. Miles Medical Co. v. John D. Park & Sons, 220 U.S. 373 (1911).

[2] United States v. Colgate & Co., 250 U.S. 300 (1919).

[3] United States v. A. Schrader's Son, 252 U.S. 85 (1920).

[4] Frey & Son, Inc. v. Cudahy Packing Co., 256 U.S. 208 (1921).

[5] F.T.C. v. Beech-Nut Packing Co., 257 U.S. 441 (1922).

[6] United States v. Bausch & Lomb Optical Co., 321 U.S. 707 (1944).

[7] 362 U.S. 29 (1960).

Anti-trust law remains an area of common law: the cases build on and modify each other. The judicial task is to achieve wholeness in the legal structure and to be properly responsive, within the framework of the law, to felt needs. The task is a traditional one, and because so little of the Supreme Court's work involves the exercise of the functions of a common-law court its decisions in this area are of particular interest. A division in the Court, of course, enhances the interest. In *Parke, Davis*, Mr. Justice Brennan spoke for himself and four colleagues; Mr. Justice Stewart concurred only in the judgment; Mr. Justice Harlan, joined by Justices Frankfurter and Whittaker, dissented.

I. The Facts of the Parke, Davis Case

The complaint in *Parke, Davis* alleged a violation of sections one and three of the Sherman Act[8] through a combination and conspiracy of the manufacturer, wholesalers, and retailers to maintain wholesale and retail prices. A "continuing agreement, understanding and concert of action" was specifically alleged.[9] This included an agreement to adhere to wholesale and retail prices, and by the retailers not to advertise the products at prices lower than the fixed prices. An agreement by the defendant and the wholesaler co-conspirators not to sell Parke, Davis products to retailers who sold or advertised below the set prices was also charged. One of the terms of the agreement alleged was that Parke, Davis would "induce, coerce and compel" wholesalers not to sell products to offending retailers. Judge Jackson of the Court of Customs and Patent Appeals, sitting in the District Court for the District of Columbia by designation,[10] granted the motion to dismiss the complaint at the conclusion of the Government's case.[11] Judge Jackson said in his opinion that it was "apparent . . . that defendant had well-established policies concerning the prices at which defendant's products were to be sold by wholesalers and retailers, and the type of retailers to whom the

---

[8] 26 Stat. 209 (1890), as amended, 15 U.S.C. §§ 1 and 3 (1958).

[9] Record, pp. 4–5.

[10] He had also been assigned to sit as one of the three-judge panel in the *Gypsum* case. See United States v. United States Gypsum Co., 53 F. Supp. 889 (D.D.C. 1943), 67 F. Supp. 397 (D.D.C. 1946), *reversed*, 333 U.S. 364 (1948).

[11] 164 F. Supp. 827 (D.D.C. 1958).

wholesalers could re-sell." But "there was no coercion by defendant and no agreement with co-conspirators. . . ." "[R]epresentatives of defendant notified retailers concerning the policy under which its goods must be sold, but the retailers were free either to do without such goods or sell them in accordance with the defendant's policy. . . . Wholesalers were likewise free to refuse to comply and thus risk being cut off by the defendant." Judge Jackson "noted that every visit made by the representatives to the retailers and wholesalers was, to each of them, separate and apart from all others."[12]

The facts in *Parke, Davis* are of importance in measuring the decision; hence they are set out here in some detail.[13] Parke, Davis sold both to wholesalers and retailers; its sales to retailers were at lower quantity prices than wholesalers could offer.[14] While Parke, Davis suggested minimum wholesale and retail prices,[15] it did not have any systematic machinery for maintaining them; that is, it did not regularly "shop" stores, nor maintain card index files with the names of price cutters, nor did it seek and obtain the co-operation of wholesalers and retailers in reporting or policing price deviations.[16] Parke, Davis and its wholesalers had continued, for a short time prior to the summer of 1956, to sell to retailers in the District of Columbia who engaged in minor price cutting.[17] But when substantial price cutting by the Dart Drug Company, a retailer, "demoralized the market," the manager of the Parke, Davis branch office "instructed his assistants and the Company's salesmen to inform the trade in the District of Columbia and Virginia that it was the policy of Parke, Davis not to sell to any retailer who sold Parke, Davis products below suggested minimum prices, and not to sell to any wholesaler who, in turn, sold

---

[12] *Id.* at 829.

[13] The "Findings of Fact" are set out *id.* at 830–35. The quotations in the description of the facts in the text and notes are taken from these findings. See notes 15–27 *infra*.

[14] The sales in question took place in the District of Columbia and Virginia, neither of which had fair trade laws for the periods involved in the litigation.

[15] Finding No. 7.

[16] Finding No. 10.

[17] Finding No. 12. But "[i]n the spring of 1956, Parke, Davis . . . had a policy of refusing to sell to retailers it deemed to be undesirable customers, including those whose failure to maintain suggested minimum retail prices disrupted the market, and of refusing to sell to wholesalers who sold to retailers who were considered undesirable." Finding No. 11.

those products to such a retailer."[18] Five retailers, however, continued to sell the products below the minimum retail price. Parke, Davis then discontinued selling to them and told wholesalers "it would discontinue selling to them also if they sold Parke, Davis products to these retailers."[19] Three wholesalers attempted to stop the sales of the products to these retailers in order not themselves to be cut off.[20]

The Government listed five drug store companies as having participated in the conspiracy. One of these was Peoples Drug Store. Judge Jackson found that the "evidence shows that a representative of Parke, Davis advised a representative of Peoples that Parke, Davis would not sell to that company if it did not observe Parke, Davis' suggested prices. The Peoples' representatives stated that Peoples would stop cutting prices . . . and Parke, Davis continued to sell to Peoples."[21] Another alleged co-conspirator was Babbitt's Cut Rate Drug Store. "[S]ales to Babbitt were curtailed for a period of time and later resumed."[22] Standard Drug Stores was "advised of [the] policy and informed that if it continued to cut prices on Parke, Davis products it would be cut off. . . . It continued to cut prices, and it was cut off for about two weeks."[23] Drug Mart, a group of some thirty independent retail pharmacies, engaged in co-operative advertising and purchasing, was advised "that Parke, Davis would refuse to sell the stores if cut-rate advertising of Parke, Davis products continued, and Drug Mart in fact discontinued such advertising for a period of several months. . . . The evidence shows that each member store of the organization was free to charge whatever prices it wished and to advertise as it wished, regardless of whether there was any joint advertising of Parke, Davis products."[24]

The fifth retailer listed as a co-conspirator was Dart Drug. The findings stated that "Dart Drug was cut off early in July when it continued to sell at cut prices after being advised of the Parke, Davis policy. Sometime later in July, and again in the later part of August,

18 Finding No. 12.
19 Finding No. 13.
20 Finding No. 14.
21 Finding No. 19.
22 Finding No. 20.
23 Finding No. 21.

24 Finding No. 22. "There is evidence that one reason for Drug Mart's discontinuing this advertising was that Parke, Davis advised the organization that it was treating as a discount item certain resale premiums which, under Parke, Davis' sales policies were required to be paid to sales personnel in the various stores, and the buyer for Drug Mart felt he was not interested in promoting Parke, Davis' goods if he could not treat these payments as a discount." *Ibid.*

Parke, Davis' representatives advised Dart Drug that, if that concern advertised Parke, Davis products at cut prices, Parke, Davis would not sell to it, but that if it did not advertise such cut prices, Parke, Davis would sell to it. Dart Drug ceased advertising Parke, Davis' products for a period of two weeks in July, and during this time purchased from Parke, Davis. . . . Parke, Davis again commenced selling to Dart Drug in August when Dart Drug ceased advertising and continued to do so after Dart resumed advertising two months thereafter. At all times, Dart Drug sold Parke, Davis' products at cut prices in its store, whether or not it was advertising them."[25]

The "no agreement" refrain ran throughout the findings. No agreement was solicited, and no "agreement or understanding of any kind" was made with Peoples concerning prices or advertising; nor with Babbitt, Standard Drug, Drug Mart, or Dart Drug. So far as the wholesalers were concerned. "The evidence shows that the wholesalers were familiar with Parke, Davis' policies . . . and had for many years . . . observed Parke, Davis' suggested minimum resale prices because . . . they desired to continue as customers of Parke, Davis. There is no evidence that any of them made any agreement with Parke, Davis as to prices or that Parke, Davis ever solicited an agreement from any of them as to this matter."[26] And there was no evidence that "Parke, Davis ever conferred or discussed its sales policies with more than one wholesaler or more than one retailer at a time, nor that it made the enforcement of its policies as to any one wholesaler or retailer dependent upon the action of any other wholesaler or retailer."[27] Indeed, in his conclusions of law Judge Jackson stated that "Parke, Davis did not combine, conspire, or enter into an agree-

---

[25] Finding No. 23. There were also findings relevant to the scope and effect of the particular price maintenance enforcement activities of the defendant. These activities took place in the period from July through the autumn of 1956, when "Parke, Davis in good faith abandoned and discontinued its efforts to maintain minimum resale prices . . . through refusals to sell." Finding No. 27. "Parke, Davis' sales constitute less than 5% of the sales of pharmaceutical products in the District of Columbia and Richmond, Virginia. There are about 2,000 different drug manufacturers selling about 178,000 different drug items in the District of Columbia." Finding No. 3. "No evidence was introduced to show that the discontinuance of advertising by a few retailers for a short period of time had any effect whatsoever on the prices charged to the public for Parke, Davis & Company products." Finding No. 25.

[26] Finding No. 28.

[27] Finding No. 31.

ment, understanding or concert of action with the alleged co-conspirators or anyone else . . ." on any relevant phase of the case.[28]

The type of problem inherent in the evidence and findings may be
seen in the testimony of the Vice-President of District Wholesale
Drug (one of the wholesalers who, it was claimed, was induced,
coerced, or compelled by the defendants not to sell to price-cutting
retailers):

> Q. Do you recall now, Mr. Levin, the precise words you used
> when you spoke to the three Parke, Davis representatives after
> they first visited your office?
> A. The precise words I used?
>
> . . . .
>
> Q. When they came and asked you not to sell to certain of these
> retailers?
> A. Yes. The one thing that did concern me, I specifically asked
> them if we were the only wholesalers who would have that request
> made. And they said no, they were visiting all three local whole-
> salers. And I said, "Well if that is the case, I will go along with
> whatever you suggest."[29]

The assistant branch manager of the Baltimore branch of Parke, Davis
testified as to his conversation with Mr. Haft, the proprietor of Dart
Drug:

> Q. Isn't it true that sometime toward the middle of July, after
> he had been cut off for a period of approximately two weeks, he
> told you he would like to conform with your policy if you would
> again ship to him?
> A. Yes.
> Q. And he told you, if you would ship to him, he would agree
> not to cut your prices in ads in the newspapers?
> A. Well, I did not ask Mr. Haft to agree to anything.
> Q. I am not using that as a nasty word, Mr. Powers. The sub-
> stance of the conversation was, sir, was it not, that, if you would
> sell to him, he would stop advertising?
> A. That is correct.
> Q. And you agreed to do this, did you not?
> A. I told him that if he wanted to go along and play the game
> regularly and play the game according to the rules, we would be
> glad to ship him.

---

[28] 164 F. Supp. at 835–36.

[29] Record, p. 202.

Q. And he said he would?
A. That is right.[30]

Mr. Haft testified that Mr. Dripps, a sales manager for Parke, Davis, and Mr. Powers, the assistant branch manager, had a conversation with him as follows: "We had a discussion of a nature that they had gotten Standard Drug, Babbitt, Tates, Peoples and all the rest of the retailers back in line as far as in reference to advertising and window displays on Parke, Davis items."[31]

These few excerpts, of course, provide no basis whatsoever for an independent evaluation of the evidence, even if that were relevant or proper. The defendant's brief before the Supreme Court made the point with respect to the testimony of the Vice-President of District Wholesale Drug, who testified that he had said he "would go along with whatever you suggest," that both he and the president of his company, "who actually made the decision to cease selling to the retailers, . . . stated that the basis of that decision was simply the knowledge that unless the company cut off the retailers' purchases of Parke, Davis products, it would itself be cut off by Parke, Davis. . . ."[32] In connection with Haft's testimony, the brief argued that the "evidence indicates that Haft instigated the present suit . . . , that he had consulted his lawyer with regard to the possibility of bringing a treble damage action . . . and that he was attempting in his dealings with Parke, Davis to lay a foundation for such a suit," and in other respects it questioned the weight to be given to his testimony.[33] The brief commented: "The Government also places a great emphasis upon statements of some of its witnesses to the effect that they did 'go along with PD' or 'agreed to abide by PD's policy.' . . . The crux of the matter is not whether the witness used the word 'agreed' or a similar term; rather it is whether Parke, Davis sought to obtain an agreement with its customers rather than merely to inform them of its policy and the action the Company proposed to take."[34] And in a footnote the brief asserted, "The Government is at pains to ridicule the testimony of a number of witnesses to the effect that they did not enter into any 'agreement' with Parke, Davis, contending in effect that it is not the use of the word 'agree' that determines whether a

---

[30] *Id.* at 224–25.

[31] *Id.* at 74.

[32] Brief for Appellee, p. 39.

[33] *Id.* at 32.

[34] *Id.* at 56–57.

conspiracy is formed, but the nature of the participants' conduct. . . . The Government's contention on this point is belied by its own excessive reliance, both here and in the court below, on the use of the word 'agree.' "[35] But, the brief went on to say, Parke, Davis agreed fully that the critical question was not the specific words but the nature of the events.

So far as the relationship between the evidence and the law was concerned, the defendant's brief put the issues in this way:

> Whether an agreement or conspiracy existed depends upon facts and cannot be resolved by name calling. . . . To be sure, Parke, Davis announced its policy generally to all customers in advance, but its right to do so was expressly recognized in *Colgate* and subsequent cases. To be sure, customers who had been cut off wanted to be reinstated and Parke, Davis was thus obliged to reiterate its policy and explain that customers who cut prices would not be sold. . . . Nor does it change matters to characterize the recognition of this policy by some customers as "forced cooperation." This Court held very explicitly in *Frey & Son, Inc. v. Cudahy Packing Co.* . . . , that adopting a policy of refusals to sell, calling the attention of customers to this policy and the customers' acquiescence in it are not sufficient to establish a violation of the Sherman Act. . . . The Government seeks to attach the label "concerted action" to Parke, Davis' dealings with the retailers on the subject of prices by emphasizing the concern of some of the retailers for what their competitors were doing. But the fact that a businessman is concerned about what his competitors are doing, and governs his behavior in part according to theirs, does not of itself give rise to an inference of conspiracy. . . . Similarly, the facts that no retailer was willing to cease advertising until he thought his competitors were doing the same, and that each was determined to advertise as soon as anyone else did, merely show normal, predictable, competitive behavior to be expected from sensible businessmen, and give rise to no inference of deliberately concerted action. . . . The situation as to wholesalers is the same: although one wholesaler, concerned about its competitors, twice asked Parke, Davis representatives whether other wholesalers were also being informed of the policy. . . . It was clear at all times that Parke, Davis' policy was applicable to each wholesaler separately, whether or not retailers or other wholesalers responded to the policy . . . as at least one wholesaler, in fact, did not. . . .[36]

---

[35] *Id.* at 56, n. 36.

[36] *Id.* at 54–56.

In granting the motion to dismiss, Judge Jackson proceeded on the ground that "the actions of defendants were properly unilateral and sanctioned by law under the doctrine laid down in the case of United States v. Colgate Co. . . . That doctrine continues to be the law."[37]

The *Colgate* doctrine, in the language of Mr. Justice McReynolds, was that "in the absence of any purpose to create or maintain a monopoly, the [Sherman] act does not restrict the long-recognized right of trader or manufacturer engaged in an entirely private business, freely to exercise his own independent discretion as to parties with whom he will deal. And, of course, he may announce in advance the circumstances under which he will refuse to sell."[38] The Supreme Court did not agree with Judge Jackson that *Parke, Davis* fell within the *Colgate* doctrine; it reversed and remanded.

II. THE JUDICIAL HISTORY BEHIND THE DR. MILES– COLGATE DOCTRINE

The problems of and decisions on resale price maintenance run as a central theme through the history of anti-trust law. The relationship between the law of resale price maintenance and other anti-trust doctrines is one of intricate interaction. Important doctrines were still in the process of crucial evolution at the time *Dr. Miles* was decided in 1911 and *Colgate* in 1919, and this evolution was to continue. Resale price cases must be viewed against this background. During the period controlled by *Dr. Miles* and *Colgate* there was a particular consciousness that the underlying law of restraint of trade had been changing. The *Nordenfelt*[39] decision by the House of Lords, before the turn of the century, was one important indication of change. Mr. Chief Justice White in *Standard Oil*,[40] decided just one month after *Dr. Miles*, stressed the evolutionary nature of the basic concept. The

---

[37] 164 F. Supp. at 829. An additional reason for the judgment was that the allegedly unlawful conditions no longer existed. This was the main thrust of Judge Jackson's oral ruling. See Record, p. 300. His reliance on *Colgate* was similar to the position taken by Judge Tamm in a companion criminal case. See United States v. Parke, Davis & Co., CCH Trade Reg. Dec. ¶ 68,856 (D.D.C. 1957).

[38] 250 U.S. at 307.

[39] Nordenfelt v. Maxim Nordenfelt Guns & Ammunition Co., Ltd. [1894] A. C. 535 (H.L.).

[40] Standard Oil Co. of New Jersey v. United States, 221 U.S. 1 (1911).

frequent citation of such cases as *Horner v. Graves*,[41] *Oregon Steam Navigation Co. v. Winsor*,[42] and *Diamond Match Co. v. Roeber*[43] reflected the thought of bench and bar that restraints at one time unlawful, albeit perhaps a long time ago, might now be considered partial and reasonable, even though price fixing or resale price restriction was involved. Mr. Chief Justice Holmes of the Supreme Judicial Court of Massachusetts in *Garst v. Harris*,[44] in 1900, had sustained the right of a manufacturer to collect liquidated damages from a purchaser who had violated the stipulated price. So far as the restraint of trade aspect was concerned, Mr. Chief Justice Holmes stated that "some limits were set to the inherited doctrine on this subject by the recent case of *Anchor Electric Co. v. Hawkes*,"[45] which approved restrictive agreements by sellers of a business not to compete with the purchaser for five years, and which proclaimed that "arbitrary rules . . . have thus been made to yield to changed conditions. . . ."[46] Consciousness of a malleable background gave added strength to arguments justifying restraints.

Open Issues at the Time of the Colgate Case. One question, still open when *Dr. Miles* and *Colgate* were decided, was whether price-fixing agreements might be lawful because reasonable. In 1889, in *Fowle v. Park*,[47] the Supreme Court, speaking through Mr. Chief Justice Fuller, had found an agreement dividing territories and fixing prices to be enforceable where a secret medicinal preparation was involved. The restraints were limited as to the geographic area within which they were to operate. The Court was "unable to perceive how they could be regarded as so unreasonable as to justify the Court in declining to. enforce them."[48] Despite the *Joint Traffic*,[49] *Trans-Missouri*,[50]

---

[41] 7 Bing. 735, 131 Eng. Rep. 284 (C.P. 1831).

[42] 20 Wall. 64 (1873).

[43] 106 N.Y. 473 (1887).

[44] 177 Mass. 72 (1900).

[45] *Id*. at 74. The *Anchor Electric* case is reported at 171 Mass. 101 (1898).

[46] 171 Mass. at 106.

[47] 131 U.S. 88 (1889).

[48] *Id*. at 97.

[49] United States v. Joint Traffic Ass'n, 171 U.S. 505 (1898).

[50] United States v. Trans-Missouri Freight Ass'n, 166 U.S. 290 (1897).

and *Addyston*[51] cases, the problem of the legality of "reasonable" price-fixing agreements remained undecided until Mr. Justice Stone's opinion in 1927 in *Trenton Potteries*.[52] And *Trenton Potteries* did not come until after the cluster of resale price cases which began with *Colgate* in 1919. The unresolved nature of the question when *Colgate* was decided is underscored by the 1918 *Board of Trade*[53] decision, where Mr. Justice Brandeis, speaking for the Court, strongly implied that some price fixing might be reasonable and lawful. In his opinion in *Trenton Potteries*, Mr. Justice Stone relied to a considerable extent for his conclusion of illegality without regard to reasonableness on *Dr. Miles* and other resale price cases;[54] *Dr. Miles* in turn had relied on the assumed rule of illegality of horizontal price arrangements.

The related question whether market control was an indispensable ingredient of the illegality of price fixing was still unsettled in 1919, and remained so even after *Trenton Potteries*. Indeed, the vitality of that question was demonstrated as late as 1933 in *Appalachian Coals*.[55] In 1895, in the *Dueber Watch* case,[56] the Court of Appeals for

---

[51] United States v. Addyston Pipe & Steel Co. 85 Fed. 271 (6th Cir. 1898), *affirmed*, 175 U.S. 211 (1899).

[52] United States v. Trenton Potteries Co., 273 U.S. 392 (1927).

[53] Board of Trade of the City of Chicago v. United States, 246 U.S. 231 (1918).

[54] In United States v. Trenton Potteries, 273 U.S. 392, 399–401 (1927), Mr. Justice Stone said: "In *Dr. Miles* . . . contracts fixing reasonable resale prices were declared unenforceable upon the authority of cases involving price-fixing arrangements between competitors. . . . In the second circuit the view maintained below that the reasonableness or unreasonableness of the prices fixed must be submitted to the jury has apparently been abandoned. . . . While not necessarily controlling, the decisions of this Court denying the validity of resale price agreements, regardless of the reasonableness of the price, are persuasive." In the Second Circuit case referred to by Mr. Justice Stone, Live Poultry Dealers' Protective Ass'n v. United States, 4 F. 2d 840, 842–43 (2d Cir. 1924), Judge Learned Hand had written: ". . . it is somewhat surprising at this day to hear it suggested that a frank agreement to fix prices and prevent competition as regards them among one-half the buyers in a given market may be defended, on the notion that the results are economically desirable. . . . The suggestion is that, since *Standard Oil* . . . such a combination may be justified. . . . That might be the law, but we do not so understand it. In numerous instances since that case the Supreme Court has held that such a combination is unlawful of itself. . . . Indeed, many of them were cases where the manufacturer of a product in which he had a natural or legal monopoly attempted to control its resale prices, a weaker case than this at bar."

[55] Appalachian Coals, Inc. v. United States, 288 U.S. 344 (1933).

[56] Dueber Watch-Case Mfg. Co. v. E. Howard Watch & Clock Co., 66 Fed. 637 (2d Cir. 1895).

the Second Circuit, each of the three judges going his own way, held that a treble-damage action would not lie against manufacturers of watchcases who had combined to fix prices. In order to force the plaintiff manufacturer to join with them in fixing prices, the defendants had refused to sell to dealers who bought from the plaintiff. Judge Lacombe emphasized that the goods were not of prime necessity; it was difficult to see how the public would be affected by a combination, for if the price were too high the public would buy from their competitors. There was nothing to show that all or substantially all of the manufacturers of watchcases in the United States or even in a single state were included; they might represent only a small part of the watchcase industry. The view that a distinction should be drawn in price-fixing cases between common articles and those of prime or public necessity was criticized in *Addyston* three years later by Judge Taft, speaking for a court that included Judges Harlan and Lurton, because it furnished "another opportunity for courts to give effect to the varying economical opinions of its individual members."[57] But emphasis on this distinction between necessaries and "common articles" kept appearing. It is to be found, for example, in Mr. Justice Holmes's dissent in *Dr. Miles*.[58] Traces of the argument that, monopoly aside, legally unenforceable price agreements involving no coercion may not be illegal can be found in the *Joint Traffic* case,[59] in Mr. Justice Holmes's dissent in *Northern Securities*,[60] and in *American Column*.[61]

Despite *Montague & Co. v. Lowry*[62] in 1904, the scope of the doctrine of illegality of collective refusals to deal, or boycott, had not been determined when *Dr. Miles* or *Colgate* were decided. Again there were then important open questions concerning the relevance of market control or reasonableness. The relevance of the law of boycott, or of collective refusals to deal, to resale price maintenance is close. For example, the doctrine gives added significance to the inclusion of retailers as well as wholesalers in a resale price arrangement, for if the wholesaler may not deal with recalcitrant retailers, in modern eyes

---

[57] 85 Fed. at 286–87.

[58] 220 U.S. at 412.   [59] 171 U.S. 505 (1898).

[60] Northern Securities Co. v. United States, 193 U.S. 197, 400 (1904).

[61] American Column & Lumber Co. v. United States, 257 U.S. 377, 412 (1921).

[62] 193 U.S. 38 (1904).

the manufacturer may have organized a boycott illegal in itself. This growth of doctrine thus helped to make of *Bausch & Lomb*[63] in 1944 a case somewhat different from its resale predecessors of more than twenty years earlier, which necessarily had been decided without the benefit of *Fashion Originators' Guild*.[64] That case almost made any organized collective refusal to deal unlawful without regard to reasonableness. The strong emergence of the doctrine of concert of action, important both for collective refusals to deal and price-agreement cases, came twenty years after the *Colgate* case. Resale price proposals, observed by numerous dealers each aware of collective participation, take on a new, although perhaps not decisive, aspect under the impact of this doctrine.

Restraints on Alienation. Resale price cases involve patents, copyrights, trade-marks or brands, or secret processes. These are important as providing reinforcing answers to the two questions involved in all of the cases. The first question is by what right the manufacturer asserts his continuing interest in the commodity; the second is through what means does he remove his restriction from the general law of restraint of trade, or make it appear more reasonable within the terms of the law. Here the patent holder for many years held the more protected position. "Within his domain, the patentee is czar," Judge Baker wrote in a much-quoted phrase intended to explain why, in the *Victor Talking Machine* case[65] in 1903, an action for infringement would lie against a remote purchaser for selling patented machines at a price below the minimum set in a license notice. The assumed strength of the patentee's position naturally led proponents of resale price agreements in non-patent cases to lean heavily on the patent analogy. When Judge Lurton wrote the opinion for the Court of Appeals in *John D. Park & Sons v. Hartman*[66] in 1907 and in the closely related *Dr. Miles* case[67] in 1908, he thought these cases turned on whether there was an identity of character between the statutory monopoly of articles made under a valid patent or copyright and articles made according to some private formula. Previously, in *Bobbs-*

---

[63] 321 U.S. 707 (1944).

[64] Fashion Originators' Guild of America v. F.T.C., 312 U.S. 457 (1941).

[65] Victor Talking Machine Co. v. The Fair, 123 Fed. 424, 426 (7th Cir. 1903).

[66] 153 Fed. 24 (6th Cir. 1907).

[67] 164 Fed. 803 (6th Cir. 1908), *affirmed*, 220 U.S. 373 (1911).

Merrill,[68] the court of appeals in 1906, and the Supreme Court in 1908, had held resale price maintenance unenforceable where it was attempted under a copyright through notice of the restriction to a remote purchaser. Nevertheless, Judge Lurton thought "the statutory right to exclusively publish and vend copies of a copyrighted production would seem to take direct contracts between the publisher and his vendees in respect to the price at which subsequent sales shall be made outside of the rule as to restraints of trade. . . ."[69] There were, he recognized, wide differences between copyrights and patents.[70] It was well settled, he thought, that articles made under patents may be the subject of contracts by which their use and price on resale could be controlled by the patentee. This was shown by the *Peninsular Button Fastener* case[71] in which he had written the opinion, and such cases as *Victor Talking Machine*[72] and *Bement v. National Harrow Co.*[73] It would be shown also by *Henry v. A. B. Dick Co.*,[74] where Mr. Justice Lurton spoke for the Supreme Court. But then through *Bauer & Cie*[75] in 1913, *Straus v. Victor Talking Machine Co.*[76] and *Motion Pictures Patents*[77] in 1917, and finally in the *Boston Store* case,[78] the patentee lost

---

[68] Bobbs-Merrill Co. v. Straus, 147 Fed. 15 (2d Cir. 1906), *affirmed*, 210 U.S. 339 (1908).

[69] 153 Fed. at 29.

[70] Judge George Ray was the trial judge in Bobbs-Merrill Co. v. Straus, 139 Fed. 155 (C.C.S.D. N.Y. 1905); Scribner v. Straus, 139 Fed. 193 (C.C.S.D. N.Y. 1905); Cortelyou v. Charles E. Johnson Co., 138 Fed. 110 (C.C.S.D. N.Y. 1905); A. B. Dick & Co. v. Henry, 149 Fed. 424 (C.C.S.D. N.Y. 1907). As these cases show, his construction of the meaning of a notice differed markedly depending on whether a copyright or a patent was invoi ed.

[71] Heaton-Peninsular Button-Fastener Co. v. Eureka Specialty Co., 77 Fed. 288 (6th Cir. 1896).

[72] 123 Fed. 424 (7th Cir. 1903).

[73] 186 U.S. 70 (1902).   [74] 224 U.S. 1 (1912).

[75] Bauer & Cie v. O'Donnell, 229 U.S. 1 (1913).

[76] 243 U.S. 490 (1917).

[77] Motion Picture Patents Co. v. Universal Film Mfg. Co., 243 U.S. 502 (1917).

[78] Boston Store of Chicago v. American Graphophone Co., 246 U.S. 8 (1918). Earlier patent cases drew a distinction between the purchase of the right to use and the purchase of the right to make and vend, in an effort to avoid the widespread effect which curtailing the right of use would have on purchasers of patented items. These were not resale price cases. Wilson v. Rousseau, 4 How. 645 (1846); Bloomer v. McQuewan, 14 How. 539 (1852); *cf.* Evans v. Jordan & Morehead, 9 Cranch 199 (1815). In Mitchell v. Hawley, 16 Wall. 544 (1872), the purchaser of patented machines was enjoined from their continued operation during the new term of the patent. The purchaser had bought the machines from a licensee given the right "to make and use and to license to others the right to use," but

most, although not all, of his preferred position. Beginning with situations in which the restriction was imposed on remote vendees, and proceeding to a more direct relationship, the interest of the patentee

---

with the limitation that the licensee could not "dispose of, sell or grant any license to use" beyond the original period. *Id.* at 545. In Adams v. Burke, 17 Wall. 453 (1873), an undertaker, who had bought patented coffin lids from manufacturers having only the right to make, use, and vend within a ten-mile radius of Boston, was found to have the right to use these lids outside the radius. The essential nature of things, the Court said, indicated that when a patentee sells a machine "whose sole value is in its use" and "receives the consideration for its use . . . he parts with the right to restrict that use. The article, in the language of [*Bloomer v. McQuewan*], passes without the limit of the monopoly." *Id.* at 456. Mr. Justice Black, dissenting in General Talking Pictures Corp. v. Western Electric Co., 305 U.S. 124 (1938), in which Mr. Justice Brandeis for the majority had relied on *Mitchell v. Hawley, supra,* as authority for a restrictive license, sought to explain the validity of the restriction in *Mitchell v. Hawley* on the ground that there the licensee only had been given the right to make and use; the patentee's power to vend had not been transferred and exercised. In later cases, such as United States v. Masonite Corp., 316 U.S. 265 (1942), the exercise of the right to vend by the patentee is taken as determinative that the patentee may no longer continue his control. This is a reflection of the "adequate compensation" theme presented as far back as *Bloomer v. McQuewan.* See also United States v. General Electric Co., 272 U.S. 476, 486, 490, 494 (1926).

The defendant's brief in the Supreme Court in United States v. A. Schrader's Son, 252 U.S. 85 (1920), attempted to justify the resale price maintenance there on the basis of the patents. "It will be observed that the royalties under the agreements . . . are in addition to the initial price and are not payable unless and until the goods have been used or sold by the defendant's vendees and that the percentage of the resale price which defendant is to receive is based on the amount of the resale price which the vendee *actually receives.* . . ." Brief for Appellee, pp. 21–23. The brief seeks to distinguish prior copyright and patent cases where resale price maintenance failed on the point that in each case the manufacturer had received adequate compensation. Thus, from *Bobbs-Merrill,* the brief quotes: "The facts disclose a sale of a book at wholesale . . . at a satisfactory price. . . ." 210 U.S. at 343. From *Dr. Miles:* "The complainant having sold its products at a price satisfactory to itself. . . ." 220 U.S. at 409. From *Bauer & Cie:* ". . . such article being in the hands of a retailer by purchase from a jobber who has paid to the agent of the patentee the full price asked for the article sold." 229 U.S. at 11. From *Straus v. Victor Talking Machine Co.:* ". . . the plaintiff makes sure, that the future shall have no risks, for it requires that all that it asked or expects at any time to receive for each machine must be paid in full. . . ." 243 U.S. at 498. From *Motion Pictures Patents:* "It is admitted . . . when sold it was fully paid for. . . ." 243 U.S. at 507. From *Boston Store:* "Can a patentee, in connection with the act of delivering his patented article to another for a gross consideration then received, lawfully reserve by contract a part of his monopoly right to sell?" 246 U.S. at 27.

The reward theme is reflected in Ethyl Gasoline Corp. v. United States, 309 U.S. 436, 459 (1940) ("It has chosen to exploit its patents by manufacturing the fluid covered by them and by selling that fluid to refiners for use in the manufacture of motor fuel."); and in *Masonite,* 316 U.S. at 278 ("The test has been whether or not there has been such a disposition of the article that it may fairly be said that the patentee has received his reward for the use of the article.").

was said to cease when he had sold the article and received full compensation for it. Attempted conditions under patents or copyrights, imposed by notice and threat of infringement actions, were thought to constitute restraints on alienation or qualifications of title more clearly even than would contractual limitations; hence these restrictions were regarded as more vulnerable than contract restrictions once the preferred position for patent or copyright appeared to have been removed.

But, functionally, resale price maintenance was much the same, whether involving patents or copyrights or secret processes covered by brand marks. Mr. Louis D. Brandeis, when he took to *Harper's Weekly* in 1913 to lament the lack of control over cutthroat prices—"the most potent weapon of monopoly"—treated cases dealing with each of the three areas as significant defeats.[79] The pervasive argument for resale price maintenance gained its greatest support in the patent field, but it was advanced across the board. One argument unifies the cases and suggests the propinquity of the subject to the right to refuse to deal. It is that the manufacturer, since he may refuse to sell altogether, should be allowed to take the lesser step of selling upon restriction. The argument appears in Mr. Justice Holmes's dissent in *Beech-Nut*. The restriction may hinder competition from those who purchase from him, but "I cannot see," he wrote, "what that policy has to do with a subject-matter that comes from a single hand that is admitted to be free to shut as closely as it will."[80]

In considering the theories for the enforceability or legality of resale price agreements, form and circumstance make a difference. The restriction may be on a purchaser in privity with the manufacturer who imposed it; it may be on a remote vendee. In the latter event, the restriction, if it is to be enforced, may raise the question whether it runs with the chattel. In any event, the restriction appears to be greater as the vendee becomes more remote from the manufacturer. Where remote vendees are involved, notice of the restriction becomes important, as a matter of fairness, or perhaps as suggesting an implied contract, or as providing the means for the downward reach, when allowed, of some government-granted monopoly. The restrictions might involve horizontal collaboration among manufacturers or

---

[79] *Competition that Kills*, in BRANDEIS, BUSINESS—A PROFESSION 236, 254 (1914).

[80] 257 U.S. at 457.

distributors, on all or only part of a market, and possibly be combined with other arrangements, as, for example, an exclusive agreement preventing the sale of a competitor's goods. Protection for the agreement may be urged not only against parties to it but against those who may be said to have fraudulently induced its breach. Mr. Justice Holmes, in his dissent in *Dr. Miles*,[81] refers to *Garst v. Harris*[82] and *Garst v. Charles*,[83] decided by the Massachusetts Supreme Court. In *Garst v. Charles*, decided after Mr. Justice Holmes had gone to the Supreme Court of the United States, the Massachusetts court protected a resale price agreement against a purchaser from a purchaser on the ground that this was "a conspiracy to deprive one of the benefit of a contract with another. . . . The defendant was a party to this scheme of fraud, and presumably was the author of it."[84] Holmes did not cite *Garst v. Hall & Lyon Co.*,[85] in which he had participated, and in which an unsuccessful attempt was made to enforce a resale price against a retailer who had made no contract with the manufacturer. The retailer had not bought the article directly from the wholesaler who received with it the restriction, stated on the box, from the manufacturer. "The purchaser from a purchaser," the Court said, "has an absolute right to dispose of the property."[86]

The question whether conditions may run with goods as a type of negative easement or whether this kind of qualification of title is a

---

[81] 220 U.S. at 413.

[82] 177 Mass. 72 (1900).   [83] 187 Mass. 144 (1905).

[84] *Id.* at 149–50. Sir Frederick Pollock wrote Mr. Justice Holmes on May 3, 1911: "Either your dissenting opinion in the Miles Medical Co.'s case is right or much of our recent authority here is wrong." 1 HOLMES-POLLOCK LETTERS 178 (Howe ed. 1942). In his *Dr. Miles* dissent, 220 U.S. at 413, Mr. Justice Holmes wrote: "I think that my view prevails in England," citing Elliman, Sons & Co. v. Carrington & Son, Ltd. [1901] 2 Ch. 275. Judge Lurton, in John D. Park & Sons v. Hartman, 153 Fed. 24, 43 (6th Cir. 1907), had written: "A general system of contracts, such as that which the complainant seeks to enforce and which the bill avers is a method generally adopted in his line of business, involves very different questions from those which arise when a single contract only is involved and when the action is between the contracting parties for a breach, as was the case in Garst v. Harris [note 82 *supra*] and Elliman v. Carrington [*supra*]." Mr. Justice Holmes, in *Dr. Miles*, also put to one side the combination cases "entered into with intent to exclude others from a business naturally open to them, and we unhappily have become familiar with the methods by which they are carried out." 220 U.S. at 413. At this point he cited Jayne v. Loder, 149 Fed. 21 (3d Cir. 1906), where, upon suit by an "aggressive price cutter," a combination among proprietary companies, wholesale druggists, and retail druggists was held unlawful.

[85] 179 Mass. 588 (1901).   [86] *Id.* at 591.

fatal restriction on alienation is in the background of the resale price cases. Mr. Justice Hughes, whose opinion in *Dr. Miles* relied heavily on Judge Lurton's opinion in *Park v. Hartman*,[87] buttressed the argument against the enforceability of the restrictions with a much used quotation from *Coke on Littleton*:[88] "If a man be possessed of a horse or of any other chattel, real or personal, and give his whole interest or property therein upon condition that the donee or vendee shall not alien the same, the same is void, because his whole interest and property is out of him, so as he hath no possibility of a reverter; and it is against trade and traffic and bargaining and contracting between man and man."[89] Professor Chafee was critical of the reliance on this quotation. "It does seem possible," he wrote, "that the nineteenth and twentieth centuries have contributed legal conceptions growing out of new types of business which make it inappropriate for Justices Lurton and Hughes to base their sweeping overthrow of contemporary commercial policies on judicial views of the reign of Queen Elizabeth."[90]

There are, in any event, some contrary quotations indicating that under special circumstances, of which *Garst v. Charles* is an example but *Board of Trade v. Christie*[91] is a better one,[92] conditions may attach, whether or not they strictly run with the goods. One such statement is by Lord Justice Knight Bruce in *De Mattos v. Gibson*,[93] a

---

[87] See text *supra*, at note 66.

[88] The quotation is from § 360 of 2 COKE ON LITTLETON, as quoted by the Supreme Court in *Dr. Miles*, 220 U.S. at 404–5, taken from Judge Lurton's decision in the *Park* case, 153 Fed. at 39.

[89] Defendant's Brief on the Merits, in *A. Schrader's Son*, 252 U.S. 85 (1920), comments, p. 26: "Lord Coke, however, did not say that it is unlawful for a man who is possessed of a chattel to sell the same on the condition that it shall be resold by the vendee at not less than a certain price and that a percentage of such resale price shall be paid over to the vendor by his vendee after the resale is made."

Much quoted also was the language of Swinfen Eady, J., in Taddy & Co. v. Sterious & Co. [1904] 1 Ch. 354, 358: "Conditions of this kind do not run with the goods, and cannot be imposed upon them." See also McGruther v. Pitcher, [1904] 2 Ch. 306.

[90] Chafee, *Equitable Servitudes on Chattels*, 41 HARV. L. REV. 945, 983 (1928).

[91] 198 U.S. 236 (1905).

[92] See also Murphy v. Christian Press Ass'n Pub. Co., 38 App. Div. 426 (N.Y. 2d Dept. 1899); Capitol Records, Inc. v. Mercury Records Corp., 221 F. 2d 657 (2d Cir. 1955).

[93] 4 de G. & J. 276, 282, 45 Eng. Rep. 108, 110 (Ch. 1859): "Reason and justice seem to prescribe that, at least as a general rule, where a man, by gift or purchase, acquires property from another, with knowledge of a previous contract, lawfully and for valuable con-

typical nineteenth-century pronouncement of a general standard concerning reason and justice which, at least in the case at hand, seemed to serve as a substitute for the relief desired. But in 1926 relief was given in the *Strathcona Steamship*[94] case by the Privy Council. Lord Shaw's statement, affirming the appropriateness of a charter-party obligation imposed upon a purchaser, touches upon the vital question when any application is made to resale price situations. "It has been forgotten," Lord Shaw wrote, "that—to put the point very simply—the person seeking to enforce such a restriction must, of course, have, and continue to have, an interest in the subject matter of the contract."[95]

There is a close relationship between the doctrines relating to restrictions on alienation or qualification of title, particularly in the hands of remote vendees, and unreasonable restraints of trade. When Charles Evans Hughes, who had resigned from the Supreme Court three years before, argued *Colgate* on behalf of the defendant, he linked the two doctrines.[96] As Professor Chafee wrote, in piloting "the battered hulks of price maintenance up a tortuous channel between the familiar rocks and shoals presented by his former colleagues,"[97] Hughes laid great stress on the absence of any agreement "which, if valid, would have constituted any restraint on alienation."[98] There was "no agreement whatever which, if valid, would in the slightest

---

sideration made by him with a third person, to use and employ the property for a particular purpose in a specified manner, the acquirer shall not, to the material damage of the third person, in opposition to the contract and inconsistently with it, use and employ the property in a manner not allowable to the giver or seller."

[94] Lord Strathcona S.S. Co. v. Dominion Coal Co., Ltd. [1926] A.C. 108 (P.C. 1925) (N.S.).

[95] *Id.* at 121.

[96] Hughes also argued reasonableness as a defense to price fixing in the *Trenton Potteries* case, note 52 *supra*, where he was counsel for the defendants, and in the *Appalachian Coals* case, note 55 *supra*, where he spoke for the Court as its Chief Justice, reasonableness almost became a defense to a price-fixing charge. As Mr. Justice Hughes, he had dissented in the *Dick* case, note 74 *supra*. The distinction that Mr. Hughes saw between *Dr. Miles* and *Colgate* is emphasized by the following quotation from his biographer: "Nor would he pit Hughes the lawyer against Hughes the judge. If a case required arguments at variance with legal principles he had enunciated as Associate Justice, he declined it. This self-imposed rule did not, however, prevent him from arguing a case if he saw an honest distinction between the principle he had laid down for the court and the new point at issue." 2 PUSEY, CHARLES EVANS HUGHES 634 (1951).

[97] Chafee, *supra* note 90, at 990.

[98] Brief for Defendant-in-Error, in *Colgate*, p. 12; see *id.* at 39.

degree have affected or qualified the title of the purchaser or his freedom to sell."[99] *Dr. Miles*, in which he had written the opinion, involved, Mr. Hughes explained, "the restraint upon the right of alienation of property sold, not the right of the manufacturer to refuse to
sell. . . ."[100] This argument as to the crucial significance of the restraint on alienation, or qualification of title, was a variation of that
unsuccessfully employed by Mr. Beck in *Boston Store* one year earlier
and before that by Mr. Justice Holmes in his dissent in *Dr. Miles*.[101]
As used in *Colgate*, the argument, while consistent with a distinction
between an informal agreement, on the one hand, and formal contracts, on the other, nevertheless emphasized the greater vulnerability
of restraints which were less consensual, *e.g.*, where an attempt was
made to impose a restriction through mere notice, as under a patent,
or upon remote vendees. In its insistence upon the crucial significance
of an enforceable qualification of title, the argument impliedly distinguishes vertical price understandings from horizontal price arrangements. As such the argument may be taken as an approach to a larger
problem. It suggests that understandings unlawful as agreements fixing prices when made horizontally need not be considered unlawful,
although unenforceable, when made vertically. The justification
would be that vertical price arrangements are really not price fixing,
and not unreasonable restraints of trade, unless there is evidence of
such widespread effect as to have the same general consequences as
horizontal arrangements among the buyers setting a general market
price. Mr. Justice Holmes made the point in *Dr. Miles* when he
wrote: "I suppose that in the case of a single object such as a painting
or a statue the right of the artist to make such a stipulation hardly
would be denied. . . . I suppose that the reason why the contract is

---

[99] *Ibid*.

[100] *Id*. at 25.

[101] See 224 U.S. at 12–15. The rule of *Dr. Miles*, Mr. Beck had said, operated against
limitations and qualifications of the property interest; against attempts by contract to
control subpurchasers as distinguished from purchasers. Then, departing from this line, he
pointed out that in *Boston Store* the monopolistic features were absent which had been
present in *Dr. Miles*, where the articles of commerce were absolutely monopolized by the
producer. But in any event, went Mr. Beck's argument, the erroneous idea that any restraint on the alienation of personal property was void at common law arose out of a
misconception of a passage from *Coke on Littleton;* that passage referred only to total restraints. See text *supra*, at notes 88 and 89. Mr. Beck was later to argue the *Beech-Nut* case
on behalf of the Government.

held bad is that it is part of a scheme embracing other similar contracts . . . with the object of fixing a general market price."[102] But Mr. Justice Holmes was out of sympathy with the law against resale price maintenance, believing that "we greatly exaggerate the value and importance to the public of competition in the production or distribution of an article . . . as fixing a fair price. What really fixes that is the competition of conflicting desires."[103]

III. The Opinions in Parke, Davis

Mr. Justice Brennan's opinion for the Court in *Parke, Davis* sketched the growth of the relevant segment of resale price doctrine through three stages. First there was the unprotectability of an elaborate price structure. This was followed by the emphasis on the illegality of resale price agreements, but also on the legality of the right to announce in advance the circumstances under which there will be a refusal to deal. Third was the proposition that illegality may be caused by any methods as effectual as agreements.

The history was set forth in terms of six resale price cases. *Dr. Miles*, according to Mr. Justice Brennan, held written price contracts "void because they violated both the common law and the Sherman Act."[104] But then there was *Colgate*, where the district court had "construed the indictment as not charging a combination by *agreement* between Colgate and its customers to maintain prices."[105] The Supreme Court held that it was bound by this interpretation "and that without an allegation of unlawful *agreement* there was no Sherman Act violation charged."[106] Mr. Justice Brennan quoted from *Colgate* the passage concerning the right of a trader to exercise his own independent discretion and to announce in advance the circumstances under which he will refuse to sell. The *Colgate* decision "created some confusion and doubt as to the continuing vitality of the principles announced in *Dr. Miles*."[107]

In *Schrader's Son*, Mr. Justice Brennan went on to say: "We had no intention to overrule or modify the doctrine of *Dr. Miles* . . . where the effort was to destroy the dealers' independent discretion

---

[102] 220 U.S. at 411.

[103] *Id*. at 412.

[104] 362 U.S. at 38.

[105] *Id*. at 37.

[106] *Ibid*.

[107] *Id*. at 38.

through restrictive agreements.[108] [A] manufacturer is not guilty of a combination or conspiracy if he merely 'indicates his wishes concerning prices and declines further dealings with all who had failed to observe them . . .' ; however, there is unlawful combination where a manufacturer 'enters into agreements—whether express or implied from a course of dealings or other circumstances—with all customers . . . which undertook to bind them to observe fixed resale prices.' "[109] But then, in *Cudahy*, the Court, while emphasizing that the essential agreement, combination, or conspiracy might be implied by the jury from a course of dealings or other circumstances, held that the trial judge had given an erroneous instruction. The erroneous instruction went as follows: "I can only say to you that if you shall find that the defendant indicated a sales plan to the wholesalers and jobbers, which plan fixed the price below which the wholesalers and jobbers were not to sell to retailers, and you find defendant called this particular feature of the plan to their attention on very many different occasions, and you find the great majority of them not only expressing no dissent from such plan, but actually cooperating in carrying it out themselves selling at the prices named, you may reasonably find from such that there was an agreement or combination forbidden by the Sherman Anti-Trust Act."[110]

Mr. Justice Brennan found, however, that the authority of the holding in *Cudahy* was "seriously undermined by subsequent decisions. . . . Therefore, [it] does not support the District Court's action in this case, and we cannot follow it here."[111] *Cudahy* was undermined and *Colgate* limited by *Beech-Nut*. There the company "had adopted a policy of refusing to sell its products to wholesalers or retailers who did not adhere to a schedule of resale prices. Beech-Nut later implemented this policy by refusing to sell to wholesalers who sold to retailers who would not adhere to the policy. To detect violations the company utilized code numbers on its products and instituted a system of reporting. When an offender was cut off, he would be reinstated upon the giving of assurances that he would maintain prices in

---

[108] *Id.* at 39.

[109] *Ibid.*, quoting from 252 U.S. at 99.

[110] 256 U.S. at 210–11. A foreshortened version is set out at 362 U.S. at 40.

[111] 362 U.S. at 40.

the future."[112] Beech-Nut's program was held to be an unfair method of competition, violative of the Federal Trade Commission Act, because Beech-Nut's practices violated the Sherman Act. Mr. Justice Brennan construed *Beech-Nut* as holding "that the nonexistence of contracts covering the practices was irrelevant."[113] For this important point, Mr. Justice Brennan quoted from the *Beech-Nut* opinion: "The specific facts found show suppression of the freedom of competition by methods in which the company secures the cooperation of its distributors and customers, which are quite as effectual as agreements express or implied intended to accomplish the same purpose."[114] Summarizing, Mr. Justice Brennan wrote: ". . . because Beech-Nut's methods were as effective as agreements in producing the result that 'all who would deal in the company's products are constrained to sell at the suggested prices' . . . the Court held that the securing of the customers' adherence by such methods constituted the creation of an unlawful combination to suppress competition among the retailers."[115]

The construction of *Beech-Nut* as narrowly limiting *Colgate*, by subjecting to Sherman Act liability the producer who gains "adherence to his resale price by methods which go beyond the simple refusal to sell to customers who will not resell at stated prices, was made clear in *United States v. Bausch & Lomb Optical Co. . . .*"[116] In *Bausch & Lomb*, a Sherman Act violation was found when "the refusal to sell to wholesalers was not used simply to induce acquiescence of the wholesalers in the . . . published resale price, . . . [but] the wholesalers 'accepted [the] proffer of a plan of distribution by cooperating in prices, limitation of sales to and approval of retail licensees. . . . Whether this conspiracy and combination was achieved by agreement or by acquiescence of the wholesalers coupled with assistance in effectuating its purpose is immaterial.' "[117] "Thus," Mr. Justice Brennan concluded, "whatever uncertainty previously existed as to the scope of the *Colgate* doctrine, *Bausch & Lomb* and *Beech-Nut* plainly fashioned its dimensions as meaning no more than that a simple refusal to sell to customers who will not resell at prices suggested by the seller is permissible under the Sherman Act."[118] The

---

[112] *Id.* at 40–41.

[113] *Id.* at 41.

[114] *Ibid.*, quoting from 257 U.S. at 455.

[115] 362 U.S. at 42.

[116] *Ibid.*

[117] *Id.* at 43.

[118] *Ibid.*

unlawful combination would not have to arise from a price-main-tenance agreement, express or implied, for "such a combination is also organized if the producer secures adherence to his suggested prices by means which go beyond his mere declination to sell to a customer who will not observe his announced policy."[119] *Bausch & Lomb* and *Beech-Nut* are not to be read as teaching that particular "fact complexes" justify "the inference of an agreement." Rather, they reach "combinations of traders to suppress competition" when "the manufacturer's actions, as here, go beyond mere announcement of his policy and the simple refusal to deal. . . ."[120]

In this structure of changing or developed doctrine, Parke, Davis' program violated the limitations of *Colgate's* permissive area in two respects. "Parke, Davis used the refusal to deal with the wholesalers in order to elicit their willingness to deny Parke, Davis products to retailers and thereby help gain the retailers' adherence to its sug-gested minimum retail prices."[121] Moreover, Parke, Davis, "with re-gard to the retailers' suspension of advertising . . . first . . . discussed the subject with Dart Drug. When Dart indicated willingness to go along the other retailers were approached and Dart's apparent willing-ness to cooperate was used as the lever to gain their acquiescence in the program."[122] "Affirmative action" was thus taken "to achieve uniform adherence by inducing each customer to avoid price competi-tion. . . . [T]he customers' acquiescence is not then a matter of indi-vidual free choice prompted alone by the desirability of the product. The product then comes packaged in a competition-free wrapping. . . ."[123] Mr. Justice Brennan "admitted that a seller's announcement that he will not deal with customers who do not observe his policy may tend to engender confidence in each customer that if he complies his competitors will also."[124] And earlier in the opinion he had writ-ten: "True, there results the same economic effect as is accomplished by a prohibited combination to suppress price competition if each cus-tomer, although induced to do so solely by a manufacturer's an-nounced policy, independently decides to observe specified resale prices. So long as *Colgate* is not overruled, this result is tolerated but only when it is the consequence of a mere refusal to sell. . . . When

---

[119] *Ibid.*

[120] *Id.* at 44.

[121] *Id.* at 45.

[122] *Id.* at 46.

[123] *Id.* at 47.

[124] *Id.* at 46.

the manufacturer's actions . . . go beyond mere announcement of his policy and the simple refusal to deal, and he employs other means which effect adherence to his resale prices, this countervailing consideration is not present and therefore he has put together a combination in violation of the Sherman Act."[125] The countervailing consideration is the "manufacturer's right 'freely to exercise his own independent discretion as to parties with whom he will deal.' "[126]

Mr. Justice Harlan's dissent was a four-pronged attack on the majority opinion. First, the majority was charged with introducing a new standard or meaning into the phrase "contract, combination . . . or conspiracy" without elucidating this new standard. For Mr. Justice Harlan found no "new narrowing concept" read into the *Colgate* doctrine by *Beech-Nut* or *Bausch & Lomb*. "Until today I had not supposed that any informed antitrust practitioner or judge would have had to await *Beech-Nut* to know that the concerted action proscribed by the Sherman Act need not amount to a contractual agreement. But neither do I think that it would have been supposed that the Sherman Act does not require concerted action in some form."[127] *Beech-Nut* rested on co-operative methods that constituted concerted action. In *Bausch & Lomb* there was a finding by the district court of agreements with wholesale customers to fix prices and boycott retailers. It rested on " 'an agreement between the seller and purchaser to maintain resale prices.' . . . It justified the finding of concerted action on the ground that '[T]he wholesalers accepted Soft-Lite's proffer of a plan of distribution by cooperating in prices, limitation of sales to and approval of retail licensees.' "[128] Thus these two cases "turned on the application of established standards of concerted action to the full sweep of the particular facts . . . and not upon any new meaning given to the words 'contract, combination . . . or conspiracy.' "[129] Now the Court has said that any additional step "beyond mere announcement of this policy and refusal to sell" puts the seller in violation of the Sherman Act, "[b]ut we are left wholly in the dark as to what the purported new standard is" that makes this so.[130]

Second, the majority brushed aside the findings of the district court on the ground that the ultimate findings were premised on an

---

[125] *Id.* at 44.

[126] *Ibid.*

[127] *Id.* at 52.

[128] *Id.* at 53.

[129] *Ibid.*

[130] *Ibid.*

erroneous interpretation of the standard to be applied.[131] According to Mr. Justice Harlan, the majority was "mistaken in attributing to the District Court the limited view that Parke, Davis' activities should . . . be upheld unless they involved some express or implied 'contractual arrangement.' . . ."[132] A " 'combination and conspiracy' . . . comprising a 'continuing agreement, understanding and concert of action,' " had been charged; "the District Court repeatedly emphasized that Parke, Davis did not have an 'agreement or understanding of any kind.' . . . It determined . . . that 'there was no coercion' and that 'Parke, Davis did not combine, conspire or enter into an agreement, understanding or concert of action' with the wholesalers, retailers, or anyone else. I cannot detect . . . any indication that the District Court . . . applied anything other than the standard which has always been understood to govern. . . ."[133]

Third, the majority was wrong in its analysis of Parke, Davis' activities beyond the simple refusal to sell. These consisted of the company's announcement that it would "cut off wholesalers who continued to sell to price-cutting retailers," followed by a refusal to sell to such wholesalers, and reporting by the company of "its talks with one or more retailers to other retailers," seeking "assurances of compliance," and getting them, thus gaining adherence to its policy only " 'by actively bringing about substantial unanimity among the competitors. . . .' "[134] But as to the refusal to sell to wholesalers who sold to price-cutting retailers, the district court found "such conduct did not involve any concert of action but was wholly unilateral on Parke, Davis' part. And I cannot see how such unilateral action, permissible in itself, becomes any less unilateral because it is taken simultaneously with similar unilateral action at the retail level."[135] As to the reporting of talks among retailers, "the District Court found that the Company did not make the 'enforcement of its policies, as to any one wholesaler or retailer, dependent upon the action of any other wholesaler or retailer.' "[136] It stated that acquiescence came because they valued de-

---

[131] *Cf.* United States v. United States Gypsum Co., 333 U.S. 364 (1948); United States v. Griffith, 334 U.S. 100 (1948).

[132] 362 U.S. at 53.

[133] *Id.* at 54. See text *supra*, at notes 15–27.

[134] 362 U.S. at 54.

[135] *Id.* at 55.   [136] *Ibid.*

fendant's business and not through coercion or agreement. "Even if this were not true, so that concerted action among the retailers at the 'horizontal' level might be inferred, as the Court indicates, under the principle of *Interstate Circuit* . . . I do not see how that itself would justify an inference that concerted action at the 'vertical' level existed between Parke, Davis and the retailers or wholesalers."[137]

Finally, "*Beech-Nut* did not say that refusals to sell to wholesalers who persisted in selling to cut-price retailers . . . was a *per se* infraction of the *Colgate* rule, but only that it was offensive if it was the result of cooperative group action."[138] In this case, "the defensive, limited, unorganized, and unsuccessful effort of Parke, Davis . . . does not justify our disregarding the District Court's finding" of no concert of action.[139] Indeed, as Mr. Justice Harlan stated at the beginning of his dissent, "the Court's opinion reaches much further than at once may meet the eye. . . . The Court has done no less than send to its demise the *Colgate* doctrine which has been a basic part of antitrust law concepts since it was first announced. . . ."[140] And, he concluded, "contrary to the long understanding of bench and bar, the Court treats *Colgate* as turning not on the absence of the concerted action explicitly required by §§ 1 and 3 of the Sherman Act, but upon the Court's notion of 'countervailing' social policies. . . . It is surely the emptiest of formalisms to profess respect for *Colgate* and eviscerate it in application."[141]

Through this conflict between the majority and dissenting opinions Mr. Justice Stewart's three-sentence concurrence cuts a cryptic path. Since the record shows an illegal combination to maintain retail prices, Mr. Justice Stewart wrote, he found "no occasion to question, even by innuendo, the continuing vitality of the *Colgate* decision . . . or of the Court's ruling as to the jury instruction in *Cudahy*."[142]

IV. The Colgate Case and Its Progeny

The Colgate Case. The right to refuse to deal is basic. Mr. Justice Lurton in the *Grenada Lumber*[143] case suggested that the right is

---

[137] *Ibid.* Strange to say, the majority opinion did not cite the *Interstate Circuit* case for the concert-of-action point.

[138] *Ibid.*

[139] *Id.* at 56.

[140] *Id.* at 49

[141] *Id.* at 57

[142] *Id.* at 49.

[143] Grenada Lumber Co. v. Mississippi, 217 U.S. 433, 440 (1910).

constitutionally protected. The right is reflected in *Colgate*. Even so, *Colgate* involved certain difficulties which it did not solve and which have caused trouble ever since. For this reason, *Colgate* seems unworthy of being memorialized in a dissenting opinion forty years after it was decided. *Colgate* is a poor instrument with which to bring the doctrine it espouses into the general fabric of the anti-trust laws; particularly is this so because the problem of the relationships between the doctrines of price fixing and the right to refuse to deal is a serious one. Perhaps *Colgate* should be regarded solely in the light of the construction which Mr. Justice McReynolds placed upon the district court's interpretation of the indictment; namely, that the indictment was defective in failing to charge an agreement between Colgate and its dealers which obligated the dealers to resell at prices fixed by the company. But this view of *Colgate* is too simple; it obscures important inherent inconsistencies. These inconsistencies are revealed by a closer look at the indictment and at the district court's view of it. As Charles Wesley Dunn wrote some years ago, "The *Colgate* case presents a curious and extraordinary situation in that the court is compelled to hold that an indictment does not charge an offense against the anti-trust act upon the ground that, *first*, it presents but a simple refusal to sell, whereas, under the rule of the later *Schrader* and *Frey cases*, it presents a course of dealing to be submitted to the jury. . . . *Second*, it fails to aver agreements between the manufacturer and his dealers to fix and maintain prices for the resale of his products, whereas, as a matter of fact, it expressly avers such agreements."[144]

The *Colgate* indictment in fact did charge that Colgate "knowingly and unlawfully created and engaged in a combination with . . . wholesale and retail dealers . . . for the purpose and with the effect of procuring adherence on the part of such dealers . . . to resale prices fixed by the defendant, and of preventing such dealers from reselling such products at lower prices, thus suppressing competition amongst such wholesale dealers and amongst such retail dealers. . . ."[145] The indictment specified that Colgate "requested . . . dealers whom it ascertained to have made" sales below the resale price "to give it assurances and promises that they would in the future resell its products

---

[144] *Resale Price Maintenance*, 32 YALE L. J. 676, 690 (1923). Mr. Dunn was, along with Charles Evans Hughes, among counsel for Colgate at the trial.

[145] Record, p. 3.

at the prices which it indicated."[146] It stated that Colgate "uniformly refused to sell its products to dealers who had made sales at prices other than those indicated . . . until such dealers gave assurances and promises. . . . Induced by such requests and by such refusals, many dealers, wholesale and retail, who had sold such products at prices other than those indicated . . . gave to defendant assurances and promises that they would thereafter resell such products at the prices indicated by defendant. Defendant thus procured many such assurances and promises from dealers. . . ."[147]

Judge Waddill sustained the demurrer to the indictment because the indictment did not charge an offense and was too indefinite in form. His opinion was written with respect to an indictment not brought before the Supreme Court. A second indictment was returned with this variation: it added the names of three dealers who "[a]mongst other dealers, wholesale and retail, . . . agreed with the defendant to resell its products at the prices fixed by it as aforesaid."[148] Judge Waddill then sustained the demurrer to this second indictment "in so far as it avers that the indictment fails to charge any offense under the Sherman Act or any other law of the United States."[149] So far as the substance of the indictment was concerned, he said, I construe "this indictment as [I] construed the former indictment."[150] The addition of the names of three who agreed "as aforesaid" cured the indictment of indefiniteness; it did not change Judge Waddill's view that no violation of law was charged. Since the *Colgate* case came to the Supreme Court from the district court under the Criminal Appeals Act, the construction of the indictment by the district judge was not subject to review.[151]

"This, at the threshold," the trial judge wrote, "presents for the

---

[146] *Id.* at 4.

[147] *Ibid.* The indictment, as indicated in Judge Waddill's opinion, sets forth a variety of means used by Colgate to carry out the combination, such as distributing telegrams and lists of uniform resale prices; urging adherence; informing dealers that defendant would refuse to sell to those who did not adhere; requesting dealers to inform Colgate of sales at other prices; investigating sales; placing offending dealers on suspended lists and refusing to sell to such dealers until they gave assurances and promises. 253 Fed. 522, 523 (E.D. Va. 1918).

[148] Record, p. 5.

[149] *Id.* at 8.   [150] *Ibid.*

[151] ROBERTSON & KIRKHAM, JURISDICTION OF THE SUPREME COURT OF THE UNITED STATES § 185 (Wolfson & Kurland ed. 1951).

determination of the court how far one may control and dispose of his own property; that is to say, whether there is any limitation thereon, if he proceeds in respect thereto in a lawful and bona fide manner. That he may not do so fraudulently, collusively, and in unlawful combination with others, may be conceded [citing *Eastern States Lumber Association*].[152] But it by no means follows that, being a manufacturer of a given article, he may not, without incurring any criminal liability, refuse absolutely to sell the same at any price, or to sell at a named sum to a customer, with the understanding that such customer will resell only at an agreed price between them, and, should the customer not observe the understanding as to retail prices, exercise his undoubted right to decline further to deal with such persons."[153]

Three other quotations are relevant to Judge Waddill's view of the indictment. At one point he wrote that "the averment [was], in effect, that [Colgate] knowingly and unlawfully created and engaged in a combination with certain of its wholesale and retail customers, to procure adherence on their part, in the sale of its products sold to them, to resale prices fixed by the defendant, and that, in connection therewith, such wholesale and retail customers gave assurances and promises, which resulted in the enhancement and maintenance of such prices, and in the suppression of competition by wholesale dealers and retail dealers, and by the latter to the consuming public."[154] Later he stated that in "the view taken by the court, the indictment here fairly presents the question of whether a manufacturer . . . is subject to criminal prosecution . . . for entering into a combination in restraint of . . . trade . . . because he agrees with his wholesale and retail customers upon prices claimed by them to be fair and reasonable, at which the same may be resold, and declines to sell his products to those who will not thus stipulate as to prices."[155] Finally: "The pregnant fact should never be lost sight of that no averment is made of any contract or agreement having been entered into whereby the defendant . . . and his customers, bound themselves to enhance and maintain prices, further than is involved in the circumstance that the manufacturer . . . refused to sell to persons who would not resell at indicated

---

[152] Eastern States Lumber Ass'n v. United States, 234 U.S. 600 (1914).

[153] 253 Fed. at 525.

[154] *Id*. at 524.   [155] *Id*. at 525.

prices, and that certain retailers made purchases on this condition, whereas, inferentially, others declined so to do. No suggestion is made that the defendant, the manufacturer, attempted to reserve or retain any interest in the goods sold, or to restrain the vendee in his right to barter and sell the same without restriction. The retailer, after buying, could, if he chose, give away his purchase, or sell it at any price he saw fit, or not sell it at all; his course in these respects being affected only by the fact that he might by his action incur the displeasure of the manufacturer, who could refuse to make further sales to him, as he has the undoubted right to do."[156]

Judge Waddill's opinion refers with approval to *Great Atlantic & Pacific Tea Co. v. Cream of Wheat*[157] in the Second Circuit, and particularly to the district court opinion by Judge Hough.[158] There the court denied an injunction to restrain Cream of Wheat from refusing to sell its goods to the chain store. Cream of Wheat sold to the plaintiff upon condition that the resale price should be not less than fourteen cents per package. When plaintiff "refused to observe this agreement or request, and openly sold Cream of Wheat . . . for 12 cents per package," remained "contumacious," and refused to maintain prices, defendant cut off sales to the chain store.[159] It also attempted to keep jobbers from selling its products to the plaintiff. Judge Hough said the "premise that defendant *fixes* the resale price" was inaccurate because "*fixing* connotes enforcement."[160] The sale implied no agreement to maintain or fix prices. The request amounted to saying, " 'Keep up the retail price, or we will stop supplying you, if we think such stoppage profitable.' I do not suppose that this sales scheme was a contract, or anything enforceable against defendant. . . ."[161] The opinion expressed the view that "definite, positive, and admitted price regulation"[162] would not be an unreasonable restraint of trade since "Cream of Wheat is not a necessity; it is not even a staple article of commerce . . . ; collectively . . . grocery keepers are more important to the public and the defendant than is the plaintiff."[163] A much later case recorded a letter from the president of the

---

[156] *Id.* at 527.

[157] 227 Fed. 46 (2d Cir. 1915).

[158] 224 Fed. 566 (S.D. N.Y. 1915).

[159] *Id.* at 570.

[160] *Id.* at 572. The case was considered as arising under the Clayton Act rather than the Sherman Act.

[161] 224 Fed. at 569.

[162] *Id.* at 573.

[163] *Ibid.*

Cream of Wheat company in which he stated: "we have continued to sell the American Stores Company and the National Grocery Company because they have kept their promise with regard to resale price. We have refused to sell the Great Atlantic and Pacific Tea Company because they did not keep their promises."[164] Such a promise would not be inconsistent with Judge Hough's analysis. The promise would not be enforceable and, as Judge Hough wrote, "it is not necessarily unlawful for a man to do voluntarily what he cannot be compelled to do."[165]

Judge Waddill's opinion in *Colgate* may be thought to reflect views concerning the legality of reasonable partial restraints of trade and the more vulnerable and distinguishing characteristics of attempts to reserve or retain an interest in the goods sold or to impose restrictions on remote vendees. To some extent, although not completely, he appears to reflect a position comparable to that taken by the Washington Supreme Court five years before in *Fisher Flouring Mills Co. v. Swanson*,[166] a common-law case. There a manufacturer was permitted to enjoin a retailer from selling at a lower price than he had agreed with the

---

[164] Cream of Wheat Co. v. F.T.C., 14 F. 2d 40, 42 (8th Cir. 1926).

[165] 224 Fed. at 573 n. 9. Judge Hough appears to have adopted a version of the argument rejected in United States v. Kellogg Toasted Corn Flake Co., 222 Fed. 725, 730 (E.D. Mich. 1915), that there would have to be a valid contract before there could be a violation of the Sherman Act. Compare also the language in United States v. Keystone Watch Case Co., 218 Fed. 502, 512 (E.D. Pa. 1915), discussing the effect of a circular in which the company stated its intention to sell thereafter only to those dealers who conformed voluntarily to its wishes for resale price maintenance and exclusivity: "We regard it, not as a request, but as a threat; and not as an empty threat, but as a real menace from a strong manufacturer."

On the appeal from Judge Hough's decision, Judge Lacombe, who had written the opinion in *Dueber Watch*, note 56 *supra*, in which he had sustained the validity of a combination of manufacturers to fix prices, wrote: "We had supposed that it was elementary law that a trader could buy from whom he pleased and sell to whom he pleased, and that his selection of seller and buyer was wholly his own concern. . . . Before the Sherman Act it was the law that a trader might reject the offer of a proposing buyer for any reason that appealed to him; it might be because he did not like the other's business methods, or because he had some personal difference with him, political, racial, or social. . . . We have not yet reached the stage where the selection of a trader's customers is made for him by the government." 227 Fed. at 48–49. *Cf.* United States v. New York Great Atlantic & Pacific Tea Co., 173 F. 2d 79, 87 (7th Cir. 1949), where Minton, J., said of the purchaser defendant: "It went further and served notice on the supplier that if the supplier did not meet the price dictated by A & P, not only would the supplier lose the business at the moment under negotiation, but it would be put upon the unsatisfactory list or private blacklist of A & P and could expect no more business from the latter. This was a boycott and in and of itself is a violation of the Sherman Act."

[166] 76 Wash. 649 (1913); see also Grogan v. Chaffee, 156 Cal. 611 (1909).

manufacturer to maintain. The court realized that a non-ancillary price agreement of the *Addyston* type, which would not be a "partial restraint" having "a main lawful purpose," would be invalid. But it did "not follow that every contract restraining competition as to an insignificant part of the total of a given commodity, in a given market" would be "obnoxious."[167] "If a controlling number of manufacturers or wholesale dealers in a given commodity should make identical contracts with the retailers of that locality, it would doubtless be the result of an agreement, secret or otherwise, between them" and would be "a combination in restraint of competition."[168] The Washington court distinguished *Park & Sons*[169] because "it involved a monopoly . . . a complete or general restriction as to Peruna. . . ."[170] *Dr. Miles* was distinguished because it concerned a system of "interlocking restrictions," involving sales "by all dealers at wholesale or retail, whether purchasers or subpurchasers."[171] It involved "four hundred jobbers and wholesalers, and retail agency contracts with twenty-five thousand retail dealers. . . . [T]he system . . . had no purpose save to create and perpetuate a monopoly."[172] *Bobbs-Merrill*[173] was an attempted notice restriction under copyright upon future purchasers with whom there was no privity of contract; "the distinction" was "too plain to require further comment."[174] "Finally," the Washington court said, "it seems to us an economic fallacy to assume that the competition which, in the absence of monopoly, benefits the public, is competition between rival retailers. The true competition is between rival articles. . . ."[175]

To be sure, in Judge Waddill's view he was dealing in *Colgate* with the subject of a manufacturer's rights with respect to his own products. The seller had an interest in his property and in preventing price cutting. The defendant "might have been more injuriously affected . . . than the public would be benefited by a temporary reduction in the prices. . . ."[176] The seller had no monopoly; it was not shown that he had any appreciable proportion of the soap business. His goods were not a necessity. But this does not mean that Judge Waddill thought there was no agreement. The opinion indicates fairly clearly

[167] 76 Wash. at 655.

[168] *Id.* at 659–60.

[169] Note 66 *supra*.

[170] 76 Wash. at 664–65.

[171] *Id.* at 667.

[172] *Ibid.*

[173] Note 68 *supra;* see also note 78 *supra*.

[174] 76 Wash. at 666.

[175] *Id.* at 668–69.

[176] 253 Fed. at 527.

that Judge Waddill was not greatly disturbed by the word "agree-ment." He thought it was not necessarily an offense—certainly not a criminal offense—under the Sherman Act for a trader to refuse to sell his own property unless assurances, promises, or agreements were given or made that resale prices would be maintained. The agreement would not be enforceable except through the sanction of refusing to deal. The conception seems to be that the individual trader's right to refuse to deal includes the right to make an unenforceable agreement to maintain resale prices. At least this would not be a violation of the Sherman Act. In a probable allusion to the patent or copyright cases, or perhaps to other situations like *Dr. Miles*, Judge Waddill wrote that here there was no suggestion of an attempt "to reserve or retain an interest in the goods sold, or to restrain the vendee in his right to barter and sell the same without restriction."[177] But this did not mean that an allegation of an agreement, or a specification of those who agreed in this manner, would be fatal to the seller's position. Thus the designation of some who actually did agree in the second indictment made no difference so far as the substance of the charge was con-cerned.

The view that Judge Waddill, without much qualm, accepted the existence of an agreement by the buyer under these circumstances is supported by his itemization of the particular agreements which were not charged. There was no agreement with other manufacturers; no agreement between the retailers. The combination involved whole-sale and retail dealers. If assurances were given by the first buyers, there was no charge that they in turn were required to obtain similar assurances from their buyers. There was no charge that the buyers giving the assurances would also stipulate to buy only from the de-fendant or sell only to customers selected by it.[178] "What the public is interested in is that only reasonable and fair prices shall be charged . . . and it is not claimed that the defendant's manner of conducting its business has otherwise resulted."[179] Possibly in Judge Waddill's

---

[177] *Ibid.*

[178] At this point in the opinion, Judge Waddill wrote that "no charge is made that any contract was entered into by and on the part of the defendant, and any of its retail cus-tomers. . . ." *Id.* at 524. The omission of wholesalers from this clause was probably intentional, but this, of course, does not mean that he thought a contract had been entered into with the wholesalers. The mention of the absence of exclusive arrangements is prob-ably an oblique reference to the *Keystone Watch* case.

[179] 253 Fed. at 527.

view it would have made no difference if the agreements charged had been enforceable, since they were not sufficiently widespread or interlocking to constitute indictable restraints. The conception, as it turns out, seems to involve unenforceable agreements, but agreements nevertheless.[180]

In the Supreme Court, Mr. Hughes for Colgate emphasized the absence of any "imposition and enforcement of a restraint upon the right of alienation of movables sold. . . ."[181] The district court's statement that the "manufacturer 'agrees' with his wholesale and retail customers" was not to be taken to mean "that there was any qualification of the customer's title or right to alienate, but simply a recognition of the manufacturer's right to decline to make future sales."[182] In *Dr. Miles*, "[t]his Court fully recognized the right of the manufacturer to sell or not, as he pleased."[183] When it did sell, "[e]ach buyer received a full and unqualified title and possessed complete and unrestricted liberty of alienation."[184] There was no "system of restrictive contracts or notices attempting to restrict title such as had received the condemnation of this Court. But, unable to charge any such violation of law, the Government sought, by vague generalities and use of the words 'agree' and 'understanding' and 'assurances and promises,' to make a case, when in fact there was no restrictive agreement whatever."[185] "The 'assurances' and 'promises' . . . were only declarations of intention, not a qualification of title."[186] The Government had cited the *Kellogg Toasted Corn Flakes* case,[187] where a federal court had rejected the argument that there was no restraint of trade because the notice of resale price on the carton did not constitute a valid contract. "But," said the Hughes brief, "in that case, there was a restriction attempted to be imposed upon the right of alienation as an express condition of the sale, and notice was given that re-sale

---

[180] Among its assignment of errors, the Government asserted that the district court had distinguished between contracts and informal agreements or understandings, and between the interpretation of the Sherman Act in civil and criminal proceedings, with the result that the illegality of resale price combinations depended upon the presence of monopoly, the existence of concerted action with other manufacturers, the imposition of restrictions upon dealers to whom the manufacturer does not sell directly, and upon the magnitude of the prices fixed. Record, pp. 35–36.

[181] Brief for Colgate & Company, Defendant-in-Error, p. 23.

[182] *Id*. at 10.

[183] *Id*. at 25.

[184] *Id*. at 23.

[185] *Id*. at 8–9.

[186] *Id*. at 13.

[187] Note 165 *supra*.

at a lower price than that fixed by the manufacturer would be regarded as 'an infringement of our patent rights' and would render 'the vendor liable to prosecution as an infringer.' The pith of the decision lay in the invalidity of the restrictions sought to be imposed upon the title by the notices used. . . ."[188] There was no combination. " 'Combination' is a term which fits the concerted action of rival producers. It fits the concerted action of competing dealers. It may fit a system of restrictive contracts tying the dealers together through interlocking restraints imposed by their mutual stipulations qualifying their title."[189] "The absence of monopoly and of monopolizing intent, and of any concert with other manufacturers was commented upon" by the district court.[190] "So far as 'prices' are concerned, there is no charge—as the District Court held—that any prices suggested were not fair and reasonable."[191]

The Government's brief stressed combination and agreement. It urged the *Boston Store* case,[192] outlawing patent resale price restrictions, as resting upon the fundamental ground that the form of the arrangement was unimportant; therefore a formal contract was not required to prove a violation. It attempted to answer the point that prior cases, particularly *Dr. Miles*, held only that the agreements were unenforceable, by citing three district court cases from which the conclusion might be drawn that they were unlawful as well.[193] It quoted the district court in each of these cases; from *Kellogg*,[194] to the effect that a legally enforceable contract was not required, and from *Frey & Son v. Welch Grape Juice* and *Lowe Motor Supplies Co. v. Weed Chain Tire Grip Co.*, on the point that no written and signed agreement was necessary.[195] The agreement or understanding could be a restraint, Judge Mack had said in *Lowe*, "whether it is in writing, whether it is by word of mouth, whether it is by looking into each other's eyes, or in any other way in which men come to an understanding or agreement. . . ."[196] But when it was all over, Mr. Justice McReynolds concluded that in *Colgate* there was an absence of agree-

---

[188] Brief for Colgate & Company, Defendant-in-Error, p. 32.

[189] *Id.* at 40.   [192] Note 78 *supra*.

[190] *Id.* at 9.   [193] Brief for the United States, pp. 16–17.

[191] *Id.* at 13.   [194] Note 165 *supra*.

[195] Brief for the United States, pp. 13–15. These cases are unreported.

[196] *Id.* at 15.

ments which obligated the purchaser not to resell except at prices fixed by the company. In the absence of monopoly, the trader could decide with whom he would deal. "[A]nd, of course, he may announce in advance the circumstances under which he will refuse to sell."[197] By this means the law of resale price maintenance was made to turn on an imaginary inference, all askew from the normal meaning of "agreement."

The decision, as Mr. Justice Brennan wrote with understatement, "created some confusion and doubt," and not only "as to the continuing vitality of the principles announced in *Dr. Miles*,"[198] but as to what *Colgate* was all about. This was immediately reflected in *Cudahy*, *Schrader's Sons*, and *Beech-Nut*.

From Cudahy to Bausch & Lomb. In *Frey & Son. v. Cudahy Packing Co.*,[199] a jobber, claiming damages for having his supply cut off for failure to abide by a resale plan for wholesalers and jobbers of Old Dutch Cleanser, won a treble-damage action in the district court.[200] District Judge Rose made the point in his instructions to the jury that "[b]y the nature of things . . . defendant has a monopoly in the original production of Old Dutch Cleanser. . . ."[201] He told the jury they might find an agreement or combination if they found the defendant called the sales plan, which fixed minimum resale prices, to the attention of the purchasers "on very many different occasions," and they not only expressed "no dissent" but actually co-operated in carrying it out.[202] The Court of Appeals for the Fourth Circuit, one month after Mr. Justice McReynolds' decision in *Colgate*, reversed. Speaking through Judge Woods, it pointed out that "[t]here was no formal written or oral agreement with jobbers for the maintenance of prices."[203] "The vital question," the court said, was "whether defendant's method of business coupled with the acquiescence of its customers . . . was such cooperation . . . as amounted to a combination in restraint of trade. . . ."[204] And *Colgate* had "clearly answered" this question "in the negative."[205]

---

[197] 250 U.S. at 307. *Cf.* F.T.C. v. Gratz, 253 U.S. 421 (1920).

[198] 362 U.S. at 38.   [199] 256 U.S. 208 (1921).

[200] A demurrer to the complaint had been overruled. 232 Fed. 640 (D. Md. 1916).

[201] Record, p. 437.   [203] *Id.* at 556.

[202] *Id.* at 442.   [204] *Ibid.*

[205] *Ibid.* Messrs. Hughes and Dunn were counsel for Colgate in *Cudahy* as *amicus curiae*. The *Cudahy* case shows the problem of "agreement." A jobber was asked to sign a

Three months after *Colgate*, District Judge Westenhaver, in *Schrader's Son*,[206] said, "Personally, and with all due respect, permit me to say that I can see no real difference upon the facts between *Dr. Miles* . . . and *Colgate*." As he read the cases, the difference could not be that in *Dr. Miles* the arrangement was put in writing whereas in *Colgate* the wholesale and retail dealers observed the prices fixed by the vendor. That would be "a distinction without a difference." "It is a little difficult," he said, "to perceive why an invalid stipulation in a contract could become a contract in restraint of trade, although one can readily see why a combination or conspiracy using invalid ar-

---

paper stating: "We understand that in the distribution and sale of your product . . . you make same uniformly through jobbing distributive channels and that you suggest certain retail selling prices and terms. . . . we further understand that while you require no agreement from any customer respecting the retail price and terms at which he will sell, you nevertheless maintain a special price for such jobbers as co-operate with you. . . . I understand the selling prices and terms to be as per list attached hereto, and that I (or my firm) have given positive instructions to every salesman to adhere absolutely to these prices and terms and to the office staff as it may affect the settlement of accounts." Record, pp. 184–85. The jobber to whom this was given refused to sign.

The testimony of a representative of Cudahy was that it "was up to me to keep [jobbers] on the list unless they were violating some agreement."

"Q. What do you mean by that, violating some agreement?"

"MR. MONTAGUE: I object to the word 'agreement' as a very large word. It is not for this witness to characterize a thing as an agreement."

"THE COURT: Pardon me. There are some things that he can characterize as agreements without any trouble in the world, for instance, you ask him to dinner, and he said he would go."

"THE WITNESS: I mean, by violating agreement, if they were abiding by the instructions issued by the Cudahy Packing Company, and the instructions were that jobbers were to maintain the prices." *Id.* at 211.

One wholesaler testified: "Around that time I had one of their salesmen approach me and state definitely what their policy had always been. That was as far as it got. Had I known that policy at the time I would not have cut Old Dutch Cleanser. You ask me what policy did he state? He said, 'We always in the past have gone along certain lines with our selling end of it and of course we know that certain parties in the city have been getting Dutch Cleanser, we will not say who they are, but we have definite data as to who they are. The cases are numbered and we know who gets the stuff. We will not say who they are, but we know it is being done. Now I just want to present our policy so that you will be fully informed on that, and of course I would not want you to be one of those whom we suspicion of cutting.' He said nothing about what the consequences would be if we did not take that advice. After that, we pretty much observed the advice." *Id.* at 285. He said: "I certainly regard myself as absolutely free to sell that Old Dutch Cleanser at any price I choose." *Id.* at 286. The Court asked, "Did you feel yourself, after that conversation with the agent, in honor free to cut the price?" The witness answered, "Not honor free, no sir." *Id.* at 288.

[206] 264 Fed. 175, 183 (W.D. Ohio 1919).

rangements might result in such a violation."[207] He said that he noted this in passing "because of the insistence of counsel for the government that a combination or conspiracy, such as was clearly disclosed in the Colgate Case, might not be a violation of the Sherman Anti-Trust Law, whereas if that combination and conspiracy had been put in writing in the form of an agreement, it would be a violation, notwithstanding such provisions in the agreement were themselves void."[208] The real difference, he felt, was that there had to be a purpose to create and maintain a monopoly. On this basis he sustained the demurrer in *Schrader's Son*, even though the manufacturer of valves and accessories there had identical written contracts with jobbers and tire manufacturers requiring resale price maintenance. Judge Westenhaver felt that some significance attached to the fact that retailers were not included in the arrangement: "They may compete freely with one another, and may even give away the articles purchased by them."[209]

Then the Court of Appeals for the Second Circuit (Messrs. Hughes and Dunn representing the petitioners) reversed the order of the Federal Trade Commission in *Beech-Nut*.[210] Judge Ward said the obvious purpose of Beech-Nut was to prevent any competition as to the resale price between purchasers of its product. If founded on an agreement between the manufacturer and purchasers severally, this was a violation of the Sherman Act under *Dr. Miles*. It was "difficult to say why a different conclusion should be reached, if the same result is attained by acquiescence and co-operation without express agreement. . . . But we understand the Supreme Court to hold in . . . [*Colgate*] that a similar, but less drastic, method of sale constitutes merely the exercise of a man's right to do what he will with his own, and is not obnoxious to the Sherman Act."[211]

In *Schrader's Son*[212] and *Cudahy*[213] Mr. Justice McReynolds said he had been misunderstood. *Colgate* rested on the absence of agreements,

---

[207] *Id.* at 180.   [208] *Ibid.*

[209] *Id.* at 183. This was not the view of the majority in *Parke, Davis: Schrader's Son* "involved the prosecution of a components manufacturer for entering into price-fixing arrangements with *retailers*, jobbers and manufacturers who used his products." 362 U.S. at 38. (Emphasis added.)

[210] 264 Fed. 885 (2d Cir. 1920).

[211] *Id.* at 889. Judge Manton, concurring, referred to a "tacit understanding." *Id.* at 891.

[212] 252 U.S. 373 (1920).   [213] 256 U.S. 208 (1921).

whether express or implied, from a course of dealings or other circumstances. *Schrader*, where the district judge had said there had to
be a purpose to create and maintain a monopoly, was reversed and
remanded. Mr. Justice Holmes and Mr. Justice Brandeis dissented
without opinion. Except by inference, the opinion ignored arguments
of counsel which raised questions concerning whether retailers had to
be included, a tendency to enhance prices shown, [214] or the scope of the
restraint spelled out in terms of the percentage of trade covered because price fixing could be a reasonable partial restraint of trade. [215]
Cudahy [216] was affirmed. But Mr. Justice McReynolds said both the

[214] The Government argued: ". . . the tendency to enhance prices paid by the public
not only exists in a combination, but is fulfilled, although no retailers are included in the
combination. . . . The enhancement of the prices at which the wholesalers sell to the
retailers is, of course, transmitted by the retailers to the public. . . ." Brief for the United
States, p. 12.

[215] The defendant cited North Western Salt Co. v. Electrolytic Alkali Co. [1914]
A.C. 461 (H.L.), for the point that "it is well established that a covenant in partial
restraint of trade is to be regarded as *prima facie* reasonable." Brief for A. Schrader's Son
(Inc.), Defendant-in-Error, p. 13. The House of Lords had there decided that a price-
fixing agreement between salt manufacturers was not necessarily void on its face. The
defendant also argued: "There is not a fact in the record from which the Government is
entitled to assert the conclusion that there is here disclosed an unreasonable combination
to restrain interstate trade. . . . There is no showing here as to the extent of defendant's
trade, . . . nothing to show but that sales to the retail trade constitute 90 per cent of the sales
by tire makers and jobbers of the defendant's goods, the retail trade being wholly
unrestrained. . . ." *Id*. at 31.

[216] The plaintiff in *Cudahy* argued: "Except that the resulting contract is in its nature
unlawful, the distribution by the defendant among jobbers of its circulars stating the
terms on which it would sell . . . comprises all the elements of a *legal* contract on the part
of such jobbers . . . to observe the terms of the circulars, including the maintenance of
resale prices. . . . The defendant's circulars are the complete, though circumlocutory,
equivalent of the written statement of terms in *Garst vs. Harris*." Brief for Plaintiff-in-
Error, pp. 31, 33. It also argued: "The *mutual* character of the *combination* . . . is still
further illustrated by what the defendant *did* when a jobber failed to maintain prices.
Instead of 'refusing to deal with anyone who *failed* to maintain resale prices specified by
it' . . . the defendant, when a jobber first failed to maintain prices, *did not refuse* to deal
with such jobber, but *did* by written communications and by personal interviews try to
effect an understanding that such jobbers would maintain prices." *Id*. at 35. The plaintiff's
brief also asserted: "It is, of course not overlooked that this Court itself has been divided
in opinion as to the legality of price maintenance agreements. . . . No member of this
Court, however, has suggested that the legality or illegality of such agreements should be
determined by the Court or jury in each case by weighing the supposed economic advantages and disadvantages resulting therefrom in the particular case. . . . It is safe to
say that *either prohibition* or *permission* . . . would be *preferable*. . . ." *Id*. at 50–51. The
defense brief argued not only that there was no restraint upon future alienation, but that
"No 'understanding and agreement' in the nature of so-called resale price maintenance
violates the anti-trust laws unless, in the light of reason . . . it constitutes such an undue
restriction . . . as to monopolize or (unduly) restrain trade." Otherwise it would constitute the "single, unique and anomalous exception to the . . . 'light of reason' set up by
the Supreme Court. . . ." Brief on behalf of Defendant-in-Error, pp. 78, 79.

district court and the court of appeals were wrong—the court of appeals because the question whether there was an unlawful combination or agreement was for the jury to decide, the district court because the jury was erroneously instructed that the necessary combination or agreement could be found from the resale plan, together with frequent notice of it to purchasers, no dissent by them, and actual co-operation.[217] Mr. Justice Pitney, joined by Justices Day and Clarke, dissented, in part on the ground that the district court's instruction "suggested a perfectly natural and legitimate inference. . . . Concerted action is of the essence of a conspiracy. . . ."[218]

In *Beech-Nut*, the Supreme Court said that *Colgate* had been misunderstood. The court of appeals had assumed that the difference was between a written agreement and a tacit understanding. But Mr. Justice Day explained that the specific facts assumed in the *Beech-Nut* case went "far beyond the simple refusal to sell goods to persons who will not sell at stated prices, which in the *Colgate case* was held to be within the legal right of that producer."[219] "The specific facts found showed suppression of . . . competition by methods in which the company secures the cooperation of its distributors and customers, which are quite as effectual as agreements express or implied intended to accomplish the same purpose."[220] Now Mr. Justice McReynolds was in dissent. In something of a reversal of *Colgate*, in which there were two

---

[217] See text *supra*, at note 202.

[218] 256 U.S. at 217. In *Binderup v. Pathe Exchange*, 263 U.S. 291, 312 (1923), the Supreme Court held in favor of an exhibitor who brought an action against distributors who had refused to sell to him. The Court said: "It is doubtless true that each of the distributors, acting separately, could have refused to furnish films to the exhibitor without becoming amenable to the provisions of the act, but here it is alleged that they combined and conspired together to prevent him from leasing from any of them." The Court cited *Schrader's Son* and District Judge Ray's opinion in *Bobbs-Merrill Co. v. Straus*, note 68 *supra*, which had said that the combination among booksellers and publishers was in itself unlawful. Defendants' brief in the Supreme Court described Colgate as having "fixed and set a re-sale price upon its articles, and although it did not exact a positive agreement on the part of the jobber or retailer . . . it did announce that any jobber or retailer who did cut the prices fixed by it would be cut off of its list. . . . In the case at bar there is no allegation to the effect that the defendants agreed among themselves not to supply the plaintiff with films and the facts alleged give rise to no such agreement by implication. . . The re-sale price maintenance cases illustrate attempts to retain the incidents of ownership in an article of personal property after a completed sale of the article had been made, and it is this vice that renders agreements to maintain a fixed re-sale price illegal and not the incidental effect or consequence of breaching the agreement which results frequently in a refusal to deal with those breaching the agreement." Brief for the Defendants-in-Error, pp. 81, 82–83.

[219] 257 U.S. at 454.   [220] *Id.* at 455.

complaints, the original complaint in *Beech-Nut* had charged an agreement; then, in the amending stipulation and in the findings of fact, the Federal Trade Commission had said the merchandising conduct of Beech-Nut did "not constitute a contract or contracts whereby resale prices are fixed, maintained and enforced."[221] "How," Mr. Justice McReynolds asked, "can there be methods of cooperation . . . or the cooperation of customers with a view to prevent others, when the existence of essential contracts is definitely excluded?"[222] Possibly in the light of Mr. Justice McReynolds' dissent, Mr. Justice Harlan's statement concerning informed anti-trust practitioners, judges, concerted action, and contractual agreements is dubious.[223] Mr. Justice McKenna and Mr. Justice Brandeis joined Mr. Justice Holmes in his separate dissent based on the doctrine of the "single hand that is admitted to be free to shut as closely as it will."[224]

It must be said that *Beech-Nut* was much more like *Dr. Miles* than were *Colgate*, *Schrader's Son*, and *Cudahy*. *Beech-Nut*, like *Dr. Miles*, involved wholesalers and retailers in interlocking restraints. In *Colgate*, Judge Waddill had stressed that the wholesalers had not been required to obtain assurances from the retailers. In *Schrader's Son*, Judge Westenhaver said, "Let me repeat: The retailers are not in the present case included."[225] In *Cudahy* the complaint did charge that the retailers were required to promise to sell at fixed prices, but the decision did not turn on this. The use of soliciting agents who obtained orders from retailers and forwarded them to jobbers was the closest approach to an interlocking restriction in that case. But in both *Beech-Nut* and *Dr. Miles* wholesalers were not permitted to sell to offending retailers. Moreover, the retailers in *Dr. Miles* also contracted with the manufacturer as to what the retailers would pay wholesalers, and *Beech-Nut* involved diversion of retailer's orders from offending jobbers and wholesalers. The main difference between *Dr. Miles* and *Beech-Nut*, as has been pointed out so often, was that there were written contracts in *Dr. Miles*, including, in the case of the retailers, stipulated damages for each violation; in *Beech-Nut* there was an assumed elaborate system in operation, tracing price cutters, separating retailers from banned wholesalers, and requiring whole-

---

[221] *Id.* at 458.

[222] *Id.* at 459.

[223] See text *supra*, at note 127.

[224] 257 U.S. at 457.

[225] 264 Fed. at 183.

salers not to sell to price-cutting retailers until (after assurances as to future conduct) they were restored.[226]

In *Beech-Nut* the Government could, and did, argue that:

> Perhaps the most "drastic" of these practices is that of a virtual boycott, for failing to observe resale prices, of retail dealers with whom respondent has no direct dealings, but who purchase their supplies of Beech-Nut products from the jobbers.
>
> In this way, by the joint action of the competing retailers, the respondent and the jobbers, a general "embargo" is established against recalcitrant retail dealers, and, in some instances against jobbers, whose only offense is that they have disposed of their own goods at prices satisfactory to themselves.
>
> In addition to this blacklisting and boycotting of dealers with whom respondent in many cases has no business relations whatever, we have also the practice indulged in by respondent, in aid of its price-maintenance scheme, of interfering in the relations between retailers and jobbers by diverting the retailers' order from one jobber to another.[227]

It is one thing, therefore, to say that *Beech-Nut* involved methods quite as effectual as agreements, express or implied, and quite another thing to say that any contract or combination which goes beyond a refusal to sell to price cutters is an actionable restraint of trade. Indeed, *Beech-Nut* limits the illegal contracts or combinations which go beyond the simple refusal to sell to those which "unduly" hinder or obstruct the free and natural flow of commerce. Competition, the Court concluded, was practically suppressed among retail distributors by the methods used; jobbers and wholesalers who did not comply were effectively cut off until they were restored to favor. This was an echo of the reasoning employed by Judge Lurton in *Park v. Hartman* when he wrote, "The plain effect . . . is, first, to destroy all

---

[226] "It may be that the mention of coöperative methods does not prevent a manufacturer from getting the facts merely through his own employees, so long as he does not turn his dealers into spies upon their rivals, but such a view would operate unduly in favor of the large corporation which can afford to employ its own 'spotters' as against a small competitor. This case and another ruling by the Commission even make it illegal for the producer to record the names of the price-cutters in a card catalogue. Apparently someone must keep them all in his head, which must enhance the salary of clerks endowed with a memory like Lord Macaulay." Chafee, note 90, *supra*, at 991. In dissent, Mr. Justice McReynolds said: "Having the undoubted right to sell to whom it will, why should respondent be enjoined from writing down the names of dealers regarded as undesirable customers?" 257 U.S. at 459.

[227] Brief for the Petitioner, p. 27.

competition between jobbers or wholesale dealers. . . . Next, all competition between retailers is destroyed. . . ."[228] And it echoed, too, the Court in *Dr. Miles*, when in answering the contention that the arrangement was reasonable, it said: "[T]he complainant can fare no better . . . than could the dealers themselves if they formed a combination and endeavored to establish the same restrictions, and thus to achieve the same result, by agreement with each other."[229] It was the specific facts found which showed this widespread suppression of competition.

The emphasis in *Beech-Nut* on methods was made necessary by the stipulation, and therefore the findings of fact: "That the merchandising conduct of respondent heretofore defined and as herein involved does not constitute a contract or contracts whereby resale prices are fixed, maintained and enforced."[230] As Mr. Justice McReynolds wrote in his dissent, "the detailed facts [were] sufficient to support a finding that there were such agreements."[231] The effect of *Beech-Nut*

---

[228] 153 Fed. at 42.

[229] 220 U.S. at 408.   [230] 257 U.S. at 458.

[231] *Ibid*. These were years of transition and uncertain direction concerning the law of price fixing and the inferences to be drawn from concerted action. This is reflected in the trade association cases where many of the same policy issues advanced by those in favor of resale price maintenance as protection of the small against the large were involved. *American Column & Lumber*, note 61 *supra*, was decided by the Court less than one month prior to *Beech-Nut*. There, Mr. Justice Clarke had written of the operations of an open-price competition plan ". . . the only element lacking in this scheme . . . is a definite agreement as to production and prices. But this is supplied: by the disposition of men 'to follow their most intelligent competitors,' especially when powerful; by the inherent disposition to make all the money possible, joined with the steady cultivation of the value of 'harmony' of action. . . ." 257 U.S. at 399. Mr. Justice Holmes had dissented in part because ". . . the parties to the combination are free to do as they will." *Id*. at 413. Mr. Justice Brandeis, joined by Mr. Justice McKenna, dissented not only because there was no coercion but because of the benefits of rationalization of competition which would result. He pointed to the concentration which might result from the refusal to permit small firms to co-operate. After all, United States v. United States Steel Corp., 251 U.S. 417 (1920), which held that "it was not unlawful to vest in a single corporation control of 50 per cent. of the steel industry," *id*. at 419, had been decided less than one year before, on the same day as *Schrader's Son*. In 1925, when the Government sought to extend the ruling in *Column & Lumber* to cover combinations for the exchange of cost and price data, Mr. Justice Stone emphasized that it was not alleged or proved that there was any agreement among the members affecting production, fixing prices, or for price maintenance. Maple Flooring Ass'n v. United States, 268 U.S. 563 (1925). Mr. Chief Justice Taft, Mr. Justice Sanford and Mr. Justice McReynolds dissented. Mr. Justice McReynolds wrote that the members were "parties to definite and unusual combinations and agreements, whereby each is obligated to reveal to confederates the intimate details of his business and is restricted in his

was to concentrate the attention of the Federal Trade Commission and the courts on the particular enforcement measures used in resale price agreements. Attention was focused on the securing of reports from independent dealers concerning price cutters, the use of other investigating measures sometimes called espionage, and the procurement of assurances and promises of future good behavior before price cutters were restored. In the *American Tobacco* case[232] in 1925, the Second Circuit, in a questionable decision delivered by Judge Rogers, found nothing wrong in a manufacturer's implementing a price agreement among wholesale dealers by enforcing it through his right to refuse to deal. The court said that *Beech-Nut* was radically different because in *American Tobacco* there was no attempt to impose price maintenance on retail dealers. The court remarked in passing that, so far as *Colgate* was concerned, the Supreme Court "has had occasion in a number of subsequent cases to point out that this case has been misunderstood by the profession, and it has explained, if not what the case means, what it does not mean."[233]

In the *Hudnut* case,[234] decided in the district court by Judge Augustus Hand, and in *Ayer*[235] decided by the Second Circuit, emphasis was placed on the isolated character of those instances in which assurances and promises perhaps were required for reinstatement. In *Hudnut*, Judge Hand said that of forty thousand customers there were only seventy-three cases of retailers cut off and then reinstated. In addition, "it is true that the distinction between an agreement by word or conduct to maintain a reselling price on merchandise sold and delivered, and a warning that, if such price is not maintained, future sale will be withheld, is delicate, and the second may be accompanied by such circumstances as to show conclusively that a contract really is made. Yet there is a difference, and, if it is not observed, the right to refuse to sell to a customer, who does not by his conduct satisfy his vendor, will disappear."[236] Here "there were among the

---

freedom of action. . . . Pious protestations and smug preambles but intensify distrust when men are found busy with schemes to enrich themselves through circumventions." *Id*. at 587.

[232] American Tobacco Co. v. Federal Trade Commission, 9 F. 2d 570 (2d Cir. 1925).

[233] *Id*. at 583.

[234] United States v. Hudnut, 8 F. 2d 1010 (S.D. N.Y. 1925).

[235] Harriet Hubbard Ayer, Inc. v. F.T.C., 15 F. 2d 274 (2d Cir. 1926).

[236] 8 F. 2d at 1010.

73 cases very few instances indeed where Hudnut's salesmen, even with the inevitable enthusiasm of such persons, did anything like make an agreement to fix a resale price."[237] Judge Hand therefore thought the facts were more nearly like those in *Colgate* and *Cudahy* than in *Beech-Nut*.

In the *Ayer* case, three visits by a salesman to offending retailers were insufficient to bring the program under the ban of *Beech-Nut*. The court said: "There is testimony that a price list of petitioner's products was sent out in some of the packages, but there is no evidence to show that there was anything by way of direction in their merchandising system to compel, or even request, retail dealers to adhere to these prices in their resales. . . . In each instance where the salesman visited the retailer, the latter assured petitioner that they would not offend further by a continuing price-cutting. In two instances the customers' order was refused on the ground that they were price cutters. There were some 29 letters offered in evidence of the same purport as the samples referred to. From this it is clear that there was no established unlawful method of merchandising in petitioner's business. . . . Out of thousands of sales made with some 8,000 customers, but a few are referred to as instances of an effort to eliminate the price cutter."[238]

In *J. W. Kobi Co. v. F. T. C.*,[239] decided the next year, the Second Circuit upheld the order of the commission because agreements or understandings to observe fixed resale prices had been proved. "There was also a method employed in reporting on price cutters and a continuous request of dealers and jobbers to report the competitors who did not observe the resale prices suggested . . . and a threat to refuse sales to dealers so reported on."[240] Similarly, in 1935 the Second Circuit affirmed the commission's determination of illegality in *Armand Co. v. F. T. C.*[241] The manufacturer had requested a written "declaration of intention," to be signed by dealers, "freely and voluntarily" and "not to be understood as either an express or implied obligation or agreement on the part of the dealer."[242] In fact, the declaration stated that it was "in recognition of petitioner's right to refuse to sell to dealers who did not charge suggested resale prices."[243] The sales-

[237] *Ibid.*

[238] 15 F. 2d at 278.

[239] 23 F. 2d 41 (2d Cir. 1927).

[240] *Id.* at 43.

[241] 78 F. 2d 707 (2d Cir. 1935).

[242] *Id.* at 708.

[243] *Ibid.*

men were told they might inquire prior to a sale whether a dealer intended to conform; the dealer might write a declaration of intention, but the salesman was directed not to make " 'any agreement with the dealers as to the resale prices.' "[244] After 1922 the declaration of intention had been abandoned, but "the record is replete with evidence that . . . agreements or understandings were entered into between the petitioner and certain dealers [who] . . . agreed to refuse to resell petitioner's products to retail stores which did not . . . charge the retail prices suggested. . . ."[245] Pursuant to one such agreement, a drug company in Seattle kept a list of retailers in the territory who were known to be price cutters. The evidence indicated a desire to have "a tacit or oral agreement for the fixing of prices on resale. . . ."[246] In many instances price cutters were dropped but later reinstated upon satisfying the company of their willingness to comply. Here the petitioner dealt with 39,000 retail druggists out of a total of 56,000, and 247 wholesale druggists out of a total of 550. "This is a kind of competition between wholesalers and retailers of a product of a single manufacturer which was intended by the decisions of the courts to be free and open."[247]

The Fourth Circuit in 1925, in *Oppenheimer, Oberndorf & Co. v. F. T. C.*,[248] upheld the commission's order against a resale price program where jobbers were cut off, a reporting system used, and attempts made to get assurances of no price cutting. No retailers were involved in the program. "This difference," the court said, "of course, cannot affect the principle."[249] There was no marking of packages under a key system, as there had been in *Beech-Nut*, but that "was only one of the means of throttling competition, and its absence here does not affect the illegality of the other means to that end condemned by the Supreme Court."[250]

In the Ninth Circuit, in *Hills Bros. v. F. T. C.*[251] in 1926, the court upheld the order of the commission against the operation of a mini-

---

[244] *Ibid.*

[245] *Id.* at 709.   [246] *Ibid.*

[247] *Id.* at 710. See also Forstmann Woolen Co. v. Murray Sices Corp., 10 F.R.D. 367 (S.D. N.Y. 1950).

[248] 5 F. 2d 574 (4th Cir. 1925). See also McElhenney Co. v. Western Auto Supply Co., 269 F. 2d 332 (4th Cir. 1959).

[249] 5 F. 2d at 575.

[250] *Ibid.*   [251] 9 F. 2d 481 (9th Cir. 1926).

mum retail price program made known to the retail trade by a bulletin issued to all salesmen and through advertisements published in trade journals. Since adopting the program, the company had refused to sell to approximately one hundred dealers in various states for their failure to maintain prices. "The petitioner learns of instances where its minimum resale price is cut, through its salesmen and from competing retail dealers located near the dealer who may be cutting the price, and salesmen report instances of price cutting in their respective territories and invite and procure from retail dealers upon whom they call reports of the failure of other competing dealers to maintain the minimum price. . . . Retail dealers continually advise salesmen whenever a competitor cuts the minimum price . . . and often telephone to one of the branch offices. . . . These reports by retail dealers are solicited and requested by the salesmen. . . ."[252] The court held that the arrangement differed "in degree and not in kind from the Beech-Nut Co. case."[253]

The Sixth Circuit, in *Toledo Pipe-Threading Mach. Co. v. F. T. C.*[254] in 1926 and *Shakespeare Co. v. F. T. C.*[255] in 1931, found price programs unlawful by reason of the requirement of assurances before price cutters were reinstated. In *Toledo Pipe-Threading* the court said the *American Tobacco* case,[256] which had allowed the implementation of the jobbers' price program, and *Hills Bros.*[257] were fundamentally in conflict. The tobacco company and its wholesale association did indulge in a concert of action to constrain price cutters as much as did the Toledo Company and its distributors in the case before the court. So far as *Hills* was concerned, "the cooperation between [the manufacturer] and its customers was no more in kind, though probably greater in amount, than we have here. . . ."[258] The methods of Colgate as described in the indictment probably went further than the methods used in *Oppenheimer*, but nothing much could be made of this because the conclusion that the Colgate program did not amount to a system of co-operation was that of the district court and not of the Supreme Court. *Beech-Nut* was not completely parallel, because in *Oppenheimer* there was no system of identifying marks, no group of

---

[252] *Id.* at 482–83.   [253] *Id.* at 485.

[254] 11 F. 2d 337 (6th Cir. 1926). See also Crane Distributing Co. v. Glenmore Distilleries, 267 F. 2d 343 (6th Cir. 1959).

[255] 50 F. 2d 758 (6th Cir. 1931).   [257] Note 251 *supra.*

[256] Note 232 *supra.*   [258] 11 F. 2d at 341.

salesmen or agents reporting violators or penalizing them by diverting retail business, and there was no "don't sell" list with the accompanying co-operative effort to prevent other dealers from selling to the price cutter. But there was the generally encouraged practice of dealers to report price cutters. The court said it was agreed that a dealer might say to a price cutter, " 'I have cut you off from my list, I will sell you no more.' There seems no reason why this exclusion must be permanent. . . . Yet the difference between his express promise to observe . . . and the implied promise which he quite obviously makes to the same effect, if he asks for the acceptance of a further order, is not a sharp distinction. It may be that ultimately either the principle that price maintenance is an evil, and may not be accomplished in any manner, or the principle that such a system may be established and enforced in any nonoppressive way will clearly prevail."[259] For this case, there was "room to think that requirement of promises from price cutters, and the assurances in a number of cases received by them, go far enough so that they constitute a system of co-operative effort not protected by the manufacturer's individual right of arbitrary selection of customers, and, though with hesitation, we accept that view."[260] Similarly, in *Shakespeare Co.*, there were several instances in which the petitioner refused to sell orders except upon assurance by the customer that he would discontinue selling below the suggested minimum price. "There are to be found, too," the court said, "instances of the refusal of the petitioner to make further shipments on orders that had been accepted until such assurances were given. . . . Thus, while the petitioner had the right to refuse to sell its goods to those who did not sell them at the suggested resale price, with the further right, we think, to state to them its reasons for so doing, the evidence . . . shows that it put into practice 'a system of co-operative effort,' within the meaning . . . of the decision in Toledo Pipe-Threading. . . ."[261] "The line of demarcation between the permissible and the prohibited, under principles already suggested, is indistinct, and rather baffles definition. . . . If some customer cuts prices below

---

[259] *Id.* at 342.

[260] *Ibid.* The court said that the opinion in F.T.C. v. Raymond Bros.-Clark Co., 263 U.S. 565 (1924), was helpful because it "emphasized concert of action among several to constrain another as being the feature distinguishing between the permitted and the forbidden." *Id.* at 341.

[261] 50 F. 2d at 759.

the requested minimum, the petitioner may refuse to make additional sales to such customers, but may go no further. Assurances as to future conduct may not be solicited. Should such assurances be given by the customer, . . . they must be considered as gratuitous and as not involving the petitioner in a violation of the Commission's order."[262] The Eighth Circuit held that, after an illicit price program had been in operation, information as to price cutting could not be solicited, but could be received and acted upon.[263]

---

[262] *Id.* at 760. In Q. R. S. Music Co. v. F.T.C., 12 F. 2d 730 (7th Cir. 1926), the court also upheld an order striking down an arrangement whereby price cutters, when reported, had to give assurances.

In A. C. Becken Co. v. Gemex Corp., 272 F. 2d 1 (7th Cir. 1959), a treble-damage suit resulted in judgment for the defendant in the district court. The plaintiff's theory was that defendant had attempted to force him into a price-fixing agreement for the establishment and maintenance between wholesalers of minimum resale prices on Gemex products and competitive products. The plaintiff asserted that when it had refused to join such a conspiracy, the defendant carried out its threat to drop him. "Tower, defendant's representative, . . . visited plaintiff's office, and told its vice-president Bohlander that plaintiff would be expected to sell lines competitive to defendant's lines at manufacturer-suggested prices. On the following day, Swartman, defendant's sales manager, and Tower talked to President Clark and others, of plaintiff. . . . Tower stated that 'it is the philosophy of our company' that to be a Gemex distributor, plaintiff would have to sell competing lines of watch bracelets at prices suggested by manufacturers. Tower also said that he had talked to Stein & Ellbogen Company and The Ball Company, competitors of plaintiff, and, when asked how he knew that they would uphold, or how they would stop doing this, and he said they had shook hands over it. And he said, 'That is good enough for me.' Bohlander suggested that . . . 'if they would not allow us to sell the line through the salesman, that they at least allow us to show the line in our catalog.' . . . At that point Mr. Tower stood up and he said, 'Well,' he said, 'we are at an impasse, this is it.' " *Id.* at 3. Judge Schnackenburg, speaking for the court of appeals, reversed the judgment: "A wrench can be used to turn bolts and nuts. It can also be used to assault a person in a robbery. Like a wrench, a manufacturer's right to stop selling to a wholesaler can be used legitimately; but it *may not* be used to accomplish an unlawful purpose." *Id.* at 3–4.

[263] The setting for this holding was Cream of Wheat Co. v. F.T.C., 14 F. 2d 70 (8th Cir. 1926), involving practices which set off the chain of events which made for Judge Hough's and Judge Lacombe's opinions on the rights of individual traders in the *Great Atlantic & Pacific Tea Co.* cases. The Cream of Wheat Company had informed itself of price cutting through advertisements and lists of prices put out by customers; it had solicited or had been furnished with reports concerning price cutting by its customers. These reports came from other customers, from dealers, and from its sales agents. At times it had sought and received from customers and prospective buyers assurances to observe resale prices. A letter to one customer in the record read: "Please understand that we do not want any agreement with you, or anything like an agreement, as to how you shall resell our product. We simply reserve the right to refuse to sell you any more of our products in the event you did not see fit to comply with any request which we make of you. . . ." *Id.* at 43. The First Circuit, in Moir v. F.T.C., 12 F. 2d 22 (1st Cir. 1926), upheld

It cannot be said that the law of resale price maintenance was unworkable after *Beech-Nut*, but the theory of the law was uncomfortably indistinct and confused. *Dr. Miles, Colgate, Schrader's Son,* and *Cudahy* had based the illegality of resale price arrangements on agreements; *Colgate* and *Cudahy* together had created in effect a protected area for the trader in which implied agreements would not be seen. This protected area extended at least to relationships with the first vendee. It consisted of acknowledgment of the legitimacy of the trader's weapon of refusal to deal. His use of it was not improper coercion, at least if he had no monopoly, and did not have the specific intent for an attempt to monopolize. Conformity gained thereby was no agreement, despite the inducement always present to vendees to conform to avoid competition among themselves. The situation in *Dr. Miles* and *Beech-Nut* was different because the restrictions were interlocking, the restraints widespread. By involving the first vendees in enforcement against subsequent purchasers, the restrictions, in terms of the earlier arguments, imposed greater restraints on alienation. *Beech-Nut*, in the situation created by the commission's stipulation that there were no contracts, provided a bypass around *Colgate*, at least for commission cases, by emphasizing means. But the theory, and therefore the scope, importance, and predictability of the bypass was unclear. Was illegality limited to those cases in which methods worked widespread restraints, as in *Dr. Miles* and *Beech-Nut?* Were methods of co-operative enforcement, indicating concerted action, important as substitutes for—because signs of—agreement, or as exhibiting a combination with too much reliance upon the help, coerced or not, of independent dealers? Were the methods specified in *Beech-Nut* important because unfair or too effective, although perhaps no more effective than the methods portrayed in *Cudahy*, and therefore

the order of the commission in a resale price maintenance case against Chase & Sanborn. There was said to be evidence not only of implied but of express agreements. Chase & Sanborn in one communication had written: ". . . we have taken this opportunity to express our feeling on the subject frankly, and are writing to receive your assurance of co-operation in maintaining this minimum price in the future. . . ." *Id.* at 24. In A. H. Grebe & Co. v. Siegel, 14 F. 2d 175 (D.R.I. 1926), the district court refused a preliminary injunction against a price cutter who was removing identifying marks from the plaintiff's radio sets. The court proceeded on the basis that the use of identifying marks to prevent price cutting was one of the co-operative means of enforcement banned by the *Beech-Nut* case. See also Advertising Special. Nat. Ass'n v. F.T.C., 238 F. 2d 108 (1st Cir. 1956); *cf.* B.V.D. Co. v. Isaac, 257 Fed. 709 (6th Cir. 1919).

when used by the trader would operate as a forfeiture of the trader's privilege?

The Supreme Court decided the *Ethyl* case[264] in 1940 and the *Bausch & Lomb* case[265] in 1944. If isolated from the stream of other anti-trust cases, neither opinion need be taken as working any change in the law of resale price maintenance. Both cases involved first vendees in the enforcement of restrictions upon subsequent purchasers. They were situations therefore of the *Dr. Miles* type. In *Ethyl* the manufacturer had licensed 123 refiners, who in turn sold to 11,000 jobbers, also licensed by the manufacturer. The 123 refiners sold "about 88% of all the gasoline sold in the United States."[266] The manufacturer sold patented fluid to the refiners, who in turn sold the fluid mixed with their gasoline to the jobbers. The manufacturer specified that the refiner must "maintain a minimum differential between his Ethyl gasoline and his best non-premium grade of gasoline."[267] The refiner was not permitted to sell to unlicensed jobbers. The defendants argued there was no agreement concerning this limitation; it was merely a limitation in the refiner's license. Applications by jobbers for licenses were turned down for a variety of reasons, but among them was failure to maintain retail prices on gasoline, "not of defendant's patented fuel," as the defense brief pointed out, "because they have never sold any, but of other motor fuels."[268] Licensed jobbers were also investigated to determine whether they were maintaining " 'the marketing policies and prevailing prices of the petroleum industry.' "[269] There were sporadic instances in which representatives of the manufacturer joined with the refiner to help persuade jobbers to abide by the refiner's marketing practices. The case was submitted to the district court on agreed "elaborate, overlapping, and to some extent inconsistent, statements of fact designed to support the respective positions."[270]

District Judge Bondy concluded that, so far as the relationship between the manufacturer and the jobbers was concerned, a clear case of price maintenance was not made out. This was because "in the absence of an agreement or understanding between them, or of the

[264] 309 U.S. 436 (1940).

[265] 321 U.S. 707 (1944).

[266] 27 F. Supp. 959, 961 (S.D. N.Y. 1939).

[267] *Ibid.*

[268] Brief for the Appellants, p. 62.

[269] 309 U.S. at 453.

[270] Brief for the Appellants, pp. 4–5.

suppression of the freedom of competition by methods in which the manufacturer secures the cooperation of his distributors and customers," suggested resale prices, refusals to sell to price cutters, announcements of this policy, and investigation of the price policies of his dealers, without more, were not unlawful.[271] It was not a necessary, although perhaps a permissible, conclusion from the stipulation that an agreement or understanding for the maintenance of prices existed between the manufacturer and the jobbers. But the case could be disposed of on other grounds. "Each of the refiner license agreements provides that lead-treated gasoline may be sold to those jobbers only who are licensed by the defendant corporation and this provision is almost invariably complied with by the refiner licensee. . . . This provision of the refiner license agreements clearly is in restraint of trade. Each agreement calls for cooperative action between the defendant corporation and its refiner licensee in the exclusion of unlicensed jobbers from the market. While a manufacturer or trader may refuse to deal with those who do not observe the resale prices suggested by him, he may not combine or enter into agreement with intermediate distributors to cut off the supplies of such dealers. . . . The defendants can fare no better with their system of separate agreement than could the refiners if they formed such a corporation."[272]

The Supreme Court affirmed. The record left no doubt, it said, that the manufacturer had made use of his dominant position to exercise control over prices and marketing policies of jobbers sufficiently to make its attitude towards price cutting a pervasive influence in the jobbing trade. "The picture here revealed is not that of a patentee exercising its right to refuse to sell or to permit his licensee to sell the patented products to price-cutters."[273] The "scene [was] one in which appellant has established the marketing of the patented fuel in vast amounts on a nationwide scale through the 11,000 jobbers and at the same time, by the leverage of its licensing contracts resting on the fulcrum of its patents, it has built up a combination capable of use, and actually used, as a means of controlling jobbers' prices and suppressing competition among them."[274] The manufacturer had patents not only on the fluid which it sold but also on the fuel produced by

---

[271] 27 F. Supp. at 964.

[272] Id. at 965.

[273] 309 U.S. at 457.

[274] Ibid.

mixing the fluid with gasoline, and an additional patent on the method of using fuel containing the patented fluid in combustion motors, but it had chosen to derive its profits from sale of the fluid. It could not use a license under the fuel patent in order to benefit the refiners or to enhance its enjoyment of the fluid patent. Having sold the fluid to the refiners, its attempted regulation, by contracts or combination with the refiners, of the market prices and practices of subsequent purchasers was a violation of the Sherman Act.

In *Bausch & Lomb*, Soft-Lite purchased tinted lenses from the manufacturers and sold them to jobbers who were permitted to resell them only to retailers licensed by Soft-Lite. Each pair of Soft-Lite lenses was accompanied by a "Protection Certificate" which, the wholesalers were informed, could be used to trace wholesale lenses found in the hands of unlicensed retailers. Soft-Lite designated to the wholesalers the prices to be received by them from the retailers by means of published price lists available to the retailers as well; the wholesalers understood they would be cut off if there were material deviations. Licensed retailers were required to maintain prevailing local price schedules. Judge Rifkind found that, while there was no written resale price agreement between Soft-Lite and the wholesalers, "agreement is implicit in the operation of the system. The living reality of uniform prices from wholesalers to retailers, corresponding to the written instructions of the distributor, of wholesalers' refusal to sell to unlicensed dealers, of surveillance of wholesalers by means of protection certificates and over retailers by 'shopping,' compel the conclusion that between the wholesalers and [Soft-Lite] there was agreement or at least acquiescence in a program of concerted action."[275]

In the Supreme Court, Mr. Justice Reed said: "Our task of examining Soft-Lite's objections is simplified by the frank recognition of those appellants that 'the retail license provisions binding dealers to sell at locally prevailing prices and only to the public constitute illegal restraints.' . . . The retailer's price to his customer is the single source of stable profits for all handlers."[276] It was plain that the arrangements for price maintenance in the wholesalers' sales to retailers were an integral part of the whole distribution system. "The requirement of the wholesalers' recommendation as to the business

---

[275] 45 F. Supp. at 396.   [276] 321 U.S. at 719–20.

character of the applicant for a retail license, the evidence of espionage, the limitation of resales to Soft-Lite retail licensees, the existence of the 'Protection Certificate' to mark the wholesaler who might violate the arrangement, the uniformity of the prices, as prescribed in Soft-Lite's published lists . . . all . . . require the inference . . . that a conspiracy to maintain prices down the distribution system existed. . . ."[277]

Soft-Lite had urged that it came within the scope of cases permitting refusal to sell to customers who did not maintain prices. These cases, Mr. Justice Reed wrote, did not involve "as the present case does, an agreement between the seller and purchaser to maintain resale prices."[278] *Beech-Nut* "recognizes that a simple refusal to sell to others who do not maintain the first seller's fixed resale prices is lawful but adds as to the Sherman Act, 'He [the seller] may not, consistently with the act, go beyond the exercise of this right, and by contracts or combinations, express or implied, unduly hinder or obstruct the free and natural flow of commerce in the channels of interstate trade.' "[279] Beech-Nut, without agreements, was found to suppress this freedom by coercion of its customers, by reports of competitors about customers, and by boycotts of price cutters. Here, as in *Beech-Nut*, there was more than mere acquiescence of wholesalers in the published resale price list. Then Mr. Justice Reed used the language later picked up by Mr. Justice Brennan in *Parke, Davis:* "The wholesalers accepted Soft-Lite's proffer of a plan of distribution by cooperating in prices, limitation of sales to and approval of retail licensees. That is sufficient. . . . Whether this conspiracy and combination was achieved by agreement or by acquiescence of the wholesalers coupled with assistance in effectuating its purpose is immaterial."[280]

To Mr. Justice Brennan, in *Parke, Davis*, the crucial importance of *Beech-Nut* and *Bausch & Lomb* was that, under their doctrine, an unlawful combination arises not only from an agreement but without an agreement "if the producer secures adherence to his suggested prices by means which go beyond his mere declination to sell to a customer who will not observe his announced policy."[281] This seems

[277] *Id.* at 720.

[278] *Id.* at 721.

[279] *Id.* at 722.

[280] *Id.* at 723, quoted at 362 U.S. at 42.

[281] 362 U.S. at 43.

to be a rather mechanical application of language if applicable to situations where restraints were less widespread and first vendees were not incorporated into an enforcement system over subsequent purchasers. Yet both *Ethyl* and *Bausch & Lomb* do reflect changes in the law which could not help but have an impact on resale price situations.

In *Trenton Potteries*,[282] in 1924, the Court of Appeals for the Second Circuit had held that, in a price-fixing case, the trial judge should have submitted to the jury the question whether the price agreement complained of constituted "an unreasonable restraint of trade." The trial judge had instructed the jury: "the law is clear that an agreement on the part of the members of a combination controlling a substantial part of an industry, upon the prices which the members are to charge for the commodity, is in itself an undue and unreasonable restraint of trade and commerce. . . ."[283] On certiorari, the Supreme Court, through Mr. Justice Stone, reversed the Second Circuit. "Whether the prices actually agreed upon were reasonable or unreasonable was immaterial in the circumstances charged in the indictment and necessarily found by the verdict."[284] Mr. Justice Stone's opinion relied somewhat on resale price agreement cases, and noted that "in the second circuit the view maintained below that the reasonableness or unreasonableness of the prices fixed must be submitted to the jury has

---

[282] 300 Fed. 550, 553–54 (2d Cir. 1924).

[283] 273 U.S. at 396.

[284] *Id.* at 401. Mr. Hughes was counsel for the respondents. He argued: "The petitioner's brief cites a number of decisions of this Court as authority for the proposition that any price fixing agreement is *per se* an unlawful restraint of trade. A careful examination of those decisions, however, discloses that they do not sustain the Government's view." Respondents' Brief, p. 33. "This Court cannot hold that no rule of reason is to be applied in an equity suit to restrain a price fixing arrangement, without repudiating the *Chicago Board of Trade* case. But if it holds that the considerations of reason there applied cannot be applied in a criminal case, then it must be prepared to hold that the defendants in that case could be indicted, convicted and sent to jail for doing the very things which this Court refused to enjoin because, being reasonable, they were not in violation of the statute. It is easy to conceive of cases involving an agreement as to prices that would be *per se* unlawful. But is the Court to hold that no price fixing agreement can ever be lawful?" *Id.* at 39–40. "An examination of all the indictments found under the Sherman Act in which price fixing was charged between the date of the *Standard Oil* decisions and the date of the indictment of these defendants, shows that every one of them which ever went to trial contains an allegation that excessive, extortionate, or unreasonable prices were exacted, or that the restraint was in other ways unreasonable." *Id.* at 38.

apparently been abandoned."[285] *Ethyl*, unlike *Beech-Nut* (*Trenton Potteries* had been decided in the interim), recognized that "Agreements for price maintenance of articles moving in interstate commerce are, without more, unreasonable restraints . . . and agreements which create potential power for such price maintenance exhibited by its actual exertion for that purpose are in themselves unlawful restraints. . . ."[286]

After *Ethyl*, the Supreme Court decided *United States v. Socony-Vacuum Oil Co.*[287] There an indictment viewed a combined buyer program by oil companies as price fixing. The court of appeals reversed the judgment of conviction on the ground that, since such a combination was not illegal in itself, the question of reasonableness should have been submitted to the jury. The Supreme Court disagreed and in doing so repeated not only what it had said in *Trenton Potteries* but announced that market power was not essential to the illegality of price fixing. "[T]here may be effective influence over the market though the group in question does not control it," Mr. Justice Douglas wrote.[288] "Price fixing agreements may have utility to members of the group though the power possessed or exerted falls far short of domination and control. Monopoly power . . . is not the only power which the Act strikes down. . . ."[289] Then, in a footnote, he attached this observation: "In view of these considerations a conspiracy to fix prices violates § 1 of the Act though no overt act is shown, though it

---

[285] *Id.* at 400–401.

[286] 309 U.S. at 458. The defendants' brief in *Ethyl*, resting on Judge Bondy's finding that no resale price agreements with jobbers were present, slyly suggested in a footnote that the Miller-Tydings amendment had changed the law that "any express contract between a seller and his *existing customers* was illegal." Brief for Appellants, p. 64 n.36. The brief added: ". . . in view of the lower court's refusal to find any actual price maintenance, or any kind of implied agreement between defendant and any refiner or jobber licensee, there is no need to examine those cases—probably no longer controlling—which deal with the niceties of how far a seller may go in espionage among his existing customers before an implied agreement will be charged." *Ibid.* Earlier, the brief had said: ". . . the public interest in permitting a manufacturer by express contract to protect himself against price cutters has come to be widely recognized by federal and state enactment." *Id.* at 45. This argument was answered in United States v. McKesson & Robbins, 351 U.S. 305, 310–11 (1956), where the Court said "There is no basis for supposing that Congress, in enacting the Miller-Tydings and McGuire acts, intended any change in the traditional *per se* doctrine." It should be added that statements about the illegality of resale price contracts, at a time when there was uncertainty as to the illegality under some conditions of horizontal price agreements, carried a different meaning, because in a different setting, than they do now after *Trenton Potteries* and *Socony*.

[287] 310 U.S. 150 (1940).

[288] *Id.* at 224   [289] *Ibid.*

is not established that the conspirators had the means available for accomplishment of their objective, and though the conspiracy embraced but a part of the interstate or foreign commerce in the commodity."[290] In *Bausch & Lomb*, price fixing was considered, under the rule of *Socony*, as "unlawful *per se*," and Judge Rifkind's opinion added the observation, citing *Socony*: "It does not matter whether the market in the commodity involved is or is not dominated by the parties to the agreement."[291]

In *Ethyl* the Government urged the illegality of the arrangement with the refiners as a boycott against unlicensed jobbers, participated in by those "occupying a dominant position in the industry."[292] "It may be true," the Government said, "that a trader, acting alone, has the right to select the parties with whom he will deal [citing *Colgate*]. But the action of appellant in denying jobbers access to the market cannot be justified under this rule. . . . It is the kind of combination or organized boycott which this Court has consistently held to be illegal."[293] But in *Ethyl* the defendant could still urge with some authority the reasonableness of the exclusion: "unreasonableness may be determined from its effect upon trade or from the justifiableness of the act—the balancing of the interests which are secured and impaired by it—in much the same way that unfairness or an unfair method of competition is judged."[294] "The restraint is reasonable and justifiable by reason of defendant's direct interest in and admittedly legal power over the sale and use of its patented fuel."[295] Even the Government's brief inferentially concedes, for some joint exclusion cases, the relevance of the reasonableness argument: "In

---

[290] *Id.* at 225 n. 59.   [291] 45 F. Supp. at 396.

[292] Brief for the United States, p. 36. The Government referred to United States v. First National Pictures, 282 U.S. 44 (1939), and later cited *Dr. Miles, Eastern States Lumber Ass'n, Beech-Nut, Trenton Potteries*, and *Interstate Circuit*, in support of the proposition. *Id.* at 46. Acceptance of this view is reflected in Mr. Justice Stone's opinion, 309 U.S. at 455–56, through the citation of Paramount Famous Pictures Corp. v. United States, 282 U.S. 30 (1930), and *First National Pictures*. The Government also argued that it was ". . . unnecessary to decide whether such an agreement existed. By combining with refiners appellant has forced the jobbers to accept its dictates if they wish to continue in business. This is not a case of agreement but of coercion." Brief for the United States, p. 42 n. 20.

[293] *Id.* at 85.   [294] Brief for Appellants, p. 62.

[295] *Id.* at 66. The brief cited Wm. Filene's Sons Co. v. Fashion Originators' Guild, 90 F. 2d 556 (1st Cir. 1937), with the comment ". . . boycott of style copyist held justifiable." The Supreme Court later rejected this in *Bausch & Lomb*.

the absence of some special justification, this Court has consistently condemned such arrangements."[296] This view of the relevance of reasonableness to collective exclusion cases was almost foreclosed by the *Fashion Originators' Guild*[297] case prior to the decision in *Bausch & Lomb*. In *Fashion Originators' Guild*, where it had been sought to justify collective refusals to deal with those who traded with copyists, Mr. Justice Black had written for the Court, "The reasonableness of the methods pursued by the combination to accomplish its unlawful objective is no more material than would be the reasonableness of the prices fixed by an unlawful combination. . . . Even if copying were an acknowledged tort under the law of every state, that situation would not justify petitioners in combining together to regulate and restrain interstate commerce in violation of federal law."[298] In *Bausch & Lomb*, the Court held: "A distributor of a trade-marked article may not lawfully limit by agreement, express or implied, the price at which or the person to whom its purchasers may resell, except as the seller moves along the route which is marked by the Miller-Tydings Act. . . . The same thing is true as to restriction of customers."[299] It cited *Fashion Originators' Guild*, among other cases.

Moreover, *Bausch & Lomb* recognized the *Interstate Circuit* and *Masonite* doctrine of concert of action as a conspiracy, possibly without agreement, by knowing participants in a program. In *Interstate Circuit*, distributors were charged with a conspiracy to enforce similar admission-price restrictions on their exhibitor licensees in response to an exhibitor's demand. Mr. Justice Stone wrote: "While the District Court's finding of an agreement . . . is supported by the evidence, we think that in the circumstances of this case such agree-

---

[296] Brief for the United States, p. 36.

[297] Fashion Originators' Guild v. F.T.C., 312 U.S. 457 (1941).

[298] *Id.* at 468. The defendant had argued: "Nothing is done in the execution of the program which each petitioner could not do alone without danger of criticism. *United States* v. *Colgate & Co.*, 250 U.S. 301, 307; *Federal Trade Commission* v. *Raymond Bros.-Clark Co.*, 263 U.S. 565. Cf. *Grenada Lumber Co.* v. *Mississippi*, 217 U.S. 433. Indeed, morality is on the side of the petitioners. A boycott like any combination can be justified; it is only *prima facie* unlawful." Brief for Petitioners, p. 42. The argument was made that "recent decisions of the Court show that a cooperative endeavor to regulate others' competitive practices by a concerted refusal is not *per se* a violation of the Sherman Act." *Id.* at 50–51. The reference was to Sugar Institute v. United States, 297 U.S. 553 (1936); Interstate Circuit v. United States, 306 U.S. 208 (1939); and Apex Hosiery Co. v. Leader, 310 U.S. 469 (1940).

[299] 321 U.S. at 721.

ment for the imposition of the restrictions . . . was not a prerequisite to an unlawful conspiracy. It was enough that, knowing the concerted action was contemplated and invited, the distributors gave their adherence to the scheme and participated in it. Each distributor was advised that the others were asked to participate; each knew that cooperation was essential to successful operation of the plan."[300] This was followed in *Masonite*, where similar patent-license arrangements setting the price among competitors, designated as *del credere* agents, were held unlawful. Mr. Justice Douglas wrote, "the District Court found that, in negotiating and entering into the first agreements, each appellee, other than Masonite, acted independently of the others. . . . But it is clear that, as the arrangement continued, each became familiar with its purpose and scope."[301] The opinion in *Masonite* then applied the *Interstate Circuit* doctrine of contemplated and invited concerted action. *Interstate Circuit* had been decided prior to *Ethyl*, and indeed use of it was made in the opinion, although not on the concerted action point.[302] But *Masonite* came between *Ethyl* and *Bausch & Lomb*. The last of these applied the doctrine of concerted action to the wholesalers' participation in Soft-Lite's program. "The wholesalers accepted Soft-Lite's proffer of a plan of distribution by cooperating in prices, limitation of sales to and approval of retail licenses. That is sufficient,"[303] wrote Mr. Justice Reed, citing *Interstate* and *Masonite*. As the Government had argued in its brief in *Bausch & Lomb*, "While . . . *Cudahy* . . . held that it was error to charge the jury that it might find a violation of the Sherman Act if it found that the defendant had frequently called to the attention of the wholesalers a sales plan which fixed minimum resale prices and that the great majority of the wholesalers had sold at the prices named, this holding provoked a vigorous dissent, has never since been referred to by this Court, and is difficult to reconcile with its recent decisions

---

[300] 306 U.S. at 226.   [301] 316 U.S. at 274–75.

[302] *Interstate Circuit* was cited for the point that the benefit of a patent, like the benefit of a copyright, could not be used "for the exploitation or promotion of a business not embraced within the patent." 309 U.S. at 459. See also *id.* at 456. *Interstate Circuit*, itself referring to the control of admission prices through distributor's licenses, held: "The consequence of the price restriction, though more oppressive, is comparable with the effect of resale price maintenance agreements, which have been held to be unreasonable restraints in violation of the Sherman Act." 306 U.S. at 232. See also Brief for the United States, pp. 73–74.

[303] 321 U.S. at 723.

in the *Interstate Circuit* and *Masonite* cases."³⁰⁴ It is the impact of these surrounding but relevant doctrines³⁰⁵ that raises new questions or requires different meaning in resale price cases.

---

³⁰⁴ Brief for the United States, p. 33. In United States v. Paramount Pictures, Inc., 334 U.S. 131, 144 (1948), Mr. Justice Douglas applied the concert-of-action theory to the relationship between licensees under similar price restrictions imposed by the distributor. As to concert of action, see Johnson v. J. H. Yost Lumber Co., 117 F. 2d 53 (8th Cir. 1941); Theatre Enterprises v. Paramount, 346 U.S. 537 (1954).

³⁰⁵ Kiefer-Stewart v. Seagram & Sons, 340 U.S. 211 (1951), and United States v. McKesson & Robbins, Inc., 351 U.S. 305 (1956), must now be added to *Socony* to show that market power is not required for price fixing. Associated Press v. United States, 326 U.S. 1 (1945), *Kiefer-Stewart*, and Klor's Inc. v. Broadway Hale Stores, Inc., 359 U.S. 207 (1959), must be added to *Fashion Originators' Guild* on the illegality of collective refusals to deal. *Associated Press* and *Kiefer-Stewart* close the door somewhat more—it is not clear that it is absolutely closed—on the reasonableness argument for collective exclusion. *Klor's* may show that market power is not required in boycott cases.

In the *Associated Press* case, Judge Learned Hand in the district court wrote, relevant to both price fixing and boycott: "There are some situations in which the liabilities have now become settled. No combination fixing prices is valid. . . . Whatever doubts were thrown upon . . . Trenton Potteries . . . by Appalachian Coals . . . and Sugar Institute . . . have been finally laid in . . . Socony-Vacuum. . . . Again, if a combination effectively excludes, or tries to exclude, outsiders from the business altogether, it is a monopoly, or an incipient monopoly, and it is unconditionally unlawful. . . . That is indeed the standard type of an illicit combination. . . . Finally, a combination may be illegal because of the means used to effect purposes lawful in themselves; and the means may be unlawful although it would not be, if used by a single person. It is arguable that a boycott, for instance, is always such a means: i.e., any use by a combination of its economic power to force a third person not to deal with another whom the combination wishes to coerce. At least, there is language in the books which lends itself to such a conclusion. . . . But these settled instances are not exhaustive; they are only illustrations of a general doctrine, whose scope they do not measure. When a situation does not fall within one of them, a court is forced to weigh the advantages gained by the combination against the injury done to the public, and apparently in this connection the public is the 'purchasers or consumers' whom the combination will deprive 'of the advantages which they derive from free competition.' " 52 F. Supp. at 369.

In the *Associated Press* case, *The Tribune* and McCormick brief in the Supreme Court argued that Associated Press and the defendants were not engaged in a boycott. They said: "This is stretching the meaning of boycott beyond the breaking point." P. 34. The Government's brief argued: "A combined refusal to deal which excludes others from that part of the market within the scope of the agreement has repeatedly been held to be a restraint of trade prohibited by the Sherman Act. Whether or not it is the kind of restraint, like price-fixing, which permits of no justification has not been specifically declared by this Court. But in those cases where the defendants have attempted justification of this kind of restraint, the command of the statute has been held to prevail." Brief for the United States, pp. 68–69. "We believe the rule to be drawn from the cases, taking them as a whole, is that an agreement to exclude others from certain trade is a restraint prohibited by the Sherman Act if the actual and intended effect is to restrain the competition of those excluded. There may, of course, be question whether a particular combination is of this

V. The Meaning and Effect of Parke, Davis

When *Dr. Miles*, *Colgate*, and *Beech-Nut* were decided, the law of price fixing was not clear in anti-trust cases. To be sure, *Addyston* and other cases had sought to exclude price fixing from the freedom given by the doctrine of reasonable restraints. There was some doubt after *Standard Oil* whether this question might not be reopened. Indeed, *Trenton Potteries* in 1927 was followed by the doubts engendered by *Appalachian Coals*, which presumably were finally put to rest by *Socony-Vacuum* and subsequent cases. But even under *Addyston* and *Trenton Potteries*, market control, which meant widespread restraints, was a legitimate basis for the decisions reached. As to collective refusals to deal as enforcement measures for resale price programs, one might have distinguished between those which were the result of agreement between major factors in the industry—and thus involved market control—and more incidental arrangements. Moreover, assuming that some control over the resale price was legitimate, it was tempting, as counsel argued in *Ethyl*, to assume that in this area of boycott reasonableness would be a justification. The lack of clarity in anti-trust law put the ban on resale price agreements in a rather ambiguous position. Perhaps all formal agreements attempting to qualify title in the purchaser—whatever that might mean—were void, even illegal, as restraints on alienation. This argument was more persuasive when restrictions were attached to goods in the hands of remote vendees rather than first purchasers. It helped carry the day in *Dr. Miles* and *Beech-Nut*, where the restrictions were interlocking, involving the purchasers through boycotts in the enforcement process against each other. The restraint-on-alienation argument did not have to be limited

---

character, as there may be room for doubt whether an agreement is a price-fixing one. *Cf. United States* v. *Socony-Vacuum Oil Co.* 310 U.S. 218–223." *Id.* at 74–75.

On collective refusals to deal, see United States v. Columbia Steel, 334 U.S. 495, 522 (1948); United States v. General Motors Corp., 121 F. 2d 376, 404, 411–12 (7th Cir. 1941); Gamco, Inc. v. Providence Fruit & Produce Bldg., 194 F. 2d 484 (1st Cir. 1952); *cf.* Packard Motor Car Co. v. Webster Motor Car Co., 243 F. 2d 418 (D.C. Cir. 1957); Orbo-Theatre Corp. v. Loew's Inc., 261 F. 2d 380 (D.C. Cir. 1958); *cf.* also United States v. Central Supply Ass'n, 6 F.R.D. 526 (N.D. Ohio 1947); United States v. New York Great Atlantic & Pacific Tea Co., 173 F. 2d 79, 87 (7th Cir. 1949); Lorain Journal v. United States, 342 U.S. 143 (1951); Times-Picayune Pub. Co. v. United States, 345 U.S. 594, 625 (1953).

On the illegality of price-fixing agreements, see United States v. Line Material, 333 U.S. 287, 307–8 (1948); Banana Distributors Inc. v. United Fruit Co., 269 F. 2d 790 (2d Cir. 1959); Klor's Inc. v. Broadway Hale Stores, Inc., 359 U.S. 207, 213 n. 7 (1959).

to widespread restraints. *Colgate* raised the question whether agreements, which so far as the trial judge could see were not required of the remote vendees, were not only invalid but criminal, even though the interlocking, self-policing, and widespread restraints of *Dr. Miles* were not spelled out in them. Perhaps *Colgate*, *Schrader's Son*, and *Cudahy* concluded that such assurances and promises were illegal if they were found to be agreements, express or implied, but with the clear indication that promises or assurances, at least from the first vendee, need not be regarded as agreements. Indeed, the promises and assurances which make for mutual trust—when a program is announced, price cutters are restored, and adherence is widespread—in *Colgate* and *Cudahy* were labeled as no agreements by themselves. In *Dr. Miles* and *Beech-Nut*, also, the vertical agreements, or methods which substituted for them, were combined with the effect of the widespread restraints on competition between the wholesalers and retailers. In *Dr. Miles* the argument was put in terms of an answer to the contention that reasonableness should be a factor. But the conception of the restraints in both *Dr. Miles* and *Beech-Nut* as equivalent to the market control of horizontal price fixing was certainly evident. This served to emphasize the importance of the widespread restraints, because at that time price fixing on a horizontal level, without market power or control, might have been lawful. Today the surrounding theory has changed. Agreements among wholesalers and among retailers, even if incidental, would be unlawful as horizontal price fixing. Boycott by purchasers of subsequent vendees as part of the enforcement process, even though not of market-control dimension, might be illegal in itself. And the doctrine of concert of action might be used to label common adherence to a program, which *Cudahy* permitted, as participation in a conspiracy.

In this world of changed legal doctrine, *Colgate* and *Beech-Nut* both need restatement or explanation. *Colgate* and *Cudahy* together have always been anomalous because they attempted to avoid a question of law by compelling or banning inferences of fact. It is still not known how widespread and of what character are the vulnerable restraints which condemn resale price fixing under the *Beech-Nut* doctrine. Mr. Justice Harlan, in his dissent in *Parke, Davis*, commented that "*Colgate*, decided more than 40 years ago, has become part of the economic regime of the country upon which the commercial community and the lawyers who advise it have justifiably relied."[306] From its inception the *Colgate* doctrine has been confused both in application and theory. Since the inference that *Colgate* permitted concerned the absence of an agreement, *Beech-Nut*, which allowed the examination of methods as effective as agreements, made *Colgate*'s doctrine even more uncertain. Indeed, Professor Chafee, who in this matter may have been too decisive, wrote after *Beech-Nut:* "The Supreme Court . . . has virtually declared illegal all effective methods of exercising the right which it unanimously approved in the *Colgate* case."[307] There have been numerous indications of *Colgate*'s doubtful status. Since *Parke, Davis* was decided, Judge Moore of the Second Circuit has commented on the lawyers who relied on *Colgate:* "That they did so advise and did rely is not open to doubt; whether they did so 'justifiably' in the light of warning signals during this period is more debatable. Even in 1926 an appellate court said that 'the state of the law as to price fixing may rightly be said to be in confusion.' . . . The status quo—at least as to confusion—was rather well maintained throughout the years although the encroachments were so numerous as to cause serious doubt that Colgate reflected then current judicial opinion."[308] Pride in one's pro-

---

[306] 362 U.S. at 57.

[307] Chafee, note 90 *supra*, at 991.

[308] George W. Warner & Co. v. Black & Decker Mfg. Co., 277 F. 2d 787, 789 (2d Cir. 1960). In this case it was charged that the manufacturer directed the complaining and other distributors to adhere to resale prices. The manufacturer was charged with threatening the loss of the distributorship, elimination or reduction of the price discount, surveillance of bids, and blacklisting and boycotting of nonconformers. This was held to state a cause of action.

In his opinion Judge Moore also quoted the dissent of Judge Jerome Frank in Adams-Mitchell Mfg. Co. v. Cambridge Distributing Co., 189 F. 2d 913, 917 (2d Cir. 1951). A liquor wholesaler brought an action to rescind an oral contract for the purchase of 1,100 cases of "Auld Malcolm" Scotch-type whiskey, basing his claim on the defendant-distributor's failure to maintain the price and to limit the number of distributors in the Boston area. The court in denying a motion by the defendant to dismiss the action said: "There are legitimate means of price maintenance in spite of the provisions of the Sherman Act. . . . Such means include a refusal to sell in the future to those who had not maintained a suggested price." 189 F. 2d at 916. Judge Frank wrote: "I think the anti-anti-trust lawyers and their clients will welcome the foregoing decision for two reasons; first, it breathes new life into the remains of the decrepit doctrine of United States v. Colgate . . . thereby condoning a form of price fixing which will simplify evasion of the antitrust laws. . . ." *Id.* at 917. "[T]he controlling inquiry then becomes the present state of vigor of the doctrine of United States v. Colgate. . . . The rationale of that decision is not easily discerned. For, obviously, a threat of withholding further supplies will coerce price maintenance just

fession suggests there must have been more caution than reliance.

In view of the history of resale price maintenance and of *Colgate*, Mr. Justice Harlan's dissent in *Parke, Davis* may seem puzzling. He made the point, in effect, that he did not see the significance of Parke, Davis' announcement that it would refuse to sell to wholesalers who sold to price-cutting retailers. Because the district court had found that Parke, Davis dealt with each wholesaler unilaterally, Mr. Justice Harlan wrote: "I cannot see how such unilateral action, permissible in itself, becomes any less unilateral because it is taken simultaneously with similar unilateral action at the retail level."[309] But it is just this involvement of purchasers in the enforcement of price restrictions on sub-vendees that could be said to be of importance in resale price cases. Along the same line, Mr. Justice Harlan was critical of the importance attached to Parke, Davis' attempt to secure substantial unanimity among the retailers with regard to the suspension of cut-price advertising. As to this, Mr. Justice Harlan recorded the findings of the district judge that the company "did not make 'the enforcement of its policies, as to any one wholesaler or retailer dependent upon the

---

about as well as a forthright agreement to maintain a price. The difference, for practical purposes, is shadowy. . . . Considering the course of Supreme Court anti-trust decisions on the subject of price fixing since Colgate was decided, it seems to me that, although that doctrine may not be wholly dead, yet, by distinctions stopping just short of extinction, it has been reduced to almost imperceptible proportions. . . ." *Id.* at 924. Judge Moore also quoted a comment in 58 YALE L. J. 1121, at 1128–29: "When a leading case is beset by qualifications and then atrophied by lack of use, its final demise is difficult to detect. Perhaps the Colgate case is dead, despite frequent citations. But doubt remains. The Colgate case, still a symbol of special immunity for all refusals to sell, should be expressly overruled at the earliest opportunity." 277 F. 2d at 790.

In the Robinson-Patman Act case against Standard Oil of Indiana, Standard Oil Co. v. F.T.C., 340 U.S. 231 (1951), for price discrimination in the Detroit area, the order of the commission would have prohibited Standard from selling to a wholesaler at less than Standard's tank wagon prices where the wholesaler resold to its retailers at less than Standard's posted tank wagon prices. The brief of Standard in the Supreme Court commented: "No supplier in his right mind would embark upon a price maintenance system to see to it that the wholesaler maintained the supplier's retailer prices. An agreement by the wholesaler to maintain prices would doubtless be unlawful. . . . Nor would the petitioner be safe in establishing an espionage system over its jobbers and in 'cutting off' any wholesaler who does not maintain them. . . ." Brief for Petitioner, pp. 46–47.

In Kiefer-Stewart Co. v. Joseph E. Seagram & Sons, 340 U.S. 211, 214 (1951), Mr. Justice Black wrote, in a manner not reassuring for resale price restriction, "Seagram and Calvert acting individually perhaps might have refused to deal with petitioner or with any or all of the Indiana wholesalers."

[309] 362 U.S. at 55.

action of any other wholesaler or retailer,' " and "that such acquiescence was not brought about 'by coercion' or 'agreement.' "[310] Perhaps this approach records satisfaction with the method of handling
promises or assurances obtained in this manner as though a purely factual question were involved. But special significance could attach to
assurances sought and received not from the first vendees but rather
from subsequent purchasers. Indeed, this may be, although one cannot
be sure, what Mr. Justice Stewart meant in his separate opinion. And
as Mr. Justice Harlan himself suggested, the *Interstate Circuit* doctrine
needs to be reckoned with when wholesalers and retailers with knowledge are involved in one program. Mr. Justice Harlan's answer was
that "even if . . . concerted action among the retailers at the 'horizontal' level might be inferred . . . under the principles of *Interstate Circuit*
. . . I do not see how that itself would justify an inference that concerted action at the 'vertical' level existed between Parke Davis and
the retailers or wholesalers."[311] But the arrangement, organized by a
manufacturer, of an illegal concert of action among its purchasers and
with it, the manufacturer, would be both vertical and horizontal.

This is not to argue that the *Interstate Circuit* doctrine necessarily
applies. The argument has sometimes been made that in normal
course resale price fixing always springs from the desires of purchasers and therefore reflects a kind of collusive behavior.[312] Earlier
cases, as Mr. Justice Holmes remarked in his dissent in *Dr. Miles*,
reflected this kind of combination.[313] Nevertheless, when the activities by the wholesalers and retailers are incidental and not widespread, it could be argued that *Interstate Circuit* should not be used to
stigmatize as unlawful the harmony that springs in the main not from
these incidental activities but from suggestions made by the seller.
This, of course, was the teaching of *Cudahy*. It can be said, also, that
congressional action in outlawing vertical resale price fixing, when
horizontal agreements are present, shows a conclusion that the apparent understandings and concert of action among purchasers, always

[310] *Ibid.*

[311] *Ibid.*

[312] See Bowman, *The Prerequisites and Effects of Resale Price Maintenance*, 22 U. CHI. L.
REV. 825 (1955).

[313] See Park & Sons v. National Wholesale Druggists' Ass'n, 175 N.Y. 1 (1903);
Straus v. American Publishers' Ass'n, 177 N.Y. 473 (1904); Jayne v. Loder, 149 Fed. 21 (3d
Cir. 1906).

present whenever there is successful resale price maintenance, are not to be considered unlawful. But presumably the main thrust of Mr. Justice Harlan's dissent was his point, which seems well taken, that "the defensive, limited, unorganized, and unsuccessful effort of Parke Davis" is quite different from the "aggressive, widespread, highly organized, and successful merchandising programs" in *Beech-Nut* and *Bausch & Lomb*.[314] It may not be relevant that Parke, Davis' conduct was "defensive," but certainly the concerted action in *Parke, Davis* was of a different order from that present in *Dr. Miles, Beech-Nut, Bausch & Lomb*, or even *Ethyl*.

The theory of the majority opinion appears to be that the protective area provided by *Colgate* is pierced if the producer "secures adherence to his suggested prices by means which go beyond his mere declination to sell to a customer who will not observe his announced policy."[315] This would be because the countervailing policy in favor of the seller's discretion is no longer present. Possibly this means any step, so pronounced as to be observed, beyond the announcement of the program and refusal to sell, will make the whole program vulnerable. That it may mean this, in addition to the fact that this is the language used, is suggested by the implication that *Colgate* itself, while not now overruled, has only a tenuous status. It is suggested also by the Court's deliberate statement that *Cudahy* has been limited and will not be followed. It is certainly possible to read *Beech-Nut* and *Bausch & Lomb* as having very little to do with *Cudahy*, and not limiting it. Yet if the theory now is that any step that goes beyond the announcement and refusal to sell makes the whole arrangement vulnerable, *Cudahy* might be an embarrassment; it would be obvious that the principal restraining effects stemmed from the acquiescence which *Cudahy* allowed. But this interpretation of the majority opinion is uncertain because the opinion is cast on the basis that *Beech-Nut* and *Bausch & Lomb* compel the result.

Beech-Nut and *Bausch & Lomb* do not compel the result that any activity by the seller beyond that permitted in *Colgate* frustrates the

---

[314] 362 U.S. at 56.

[315] *Id.* at 43. The Acting Assistant Attorney General in charge of the Anti-trust Division has interpreted *Parke, Davis* as sounding "the death knell for vertical price fixing activities—except to the extent protected by state law—beyond the manufacturer's simple unilateral refusal to deal with price cutting retailers." 16 A.B.A. ANTI-TRUST SECTION 55 (1960)

whole arrangement. Their factual situations were far different from *Parke, Davis*. Their restraints were much more widespread, and the results would have qualified more easily as equivalent to the type of horizontal price-fixing arrangements then unlawful. They could be said to be similar to *Parke, Davis* in that they involved, first, dealings to secure restraints on remote vendees, and second, the use, to some degree, of purchasers in a boycott as part of the enforcement process. If the dealing with remote vendees is the distinguishing point, as Mr. Justice Stewart's opinion perhaps meant to suggest, this seems to hark back to older ideas concerning restraint on alienation, or perhaps it was a means of asserting that the protected area of *Colgate* extends only to first purchasers. It could be a way of saying that the assurances and promises which are not viewed as agreements or methods as effective as agreements, when obtained from first purchasers, are to be seen in a different light when they are procured from subsequent vendees. On this it is pertinent to remark again in passing that *Schrader's Son* did not involve agreements with retailers, although, of course, *Bausch & Lomb* did. *Schrader's Son* did involve written restrictions on purchasers, however, and perhaps the uneasy distinction remaining between formal written agreements and understandings is to be preserved in practice for first purchasers. The involvement of purchasers in a boycott for enforcement would seem an even more relevant distinguishing feature of *Dr. Miles, Beech-Nut, Bausch & Lomb*, and *Parke, Davis*. This suggests, since Mr. Justice Brennan relied so heavily on the language of *Beech-Nut* and *Bausch & Lomb*, that what has been accomplished in *Parke, Davis* is not so sweeping after all. English law, which Mr. Justice Holmes pointed to as different from ours, has now taken the step of banning collective enforcement of resale price agreements, but it has done so by statute.[316]

Of course the history of the common law of resale price fixing, and of *Colgate* to a considerable extent, reflects conflicting social policies. *Colgate* is caught between the important right to refuse to deal and the antipathy to price fixing. The social policy is mixed.[317] Legislation

---

[316] See JOHNSON-DAVIES & HARRINGTON, RESTRICTIVE TRADE PRACTICES 137 (1950); Dennison, *The British Restrictive Trade Practices Act of 1956*, 2 J. LAW & ECON. 64, 66 (1959).

[317] *Cf.* Automobile Information Disclosure Act, Act of July 7, 1958, 72 Stat. 325. See REPORT OF THE ATTORNEY GENERAL'S NATIONAL COMMITTEE TO STUDY THE ANTI-TRUST LAWS 154 (1955).

permits resale price fixing under certain circumstances. Presumably that legislation presupposes that otherwise vertical price fixing is forbidden. But this really begs the question, and contrary arguments can be made. Furthermore, it is quite possible that, having regard for the propensity of competition to cause violations of price restrictions, laws forbidding resale price maintenance may not be worth the trouble they cause. The difficulty with *Colgate* is on a different level. As far as social policy is concerned, it would not be earthshaking, whichever direction the common law of anti-trust took with regard to resale price fixing.[318] But it is a matter of concern that the law should have failed to provide itself with a meaningful structure of theory. Beyond this, it is a matter of concern also that in an area involving important commercial practice the law should have developed so as to appear to put a premium on the avoidance of words which describe what the parties clearly intend. This must seem strange and degrading to men who take pride in their given word, and it fosters a caricatured view of the law.

The common law requires judging for its development. When an appellate court receives relatively few cases in a given area over a span of years (although this infrequency does not measure the importance of the commercial practice involved), the structure of theory becomes most important. It is to be hoped that a future case will make of *Parke, Davis* an important step in this much-needed development.

---

[318] Cf. Professor Chafee's conclusion: "Whatever solution of the price-control problem is adopted, it seems pretty sure to be unsatisfactory." Chafee, note 90 *supra*, at 992.

DEREK C. BOK

THE TAMPA ELECTRIC CASE AND THE PROBLEM OF EXCLUSIVE ARRANGEMENTS UNDER THE CLAYTON ACT

In few areas of the law are judges so caught up in the economic and social currents of the day as they are in the administration of the antitrust laws. The statutes they elucidate are not only vague but their meaning turns upon phrases such as "unfair competition" and "restraint of trade," which echo highly controverted problems of economic policy. In legal proceedings where these terms are applied and given meaning, the stakes are often high and the interests powerful. Hence, great care is taken to seek out each helpful fact and theory and to capture every movement of feeling and policy that may in some way influence the judge in passing on the case. For this reason, the course of the law in this troublesome field cannot be fully understood apart from the prevailing theories and discoveries, attitudes and prejudices that have to do with the phenomenon of competition.

The intellectual climate surrounding antitrust law has changed perceptibly since the late nineteen-thirties when Thurman Arnold

Derek C. Bok is Professor of Law, Harvard University.

launched his celebrated campaign against restraints of trade.[1] In those years, the enforcement of the Sherman Act could be widely publicized as a necessary step to relieve unemployment and to preserve our society against the threat of totalitarianism.[2] After decades of lax administration, the time seemed overripe for vigorous prosecutions and for a broad movement on the part of the law toward stricter standards of legality. As substantial steps were taken to achieve these ends,[3] however, a flurry of studies appeared from the pens of prominent professors and men of affairs questioning many of the doctrinal foundations of an aggressive antitrust philosophy. Essays were written warning that a strict application of the prevailing theories of competition might interfere with technological progress and cause destructive and harmful rivalry.[4] Other writings emphasized emerging forces in the economy: the growth of corporate morality,[5] the development of new products,[6] and the rise of countervailing blocs of power,[7] tendencies that were all said to serve, quite apart from the antitrust laws, to reduce the

---

[1] A description of the various intellectual currents of the period 1937–53 is included in the detailed discussion by Loevinger, *Antitrust and the New Economics*, 37 MINN. L. REV. 505 (1953).

[2] See, *e.g.*, ARNOLD, THE BOTTLENECKS OF BUSINESS (1940); Jackson, *Should the Antitrust Laws Be Revised?* 71 U.S.L. REV. 575 (1937). For an account of the political and intellectual background for the resurgence of antitrust regulation, see FORTUNE, Feb., 1938, p. 59.

[3] See, *e.g.*, United States v. Socony Vacuum Oil Co., Inc., 310 U.S. 150 (1940); Mandeville Island Farms v. American Crystal Sugar Co., 334 U.S. 219 (1948); United States v. National Association of Real Estate Boards, 339 U.S. 485 (1950); Fashion Originators' Guild of America, Inc. v. F.T.C., 312 U.S. 457 (1941); Associated Press v. United States, 326 U.S. 1 (1945); International Salt Co. v. United States, 322 U.S. 392 (1947); F.T.C. v. Morton Salt Co., 334 U.S. 37 (1948); Hartford Empire Co. v. United States, 323 U.S. 386 (1945); United States v. Line Material Co., 333 U.S. 287 (1948); American Tobacco Co. v. United States, 328 U.S. 781 (1946); F.T.C. v. Cement Institute, 333 U.S. 683 (1948); United States v. Aluminum Company of America, 148 F.2d 416 (2d Cir. 1945); American Tobacco Co. v. United States, 328 U.S. 781 (1946); United States v. Griffith, 334 U.S. 100 (1948).

[4] SCHUMPETER, CAPITALISM, SOCIALISM AND DEMOCRACY chs. 7, 8 (2d ed. 1947); Clark, *Toward a Concept of Workable Competition*, 30 AM. ECON. REV. 241 (1940).

[5] ALLEN, THE BIG CHANGE: AMERICA TRANSFORMS ITSELF (1952); LILIENTHAL, BIG BUSINESS: A NEW ERA 27 (1952).

[6] LILIENTHAL, *op. cit. supra* note 5.

[7] GALBRAITH, AMERICAN CAPITALISM—THE CONCEPT OF COUNTERVAILING POWER (1952).

danger that big business might exploit the public. Still other studies called for a more realistic view of competition that would take account of an increasing number of forces and circumstances helping to influence corporate behavior.[8] To complement these theoretical works, empirical data were compiled which inevitably cast doubt upon the need for an active antitrust policy by questioning such traditional notions as the belief that the economy was becoming more concentrated[9] and the assumption that large firms invariably sought to extract the highest possible profit from the market.[10]

While these writings did not succeed in commanding universal approval, they have had a considerable influence. In assessing the significance of this literature, however, one is inevitably struck by the absence of any serious effort to articulate positive proposals or policies to shape the regulation of business.[11] Instead, what is noteworthy in these works is the skepticism they express regarding the potentialities of antitrust policy and the qualifications they place on every simple generalization about the workings of competition. In sum, what has emerged from all these writings is a compelling sense of the intricacy and complexity that shroud the movements of the market place.[12]

---

[8] E.g., BAIN, BARRIERS TO NEW COMPETITION (1956); Chamberlin, *The Product as an Economic Variable*, 67 Q. J. ECON. 1 (1953). A striking example of this tendency is the attempt to apply the techniques of game theory to competitive balances. See, *e.g.*, SHUBIK, STRATEGY AND MARKET STRUCTURE (1959).

[9] Adelman, *The Measurement of Industrial Concentration*, 33 REV. ECON. & STAT. 269 (1951); NUTTER, THE EXTENT OF ENTERPRISE MONOPOLY IN THE UNITED STATES, 1899–1939 (1951).

[10] KAPLAN, DIRLAM, & LANZILOTTI, PRICING IN BIG BUSINESS—A CASE APPROACH (1958).

[11] This point is developed in greater detail by MASON, ECONOMIC CONCENTRATION AND THE MONOPOLY PROBLEM 371 *et seq.* (1957). See also Nourse, in *Symposium Review: Galbraith's "Concept of Countervailing Power" and Lilienthal's "Big Business,"* 49 Nw. L. REV. 139, 143–44 (1954) (commentary on Lilienthal's proposals for revising the antitrust laws).

[12] These developments have sometimes evoked rather pessimistic appraisals, even from well-known economists. In this regard, the following statement by Lionel Robbins is instructive: "There are branches of the subject [of economics] which have definitely passed beyond the consolidation of the intuitions and discoveries of our predecessors. I am not clear that this is so in the much discussed theory of imperfect or monopolistic competition; for all the multiplication of diagrams in recent literature, I doubt whether, analytically, we have advanced very far beyond Marshall's few lines of algebra; and I suspect that, in practical judgment and

These intellectual currents have doubtless been reinforced by changes in public sentiment that have taken place since the last war. With the depression years receding, distrust of big business has been diminished through a combination of common sense, prosperity, and public relations. Strong feelings have shifted from concern about Wall Street and the "trusts" to the problems of race and subversion, corruption and international affairs. Indeed, as events have tempered some of the hopes and claims of earlier decades, many thoughtful people have assumed an informed skepticism that emphasizes balance rather than commitment in contemplating public affairs. An attitude of this sort breeds respect for the case and analytic detail of the recent antitrust literature together with a tolerance for the inconclusiveness that pervades so much of this writing.

In such a period, the law has not been called upon to engineer a pervasive movement toward stricter or milder standards. Neither our mood nor our understanding has provided a new vision on which the law can focus. Instead, the overriding problem has been to enforce the existing law more effectively and in so doing to accommodate legal doctrine to an increasingly complex perception of reality. This task is made particularly difficult by the fact that many of the old concepts, values, and beliefs have been questioned and qualified without fresh substitutes appearing to take their place. In this way, the building blocks on which logic and analysis depend have been rendered less serviceable so that the administrator and judge are often hard put to reach a reasoned decision. The effects of these problems on the law cannot be fully understood simply by comparing Supreme Court opinions. The consequences of these opinions are fully worked out only in the myriad of case and commentary to which they give rise while the cases and comments, in turn, provide the experience that helps to shape the work of the Court. Thus, attention must be paid to all the institutions that con-

---

sense of proportion, we are often a good way behind." THE ECONOMIST IN THE TWENTIETH CENTURY 7 (1954). Even if this appraisal is justified, it does seem probable that any fundamental progress in theory and analysis that is made in the next decade or more will profit considerably from the data and analysis that have accumulated since Marshall. Moreover, there does appear to be a marked increase in the sensitivity of courts to the findings and analyses of economists, so that economics is undoubtedly making a greater contribution to antitrust law than was formerly the case.

cern themselves with antitrust law. As a means toward this end, this paper will examine one of the many antitrust topics and follow its course through the reforms of the forties and the reappraisals of the fifties to its most recent development in a Supreme Court opinion of the Term just passed.

I. THE EVOLUTION OF THE LAW OF EXCLUSIVE DEALING

Goods and commodities are sometimes sold or leased on the condition that the purchaser or lessee will not handle the products of any competing supplier. Arrangements of this sort are known as "exclusive dealing" contracts,[13] and they are forbidden under Section 3 of the Clayton Act whenever they may have the effect of substantially lessening competition or tending to create a monopoly.[14]

A. THE NATURE OF THE BEAST

Like so many phenomena in the world of antitrust law, exclusive arrangements are only partially understood. Little empirical work has been done on their nature and effects,[15] and almost no effort has been made to devise a theoretical framework in which they can be understood and evaluated.[16] On the other hand, something

---

[13] The term "exclusive dealing" is used in this paper to include requirements contracts.

[14] 38 Stat. 730 (1914), 15 U.S.C. § 14 (1958). The section reads as follows: "It shall be unlawful for any person engaged in commerce, in the course of such commerce, to lease or make a sale or contract for sale of goods, wares, merchandise, machinery, supplies, or other commodities, whether patented or unpatented, for use, consumption, or resale within the United States or any Territory thereof or the District of Columbia or any insular possession or other place under the jurisdiction of the United States, or fix a price charged therefor, or discount from, or rebate upon, such price, on the condition, agreement, or understanding that the lessee or purchaser thereof shall not use or deal in the goods, wares, merchandise, machinery, supplies, or other commodities of a competitor or competitors of the lessor or seller, where the effect of such lease, sale, or contract for sale or such condition, agreement, or understanding may be to substantially lessen competition or tend to create a monopoly in any line of commerce."

[15] Such bits and pieces of information as do exist are collected in Kessler & Stern, *Competition, Contract and Vertical Integration,* 69 YALE L. J. 1, 2–21 (1959).

[16] Some work along these lines has been done by Kessler and Stern, *supra* note 15. On a higher level of abstraction is a recent work on the somewhat analogous problem of full line forcing. Burstein, *A Theory of Full Line Forcing,* 55 Nw. L. REV. 62 (1960).

of their nature can be gathered by applying rudimentary logic. It is easy enough to understand that, as more customers or more distributors for a commodity become bound to handle the product of only one concern, other companies may find it harder to market their goods so that newcomers may be discouraged from entering the field and existing firms may decline or perish. But difficulties arise as soon as one must decide how great an impact has been produced by any particular series of exclusive arrangements. And this is precisely the assessment that appears to be called for if one is to follow the literal terms of the Clayton Act and determine in each case whether competition may be "substantially" lessened by the contracts in question.

Suppose that four manufacturers produce half of the total national output of some commodity and that each sells through a network of retail dealers pursuant to exclusive dealing contracts. Since competitors of the four can no longer sell to dealers distributing half of the national output, it would seem at first glance that these competitors have been substantially hurt. Nevertheless, if the manufacturers' success depends fundamentally on the popularity of their product among consumers, will the exclusive contracts really enable the four to slacken their efforts to lower prices or enhance the quality of their product? May not the other firms find other stores to handle their wares or succeed in increasing the volume of sales in the outlets to which they still have access? Businessmen who are thinking of moving into the industry may be discouraged from trying because they are blocked off from so many distributors. But is it not possible that they will find enough available outlets for their modest beginnings and may they not discover the means to build or expand their own outlets as their product grows in popularity and value? And can one be sure that many, or even most, of the distributors involved would not prefer to specialize in the sale of a single leading brand even if they were under no contract obligation to do so? Finally, since the exclusive arrangements probably run for a limited time, is it not conceivable that opportunities for prying loose exclusive outlets will occur with sufficient frequency to accommodate the normal rise and fall of competitive fortunes? Troublesome questions of this kind will often arise and differences of opinion will result, even before practiced eyes, as to whether the exclusive arrangements will have substantial effects upon competition. Since these knotty situations are the cases that develop most easily into litigated cases, the burden of contending with such complicated issues falls heavily upon the judges and the Federal Trade Commissioners.

B. EARLY DEVELOPMENTS

Various approaches have been tried by court and commission to resolve exclusive dealing cases. After the enactment of Section 3 in 1914, a number of actions were brought by the Federal Trade Commission, and though the Commission's opinions were too cryptic to yield any clear rationale, the Commission appeared to strike down exclusive dealing arrangements almost automatically.[17] Decisions in the federal courts, however, soon brought a halt to the trend of Commission decisions. The Supreme Court did find in one leading case that the Act was violated when the leading maker of dress patterns tied up 40 per cent of the available outlets with exclusive contracts.[18] But the Court took pains to emphasize that the Act was "not intended to reach every remote lessening of competition."[19] One year later, the Court reversed the Commission in an exclusive dealing case, pointing out that "effective competition requires that traders have large freedom of action when conducting their affairs."[20] Other proceedings in the lower federal courts resulted in further reversals of the Commission.[21] In the wake of these decisions, the Commission restricted its activities under Section 3 to cases in which the dominant seller of a particular commodity entered into widespread exclusive arrangements.[22] The scope of Section 3 remained confined in this manner until the second World War.

During the late nineteen-forties, the Supreme Court suggested that a large seller who engaged in "tying" arrangements in-

---

[17] E.g., Stanley Booking Corp., 1 F.T.C. 212 (1918); B. S. Pearsall Butter Co., 5 F.T.C. 127 (1922); Standard Electric Mfg. Co., 5 F.T.C. 376 (1923).

[18] Standard Fashion Co. v. Magrane-Houston Co., 258 U.S. 346 (1922).

[19] Id. at 357.

[20] F.T.C. v. Curtis Publishing Co., 260 U.S. 568 (1923).

[21] E.g., B. S. Pearsall Butter Co. v. F.T.C., 292 Fed. 720 (7th Cir. 1923).

[22] E.g., Q.R.S. Music Co., 7 F.T.C. 412 (1924); Pennick & Ford, Ltd., 14 F.T.C. 261 (1930); Carter Carburetor Corp., 28 F.T.C. 116 (1939).

volving a "not insubstantial" amount of commerce would be considered automatically to have violated Section 3 of the Clayton Act.[23] As a result, the possibility emerged that the same statutory language might yield an equally strict result in exclusive dealing cases. A suitable testing ground for this proposition was created in the Government's action against Standard Oil of California.[24] Evidence was introduced to show that Standard accounted for 23 per cent of the total taxable gallonage of gas sold in eleven western states, that Standard had entered into exclusive arrangements covering 16 per cent of the retail gasoline outlets in these states, and that 6.7 per cent of the retail gasoline sold in this area was handled by dealers subject to such arrangements with Standard. With these facts before it, the district court refused to entertain evidence offered by Standard to show that the contracts served beneficial purposes and that they did not in fact restrain competition. On certiorari to the Supreme Court, a bare majority upheld the district judge. Writing for the Court, Mr. Justice Frankfurter saw in the case a fundamental question as to how far courts could be expected to go in wrestling with complex economic problems:[25]

> The issue before us, therefore, is whether the requirement of showing that the effect of the agreements "may be to substantially lessen competition" may be met simply by proof that a substantial portion of commerce is affected or whether it must also be demonstrated that competitive activity has actually diminished or probably will diminish.

Having reduced the case to these alternatives, Mr. Justice Frankfurter had little difficulty in rejecting the more ambitious legal standard. Conceding that exclusive arrangements could be harmless or even beneficial, the Justice nevertheless declared:[26]

> ... to demand that bare inference be supported by evidence as to what would have happened but for the adoption of the practice ... or to require firm prediction of an increase of competition as a probable result of ordering the abandonment of the practice, would be a standard of proof, if not virtually impossible to meet, at least most ill-suited for ascertainment by courts.

---

[23] International Salt Co. v. United States, 332 U.S. 392 (1947). Tying agreements exist where a seller conditions the sale of a desirable item on the purchase of some other, less desirable, commodity.

[24] Standard Oil Co. v. United States, 337 U.S. 293 (1949).

[25] *Id*. at 299.   [26] *Id*. at 309–10.

Accordingly, Mr. Justice Frankfurter concluded "that the qualifying clause of Section 3 is satisfied by proof that competition has been foreclosed in a substantial share of the line of commerce affected."[27]

C. THE REPERCUSSIONS OF STANDARD STATIONS

The reaction of legal commentators to the *Standard Stations* case was as varied as it was vehement. The largest group of critics attacked the tendency of the Court to propound mechanical prohibitions in so subtle and complicated a field.[28] Writers in this group pointed to legitimate objectives that could underlie exclusive dealing and set out hypothetical cases in which exclusive arrangements that seemed clearly harmless would be condemned. But these critics made no effort to consider whether exceptions might be devised to cover such situations. Instead, they simply urged that every case be considered in the light of all the relevant facts and circumstances. No attempts were made to demonstrate how these facts could be combined and used as standards in concrete cases, even though the intellectual difficulties of this task were precisely what had led to the rejection of this approach in *Standard Stations*.

---

[27] *Id.* at 314.

[28] Perhaps the most prominent example in this category is the work of Lockhart and Sacks, which discusses a number of factors that the courts should take into account in passing upon exclusive arrangements: *The Relevance of Economic Factors in Determining Whether Exclusive Arrangements Violate Section 3 of the Clayton Act*, 65 HARV. L. REV. 913 (1952). See also: McLaren, *Related Problems of "Requirements" Contracts and Acquisitions in Vertical Integration under the AntiTrust Laws*, 45 ILL. L. REV. 141, 172 (1950): Violations of Section 3 should be found "only when supported by the 'substantial evidence' to be drawn from a realistic economic investigation and the fair conclusion that a particular arrangement probably will unduly restrict competition." Sunderland, *Changing Legal Concepts in the Antitrust Field*, 3 SYR. L. REV. 60, 80 (1951): "The courts should revert to the rule of reason: avoid scare words, rules-of-thumb and *a priori* assumptions, and employ doctrines of automatic illegality only with the utmost of caution. The decision in each case that is brought shall depend upon whether, under all the facts and circumstances, it is shown that competition has in fact been unduly restrained. Through a realistic, as distinguished from a doctrinaire, application of the Antitrust Laws, business transactions and practices which further competition will be approved and encouraged, and only those which in actuality stifle or restrict competition will be condemned." Oppenheim, *Federal Antitrust Legislation: Guideposts to a Revised National Antitrust Policy*, 50 MICH. L. REV. 1139, 1180–81 (1952): ". . . it is an escape unwarranted by constitutional standards and the intended congressional intention in the statutory standards of section 3 to deny the defendant a fair and full hearing on all relevant evidence. . . ."

If Mr. Justice Frankfurter's reasoning was mentioned at all, it was dismissed as unfair or "unwarranted by constitutional standards or legislative intentions."[29]

A smaller body of criticism took the position that any restrictions on exclusive dealing should provide for an inquiry into the limited question whether challenged restrictions actually interfered with competitors' efforts to distribute their products.[30] This position had the virtue of recognizing the difficulty of a wide-open economic inquiry without yielding to so drastic a limitation as had apparently been employed in *Standard Stations*. Nevertheless, proponents of this view did little to set forth a feasible method for determining the degree of foreclosure; at best, various factors were mentioned, such as the length of the agreement and the expense of setting up new channels of distribution, that might affect a final judgment on the matter.[31] Moreover, the critical problem of when foreclosure should be considered "substantial" under the statute was never answered by more than a very general admonition to the effect that competitors should have access to "sufficient" outlets to enable them to market their goods "effectively."[32]

Still other observers urged that *Standard Stations* actually stood for a somewhat different point than had been generally assumed. One writer concluded that "what was really forbidden [in *Standard Stations*] was a dominant company's using its market power to *impose* full requirements contracts as a condition of sale. . . ."[33] Two other commentators thought that the real problem in the case stemmed from the use of exclusive arrangements by so many major oil companies to freeze the great majority of existing outlets. "It was the 'collective,' even though not 'collusive,' foreclosure of the market by the majors, rather than the individual foreclosure by Standard, which offended the Clayton Act."[34]

---

[29] Oppenheim, *supra* note 28, at 1181.

[30] HANDLER, ANTITRUST IN PERSPECTIVE 35–36 (1957); ATT'Y GEN. NAT'L COMM. ANTITRUST REP. 146–47 (1955) (hereinafter "ATT'Y GEN. REP.").

[31] ATT'Y GEN. REP. 147 (1955).

[32] *Ibid.* A more precise exposition of the difficulties resulting from this formulation is set forth *infra*, at note 84.

[33] See Kahn, *A Legal and Economic Appraisal of the "New" Sherman and Clayton Acts*, 63 YALE L. J. 293, 318 (1954).

[34] Kessler & Stern, *supra* note 15, at 30.

As these varied comments accumulated, it became clear how difficult was the task of writing clearly for an unsympathetic audience. Beyond question, the *Standard Stations* opinion was in part ambiguous. But it is doubtful that the decision could have sustained so many differing interpretations had its words been oriented to principles that commanded general acceptance among the bench and bar. As it was, critics succeeded in reading the opinion to support the particular interpretations that they happened to advocate. In the course of a decade, therefore, at least five distinct interpretations of the case could be found in the legal commentaries.

Much the same reactions could be observed in the lower federal courts. Some courts applied the decision to strike down arrangements that affected only minute portions of the market;[35] others found room in the opinion to protect the struggling new competitor,[36] or to disregard the incidental restraint.[37] At least one court succeeded in avoiding *Standard Stations* altogether in a case where it seemed highly desirable to do so. Thus, when confronted with exclusive arrangements grounded upon urgent business needs, a district judge allowed a dominant producer to continue making restrictive agreements so long as they did not exceed one year in duration.[38] Still other judges refused to extend *Standard Stations* to sections of the Clayton Act that apparently turned upon the same legal standard as Section 3.[39]

More interesting than the behavior of the courts was the response of the Federal Trade Commission. Since the bulk of exclusive dealing cases has been initiated by the Commission, its interpretation

---

35 See, *e.g.,* Red Rock Bottlers, Inc. v. Red Rock Cola Co., 1952–53 CCH Trade Cases ¶ 67,375.

36 Dictograph Products v. F.T.C., 217 F.2d 821 (2d Cir. 1954), *cert. den.,* 349 U.S. 940 (1955).

37 Puett Electrical Starting Gate Corp. v. Harford Agricultural & Breeders Ass'n, 1950–51 CCH Trade Cases ¶ 62,570.

38 United States v. American Can Co., 87 F. Supp. 18 (N.D. Calif. 1949).

39 Transamerica Corp. v. Board of Governors, 206 F.2d 103, 170 (2d Cir. 1953): "The use of exclusive dealing contracts *per se* lessens competition. . . . For one who agrees to purchase all his requirements from a single seller . . . is consequently eliminated entirely from the competitive market. . . . [But] acquisition . . . is not *per se* a violation of the section." The defects in this distinction are pointed out by Kessler & Stern, *supra* note 15, at 66 n. 293.

of the Court's decision had great practical importance, and as events turned out, its views proved to be the most significant. Actually, the Commission adopted more than one approach to Section 3. In the first cases decided after *Standard Stations*, a standard similar to that of the Supreme Court was employed.[40] In fact, the Commission appeared to take an even stricter view, for the outcome in these early proceedings appeared to turn more on the large dollar amount of business involved than on percentage of sales in the market that were subject to exclusive contracts. Quite a different tack was taken by the Commission in 1954 in the *Maico* case.[41] In that proceeding, the hearing examiner had relied on *Standard Stations* to exclude evidence suggesting that competition had flourished in the face of exclusive arrangements. On appeal from this ruling, the Commission overrode the examiner and proclaimed its intention to consider all relevant factors in deciding whether exclusive arrangements had the proscribed effect upon competition:[42] "To refuse to exercise our talents as an administrative tribunal in these cases because the courts feel 'ill-suited' to weigh all of the relevant factors would deprive the country of the very services which we were created to furnish."

The *Maico* decision is interesting as another example of the willingness to indulge in dubious interpretations of opinions neither satisfying nor convincing on their face. The attempts of the Commission to reconcile its position with *Standard Stations* were highly strained[43] and had the result of creating different standards of legality under Section 3, so that the outcome of litigation might vary

---

[40] *E.g.*, Horlicks Corp., 47 F.T.C. 169 (1950); Underwood Corp., 49 F.T.C. 1123 (1953).

[41] 50 F.T.C. 485 (1953).   [42] *Id.* at 488.

[43] The Commission's interpretation rested on the following statement in the *Standard Stations* opinion: "The dual system of enforcement provided for by the Clayton Act must have contemplated standards of proof capable of administration by the courts as well as by the [F.T.C.] . . . Our interpretation of the Act, therefore, should recognize that an appraisal of economic data which might be practicable if only the latter were faced with the task may be quite otherwise for judges unequipped for it either by experience or by the availability of skilled assistance." 337 U.S. at 310 n. 13. This statement hardly leads necessarily to the conclusion drawn by the Commission. Even if it is susceptible to such an interpretation, it is difficult to conceive of Mr. Justice Frankfurter so casually authorizing the co-existence of two different standards of legality under the same statute.

fortuitously depending on whether the Justice Department or the Commission instituted the action.[44] Of greater importance, however, were the actual results obtained from the comprehensive inquiries undertaken by the Commission. In the very group of cases in which the new policy was announced, the facts presented a fair challenge to the Commissioner's expertise. Three of the largest manufacturers of hearing aids were shown to have exclusive arrangements that tied up the bulk of all dealers specializing in the sale of hearing attachments. Nevertheless, as one respondent pointed out, the number of competing producers had jumped from 20 to more than 80 during the years in which exclusive arrangements had been in use.[45] It was further shown that hearing aids were sold not merely by special dealers but through department stores and other kinds of outlets and that one firm, working through such distributors, had become the largest seller in the industry.[46] In addition, to prove that his practices had not injured competitors, one of the respondents also pointed out that he had himself established almost all his dealers so that competing manufacturers had never been displaced from their regular channels of business.[47] These facts raised difficult questions of the very sort that careful factual analysis was supposed to resolve. Could competition be harmed if the number of competitors quadrupled? Could new companies be blocked from the market if they were free to do as respondent had done and train their own distributors? Despite the importance of such questions, no serious effort was made by the Commission to answer them, though all the relevant facts were faithfully recorded in the final opinion.

Similar threads ran through the pattern of Commission cases in later years. In one opinion, the Commission impressively marshalled a variety of factors to strike down a network of exclusive arrangements.[48] But in that case every consideration pointed toward violation; none of the troublesome contradictions arose that justify the use of extended economic analysis and test its mettle.[49] When

---

[44] For criticism of the Commission's position, see ATT'Y GEN. REP. 148.

[45] Dictograph Products, Inc., 50 F.T.C. 281, 294 (1953).

[46] Id. at 294–95.   [47] Id. at 294.

[48] Harley-Davidson Motor Co., 50 F.T.C. 1047 (1954).

[49] Harley-Davidson, the largest producer of motorcycles in the United States, insisted that its dealers carry its products exclusively. To illustrate the effects of

such contradictions did arise in other cases, they were overlooked or summarily resolved in a manner that fitted uneasily with the precepts of economic logic. In particular, the Commission continued to avoid grappling with perplexing situations in which competition was increasing and new outlets were multiplying in the face of exclusive contracts.[50]

The culmination of this development came in 1960 with the decision of the Commission to abandon its policy of examining all relevant factors in exclusive dealing cases. Ironically, this reversal came in a proceeding that would have served as the classic case to justify a detailed examination of the facts. In *Mytinger & Casselberry*,[51] respondent, by far the largest firm in its field, had contracted with its distributors not to handle the products of any competitor. But the products involved were vitamin concentrates and the distributors were simply men and women of no special qualification who peddled the vitamins in their spare time in order to supplement their regular incomes. Under these circumstances, it was difficult indeed to conclude that respondent's competitors were being blocked from the market. Indeed, one competitor was said to be forming new distributorships at the rate of 100 each month while another was receiving 600–1,000 applications monthly from persons desiring to distribute its product.[52] It would be equally

these contracts, it was shown that one of respondent's few competitors, Simplex, was thereby denied access to 80 per cent of the retail outlets for its product. Evidence indicated that retail outlets were costly and difficult to establish and that dealers would have preferred to retain Simplex had they not been forced to choose between dropping Simplex or doing without the entire line of Harley-Davidson products.

[50] See, *e.g.*, Outboard Marine & Mfg. Co., 52 F.T.C. 1553 (1956). Respondent introduced evidence to the effect that its share of the market had declined by almost 12 per cent in the years leading up to the issuing of the complaint, that new competitors had entered the field, that some of these competitors had prospered, and that new dealers could be found without difficulty. These facts were for the most part rejected as immaterial by the trial examiner, whose opinion was affirmed in a brief *per curiam* decision by the Commission. See also Revlon Products Corp., 51 F.T.C. 260, 466 (1954).

[51] 1960–61 CCH Trade Reg. Rep. ¶ 29,091.

[52] Respondent's Motion to Dismiss, at p. 45. The opportunities for distribution seem endless. For example, one of respondent's competitors, Nutri-Bio, apparently arranged with the Christian Anti-Communist Crusade to have its products sold at Crusade meetings. See *The Reporter*, July 20, 1961, p. 26.

difficult to make out any injury to competition. The respondent's share of the market had fallen from 96 to 61 per cent in less than ten years and new competitors were entering the field at a rapid rate.[53] In response to these facts, which were emphasized again and again in the proceeding, counsel for the Trade Commission could only argue that similar considerations had been considered immaterial by the Commission in prior decisions.[54] The Commission itself, having once shown such independence in insisting on a full factual inquiry, now declared that opinions in the Second, Fifth, and Seventh Circuits required a retreat to the mechanical test of *Standard Stations*. Accordingly, the Commission found that respondent's exclusive arrangements had lessened competition within the meaning of the statute.

D. THE TAMPA ELECTRIC CASE

At the very moment that the Commission was announcing its decision to return to the doctrine of *Standard Stations*, the Supreme Court was making up its mind to move in the opposite direction. By the end of the nineteen-fifties, the climate of opinion surrounding Section 3 was distinctly conducive to doctrinal change. Almost no one had spoken in favor of *Standard Stations;* opposition could be found among critics, courts, and trade commissioners alike. The Supreme Court began to waver as early as 1953 in the *Motion Picture Advertisers* case.[55] Proceeding under Section 5 of the Trade Commission Act, the Federal Trade Commission had proscribed exclusive dealing contracts entered into by the leading makers of advertising films.[56] Nevertheless, the Commission gave recognition to the pressing business needs of the companies by allowing them to make such contracts for periods of no more than one year. Without mentioning *Standard Stations*, the Supreme Court affirmed

---

[53] Respondent's Oral Argument before Commission, May 18, 1960.

[54] *Id.* at 36. Counsel supporting the complaint also advanced the following argument: Mr. Suss: "I think there is a tendency toward monopoly when a corporation is able to achieve more than 50 percent of the business." Commissioner Tait: "Even though the market share declines from year to year?" Mr. Suss: "Even though it decreases and the respondent retains more than 50 percent of the business in spite of the decrease." *Ibid.*

[55] F.T.C. v. Motion Picture Advertising Co., 344 U.S. 392 (1953).

[56] *E.g.*, Motion Picture Advertising Service, 47 F.T.C. 378 (1950).

this order despite the suggestion in its earlier opinion that evidence of justification was irrelevant and that the length of the exclusive contracts would not be considered in appraising their effect on competition.

Not until 1961, however, did the Court make its next move in the direction of relaxing the rigor of the *Standard* opinion.[57] The *Tampa Electric* case involved a public utility company, Tampa, which had recently converted several generators from oil to coal. Tampa contracted with the Nashville Company—a medium-sized seller of coal—to supply all of its requirements of that fuel over the next twenty years. Not long after the contract was signed, Nashville reneged and claimed, in defending a suit on the contract, that the agreement was unlawful under the Clayton Act and therefore unenforceable. Nashville prevailed in the lower courts, because of the large amounts of coal and the long period of time involved.[58] Thus, the majority opinion in the court of appeals computed the total cost in dollars of all the coal that might be sold pursuant to the contract over the ensuing twenty years and concluded that by tying up a volume of business running into millions of dollars, the contract served as a "substantial clog" in a free, competitive market. In the Supreme Court, however, the judgment for defendant was reversed. The Court pointed out that no stark dollar figure could possibly convey the impact of the disputed contract on defendant's competitors; instead, the market walled off by the contract had to be compared with the total market served by coal mines competing with Nashville.[59] Once this was done, the impact of the challenged arrangement seemed minimal, for Nashville's competitors sold over a wide area and their combined sales were more than one hundred times larger than the amount of coal tied up by the contract between Tampa and Nashville.[60] Having made this point, the Court could easily have distinguished *Standard Stations* where the exclusive arrangements affected a far larger share of the market. The Court did not take this course. Instead, Mr. Justice Clark undertook to sketch the outlines of a new approach to the problems of exclusive dealing. Preliminarily, he said, it would

---

[57] Tampa Electric Co. v. Nashville Co., 365 U.S. 320 (1961).

[58] 168 F. Supp. 456 (M.D. Tenn. 1958), aff'd, 276 F.2d 766 (6th Cir. 1960).

[59] 365 U.S. at 331–32.   [60] *Id.* at 332–33.

be necessary to isolate the relevant line of commerce and the section of the country in which the challenged arrangements might have an effect.[61] That being done, the problem would remain of determining whether the contracts in question might substantially lessen competition. According to Mr. Justice Clark, this task would be accomplished by "taking into account the relative strength of the parties, the proportionate volume of commerce involved in relation to the total volume of commerce in the relevant market area, and the probable immediate and future effects which preemption of that share of the market might have on effective competition therein."[62] Attention would also have to be paid to any legitimate needs that might be served by the exclusive arrangements.[63] Thus, it was highly relevant that Tampa, as a public utility, had a particular need for a sure source of supply at a predictable price in order to meet its obligations to supply power continuously to the public. In view of this need, the small percentage of the market tied up by the challenged arrangement could not be considered unlawful.

It would hardly serve the end of this inquiry to peck over the details of the *Tampa* decision. What is important to grasp is the fundamental strength and weakness of the opinion. Its strength lies in the creation of a doctrinal basis that is sufficiently flexible to enable the Court to avoid the uncompromising prohibition of *Standard Stations*. Its great weakness lies in its vagueness as a prescription for future cases. Certainly, the attempts of the Trade Commission to cope with the concept of "foreclosure" revealed a need for guiding principles. But the pronouncements of the Court hardly seem adequate to resolve the sort of problem with which the Commission grappled so unsuccessfully. The "relative strength of the parties," for example, is a treacherous concept, as one can understand all too readily by asking how one would decide whether the largest producer of shirts, for example, is stronger than a leading department store to which the producer sells. Moreover, though this phrase seems designed to protect the dealer from being coerced by his supplier, no indication is given as to how such coercion is relevant to "the opportunities for other traders to enter into or remain in [the] market" which the Court declares to be the "touch-

---

[61] *Id.* at 327

[62] *Id.* at 329.   [63] *Id.* at 334.

stone" of Section 3.[64] The reference of the Court to "the proportionate volume of commerce" tied up by exclusive arrangements is also unclear without some explanation as to how this proportion can be related to the ebb and flow of competition in the market. On this score, the opinion is silent, though Mr. Justice Clark's emphasis on the justifications for the *Tampa* contract evokes the troublesome thought that even a proportion of less than 1 per cent might be found by the Court to impair "effective competition" in the absence of mitigating circumstances. The Court concludes its analysis with the adjuration to consider the "probable and immediate future effects" of the contracts on competition. This final point, of course, merely rephrases the statute instead of interpreting it, though the Court does succeed in this way in protecting itself against the kind of criticism that it received in such abundance for its opinion in *Standard Stations*.

Much the same analysis can be made of the treatment given by the Court to the question of justification. The issue was scarcely discussed in general terms, although the Court's own assessment of the Tampa contract illustrated the dangers of simply calling for an *ad hoc* appraisal in each situation. For all the Court's talk of public utilities, their obligations and their needs for a sure source of supply, the facts of the case revealed that 700 suppliers of coal had offered to sell to Tampa and that another contract had been consummated after Nashville's defection without delay or disruption in Tampa's operations.[65] In the light of these facts, one can scarcely say that a very convincing explanation was provided for abandoning the normal presumption that the best in price and service will be achieved by relying on a competitive market. The Court also failed to indicate why the needs of the parties could not be fully served by a contract of shorter duration, although this question surely deserved an answer in view of Tampa's willingness to enter into a year-to-year agreement following Nashville's default.[66] In the absence of clear reasoning on these points, one can derive little

---

[64] *Id*. at 328.

[65] Brief for Petitioner, at p. 6; Brief for Respondents, at pp. 6–7.

[66] After Nashville's defection, Tampa Electric made a contract with Love & Amos Coal Co., "Cancellable on 12 months notice by supplier or purchaser." Record, at p. 27.

guidance from the *Tampa* case as to what form or degree of justification will suffice in future cases.

II. Defects in the Law: Probable Causes and Possible Cures

Judged from almost any perspective, the progress of the law in the field of exclusive dealing seems deficient. A number of cases have been resolved on very questionable grounds, and there is little assurance where the legal boundaries lie. Indeed, after watching the Court and Commission pass each other like ships in the night, one is left with all the major questions still unresolved: what interests will be protected; what mitigating circumstances will justify exclusive dealing; what is "foreclosure" and how can it be measured?

A. DIAGNOSIS OF THE PROBLEM

Without doubt, difficulties of the sort that have arisen under Section 3 result in large part from the complexities that presently cloud our understanding of economic issues.[67] In the face of these complications, however, our reaction has too often been confined to a debate over the extremes of *per se* prohibitions and the rule of reason. Each of these extremes represents a response to the puzzling intricacies of antitrust law, but each often degenerates into a blind escape from the problems involved.

The dangers of the *per se* rule are well known. It is rare that a stark and sweeping prohibition can be phrased to do justice to the varying situations to which it must be applied. Hence, such a rule may be mechanically impressed upon situations, to which its purpose does not truly apply. Moreover, exceptions are often created *sub silentio;* cases around the edges of the prohibition grow like weeds with little order or consistency. In view of these difficulties, a flood of literature during the past fifteen years has emphasized the virtues of a rule of reason embodying an analysis of all the facts in

---

[67] The thought is occasionally expressed that some such confusion is inevitable as the law struggles to keep pace with the continuous changes in the needs and character of business. Changes of this sort, however, would have to be very radical to succeed in casting doubt on questions as basic to the statute as those that have remained unanswered under Section 3. A careful reading of exclusive dealing cases over the years suggests that the nature of these arrangements, their uses and their purposes, have remained essentially unchanged in past decades. Hence, an explanation for our difficulties should be sought in other quarters.

each particular case.[68] This approach has won a large following among businessmen and their advocates. From an opportunistic point of view, the flexibility of this standard offers the lawyer greater scope for the practice of his art and makes it possible for the businessman to find enough support in the law to carry out his programs now and worry about the legal consequences later. In a more important sense, the rule of reason evokes a very natural sympathy from lawyers who have often had to advise against well-motivated schemes on the basis of abstract rules which they felt were ill-suited to the realities of the situation. In much the same way, an approach to the law that emphasizes facts over doctrine has great appeal for the businessman, since it corresponds with his experience that doctrines about monopoly are generally biased against business and seldom do justice to reality.[69]

Despite the attractions of the rule of reason as an antidote to *per se* rules, experience with this approach in a field such as exclusive dealing suggests that it has drawbacks that are quite as serious as those connected with sweeping prohibitions. In considering the question whether exclusive dealing contracts lessen competition, little is accomplished by suggesting an examination of all relevant facts unless one faces up to the problems of how to define "competition," how to determine whether it has been lessened, and how to ascertain whether the reduction can be attributed to exclusive arrangements. Facts alone will not resolve these issues, for the first is a delicate matter of policy while the other two are complicated enough to divide even expert economists. Not much more is added by the occasional attempt to specify the various considerations that should be taken into account. The difficulty in answering these questions lies not so much in deciding what facts to examine as in putting all the facts together in a manner which will yield a reliable decision.[70] Still less is contributed by the suggestion that the

---

[68] The leading example is Oppenheim, *supra* note 28.

[69] See Schumpeter, *Science and Ideology*, 39 AM. ECON. REV. 345 (1949).

[70] See, *e.g.*, Lockhart & Sacks, *supra* note 28. Consciously or unconsciously, these efforts proceed from a critical premise, from which I must dissent: that analysis and research can readily arrive at a solution to the questions that arise under the antitrust laws if only they are not hampered by rigid or exclusionary rules. Representative of this tendency is the following remark by Lockhart and Sacks, which appears after the authors have noted the grave deficiencies in the existing knowl-

facts be examined by the "tests" of effective competition,[71] for these tests invariably turn on such words as "workable," "reasonable," and "substantial," which again defer most of the important intellectual problems to whoever is charged with deciding concrete cases.[72]

So long as the rule of reason remains in such a vague and formless state, it will often fail to provide a solution to concrete problems.[73] Recourse will therefore be taken to some other basis on which to rest a decision. The alternatives that are almost invariably employed for this purpose are legislative history and judicial precedent. These sources, however, are usually of little help in resolving a complicated case, for the same intellectual problems that bedevil the judge and advocate are likely to have afflicted the legislature and the appellate tribunals, and these bodies have strong reasons of their own for wishing to defer issues of this sort.

Pressed for time and burdened with all the varying facts and opinions that encumber the complicated case, an appellate court must often feel ill prepared to impose a solution that may be considered binding in other cases involving unforeseen facts. The technique of writing opinions under such circumstances is well known,

---

edge concerning the effects of exclusive arrangements: "Modern research techniques should largely be able to overcome the difficulties in isolating the effect of exclusive arrangements from other factors affecting the competitive structure in a particular industry." *Id.* at 918–19. To my knowledge, modern research techniques have not yet succeeded in this task nor do they show any immediate prospect of doing so.

[71] See, *e.g.*, Smith, *Effective Competition: Hypothesis for Modernizing the Antitrust Laws*, 26 N.Y.U. L. REV. 405 (1951).

[72] See, *e.g.*, MASON, *op. cit. supra* note 11, at 382–88.

[73] In the absence of more explicit guidance, the actual results of cases are likely to be as questionable as the decisions of the Trade Commission during the nineteen-fifties. This troublesome problem was ignored for many years by critics, who brushed lightly and uncritically over the Commission decisions while supporting the Commission for taking a more flexible approach under Section 3. See, *e.g.*, ATT'Y GEN. REP. 142–143. In recent years, however, some recognition has been given to the dubious nature of the Commission's decisions. See especially, Kessler & Stern, *supra* note 15, at 42–51. Similar dissatisfaction has been expressed with respect to decisions by courts as well as by the Commission in the related field of mergers where flexible inquiries have also been used. See Lewyn & Mann, *Ten Years under the New Section 7 of the Clayton Act: A Lawyer's Practical Approach to the Case Law*, 36 N.Y.U. L. REV. 1067 (1961). All these critics, however, tend to explain the poor quality of the decisions by intimating that the adjudicative bodies involved are either biased or inept.

particularly in the field of antitrust law. Escape hatches are built into the opinions and key points are phrased with convenient vagueness. Doubtful conclusions are buttressed by mentioning every possible point that bears in favor of the result so that the opinion becomes too particularized to have any clear bearing upon other cases with fresh constellations of facts.[74]

Even if a decision is expressed in more general terms, difficulties often result from the attempt to cast the opinion in terms of a reasoned demonstration that the results proscribed by the statute have occurred or will probably occur. Since many cases are simply too difficult to be resolved in this fashion, the resulting opinion cannot accurately reflect the real basis for decision. Hence, precedents arise that fit the facts of a later case in a formal sense but do not yield a satisfying decision. The earlier opinion may be followed out of respect for the expectations of others, but even this is not a persuasive rationale in many cases, especially where the question is whether an exception should be made to a stringent rule. Hence, the prior case is often distinguished on some tenuous ground. In this way, precedents accumulate without apparent contradictions having been persuasively resolved. Material accumulates for each side to use in briefs and argument,[75] but the resulting conflicts cannot be convincingly resolved by the judge without going back to the very problems which led him originally into a search for guiding precedent.

Much the same difficulties beset the use of legislative history. At a very high level of generality, there are value judgments about the economy that have been proclaimed by Congress in much the same form since the passage of the Sherman Act.[76] These value judgments form a frame of reference that is sometimes helpful in answering questions of general policy not resolved by the language

---

[74] The problem has been picturesquely described by an economist, Ben W. Lewis: "You know the process: take any three of the cases, extract equal parts of intent, overt acts, power (exerted and unexerted), mitigating circumstances and *stare decisis;* correct for humidity, density of comprehension, and velocity of circulation; add a dash of bitters, stir vigorously in ice, and throw over the left shoulder." 38 AM. ECON. REV. 211 (1948).

[75] "It is easy for the skillful reader to buttress almost any preconceived notion of what the antitrust laws are about by judicious citation of chapter and verse." MASON, *op. cit supra* note 11, at 391.

[76] See, *e.g.*, the discussion in KAYSEN & TURNER, ANTITRUST POLICY: AN ECONOMIC AND LEGAL ANALYSIS 19–20 (1959).

of the statute. On the other hand, the answers to specific cases cannot be found by reference to legislative history. Legislators have even less time than judges to puzzle out the complicated problems that may arise. Nor are they pressed by their constituents to undertake the disagreeable task of resolving these unborn cases. Moreover, the alignment of forces on questions of antitrust law almost always demands a compromise if any legislation is to be enacted. Support for a new statute must usually be gathered from legislators who are primarily responsive to small business interests, congressmen who are ideologically biased against big business, persons of more independent persuasion who are pragmatically concerned with achieving economic growth and efficiency, and representatives of labor and other groups who are affected indirectly in one way or another. Inconsistencies, such as the conflict between "hard" competition and small business, or questions such as the balance to be struck between efficiency and size must generally be passed over with vague language and handed on to the judge and the administrator for resolution.

These tendencies have consistently left their mark on antitrust legislation. They have accounted for the extreme generality of the Sherman Act,[77] for the inconsistencies and tortured draftsmanship of the Robinson-Patman Act,[78] and for the defeat of measures such as the basing-point bills which were introduced to clarify the law and died because they only created more obscurity.[79] Section 3 of the Clayton Act is but another product of the same processes. Although the Act was conceived in order to clarify the rule of reason, its passage depended on an alliance between forces possessing very different objectives, and the vaguely worded compromise that finally emerged was explained in several conflicting ways by participants in the legislative debates.[80]

Despite these difficulties, judges are confronted on every side

---

[77] See, e.g., the account of Senator Hoar in, II AUTOBIOGRAPHY OF SEVENTY YEARS 364 (1903).

[78] See, e.g., EDWARDS, THE PRICE DISCRIMINATION LAW 21–53 (1959), and the analysis of the problems in obtaining legislative correction set forth at pp. 634–35.

[79] 96 CONG. REC. 8721–23 (1950). For a detailed account of this legislation, see LATHAM, THE GROUP BASIS OF POLITICS (1952).

[80] See, e.g., Levy, The Clayton Law—An Imperfect Supplement, 3 VA. L. REV. 411 (1916); Comment, Section 3 of the Clayton Act—"Law Unto Itself," 22 U. CHI. L. REV. 233 (1954).

with suggestions to follow this bit of precedent or that snatch of legislative history. In the face of very difficult problems, there is an ever present temptation to surrender to these blandishments, since judicial opinions and legislative reports provide such a widely accepted basis for decision. Thus, in the formative years of an antitrust statute, there is constant danger that the courts will rely too much upon the legislative history. The cases and commentary are filled with safaris into legislative documents that succeed only in flushing a phrase here and a sentence there whose connection with the will of Congress is questionable at best. Nevertheless, the search goes on, presumably because it has been so richly rewarded in the past. It is no longer controverted that reliance may be placed on a statement appearing in the committee report of only one of the two houses of Congress. Reference is frequently made to a particular purpose underlying a statute in complete disregard of conflicting purposes expressed by other proponents of the bill.[81] Actions of other Congresses are relied upon and witnesses are invoked who have had no authority over legislation and whose remarks are buried in voluminous hearings that could not conceivably have been read by more than a handful of legislators.[82] As the statute grows older, the emphasis on legislative documents gives way to a tendency to rely heavily on precedent to justify decisions in difficult cases. Because of the ambiguity in the opinions, this technique is not likely to be convincing. To paraphrase Chesterton, judges simply run the risk of using prior cases as a drunkard uses a lamppost, for support rather than illumination. In sum, neither precedents nor legislative history can remove the burden of devising some reasoned framework through which sound and consistent decisions can be extracted from the unruly facts that lie beneath the law.

B. TOWARD A MORE RATIONAL METHODOLOGY

In order to develop a more rational methodology, it is important initially to separate the various steps that should be followed in deciding cases. Most of these steps may seem self-evident, but it is

---

[81] A pertinent example, of course, is provided by the *Standard Stations* opinion, discussed in Lockhart & Sacks, *supra* note 28, at 933–37.

[82] See, *e.g.*, Handler & Robinson, *A Decade of Administration of the Celler-Kefauver Antimerger Act*, 61 COLUM. L. REV. 629 (1961).

surprising how few of them have ever been analyzed with care either by the proponents of *per se* rules or by those who have advocated a more flexible *ad hoc* approach.

1. *Identifying the Interests To Be Protected*. In the face of a vaguely worded statute such as Section 3, affecting several different groups, it is important to begin by deciding which of the various interests involved are to be accorded protection by the courts. Will the law pay attention only to the public concern with maintaining vigorous rivalry between competing firms? Or will recognition be given to the business needs of the producers who enter into exclusive arrangements, or to the desires of rivals who are frozen out of accustomed distribution outlets, or to dealers who are unable to handle other brands they consider attractive? This question, of course, cannot be answered by collecting and analyzing relevant facts. Though analysis can help in deciding how gravely the different interests have been affected in a particular case, the question whether certain interests should be considered at all is a matter of policy for which there is no purely logical solution. It is a matter of policy, moreover, that must be settled in advance if evidence is to be gathered and appraised in any intelligent way.

Despite the importance of the foregoing question, the law on this point has remained ambiguous during the forty-odd years in which the statute has been in force. The most influential body of commentary has simply assumed that the statute exists solely to insure rivalry between competing firms and that in effectuating this purpose the courts should restrict themselves to deciding whether sellers have ready access to sufficient markets and distributive outlets.[83] There is some question as to whether such a limited view of the statute can be justified in terms of precedent and legislative history. Putting aside these reservations for the moment, however, there is reason to doubt that the prevailing view can hold up at all in coping with actual cases.

If it were possible to decide in most cases whether competitors have been unreasonably foreclosed in the sense just described, it could be argued that such foreclosure should be prohibited regard-

---

[83] See, *e.g.*, Att'y Gen. Rep. 146, 148: "We understand Section 3 as an express condemnation of business practices demonstrably detrimental to competition regardless of countervailing considerations."

less of whether producers and dealers have a vital interest in making exclusive arrangements. By a parity of reasoning, the absence of foreclosure could be said to preclude a violation even in cases where individual competitors or dealers were perceptibly injured by the contracts in controversy. The problem is markedly altered, however, once it is recognized that there is no logical solution in a large number of cases to issues such as whether foreclosure is "substantial," whether the available markets are "sufficient," or whether access to customers is "ready."[84] When answers to these questions become obscure, no reasonable judge can avoid being influenced by the presence of legitimate interests that favor or oppose the existence of the challenged arrangements, for these interests supply the only materials with which to fashion a purposeful decision. As a result, even if the inquiry under the statute is narrowly phrased, other interests are bound to affect decisions, and only confusion will result from failing to take these interests explicitly into account.

The tendencies just mentioned have been repeatedly borne out in litigation under Section 3. A prime example was afforded by the decree of the district judge allowing the American Can Company to enter into one-year exclusive contracts.[85] While one may insist doctrinally that contracts of this duration did not substantially foreclose American's rivals, it seems strained indeed, as a practical

---

[84] Stated more explicitly, the difficulties in the standard proposed by the Attorney General's Committee, note 83 *supra*, include the following:

a) No indication is provided as to how many or what kind of competitors need to be "foreclosed" in order to invoke Section 3. This omission does not merely render the standard ambiguous; it also avoids the divisive question of whether injury to competitors or injury to competition must be shown in order to prove a violation of the Act.

b) No norm or criterion is provided to enable us to determine what number of markets or outlets are "sufficient" or whether marketing is "effective." Ideally, competitors should be able to sell as much of their commodity as would be purchased in a market where all consumers are free to select between competing brands or makes. Can some such norm be used, as a practical matter, in litigation? If not, what sort of rough approximation should be utilized, or is there some other technique by which this intellectual hurdle can be by-passed entirely?

c) Though various factors are mentioned which bear on the significance of exclusive arrangements, no method is suggested as to how these factors might be combined to yield some over-all judgment as to the effects of the contracts in question.

d) There is no satisfactory indication of how large a departure from the ideal, however defined, should be considered "substantial."

[85] United States v. American Can Co., 87 F. Supp. 18 (N.D. Calif. 1949).

matter, to suppose that the court would have allowed the dominant firm in its field to enter into such arrangements had it not been for the urgent needs of independent customers for an assured supply of cans. A more complicated example is provided by the Trade Commission's tendency to equate injury to *competitors* with injury to *competition* in cases arising under Section 3. An occasional critic has attacked the Commission for confusing these terms and for forgetting that the infliction of harm upon one's rival is the very essence of competition, in the economic sense.[86] Once again, however, where the effects upon competition are ambiguous, the dislocation resulting from the loss of familiar customers, balanced against the business needs underlying the exclusive contracts, may provide the only tangible facts that can be considered in striving for decision.[87] Under these circumstances, is it indefensible to conclude

---

[86] Kessler & Stern, *supra* note 15, at 42–51. I differ with Kessler and Stern, of course, on the critical question whether effects upon competition can be readily ascertained in the generality of cases under Section 3. These authors propose the test: "[D]oes the integration arrangement impair competition more seriously than would horizontal power on each level of production if exerted independently?" *Id.* at 16. No attempt has been made by Kessler and Stern to apply their standard rigorously to the cases heard by the Trade Commission, but the present writer is doubtful whether this standard would prove feasible in many cases under Section 3. Kessler and Stern do suggest, without pursuing the matter, that their test would probably condemn the exclusive arrangements in Dictograph Products, 50 F.T.C. 281 (1953) and Outboard Marine & Mfg., 52 F.T.C. 1553 (1956). In my opinion, however, such suggestions do not do justice to the difficulties arising from such facts as the influx of new competitors in both cases, the loss of a substantial share of the market by Outboard, the success of Zenith in becoming the largest seller of hearing aids, etc. The proposed test also seems ambiguous in the sense that it provides no indication as to what magnitude of anticompetitive effects should be considered "substantial," nor does it indicate the kind and number of competitors who must feel the effects of the exclusive arrangement before "competition" (and not just "competitors") will be considered to be injured.

[87] By deciding to take injury to competitors into account, one does not necessarily espouse "soft" competition, as Kessler & Stern seem to imply. *Supra* note 15, at 50. For example, it is quite easy to take account of injury to competitors but to consider injury to competition the more important in cases where the two interests collide. More fundamentally, it is important to observe that these interests do *not* conflict in a large number of cases. On the one hand, there are many situations in which exclusive contracts make little or no contribution to competition; they neither provide greater efficiency nor otherwise promote the public interest. See pages 307–9 *infra*. In these circumstances, the interests of competitors can determine the outcome of the case without undermining the vigor of competition in any real way. On the other hand, there are cases in which competition is injured simply because a number of competitors have been harmed.

that the law has been violated so long as there is no pressing need to justify respondent's conduct?[88] Certainly no one who has read the legislative history leading up to Section 3 will insist that the interests of the individual competitor cannot be accommodated in this fashion within the meaning of the vaguely worded statute.[89]

Thus far, it has been suggested merely that various interests will inevitably intrude in doubtful cases in order to facilitate decision. It is probable, however, that the law will go further and take account of these other interests even in cases where the economic effects of exclusive arrangements on competition are not very much in doubt. The statutory history of Section 3 does not preclude this view, for Congress has had a strong regard for the welfare of individual competitors as well as for competition itself. Moreover, a steady accumulation of precedent over the past fifteen years has made the result all but certain, even though the contribution of each decision to this goal has rarely been admitted. The tying cases afford an apt illustration, for no one can suppose that rivalry will really diminish perceptibly every time that $500,000 worth of salt or some such "not insubstantial" amount is sold each year under tying agreements.[90] Another example is the recent *Klor's* decision in which several department stores had allegedly agreed to boycott a single small retailer.[91] Though the Supreme Court spoke in sweeping

---

[88] The Commission runs into difficulty, of course, because it will not justify its decision in these terms, but implies instead that because competitors are hurt, competition, in the economic sense, has necessarily been injured. See Kessler & Stern, *supra* note 15, at 41–52. This is dubious logic and leads very naturally to criticism and misunderstanding. Moreover, it enhances the danger that injury to individual competitors will result automatically in a violation of the statute even in those cases where it can be shown that the contracts in question serve beneficial purposes. Nevertheless, these are mere errors of execution that hardly support a conclusion that the interests of individual rivals ought not to be considered at all under the Act.

[89] See, *e.g.*, H. REP. No. 627, 63d Cong., 2d Sess. 13 (1914): "[Exclusive dealing] completely shuts out competitors, not only from trade in which they are already engaged but from the opportunities to build up trade in any community in which these great and powerful corporations are operating under this system and practice." This Report reveals rather clearly that the House of Representatives attached importance to the interests of dealers and competitors as well as the interest of the public in maintaining competition. *Id.* at 10–13. See also the remarks of Senator Walsh in explaining the meaning of the qualifying proviso to Section 3, 51 CONG. REC. 16, 144–46 (1914).

[90] See International Salt Co. v. United States, 332 U.S. 392 (1947).

[91] Klor's, Inc. v. Broadway-Hale Stores, Inc., 359 U.S. 207 (1959).

terms of the dangers of monopoly, the circumstances hardly justified any concern on this score, and the decision is very difficult to
explain save on the theory that the interests of the small dealer were
believed to outweigh any interest of the department stores in gang-
ing up on him. Similar threads are apparent in the *Tampa Electric*
case, for Mr. Justice Clark admitted that the business needs of producers and customers were relevant. Though the opinion is vague,
there is also some suggestion that recognition may also be given to
the interest of the dealer in not being coerced into signing restrictive agreements.[92]

Ambiguous though the cases may be, therefore, the law has
seemingly moved away from any narrow conception of competition toward a broader view that would bring the interests of all
affected parties within the ambit of Section 3. Once this is conceded, the focus of inquiry must shift to the problem of determining what sort of investigation can fairly and profitably be made to
determine the degree to which the various relevant interests have
been affected by the existence of exclusive arrangements. Only
then can the ultimate questions of policy be answered by inquiring
into the relative importance to be accorded to each of the various
interests in striking a final balance under the Act.

2. *Exploring the Effects of Challenged Activities.* It is common
knowledge that antitrust proceedings involving highly complicated
problems often lead to much confusion and wasted time. If these
dangers are to be minimized, an effort must be made to determine
which kinds of issues invite confusion and why. The question is
hardly a simple one, but it is possible to offer some preliminary
observations on the matter.

A prime difficulty in the field of antitrust law derives from the
fact that the activities called into question are seldom familiar to the
judge. Very often they do not even occur with sufficient frequency to have been observed systematically by experts. Despite these
obstacles, the motives underlying the suspect activities may be

---

[92] 365 U.S. at 329. Mr. Justice Clark mentioned that the relative power of the
defendant and his customers would be relevant in deciding the issue of substantial
foreclosure. *Id.* at 327. Nevertheless, while this statement seems to imply a concern
with the interest of dealers in not being coerced, the implication runs counter to an
earlier statement that injury to competitors and to competition forms the touch-
stone of unlawfulness under Section 3.

ascertainable, and the very obvious and immediate results may be reasonably apparent. Nevertheless, without any opportunity for careful observation, with its process of trial and error, hypothesis and validation, no fund of experience develops to refine intuition or enable sound judgments to be made concerning the ultimate effects of the challenged activities on competition and on other firms. The judge may therefore be compelled to resort to a synthetic process in which he first seeks information about the various factors that can influence these effects and then weighs them, one against the other, in order to determine their over-all impact upon competitive behavior. In occasional cases, of course, the actions in question will have taken such an aggravated form that their effects upon competition can readily be deduced by this process. More often, however, the circumstances are highly equivocal, and a multitude of varying factors may affect the impact of the defendant's actions upon other firms or condition the ways in which these firms can respond. The intellectual problems mount as the number of relevant factors becomes larger. Many factors that seem theoretically relevant can hardly be investigated in practice, because they depend on future developments or rest on psychological reactions about which it is hard to generalize. More important still, the relative importance of the considerations that *can* be explored is seldom understood with any precision, since it is so difficult to hold all the variables constant while the impact of a single factor is explored in a systematic way. Hence, the process of "weighing" these disparate factors becomes all but impossible. Even a mass of relevant data may not be very helpful because it cannot be combined in any satisfactory way to help yield a reliable result.[93]

In the light of the preceding discussion, it is clear that certain interests under Section 3 can be adequately explored without undue difficulty. It will usually be feasible, for example, to determine the needs that cause sellers and buyers to enter into exclusive arrangements. The parties involved can always describe these needs, and while the risk of exaggeration is always present, there are methods for guarding against this danger. In particular, verification

---

[93] A much more extended analysis of this topic is set forth in Bok, *Section 7 of the Clayton Act and the Merging of Law and Economics,* 74 Harv. L. Rev. 226, 287–99 (1960).

can often be obtained by checking with other sellers and buyers similarly situated, especially if these firms have not themselves chosen to enter into restrictive contracts.

By way of contrast, there is little cause for optimism over the prospect of determining the effects of exclusive arrangements on competing firms or on competition itself. These effects have not been studied empirically with any success. Instead, there are only a number of factors that are said to bear upon the issue. The prevalence and duration of the contracts, the cost of obtaining new distribution outlets, the growth of new firms in the face of exclusive contracts, the possibility of vertical integration if "exclusives" are proscribed, the relative size of the defendant—all these and more have been declared to be relevant in case or commentary. Many other factors could conceivably be added, for the impact of exclusive arrangements upon individual competitors varies in relation to their resources, their alternative opportunities, and, in the last analysis, upon everything that influences their psychological disposition. In a similar fashion, the effect of exclusives upon competition will ultimately be governed by the initiative and capabilities of the rival firms, and these attributes will be shaped by a host of separate considerations.

Even if an issue is encumbered in this fashion with a confusing array of relevant factors, it is by no means necessary to abandon all inquiry into the matter. In some cases the desired answers can be inferred from the existence of one or two key facts.[94] In exclusive

---

[94] This type of short cut is common in antitrust law. The most familiar example—which is hardly restricted to antitrust law—is the notion that proof of intent to produce unlawful effects upon the market will provide a sufficient basis for concluding that the effects in question actually took place. The reasons for this assumption are seldom articulated but are easy enough to divine. In part, the technique is merely one of logical inference. While direct proof of unlawful effects is very difficult, the defendant presumably believed that his actions were having their intended effects, and the defendant was probably in a better position than anyone else to reach this conclusion. Nevertheless, devices of this sort are not merely based on inference but depend very much on notions of fairness. Thus, unlawful results may be inferred from unlawful intent not just because the defendant can be assumed to have succeeded in his illicit design but also because the law has little sympathy for persons who seek to violate it.

Another of these short cuts, which has not won universal acceptance, holds that, where it is difficult to determine whether certain conduct will have unlawful effects but it is apparent that any legitimate objectives of the conduct can readily be achieved in other, more innocuous, ways, the conduct will be proscribed. This form

dealing cases, for example, various observers have suggested a limited inquiry into the cost to rival companies of finding new outlets of comparable quality to replace those that have been sealed off by the challenged contracts. If the cost turns out to be very low, competitors cannot be seriously disadvantaged regardless of other complicating factors that would normally influence the overall effects of exclusive arrangements. It is true that even the cost of establishing new outlets turns on a number of separate facts, but these can generally be reduced to money value and combined to yield a total cost. It is also true that difficulties may arise in deciding whether one outlet is comparable in quality to another, but since estimates concerning the commercial potential of outlets are constantly being made and refined in the light of experience, adequate testimony can often be obtained to resolve issues of this kind.[95]

The process just described can probably be adapted for use in other situations under Section 3. For example, if defendant has lost a substantial proportion of his market share during the years leading up to litigation, there are persuasive reasons for concluding that the interests of competitors and of competition itself should be given little weight. The very fact that defendant has steadily lost

---

of reasoning has been partly responsible for the severe restrictions against tying arrangements that have grown up in the face of arguments that such arrangements were undertaken as a legitimate counting device or as a method of preserving good will.

Apart from the *Standard Stations* rule itself, short cuts of this type have not been common in exclusive dealing cases. Nevertheless, a similar process has seemingly been used by the courts in rejecting arguments by the defendant that his restrictive arrangements have no harmful effects since his dealers would not turn to rival products even if they were contractually free to do so. In ignoring this defense, the law infers that at least some dealers would turn to other brands if they were able, else the defendant would not trouble to include the restrictive clauses in their contracts. This rationale is not wholly satisfying, however, for a number of dealers might not require contracts if put to the test, though it would be impossible to determine how many. In the face of this insoluble problem, it seems wiser and fairer to disregard the defendant's argument, for if he is right in contending that all or most of his dealers do not act through compulsion, then he will not suffer much by having the compulsion removed.

[95] Once litigation commences, much light on this issue should be derived from actual experience in the market in question. If all competitors have been creating outlets at a rapid rate, the cost factor is presumably not a substantial impediment. On the other hand, if testimony or business records reveal that competitors have had to curtail expansion or keep out of new markets because of the cost of new outlets, then the opposite conclusion would follow.

ground suggests that his exclusive contracts are not sufficient to wall him off from competition.[96] Certainly, he is likely to be under pressure to improve his product or lower his price. Likewise, his rivals would seem to have both an opportunity and an inducement to continue to press for further inroads upon his share of the business. Hence, there is little reason to believe that the intensity of competition has been diminished in any way. As for individual competitors, their only concern may be an interest in hastening defendant's decline or gaining access more rapidly to his markets. While this interest is not altogether negligible, it is doubtless of far less moment to the companies involved than the dislocation of being shut off from their regular customers or the burden of being substantially hampered in their efforts to expand. Hence, in the absence of more direct evidence, much can be inferred concerning the effects of exclusive arrangements from the mere fact that defendant's market position had been suffering a marked decline.[97]

As a result of limited inquiries such as those just mentioned, there will be a number of cases in which it can fairly be said that neither competition nor competitors have been injured significantly by the contracts in question. The fact that these cases do arise occa-

---

[96] In actuality, two separate cases should be identified in considering a decline in defendant's market share. The first is where the total market for the commodity in question is expanding little, if at all. In this event, defendant is presumably very much under pressure, since his sales are declining absolutely; he is probably losing dealers and will have difficulty retaining them when the restrictive contracts expire. In the second situation, however, the market is expanding so rapidly that defendant's sales are growing absolutely even though his market share is declining. Under these circumstances, defendant may be under less pressure (though many firms fix a target share as a matter of policy and will fight to achieve and maintain it). Nevertheless, if demand in the market is growing in this fashion, it must be assumed that new outlets can be found, or old ones expanded, without much difficulty. Moreover, individual competitors are presumably suffering under no real burdens, since new demand is constantly opening up for their goods.

[97] Another fact that might arguably be used as a basis for drawing inferences as to competitive effects is the advent of new competitors during the period in which exclusives have been in force. This fact has been emphasized in several proceedings before the Trade Commission. See, e.g., Outboard Marine & Mfg. Co., 52 F.T.C. 1553 (1956). Standing by itself, however, this fact, though suggestive, is probably unreliable. For example, if defendant has maintained his share of the market despite the new rivals, the success of the new firms must have been achieved by cutting into the share of older firms, which might have reacted by gaining a part of defendant's business had they been given the chance. Hence, rather substantial interests may have been injured by defendant's contracts.

sionally is a sufficient reason for making some allowance for such inquiries under the statute. On the other hand, it is clear that most cases will not be capable of being resolved in this fashion. Few situations will arise in which the defendant's market position has deteriorated substantially. The same is true of an exception based on the cost of new outlets. There will be many cases in which the product involved is distributed through stores that handle many different items, and in these circumstances the expense of developing new distributors will normally be prohibitive. There will be other instances in which the contracts clearly foreclose competitors by tying up ultimate consumers. In still other proceedings, the cost of new outlets will at least be sufficient to raise a substantial risk that competitors will be hampered in their efforts to compete. In the majority of cases, therefore, a different and more serviceable technique must be employed to measure the impact of exclusive arrangements on competition and on individual competitors.

The point has already been made that there are many more factors conditioning the effects of exclusive arrangements than could ever be usefully employed in making a judgment in actual cases.[98] As a result, any inquiry that is designed for use in the normal case under Section 3 should embody some limit upon the range of matters to be considered. It is possible simply to leave this task to the parties and let them gather and submit all the evidence that their resources and inclinations will allow, so long as each fact bears in some way on the ultimate question to be resolved. Nevertheless, with protagonists as powerful as those opposing one another in antitrust litigation, financial burdens will seldom impose satisfactory limits on the scope of the inquiry. Doubts will be resolved in favor of submitting more evidence as each side feels impelled to add further facts to counter the data introduced by the other. Hence, if proceedings under Section 3 are not to become needlessly attenuated, the boundaries must be carefully defined in advance by court or agency.

It seems obvious that any inquiry, however narrow, should take note of the proportion of goods in the relevant market that are sold subject to restrictive arrangements.[99] For this fact, more than any

---

[98] See pp. 296–97 *supra*.

[99] Any attempt to estimate the prevalence or scope of restrictive contracts requires a prior definition of the relevant market. While this is a task that has tradi-

other, serves to give a first, general approximation of the degree to which exclusive contracts interfere both with competition and

---

tionally proved difficult in the field of antitrust law, see pages 331–32 *infra*, there is some reason to believe that the problems can be reduced to tolerable dimensions under Section 3. Although space precludes any detailed treatment of the subject, the outlines of an approach to the question can be sketched briefly.

It should be emphasized that for the purposes of antitrust law the "relevant market" is not a fixed and immutable phenomenon confronting each buyer or seller. The "market" is only intended as an analytical tool to help estimate how great a likelihood exists that some undesirable effect will take place. The market is "relevant," therefore, in the sense that it is, or should be, constructed with reference to the particular evil, or adverse effect, under investigation. Hence, several different "markets" might conceivably be constructed with respect to any given transaction or business enterprise, since several different kinds of harm are prohibited under the antitrust laws. It follows, of course, that confusion in defining a relevant market tends to increase where the courts do not clearly identify which interests—or kinds of harm—will be taken into account in applying a particular statute. These general remarks can be illustrated by considering the ways in which the market might be defined under Section 3.

Geographic Market: In cases involving restrictive contracts with dealers or other middlemen, the impact upon competition should be measured with the aid of a market consisting of the area, or any appreciable segment thereof, in which the defendant sells. The extent of the foreclosure within such a market will tend to suggest the degree of danger that consumers will be deprived of an adequate choice of product, that defendant will be shielded from the pressures of competing goods, etc. This formulation may seem to make no allowance for the fact that competitors selling outside that area may be able to enter it without difficulty and hence forestall adverse competitive effects. Nevertheless, the entry problem should not be troublesome, under the approach here suggested, since Section 3 would be invoked only in those cases where new or expanded outlets cannot be secured without substantial difficulty. See pages 297–98 *supra*. In cases of this sort, the barriers to entry should, by definition, be large enough to disregard potential competition for the purposes of the Clayton Act. As for the interests of other sellers, the problem is to determine what proportion of *their market area* is foreclosed. Where the sellers are bunched, with all or most of them selling in the same area, the matter is not difficult. Where the sellers are scattered, however, it will be difficult to find any single percentage that accurately represents the degree of foreclosure that all such firms face. Theoretically, an average figure could be derived, but it would probably be preferable to provide more than one figure in order to suggest the varying degrees of foreclosure imposed upon groups or categories of firms that are differently situated. (In cases where the restrictive contracts are signed with *consumers*, the geographic market from the standpoint of competitors would be unchanged. The market for appraising effects on competition, however, will differ from the formulation in cases involving dealers whenever the area in which defendant sells is not a "natural market" in terms of transport barriers and the like. Where no such barriers exist, it would be misleading to take account of defendant's competitors only to the extent of their sales in defendant's market area.)

Product Market: From the standpoint of competitors, substitute products are rarely relevant unless the outlets or markets for such other goods are readily avail-

with the efforts of rival producers to market their products.[100] In addition to this evidence, the duration of the contracts should pre-

able to him. This possibility, however, is taken care of by the special treatment given in cases in which alternate outlets are easily available. Hence, in all the cases in which market definition becomes necessary, substitute products should be excluded from the market in assessing effects upon competitors. In appraising the effect of "exclusives" upon competition, the problem is more difficult, for there is no sound reason in theory to exclude substitutes; the only question is whether the job of defining substitutes can be done with enough finesse in actual litigation to make it worthwhile. For the purposes of this paper, however, there is serious doubt as to whether the foregoing problem need be answered at all. In cases where the defendant's interest is rather slight, I would be inclined to invalidate the contracts on the strength of any substantial foreclosure of individual competitors (which can be determined without getting into acute analytical difficulties). On the other hand, where substantial and legitimate reasons underlie the contracts, I am inclined to believe that dangers to competition and competitors will not be sufficient to outweigh these valid objectives even though the contracts are widely used, so long as their scope and duration do not exceed what is necessary to achieve the legitimate business objectives involved. Hence, the market problem can again be avoided.

The preceding remarks suggest the possibility of attacking the troublesome market problem by utilizing rules that are sound in themselves but possess the added advantage of depending less heavily upon market definition. Thus, by taking account of all the interest to be protected under Section 3 and by causing cases to turn on such questions as whether defendant developed his own outlets and whether new outlets can be secured without difficulty (see p. 312 *infra*), the market problem is avoided in a number of cases. If this approach is sound, it provides one further argument against the proposal that exclusive contracts be judged solely in terms of their impact on competition, for a standard of that sort tends to make market definition crucial.

Similar techniques for minimizing the market problem can be illustrated by looking to the related topic of mergers. A rule condemning mergers undertaken to suppress competition can, of course, be applied without recourse to market definition since we simply presume that the defendant probably knew what he was about in seeking to reduce competition. In addition, a rule causing legality to turn on an increase in concentration over time will avoid the market problem in a few cases, at least, because concentration may have increased in each of the alternative markets that the parties might advance. Finally, a more precise rule as to what percentages violate the statute will result in cases where a merger will be seen to have violated the law under any reasonable definition of the market. On the other hand, where the rule is left vague, market definition—with all its controversy and confusion—is almost always an issue, since it is almost always conceivable that a favorable finding on the question will affect the final result.

[100] In measuring the prevalence of the contracts, difficulties may arise when the agreement with the dealer involves a commitment to take some absolute amount of the seller's product rather than the dealer's full requirements. In some cases, such arrangements can readily be treated as full-requirements cases, *e.g.*, where the absolute amount is geared to the expected requirements of the dealer or where it is obvious for some other reason that if the dealer must take some from the defendant,

sumably be considered, for not only does this fact bear a fairly clear relation to the scope or prevalence of the restrictions, but it can also have a profound effect upon their significance.[101] Beyond this point, a rather delicate judgment is called for, but there are

---

he will necessarily have to take all he needs from the same source. Where these conditions do not prevail, however, more difficult questions are presented. The wording of Section 3 presents an initial hurdle, since a buyer in this situation cannot be said to be obligated not to deal in the products of a competing seller. Nevertheless, the broad language of the Sherman Act and/or Section 5 of the Trade Commission Act should suffice to bring these cases within reach of the law if Section 3 is found wanting. A second problem is raised by the fact that partial-requirements clauses allow rivals to gain a foothold with the dealers in question, thus making it possible for them to supplant the defendant entirely in the course of time. Hence, the exclusionary effects of partial-requirements clauses are not quite the same as those of full-requirements contracts. On the other hand, the difference just noted does not seem any more significant than various other factors to be excluded from inquiry. Hence, it would not be inconsistent with this analysis simply to add the quotas imposed within the relevant market in order to derive a total that can be used to compute the proportion of the market pre-empted. A final problem, however, is posed by the fact that long-term contracts are probably very common in certain industries and have probably not been considered to fall within the ban of Section 3. This difficulty, however, should not prove fatal if, but only if, substantial business reasons are taken fully into account in assessing the legality of agreements under Section 3. See pages 309–12 *infra*. If such reasons are considered, it is doubtful that long-term contracts would be disturbed where they represent a more efficient method of doing business. On the other hand, the way would be clear to scrutinize various types of arrangements, such as loans, repayable in purchases from the creditor-seller over a long period, which seem designed merely to obtain assured markets for the goods of large and affluent sellers. Special mention might be made of the troublesome cases involving the imposition of quotas that the dealer must meet in order to keep the seller's patronage. These arrangements are considered at note 107 *infra*.

101 The question of duration is often more difficult than meets the eye. For example, an agreement may be renewable on a year-to-year basis yet provide that upon cancellation the dealer will not handle any goods of the type produced by the defendant for a period of a year or more. In view of the pressure thus exerted against cancellation by the dealer, the agreement should be treated as extending for an indefinite term. Troublesome questions also arise when the agreement is of very short duration but the defendant gives his dealers an ultimatum that they must handle his products exclusively or not at all. Certainly, such agreements have a long-term exclusionary effect vis-à-vis smaller competitors (or competitors with a shorter line); such rivals might persuade dealers to experiment on the side with their goods but might never be able to succeed in introducing their products if the dealer must thereupon give up all right to handle defendant's goods. The exclusionary effect is less obvious with respect to other large producers, but even there, the defendant often has an advantage since changeover costs may be substantial and since the dealer may have built up good will in the handling of defendant's product. For all these reasons it seems wiser in the usual case to regard contracts in this category as indefinite in their term.

strong reasons for refusing to widen the inquiry any further. In the first place, the other factors that might be considered bear no understood relationship to the prevalence and duration of the restrictive arrangements; there is no telling, for example, how much the arrival of three or four new competitors detracts from the significance to be attached to the existence, say, of two-year "exclusives" covering 40 per cent of the market. Moreover, several of the other factors cannot themselves be ascertained with any precision. The possibility that the defendant will build his own outlets, for example, must almost always be purely speculative. Finally, if special provision is made for cases in which the cost of alternative outlets is insubstantial or the defendant's market share has markedly declined, none of the remaining factors seem noticeably more significant than the others. As a result, once the scope and duration of the contracts have been considered, there is no logical stopping place short of an inquiry too cumbersome to be justified.

3. *Weighing the Interests.* Since little attention has been given to the problem of identifying the interests to be protected under Section 3, it is not surprising that even less effort has been made to determine how these interests may be weighed against one another in order to reach a final conclusion. Avoiding this problem has been no mean trick, and much distortion of fact and authority has doubtless resulted from the effort to put cases in a form in which they could seemingly be decided without any need to explain how the policy issues were resolved. Legislative history has been read to "compel" particular decisions, precedent has been found to dictate a certain result, or an assumption has been quietly made that the statute is concerned with only one of several competing interests. Most frequently, the facts have been molded by emphasis and omission to make one set of interests appear so clearly to outweigh all the others as to place the matter beyond any need for explanation and debate.[102]

The reasons for such reticence are not hard to discern. Courts,

---

[102] This tendency was evidenced in the first Supreme Court opinion interpreting Section 3, for the Court ran roughshod over the record in order to find that competition was injured and that monopoly was imminent. Standard Fashion Co. v. Magrane-Houston Co., 258 U.S. 346 (1922). See pages 321–22 *infra*. The same technique appears in the *Tampa Electric* opinion in Mr. Justice Clark's exaggeration of the justification for entering into a twenty-year contract for the supply of coal. See page 284 *supra*.

and even commissions, have long displayed great reluctance to brazen their policy-making function. Moreover, one can hardly pretend that generally accepted standards of policy are close at hand to solve a variety of cases.[103] The search for value judgments in the field of competition is particularly difficult. It is hard to know what is fair or wise without possessing a knowledge of the nature and consequence of alternative decisions, and this is precisely the kind of information that is so frequently lacking in evaluating competitive behavior. Moreover, notions of fairness borrowed from other areas of human activity are often irrelevant because competition necessarily relies upon patterns of rivalry and deliberate injury which are at war with some of the basic moral tenets that prevail in other spheres. While neither of these obstacles necessarily prevents agreement on common values, they do make consensus difficult where the issues to be resolved are of vital concern to strong and articulate groups that possess sharply differing points of view.

Notwithstanding these difficulties, value premises and notions of fairness do influence decisions and must continue to do so as long as legal issues require that choices be made between conflicting interests. There is much, then, to be gained by discussing the matter openly.[104] Critical judgments of policy must be revealed by the courts or their opinions will inevitably be misunderstood.[105] Moreover, with the multiplicity of tribunals that act on matters of antitrust law, questions of policy will have to be discussed or the law

---

[103] It seems doubtful that the development of principles of policy and fairness has received anything like an adequate trial. In part, the lack of effort along these lines results from an overemphasis upon factual analysis as a method for completely resolving antitrust cases. In addition, a possible explanation lies in the separation in this country between jurisprudence and "practical" law, for writers in jurisprudence have emphasized for decades the need to view law as a method of reconciling the interests of various groups. See POUND, SOCIAL CONTROL THROUGH LAW (1942); STONE, THE PROVINCE AND FUNCTION OF LAW 487–504 (1950). Writers in this category have also made the most notable, though for our purposes rudimentary, attempts to grapple with the value problem. See, e.g., CAHN, THE MORAL DECISION 123–54 (1955).

[104] This, of course, is a very old plea. The classic statement is that of Holmes: "I think that the judges themselves have failed adequately to recognize their duty of weighing considerations of social advantage. The duty is inevitable, and the result of the often proclaimed judicial aversion to deal with such considerations is simply to leave the very ground and foundation of judgments inarticulate and often unconscious. . . ." The Path of the Law, 10 HARV. L. REV. 457, 467 (1897).

[105] See, e.g., the widespread doubt as to whether some such value judgment does not underlie the du Pont-General Motors decision, United States v. E. I. du Pont de

will be pock-marked by random and contradictory value judgments which lack the consistent application needed to transform them into effective policy.

However cogent these arguments, it would be naïve to expect judges to decide difficult cases by referring expressly to their personal preferences on matters of economic policy. Some independent source of authority must be found. There are several directions in which the courts may turn in order to derive the necessary guidance. Perhaps the most obvious source is provided by the rather persistent pattern of values and aspirations that has marked the development of antitrust law in this country. These ideals were evident in the deliberations leading up to the enactment of Section 3, they have been traditionally reflected in congressional debates upon antitrust legislation, and they are emphasized in most of the essays that deal in general terms with the nature of our antitrust laws. It is true, of course, that inconsistencies and divisions of opinion have imparted a vagueness to these principles that often robs them of utility in deciding concrete cases and dulls their cutting edge even on such basic questions as the balance to be struck between the needs of efficiency and the social advantages of small and independent competing units. Nevertheless, these drawbacks do not deprive this source of all its usefulness. For example, in the field of exclusive dealing, some assistance can be gathered from the importance that Congress placed, both in enacting Section 3 and in passing other pieces of antitrust legislation, on maintaining competition, preserving freedom of opportunity, and protecting the welfare of small businessmen.[106] With this tradition in mind, it is pos-

---

Nemours & Co., 353 U.S. 586 (1957). For belief that the size of the defendants influenced the result, see, *e.g.*, Kessler & Stern, *supra* note 15, at 69. If indeed such decisions are influenced by the great size of the defendants, it seems probable that a grave mistake has been made. Little progress of any lasting significance can be made against the problems of size by covertly calling a few close ones against large firms. On the other hand, much injustice can be done in this way, for opinions will be written that appear to apply to much smaller firms and that may thus dissuade them from entering into transactions and activities which might be adjudged to be lawful if actually put to the test.

[106] See, *e.g.*, H. Rep. No. 627, 63d Cong., 2d Sess., 10–13 (1914); 51 Cong. Rec. 16,144–46 (1914) (remarks of Senator Walsh).

For a similar emphasis reflected in the debates leading up to the amendment of Section 7 of the Clayton Act, see Bok, *supra* note 93, at 233–38.

For recognition of the persistent emphasis placed on these objectives, see Neale,

sible to fashion a policy for dealing with several of the arguments most frequently advanced to justify the use of exclusive arrangements. Consider, for example, management's desire for a "firm market" that will relieve it of the necessity for business forecasting and permit more reliable planning. This objective, of course, cannot be truly achieved by resorting to exclusive contracts, for sellers will still have to contend with fluctuations in the ultimate demand for their goods. Whatever stability is achieved, therefore, must result from the protection that "exclusives" provide against fluctuations resulting from the loss of sales to competitors. Such stability, however, is hardly to be given much weight under a statute expressly designed to preserve competition, for the constant danger of losing business to one's rivals strikes close to the heart of what we are trying to achieve in maintaining a competitive system.

Another common explanation for "exclusives" is the desire to obtain dealers who will devote themselves wholeheartedly to promoting the seller's goods, a desire often supplemented by defendant's insistence that his product is so technical or sensitive as to demand the sort of service that only a specialist can provide. Once again, the argument weakens under analysis. Though "loyal" dealers may seem more efficient to the seller, in the sense that they market more of his particular product, it does not follow that such dealers are more efficient from the standpoint of the public. Since dealers will generally be anxious to make as much money as they can, they are not likely to push the goods of other producers unless the public desires the other goods or unless the wholesale prices on these goods provide a higher margin of profit. As a result, to insist that dealers sell defendant's product to the exclusion of others will often come close to a bare demand that more competitive goods be suppressed. Moreover, if a strong and legitimate business need for exclusive selling actually does exist, it is strange that dealers will not follow this policy without being compelled to do so by contract, for the advantages that result should benefit them as well as the firms from which they buy. Perhaps an occasional dealer will be too inept or shortsighted to perceive his best interests, but such

THE ANTITRUST LAWS OF THE U.S.A. 419–24 (1960); KAYSEN & TURNER, *op. cit. supra* note 76, at 18–22.

men could presumably be replaced for demonstrable inefficiency without resorting to a widespread use of restrictive contracts.[107]

Viewed in this perspective, the justifications just mentioned seem clearly subordinate to the interests that caused the Congress to limit the use of exclusive arrangements. By pursuing such interests as these, the seller will not make any substantial strides toward greater efficiency and lower prices. Hence, there is no serious conflict among the various objectives of the antitrust laws. Moreover, though Congress refused to prohibit *all* exclusive arrangements under Section 3, this decision was not taken in order to safeguard the interests that have been discussed.[108] Indeed, one looks in vain for any concern on the part of the legislature over the desires of established sellers to secure a "firm" market or to obtain the undivided loyalty of their dealers. As a result, when the defendant has no reason for his exclusive contracts other than these interests, it seems

---

[107] It may be argued that dealers are often hard to replace so that inefficiency cannot be corrected in this fashion. Nevertheless, if the seller is powerful enough to impose ultimatums on exclusive dealing, he should be equally able to insist on efficiency. On the other hand, if the seller obtains exclusives by offering inducements, then he should possess the wherewithal to reward efficiency rather than exclusivity, or alternatively, to spend heavily on replacing inefficient dealers instead of paying all his outlets to deal exclusively.

A special, borderline situation occurs where the seller sets quotas that dealers must meet in order to continue handling the seller's goods. In theory, such quotas may be beneficial where they are imposed with the purpose and effect of increasing sales by inducing the dealer to become more industrious in his job. On the other hand, quotas may also be used to increase defendant's sales by squeezing out competitors, in which case they should be treated as ordinary exclusive-dealing contracts (partial or total as the case may be). In practice, this distinction may prove difficult to draw in some cases, particularly where *both* motives exist simultaneously. It should be borne in mind, however, that there are a variety of alternative non-exclusionary techniques by which sellers can often obtain their legitimate objectives, *e.g.*, establishing new dealers, providing lawful quantity discounts, etc. Hence, some of the difficult cases, though perhaps not all, can be resolved against the seller without risking any substantial losses in dealer-efficiency.

[108] Though the Senate, in conference committee, insisted on substituting the qualifying proviso in place of an absolute prohibition with criminal penalties, the stated reasons for this change were to make allowance for *de minimis* cases, see, *e.g.*, 51 CONG. REC. 16,149 (1914) (remarks of Senator Walsh); to benefit the small businessman or the new competitor, see, *e.g.*, *id*. at 16,145 (remarks of Senator Walsh) *id*. at 16,002 (remarks of Senator Chilton); and to avoid singling out certain practices for criminal prosecution when equally reprehensible conduct was left to the discretion of the Trade Commission, *id*. at 16,144–45 (remarks of Senator Walsh).

sensible to conclude that if sellers have been shut off from any substantial share of existing markets and channels of distribution, their interests should normally prevail.

No one who has sensed the mood of Congress' deliberations can seriously quarrel with these conclusions. Difficulty will arise, however, when an attempt is made to extend the principle too far, for it is not without qualification. If new outlets can be found with no real difficulty at all, as in *Mytinger & Casselberry*,[109] rival sellers will not have suffered from defendant's exclusive arrangements; there is consequently no injury to which the solicitude of Congress can attach. Separate treatment may also be warranted where the parties have unusual needs running counter to the policies favoring competition and the protection of rival sellers. Thus, if it is impossible to invest in a new market without an exclusive guarantee for some minimum period, then no real opportunity for rivals could arise if restrictive agreements in that market were prohibited. Similarly, if *buyers* testify to a pressing need for exclusive arrangements, we cannot resolve the case by simply determining that the seller's interest is subordinate to the interests of his rivals. Notwithstanding these special situations, the tendency to favor small businessmen and to promote free opportunity should play an important role in developing a general attitude toward the statute and in reaching results in a number of run-of-the-mill cases.

A quite separate method for making policy judgments is provided by looking to the body of general notions of fairness that have become firmly rooted in the law. While principles of this sort may not abound in the field of antitrust law, there are some, at least, that may help to resolve exclusive dealing cases. In *Dictograph Products*,[110] for example, respondent had entered into exclusive arrangements with approximately 20 per cent of all the dealers throughout the country specializing in the sale of hearing aids. In almost every case, however, the dealers had never sold hearing aids prior to being approached and trained by respondent. Since there were no obvious limits on the locations for retail outlets and no lack of persons who could be trained as salesmen, competing manufacturers could set up comparable distribution systems with no

---

[109] 1960–61 CCH Trad. Reg. Rep. ¶ 29,091.

[110] 50 F.T.C. 281 (1953).

greater trouble or expense than respondent had undergone when it established its own outlets. Under these circumstances, the issue of policy was quite clear: should competition and freedom of opportunity be encouraged to the extent of compelling respondent to allow its competitors to avail themselves of a ready-made and therefore cheaper network of distribution? In answer to this question, the Commission would surely have been on firm ground had it posited the traditional principle that no person should ordinarily be made to give up the fruits of his labors—especially for the benefit of his rivals—in the absence of some overbalancing public need. In the light of this principle, the Commission could have argued strongly that the public interest in furthering competition could not prevail under the facts of that case, where the number of competing firms had already jumped from 20 to 80 in the face of the exclusive contracts. Much could have been said for an even more general declaration that a firm that had established its own distribution system could not lessen competition so long as its rivals could set up a comparable network with no greater trouble and expense. Certainly, such a principle could have been supported by common sense as well as by rather similar policies embodied in related legislation and judicial precedent.[111]

---

[111] Where the number of competitors has not sharply increased, one may argue that defendant's interest is countered by a valid interest in favor of encouraging competition and that nothing has been said thus far helps to overcome this conflict. The dilemma may be resolved, however, by inquiring whether competition and freedom of opportunity will be substantially furthered, as policies of general application, by requiring the defendant to unlock his distribution system. It is very possible that this inquiry can be answered in the negative, thus removing the apparent conflict of policy. In the first place, freedom of opportunity seldom implies more than giving an equal chance to competitors, and for the purpose of the issue as defined in the text, equal opportunity is already present in the sense that rivals must be able to develop comparable outlets without greater trouble and expense than defendant. Second, sellers are bound to be discouraged to some extent from establishing, training, and assisting dealers if they know that the effort and expense will simply redound to the benefit of their competitors. Hence, freedom for competing sellers may simply be purchased at the expense of diminishing the opportunities and advantages of dealers. As for the interest in promoting competition, though large sellers may have spent amounts on establishing outlets that cannot be duplicated by smaller rivals, smaller rivals need fewer outlets to market their product, and they can add new outlets gradually as they grow in size. Moreover, developing dealers is only one of many ways in which large firms can far outspend their smaller competitors. Thus, large firms can purchase more advertising space and time than small companies, but it has never been suggested

In addition to weighing interests by the methods already mentioned, it is also possible for the courts to use their flexible remedial powers in order to reduce the case to a form which permits a rational decision. This technique, of course, was illustrated very clearly by the district court in the *American Can* case.[112] In that proceeding, the needs of small canners for an assured supply of cans collided with the interest in preventing the largest seller from tying up a substantial proportion of the market. By allowing exclusive contracts to be made for one year, the court may not have removed the danger that competition might be lessened and rivals foreclosed. Nevertheless, the court probably succeeded in reducing the possibility of such damage to the point that it was counterbalanced by the business needs of the canners. Much the same technique could be used in cases where substantial selling costs are eliminated by the use of exclusives, for these efficiencies could be largely realized by simply allowing one-year contracts to be signed at the option of the dealer, with a discount no greater than the savings achieved by the contract. It is probable that similar treatment could be accorded

---

that their time and space should be shared with the smaller concerns so long as the latter can obtain advertising on comparable terms. Unless a general campaign is launched against the problem of size as such, therefore, an attack upon the large firm in the limited class of cases under discussion may simply prove inconsistent and eventually ineffective from a policy standpoint. For these reasons, then, it is possible to argue that the gains to be achieved by barring exclusives in cases of this type fail to outweigh the policies favoring the seller even if it cannot be shown that competition has flourished in the face of the exclusive arrangements.

The notion that a seller ought to be allowed to gain a firm market in return for making substantial investments in his outlets has been reflected in far more questionable situations than *Dictograph*. Consider, *e.g.*, the unqualified right to build one's own outlets that was preserved notwithstanding the amendment of Section 7 of the Clayton Act in 1950. Consider also, the recent Trade Commission cases that give producers a measure of control over their outlets in return for heavy investments that cannot be matched by smaller rivals, *e.g.*, Shell Oil Co., F.T.C. Docket No. 7044 (1960). Note that the issue under discussion is not directly analogous to the question whether exclusive protection should be given to ideas, inventions, secret processes, and the like. In those cases, rivals of the excluding firm may find it more difficult or even impossible to obtain comparable ideas, inventions, etc., for themselves. The issue being considered here, however, arises only where the defendant's rivals can obtain equally satisfactory outlets at no greater trouble and expense than were incurred by the defendant.

[112] United States v. American Can Co., 87 F. Supp. 18 (N.D. Calif. 1949). See also *Motion Picture Advertising Service*, 47 F.T.C. 378 (1950), *rev'd*, 194 F.2d 633 (5th Cir. 1952), *rev'd*, 344 U.S. 392 (1953).

in a range of cases presenting strong and unusual needs for exclusive arrangements, for the time period needed to satisfy these needs is seldom so long as to create a truly comparable threat to competition or to the interests of competitors.[113]

In summary, then, the typical cases of exclusive dealing involve combinations of interests that group themselves along a continuum of ascending difficulty. Among the easiest situations are cases such as *Mytinger & Casselberry*,[114] where distributors are so easy to come by that competitors suffer little or no inconvenience from restrictive contracts. Almost by hypothesis, the defendant must act to further legitimate rather than anticompetitive interests; at the same time, his conduct will neither harm his rivals nor injure competition itself.[115] Where this condition does not prevail, however, it is helpful to inquire whether the defendant developed his outlets himself and, if so, whether his rivals can establish comparable outlets with no greater difficulty.[116] If these prerequisites obtain, it seems fair to conclude that the interests of the defendant outweigh those of other parties. If these conditions are not satisfied, however, it may then be asked whether the exclusive arrangements serve

---

[113] A more precise conception of "strong and unusual" has been set forth in note 117 *infra*.

Certain needs, such as the buyer's desire for a sure supply at a stable price, may lead to widespread use of "exclusives," but the duration of these contracts should not have to exceed one year. On the other hand, other needs, such as the concern for protection upon entering a new market, may require longer contracts, but the need should be entertained by only a small fraction of existing sellers. Hence, in neither event would there be a very great threat to competition or to the interests of competitors.

It is by no means clear, however, that the seller should be allowed to *insist* on exclusive contracts. If the contracts are permitted in deference to the buyer's interest, the buyer should presumably be left free to take the goods on an exclusive basis or not as his own interests dictate.

[114] 1960–61 CCH Trad. Reg. Rep. ¶ 29,091.

[115] The only possible interest opposed to defendant is that of the dealers, who might wish to carry competing brands. If dealers are so easy to come by, however, it is very likely that most will be happy to have been chosen at all and will not chafe over not being allowed to handle the goods of competitors. Still more important if the seller has the power to extract an exclusive commitment, he will presumably be able to provide a lower margin or obtain other concessions from the dealer if his power to sign exclusives is denied him. Thus, there is no assurance that dealers will ultimately be any better off if they are protected from exclusive arrangements.

[116] See pages 297–98 *supra*.

some strong and unusual need and whether the duration and cover-
age of the agreements do not extend beyond what is required to
satisfy that need.[117] Should these requirements be met, it is doubtful whether the dangers to competition or to competitors will be
sufficient to outweigh the legitimate ends being served by the contracts.[118] Where no such justification appears, however, a variety
of circumstances may determine the outcome.[119] There are strong

---

[117] The term "strong and unusual need" would include the following:

a) A need on the part of customers for a guaranteed source of supply at a stable
price due to marked fluctuations in the market. (Care should be taken not to extend this case to situations in which one or very few large buyers are powerful
enough to insist on an assured source of supply although their smaller rivals are not.
In such cases, the large buyers simply shift the risk of fluctuation to their less for-
tunate rivals.)

b) A need for a guarantee of exclusivity in order to justify the investment needed
to enter a new market, *e.g.*:

1) The firm just entering into a new line of business.

2) The established firm entering a market in which only one firm can operate
profitably and in which some minimum guarantee is necessary in order to make
the initial expenditure worthwhile. For a possible example, see United States v.
Western Union Telegraph Co., 53 F. Supp. 377 (S.D.N.Y. 1943).

c) A need for a firm market in the rare case where such assurance is necessary in
order to obtain business. See, *e.g.*, Motion Picture Advertising Service v. F.T.C.,
344 U.S. 392 (1953).

d) A desire to realize cost savings (where the seller merely gives buyers an option
to purchase exclusively at a discount no larger than the savings achieved).

Since several of these needs will genuinely exist only very rarely, it is particularly
important to examine defendant's claims with care. There are various ways by
which the validity of such needs can be established. The alleged needs of a particular
firm, for example, will presumably not justify exclusive contracts if other firms that
are similarly situated are able and willing to perform the same operation without
such safeguards. Moreover, in doubtful cases involving alleged needs on the part of
customers, a conditional decree could be given requiring that buyers be given the
option of taking on an exclusive or non-exclusive basis; the possibility could be
left open of subsequently barring such agreements entirely if enough customers
bought on a non-exclusive basis to indicate that customer needs were actually not
substantial.

[118] See page 309 *supra*.

[119] No provision is suggested here for outlawing exclusive arrangements that are
"imposed" on dealers by a powerful seller. Naturally, such contracts smack of
coercion and hence may seem to run counter to established notions of fairness.
Nevertheless, since the powerful seller can take advantage of his position in so
many ways, little may be gained by forbidding him this one exaction, which, from
the dealer's point of view, may be much less onerous than many others that the
seller could impose. Hence, there is very little assurance that dealers will actually be

reasons[120] for favoring the defendant where it can be shown that he has lost a substantial portion of his market share despite the exclusive arrangements.[121] In the absence of such a decline, our traditional regard for freedom of opportunity and for the interests of small competitors should serve to render the contracts unlawful if there are enough such arrangements of sufficient duration to represent a substantial contraction in the available outlets or markets for the commodity in question.[122] What is meant by "substantial," of course, is a question which cannot be answered precisely, and it is probably a matter that is more in need of a reasonably definite answer than a painstaking, and probably hopeless, examination in each case.[123] In any event, the question may not arise very often, for if "exclusives" seem attractive to one, they are likely to appeal to many, with the result that all or most of the established competitors will tend to utilize them.[124]

---

benefited from an attempt to protect them in this fashion. See note 115 *supra*.

Actually, it is probable that cases of coercion would fall in any event under other rules proposed herein. Any seller(s) powerful enough to impose exclusive arrangements would presumably control a formidable share of the market. Moreover, such contracts should be treated as being of indefinite duration, since less powerful rivals are not really free to gain a foothold with defendant's dealers when his contracts expire in view of the leverage exerted by defendant's ultimatum. See note 101 *supra*. As a result, the contracts involved would doubtless be treated as a substantial impediment to competition and to defendant's rivals.

[120] See pages 298–99 *supra*.

[121] Presumably, if the decline is to sustain an inference that competitors do in fact have considerable access to defendant's market, the drop would have to be sustained, continuing, and substantial, *i.e.*, more than merely a few percentage points. The need for exactitude here is somewhat diminished, since sellers will rarely enter into restrictive arrangements relying on the expectation that their market share will decline. Hence what is considered a sufficient decline might well vary from case to case in relation to the extent and duration of defendant's restrictive agreements.

[122] It should be made clear that in computing the scope or prevalence of exclusive arrangements, the court should include not only the restrictive contracts of the defendant but those of his rivals as well. For a discussion of certain problems connected with the meaning of "duration" and "extent," see notes 100–101 *supra*. Reasons for doubting whether problems of market definition would loom large are set forth in note 99 *supra*.

[123] See pages 291–92 *supra*.

[124] In the following kinds of situations, only one or a very few firms might utilize exclusive arrangements so that the total share of the market foreclosed might not be truly large.

a) In some cases, only the most powerful firm might use exclusives because no

4. *The Formulation of Doctrine.* Once the relevant interests have been identified and methods have been developed for measuring and weighing them in concrete cases, the problem arises of describing these techniques in language that will give appropriate guidance to future cases without becoming inflexible to changing circumstances. A number of separate questions are involved. Initially, there is the problem of deciding whether standards should be used embodying a balancing of independent factors. Should exclusive dealing arrangements, for example, be automatically allowed when they are designed to meet some specific business necessity and last no longer than the need requires? Or should a court consider other factors, such as the pervasiveness of the exclusive contracts, in order to make sure in each case that the relevant business needs are not outweighed by the danger to competition? Another question to be resolved is whether to rely on general terms, such as "reasonable" or "substantial," or to employ more specific formulations. This issue can be more than a mere problem in phraseology. In extreme form, it may bear upon the determination whether certain factors should be considered at all, for some considerations are so vaguely understood that they simply cannot be used with any degree of specificity. Another, quite separate, problem has to do with the weight to be placed upon the legal principles that are

---

other rivals possessed the power to obtain similar agreements. In such cases, the contracts would doubtless be struck down for at least two reasons. First, the contracts would probably be considered a substantial clog in the competitive market for the reasons set forth in note 119 *supra*. Second, though the point is not wholly free from doubt, considerations of fairness would be taken to condemn contracts which were secured only by virtue of the greater power of the defendant and which gave the defendant a further advantage over his competitors.

b) In other instances, a small minority might use restrictive contracts because of special and legitimate needs peculiar to the sellers making the arrangements, *e.g.*, firms entering a new market. In this event, the case could be easily resolved as suggested at page 311 *supra*.

c) In still other situations, a small minority might use exclusives because of a particularly strong desire for stability on the part of the sellers involved. Other sellers might not follow suit in view of the costs which woud have to be incurred in the form of discounts or other concessions in order to persuade dealers to sign restrictive agreements. In these cases, the interests of a few small defendants are combined with the interest of their dealers in receiving concessions while on the other side of the scale is the desire of other sellers to have full access to all dealers coupled, perhaps, with a very slight risk to competition. It is difficult to discern any answer to cases of this sort that would seem distinctly more convincing than its opposite.

adopted. Are these doctrines to be expressed as mandatory rules, or as mere guidelines, or presumptions, of varying degrees of strength?

While each of these questions represents a different step in the articulation of legal doctrine, all must turn in the end upon a common determination as to the degree of vagueness that should be tolerated in dealing with the particular offense under consideration. It is necessary, therefore, to develop some clear conception of the effects of vagueness on the process of regulating competition. This question is rarely discussed in the antitrust literature except to make the rudimentary point that specific rules are easier to administer and understand, on the one hand, but "rigid" and "inflexible," on the other.[125] Even less attention to the subject is paid in judicial opinions. As a result, with the exception of the occasional *per se* prohibition, the tendency is to resort to vague formulations since they require less time and effort to produce and since their drawbacks rarely appear so obvious as the risk of making an explicit statement which must later be retracted.

In actual fact, the hidden costs of vagueness in antitrust matters are considerable. Clear legal standards are particularly useful in this field, because the costs of violating the law are often high and the actions that give rise to suit are usually purposeful and undertaken only upon advice of counsel.[126] In addition, since clarity generally serves to reduce litigation, it is particularly important in an area of the law where the burden of protracted litigation already weighs heavily on the federal courts and on the budgets of understaffed enforcement agencies. The matter does not end there. It is even more important to observe that as the command of the statute

---

[125] An exception to this tendency is provided by KAYSEN & TURNER, *op. cit. supra* note 76, at 234–45. For the most part, however, the literature on the question of vagueness has been built up in other quarters. See, *e.g.,* DICKINSON, ADMINISTRATIVE JUSTICE AND THE SUPREMACY OF LAW 104–156 (1927); Baker, *Policy by Rule or Ad Hoc Approach—Which Should It Be?* 22 L. & CONTEMP. PROB. 658 (1957).

[126] In this regard, the antitrust field may be contrasted with the kind of law suits with which the late Judge Frank was dealing in developing his theory of "fact skepticism." See FRANK, LAW AND THE MODERN MIND (1930). Judge Frank relied heavily on the fact that most actions giving rise to law suits are not carefully premeditated with an eye to existing law and that most facts on which law suits turn are not unequivocal but turn instead on whose memory is clearest, which witness is believed, who tells the truth, etc. In contrast, most antitrust actions are not only carefully premeditated but are often governed by rules that are fashioned out of market data that is largely undisputed.

grows vaguer, its actual effects become more haphazard. Ambiguous standards cannot in good conscience be enforced by heavy penalties. As a result, equitable enforcement becomes impossible, for firms will proceed with their plans or withdraw in the face of uncertainty depending on whether they run a risk of large treble-damage suits or fear unfavorable publicity or congressional investigation.[127] In this way, the actual conduct of firms will be influenced by factors having little rational connection with the purposes of the law. Entire categories of restraints may be affected in much the same way. Resale price maintenance, for example, has never resulted in harsh official sanctions, partly because the relevant law is ambiguous at critical points.[128] A treble-damage suit is unlikely since it is so hard to prove injury or to compute damages in cases of this sort. As a result, there is little restraint upon the businessman, and it is therefore not surprising that resale-price maintenance is rather widely practiced even in sections of the country where it has not been made lawful by statute.

There is no doubt, of course, that even a generous measure of ambiguity is often inevitable, and even desirable, in formulating rules for antitrust law. Nevertheless, the optimism that suffuses the recent literature exaggerates the virtues of very vague and formless standards. General language may sometimes be justified as a temporizing device while experience accumulates, but this is seldom a valid excuse under the antitrust laws where most offenses are of long standing and possess a substantial body of case law from which to fashion suitable doctrine. Vagueness is also justified as a necessary price to pay to reach the best possible result in each case. But the better result that is achieved in an occasional litigated case may be pyrrhic indeed if it causes sufficient ambiguity to lead to haphazard results in the planning of business decisions. Still less defensible is a vagueness born of considering "relevant" facts that do not actually assist in making more accurate judgments. By extending hospitality to such factors, the courts merely invite delay and

---

[127] This problem has become more acute in recent years with the increasing importance of the treble-damage suit.

[128] The most serious soft spot has to do with the uncertainty surrounding the use of resale-price maintenance enforced by simply refusing to deal with distributors selling below list price. See Levi, *The Parke Davis-Colgate Doctrine: The Ban on Resale Price Maintenance,* 1960 SUP. CT. REV. 258.

cause troublesome uncertainty without any compensating improvement in the soundness of their decisions.

A more important defense of ambiguity emphasizes the danger that specific rules will become rigid instead of being adapted to meet unforeseen cases and changing circumstances.[129] Like most of the arguments against more definite rules, this contention is easily overstated. The fact that methods and technology of business are constantly evolving does not mean that changes are constantly occurring of a kind that need disturb antitrust doctrines. It is doubtful, for example, that exclusive dealing contracts now serve more urgent needs than they did in the past or that foreclosure works in a different way than it once did. Significant changes will doubtless occur from time to time, but there is no real warrant for the conclusion that courts and administrators will hang on doggedly to outworn doctrine. In any event, if they have so little imagination as to behave in this fashion, little will be gained by resorting to loose formulations, for it is almost inevitable that officials of this sort will perform just as badly in the delicate task of applying a vague standard to the facts of each case.

Notwithstanding the reservations just made, there is no dispute that unforeseen cases and changed circumstances will arise. This is hardly a reason, however, to abandon precision for loosely formulated standards. A far better balance can be struck between the need for guidance and the exigencies of change by continuing to strive for precise legal principles but leaving room for either party to attempt a rebuttal. A number of variations can be played on this theme. At one extreme is the absolute prohibition that appears to leave no room for exception but which in fact is often relaxed in one way or another where compelling reasons appear. At the other extreme is the simple *prima facie* case that can be rebutted either by showing justifying circumstances or by refuting the *prima facie* case itself. The considerations underlying a choice between these varying techniques are well enough understood though seldom articulated. The rules relating to price fixing, for example, are absolute for several reasons. The conduct involved is one of the

---

[129] This concern has been emphasized by Mr. Justice Frankfurter. See Electrical Workers v. N.L.R.B., 366 U.S. 667, 677 (1961): "As is too often the way of the law or, at least, of adjudications, soon the *Dry Dock* tests were mechanically applied. . . ."

most serious varieties covered by the antitrust laws. Moreover, there is an acute and persistent temptation for large numbers of businessmen to agree with their rivals on price, and the adverse effects of these agreements are immediately felt by the public. Finally, private remedies may provide no deterrent since damages are so hard to ascertain. Hence, a clear prohibition is needed so that businessmen cannot seize upon ambiguity to justify fixing prices and so that the government can freely impose stiff and deterring penalties for violation. In this way, something is done to avoid widespread agreements on price that would lead to burdensome litigation and might work substantial harm upon the public before being discovered and condemned. In the case of exclusive dealing, however, somewhat different conditions prevail. The adverse effects of exclusive arrangements upon competition seem less serious and take longer to materialize. The desire to enter into such arrangments is also less intense and is shared by fewer firms so that the burdens and frustrations of ambiguity will fall less heavily on business and government. For these reasons, it is more appropriate to frame the legal doctrine relating to exclusive dealing in terms less absolute than those relating to price fixing. On the other hand, it is also true that dealers and rival firms can suffer immediate injury from exclusive contracts. Damages are difficult to prove, and there is seldom a danger of losing sufficient amounts through private suit to deter a large firm seeking to tie up its distribution outlets. Finally, it seems probable that enough experience has accumulated under Section 3 to reduce the number of unforeseen cases to rather small proportions. Hence, in order to minimize injury and avoid burdensome litigation, the law would seem justified in moving toward a rather precisely drafted network of rules that will admit of exception only on clear and convincing evidence that an exception should be made.

III. The Possibilities for Progress

Any effort to develop antitrust law in the manner just described would be burdensome and often controversial, at least in its initial stages. Such an endeavor would necessarily be overshadowed by a wide range of other problems with which the government is currently concerned. Hence, there is reason to examine each of the various agencies that participate in the development of the law to see whether they actually possess the time and the means to devote themselves seriously to such a task. An inventory of this sort is intended primarily as a means toward a more realistic assessment of the possibilities of doctrinal reform. Nevertheless, any effort to determine what is possible in antitrust law must inescapably cast judgment on what has actually been done by the courts, the Congress, and the Commission.

A. THE SUPREME COURT

In the last few years, increasing dissatisfaction has been expressed by careful observers over the craftsmanship of Supreme Court opinions.[130] Summary reversals in controversial cases, hasty generalizations about complicated issues, loosely analyzed opinions—all these charges and more have been laid at the door of the Justices. There is much that seems to confirm these criticisms in the recent Court decisions on exclusive dealing. In failing to explore or even recognize a tenable middle ground between stark prohibition and exhaustive inquiry, *Standard Stations* can be termed an "inadequately reasoned opinion."[131] A study of the dissent in *Motion Picture Advertising* suggests that the majority opinion in that case was characterized by "the sweeping dogmatic statement" whereby "issues are ducked which in good lawyership and good conscience ought not to be ducked." *Tampa Electric*, though it cleared the ground for doctrinal reform, can doubtless be numbered among the opinions that do not "genuinely illumine the area of law with which they deal."

Serious as these comments seem to be, one is led inescapably to wonder whether the same critique could not be made of every period in the history of the antitrust laws. True, the deficiencies may be less readily observed because of the reluctance of earlier Courts to indulge in dissenting opinions. But if one perseveres, it is easy enough to find decisions, at least in the area of exclusive

---

130 *E.g.*, Hart, *Foreword: The Time Chart of the Justices*, 73 HARV. L. REV. 84 (1959); Bickel & Wellington, *Legislative Purpose and the Judicial Process: The Lincoln Mills Case*, 71 HARV. L. REV. 1 (1957); Brown, *Foreword: Process of Law*, 72 HARV. L. REV. 77 (1958).

131 The quoted words, together with those that appear in the following sentences, can be found in Hart, *supra* note 130, at 100.

dealing, which are as vulnerable as the opinions which have just been mentioned. The *Curtis Publishing* case,[132] for example, with its exclusive networks of young newsboys, provided an excellent vehicle to discuss the meaning of "foreclosure" and an equally suitable occasion for considering whether a company that had troubled to create its own distribution system should be required to share its facilities with competitors. The Court glided noiselessly over these and other issues and disposed of the case with vague statements to the effect that "effective competition requires that traders have large freedom of action when conducting their own affairs."[133] Similar weaknesses appear in the leading case of *Standard Fashion v. Magrane Houston*,[134] where Standard and its affiliates had tied up approximately twenty thousand of the nation's fifty-two thousand pattern distributors. Faced with this situation, the Court proceeded to dispose of the case with a curious farrago of abstract pronouncements and dubious assertions of fact. The Court began with the startling announcement that the meaning of the phrase "to substantially lessen competition" was so plain as to make it quite unnecessary to examine the legislative history. This language, said the Court, was clearly designed to prohibit contracts having a substantial probability rather than a remote possibility of lessening competition. With this analytical tool, a unanimous opinion found the statute violated on the strength of the following conclusions of fact, which were adopted verbatim from the circuit court opinion:[135]

> The restriction of each merchant to one pattern manufacturer must in hundreds, perhaps in thousands of small communities amount to giving such pattern manufacturers a monopoly of business in such community. Even in the larger cities, to limit to a single pattern maker the pattern dealers most resorted to by customers whose purchasers tend to give fashions their vogue, may tend to facilitate further combinations; so that the

---

[132] F.T.C. v. Curtis Publishing Co., 260 U.S. 568 (1923). The reader may recall that these issues were not ruled out by the Court's conclusion that the newsboys were agents of Curtis; the same questions were relevant to the discussion by the Court of Section 5 of the Trade Commission Act, where the agency point was not dispositive.

[133] *Id.* at 582.

[134] 258 U.S. 346 (1922).   [135] *Id.* at 357.

plaintiff, or some other aggressive concern, instead of control-ling two-fifths, will shortly have almost, if not quite, all the pattern business.

To begin with, it is interesting to note that there was no evidence whatsoever in the 159-page record that showed that Standard had entered into contracts with the sole outlet in any community. Standard emphasized this point in its petition to the Supreme Court and argued that outlets in such small towns would in fact be un-economical.[136] Nor was there any evidence that Standard had tied up the most fashionable outlets in the larger cities. Still more strik-ing was the Court's assertion that further combinations might take place in these cities, for this point was not only bereft of supporting data but such evidence as did exist pointed strongly in the opposite direction.[137] The number of independent companies in Boston, for example, had multiplied in the preceding years and several new-comers had gained substantial shares of the national market. Hence, the conclusion that Standard Fashion "will shortly have almost, if not quite all, the pattern business" was quite incomprehensible in the light of the facts.

If the Supreme Court has perennially been vulnerable to criti-cisms of this sort, the explanation is not difficult to discern. The Court is composed of laymen with a very small staff to assist them. The Justices can give but little time to each proceeding and can hear only a random and occasional case from the stream of litiga-tion arising under every section of the antitrust laws. With limita-tions such as these, the Court is simply ill adapted as an institution to the arduous task of creating serviceable doctrine in a field as com-plicated as antitrust law. This is not to say that the Court has no useful role to play in the development of antitrust law. The Justices must necessarily accept the traditional and crucial responsibility of deciding whether the doctrine developed by one lower court should be preferred to the principles of another or whether both should give way to still another rationale proposed in other, less official, quarters. The raw material from which such choices will be made, however—the careful articulation of rival doctrines and the

---

136 Petition for Certiorari, p. 37.

137 For a summary of the evidence, see *id*. at pp. 19–22, 39–40.

exploration of their strengths and weaknesses—must ordinarily be left to other institutions.

The foregoing conclusions may seem to take too pessimistic a view of the Court's potentialities as an institution. In particular, it may be argued that the Court could do much to improve the quality of its work if it entertained fewer cases, deliberated more fully and indulged in more open-minded debate.[138] While reforms of this sort may well be valuable, their significance in the antitrust field should not be exaggerated. Certainly reflection and discussion could help to improve the discrimination and judgment that the Court displays in comparing competing principles and selecting the rationale best suited to the case at hand. Greater time and care might also protect the Court from hasty generalizations that pass over difficult problems. On the other hand, it seems unlikely that these reforms could free the Court to fashion a coherent and consistent set of principles for the various areas of antitrust law. Such a task would require a far greater effort than the Justices could conceivably devote to what is, after all, only one of many problems with which the Court must deal. As a result, it is hard to escape the conclusion that the formulation of methods and principles for resolving cases must originate from other institutions. It is only natural then that the quality of the Court's performance will seldom succeed in surpassing the quality of work performed by these other bodies.

Viewed in this perspective, the opinions of the Court seem less vulnerable than one might suppose at first glance. It is doubtful whether the Court has been very far behind the contemporary store of knowledge relating to exclusive dealing or to the legal techniques by which it might be judged. In moving from a preoccupation with the dominant firm to a concept of collective foreclosure, the Court adapted to the field of exclusive dealing the findings of economists to the effect that monopolistic behavior might characterize small groups of firms as well as a single dominating concern.[139] With the *Tampa Electric* opinion, the Court has seemingly relaxed the *Standard Stations* doctrine in answer to the criti-

---

[138] See, *e.g.*, Hart, *supra* note 130, at 123–25.

[139] These findings, of course, stem from the well-known work of CHAMBERLIN, THE THEORY OF MONOPOLISTIC COMPETITION (7th ed. 1956).

cism of lower tribunals and independent critics. In making these shifts in doctrine, the Court has been responsive to the most important lessons to be derived from its environment. If the state of the law has also been vague and erratic, responsibility should presumably fall in large part upon the other institutions that affect the development of the law.

B. THE CONGRESS

Appeals have been made periodically for clarification of the antitrust laws by legislative action.[140] The outlook for obtaining clear and specific pronouncements from this quarter, however, seems exceedingly dim. Mention has been made of the effects upon legislation that are produced by the pressures of time and by the divisions of opinion within the majorities that support legislation in this field.[141] There is little reason to expect any fundamental change in these conditions. The divisions of opinion appear to reflect rather permanent political patterns in the country as a whole, while the demands upon the legislator seem steadily to increase. Even if these limitations were not so severe, the time and difficulty involved in amending statutes affecting such widespread interests would still preclude frequent legislation. As a result Congress would remain ill equipped to shoulder the responsibility for amending the law to conform with changes in our needs, our understanding, and our policies. For all these reasons, then, improvements must come, if at all, from other institutions concerned with the development of the law.

C. THE AGENCIES OF ENFORCEMENT

Of all the government bodies that help to regulate the economy, the independent commission has probably come to be most bitterly criticized. In recent years, the disillusionment has seemed particularly acute.[142] Established with the hope of achieving a speedy and expert judgment on complex economic questions, these agencies are now assailed on every side for the delays in their proceed-

---

[140] See, e.g., Oppenheim, supra note 28.   [141] See pages 288–89 supra.

[142] See, e.g., Hector, Problems of the CAB and the Independent Regulatory Commissions, 69 YALE L. J. 931 (1960); Friendly, A Look at the Federal Administrative Agencies, 60 COLUM. L. REV. 429 (1960).

ings, for their lack of consistent policies, and for their failure to lift their opinions above the level of mediocrity. Certainly, much of this criticism is borne out by the handiwork of the Federal Trade Commission in the field of exclusive dealing. Most of the contested proceedings in the nineteen-fifties required five years between complaint and final order, even though exclusive dealing cases could hardly be numbered among the most complicated forms of antitrust litigation.[143] Equally disappointing was the failure of this expert body to utilize in any convincing way the diverse market facts that they insisted so emphatically on considering. Questionable too was the judgment displayed by the Commission in deciding with such dubious logic to depart from *Standard Stations* only to abandon this approach in the very case where extended analysis seemed most necessary.[144]

In contrast to the Commission, the Antitrust Division of the Justice Department has generally enjoyed a rather favorable reputation. Most impartial observers would probably agree that the legal staff of the Division has, on the whole, been of a higher order of competence than that of the Commission. Most would also conclude that the Division has displayed somewhat better judgment and greater effectiveness in enforcing the law. Sentiments of this sort have even led to proposals that the bulk of the Commission's responsibilities in the field of antitrust law be transferred to the Department of Justice. There is an immediate appeal in suggestions of this sort. Why not concentrate the enforcement of antitrust policy in the body that has traditionally demonstrated greater com-

---

[143] I jotted down the following dates on a recent visit to the Commission archives. The list is by no means complete.

Dictograph	Complaint Issued May 2, 1949
	Final Commission Opinion, December 15, 1954
Timken Roller Bearing	Complaint Issued February 13, 1956
	Final Commission Opinion, January 24, 1961
Insto Gas	Complaint Issued February 21, 1951
	Final Commission Opinion, December 19, 1957
Outboard Machine	Complaint Issued May 23, 1951
	Final Commission Opinion, January 10, 1956

On the other hand, some contested exclusive dealing cases have been decided more rapidly. For example, in *Mytinger & Casselberry* the complaint was issued on November 26, 1957, and the final opinion was handed down on September 25, 1960.

[144] Mytinger & Casselberry, 1960–61 CCH Trad. Reg. Rep. ¶ 29,091.

petence? It would be difficult indeed to answer this argument by disputing the ability of the Division or by denying its very large capacity to play a constructive role in rationalizing the antitrust laws. Instead, the reply must merely emphasize that a commission has potentialities as an institution which exceed those of the Division and that it is still premature to rule out the possibility that these potentialities will be realized.

However able the Division may be, its principles and policies inevitably pass through the prism of the federal court system with its multitude of separate tribunals. Since the Division must seek to win its cases, it necessarily behaves as an advocate when it participates in judicial proceedings. The Division's effort to obtain a strict, quantitative rule in the *Standard Stations* litigation affords a typical example of this tendency. Inevitably, however, the presentations of the Division will be received by the courts in the spirit of advocacy with the result that responsibility for the formulation of doctrine will pass from the Division to the judge. The judge, in turn, must often refrain from fashioning principles that reach much beyond the case before him; not only is he pressed for time and comparatively inexperienced in matters of antitrust but his responsibilities are diluted by being shared with so many other courts. In this way, the work of the district courts becomes particularized and variegated so that responsibility for developing more general principles devolves increasingly upon the Supreme Court. Since that tribunal inevitably labors under all the institutional handicaps that have already been described, any transfer of functions to the Antitrust Division only helps to perpetuate deficiencies of the sort that have been so evident in the Court's opinions on the subject of exclusive dealing.

These remarks are not intended to belittle in any way the work of the Antitrust Division or the federal courts. The point is simply that the Trade Commission has unique advantages as an institution that are well suited to the task that needs to be performed. Its members can specialize and hear sufficient cases of the same general type to permit them to synthesize methods and rules of more general application. As an administrative agency, the Commission is somewhat freer than the courts to announce policies openly and to promulgate them in the form best suited to the problem at hand. This freedom cannot help but be important to a process of adjudication that depends more upon policy-making and less upon factual analysis than has been commonly supposed.

The advantages of the Commission will never be realized if appointments are uninspired and procedures slipshod, and many observers have seemingly become disillusioned with the regulatory process for this reason. In appraising the Federal Trade Commission from this standpoint, however, one can easily overgeneralize about administrative agencies and indulge in criticism that does not proceed from an adequate historical perspective. It is tempting, for example, to fall prey to such vogues as the current theory of the rise and fall of the independent agency—a theory that depicts the organization in the dawn of new legislation, follows it through an ebullient period in which the larger problems are put to the sword, and ends by describing the never-ending dusk that descends when the pioneering figures depart for new adventures and are replaced by men of a lesser breed.[145] Theories of this sort not only make the problems of the independent agency seem more immutable than they really are, but they may not even fit the facts of any particular agency. This is particularly true of the history of the Trade Commission which reflects a rather constant improvement over the entire course of its existence. Forty years ago, the opinions of the Commission in cases of exclusive dealing were appalling.[146] The few facts that found their way into the opinion were slanted against the respondent; vital matters, such as the relative size of the respondent, were not included; the events in controversy were described in language so stilted as to deprive them of much of their meaning; arguments of the respondent were not mentioned, let alone answered; and legal conclusions were simply announced, following the findings of fact, with no reasoned explanation and no hint of any underlying principle. As time went on, facts began to

---

[145] See, e.g., BERNSTEIN, REGULATING BUSINESS BY INDEPENDENT COMMISSION 74–102 (1955).

[146] The classic description of the Commission's early deficiencies is, of course, HENDERSON, THE FEDERAL TRADE COMMISSION 315–16, 127–30 (1924). A complete appreciation of the problem, however, can only be derived from actually reading the early cases. Pertinent examples from the field of exclusive dealing include Chicago Flexible Shaft Co., 1 F.T.C. 181 (1918); B. S. Pearsall Butter Co., 5 F.T.C. 127 (1922); Standard Electric Mfg. Co., 5 F.T.C. 376 (1923). For an account of the early years by one who served on the Commission, see GASKILL, THE REGULATION OF COMPETITION (1936).

be stated more fully and the beginnings of reasoned explanation began to accompany the conclusions of law.[147] It was not until after the second World War, however, that fundamental reforms were introduced. By 1950 the rudiments of a compliance procedure had been established to check on adherence to Commission orders. Arguments by the respondent began to be mentioned in the Commission opinions and to be answered with counter-argument. Finally, in the mid-fifties written opinions in narrative form were prepared individually by the commissioners, greater efforts were made to carry out compliance proceedings, and attempts were made, with some success, to reduce the time required to dispose of contested cases.[148]

It would be fruitless to insist that all these innovations have been perfected. Nor can it be denied that there is room for further improvement. Much could be done to improve procedures for selecting cases and to provide for a more systematic formulation of the areas of the economy and the doctrinal objectives toward which the efforts of the staff should be directed. More could be done to develop the tradition of appointing able men to the Commission who have had some prior opportunity to think carefully over the problems of competition and its regulation. The very nature of these needs calls to mind a number of serious obstacles. Any reforms that depend on better appointments must be assessed with an eye to the political pressures that have so often affected the process of appointment in the past. Any prognosis of the chances of creative policy-making by independent commissions must reckon with the strong pressures that make it atractive, and at times even imperative, to be shielded by the opacity of a case-by-case analysis. Opinions will doubtless vary concerning the seriousness of these problems.[149] Nevertheless, even allowing a generous measure of cynicism for power politics and pressure groups, these obstacles seem less imposing than the institutional handicaps which burden

---

[147] See, *e.g.*, Carter Carburetor Corp., 28 F.T.C. 116 (1939).

[148] Many of these reforms are recounted by a close, though hardly disinterested, observer, in Kintner, *The Revitalized Federal Trade Commission: A Two Year Evaluation*, 30 N.Y.U. L. Rev. 1143 (1955).

[149] Some observers, with far greater experience than I, have taken a very pessimistic view of the potentialities of the Trade Commission. See in particular, ARNOLD, *op. cit. supra* note 2, at 100. Judge Arnold's argument proceeds from the premise that the public will not accept sweeping pronouncements from the Trade Commission

the Congress or the Supreme Court in work of this kind. And if the Commission still operates at a lower level of competence than other institutions in the field, it is nevertheless unwarranted to abandon the agency, with all its potential advantages, in this of all periods when recent trends give greater promise than before of realizing dividends on an institutional investment that has so often seemed unprofitable in the past.

D. LEGAL CRITICISM

In this review of the various official bodies concerned with anti-trust problems, it is apparent that much difficulty stems from the press of business that in recent decades has engulfed the legislator, judge, and commissioner alike, channeling their time and effort toward day-to-day problems at the expense of reflective synthesis.[150] For this reason, the private critic has come to occupy an enviable position, since he is better able to find time to engage in the laborious process of creating the kind of doctrinal structure that the anti-trust field demands. The practitioner-critic, of course, is generally hard pressed, but even he can husband his time over longer periods to write occasional articles of a reflective nature. Academic commentators, on the other hand, are encouraged by their institutional environment to indulge in work of this sort, and though they have been accused of paying in unrealism for what they gain in detachment, they are increasingly able to acquire a practical touch by engaging in part-time ventures in business and government.

These advantages place a rather special obligation on the critic to contribute to the development of the law, and much has certainly been done along these lines. Commentators have come to play a vigorous role in urging doctrinal change and seem to have enjoyed considerable success in this effort, if exclusive dealing is any guide. It is doubtful, for example, whether the Trade Com-

---

because it lacks the "protective symbolism" of the courts or the reverence and awe traditionally accorded to judges. These remarks seem far more applicable to a period such as 1940 when the needs of the day involved a tightening of antitrust doctrine against the interests of powerful groups. The kind of doctrinal formulation discussed in these pages, however, is generally less controversial and, when well executed, might often be greeted on all sides as a welcome substitute for vague and erratic individual decisions.

[150] It is interesting to note how all of our contemporary institutional criticism lays such heavy emphasis on the shortage of time. See, *e.g.*, Hart, *supra* note 130; Hector, *supra* note 142; GROSS, THE LEGISLATIVE STRUGGLE 94–95 (1953).

mission would have departed from the approach of *Standard Sta-tions* without finding support in the rather widespread disapproval that critics heaped upon that case. This same disapproval seems also to have contributed to the atmosphere that moved the Court to go out of its way in *Tampa Electric* to suggest a new approach to exclusive arrangements. Indeed, the attention paid to law reviews by the Court has become so familiar in antitrust cases as to arouse the ire of influential congressmen and to provoke allegations of antitrust lobbies utilizing learned journals as vehicles for their views.[151]

The influence of legal writing in the antitrust field has not always been so apparent, nor has the quality of such work displayed the critical zeal that so often pervades the current material. Early articles were often unbelievably pallid in their appraisals, contenting themselves with docile descriptions of the cases and gliding over opinions that seem, at least in retrospect, to bristle with deficiencies. While many comments of this kind still appear, there has been a recent abundance of critical work appraising the logic and economic sophistication of all manner of antitrust opinions. Much of this writing was inspired by earlier work by economists questioning many of the simple postulates that had been assumed by some of the proponents of a vigorous antitrust policy. Legal writing of this sort was unquestionably of great service in checking the over-hasty use of simple premises and thereby forestalling dubious doctrinal developments.[152] While valuable work in this vein may remain to be done, there is growing need for work of a more positive kind. Indeed, now that so many of the shafts have been hurled against what appeared to be the implications of the early postwar cases, the more constructive task bids fair to achieve a pre-eminent importance.

Work of this positive variety, of course, is painstaking and difficult, and there is serious question as to whether sufficient attention has been paid to the task by writers in the field. In this regard, the *Tampa Electric* case provides a striking illustration. An effort has been made in these pages to point out the ambiguities in Mr. Justice

---

151 The allegations are recounted and analyzed by Newland, *The Supreme Court and Legal Writing: Learned Journals As Vehicles of an Antitrust Lobby?* 48 Geo. L. J. 105 (1959).

152 For an example of this work at its best, see Adelman, *Effective Competition and the Antitrust Laws*, 61 Harv. L. Rev. 1299 (1948).

Clark's analysis of the concepts of substantial foreclosure and justification. These problems are representative enough of the kind of work that remains undone, for certainly it is hard to say that the pronouncements of the Court on either issue were much vaguer than the available legal writing on the subject. Of equal significance are the implications to be drawn from the rather bizarre attempts throughout the *Tampa Electric* litigation to define a relevant market within which to appraise the effects of the restrictive arrangements.[153] Few economists would take seriously the assertion by the dissenting judge that the geographic market relevant to the Tampa contract could be defined as the state of Florida; few would be convinced by the reasoning of the majority opinion that other boiler fuels should be excluded from the product market. For that matter, most experts would probably question the analysis of the Supreme Court itself if they troubled to examine the hard facts that underlay Mr. Justice Clark's conclusions on the matter. Amusing articles can be written with refreshingly little effort to expose the theoretical inadequacies of these opinions.[154] The only reply to barbs of this sort is to inquire how much has been done by economists to illumine the conceptual problems of market definition to a point where they can be put into practice by the average court. Indeed, how much has been done by lawyers to construct a method or a conceptual framework that will make the best possible adaptation of existing economic theory to the requirements of the legal system? The answers to these questions are not encouraging. Economists of course are necessarily handicapped by the extreme complexity of the underlying concepts on which market definition depends. Even these difficulties, however, may not fully account for the amount of systematic analysis that is available, for there are very few works indeed, and most of what has been done is of the negatively critical variety.[155] The legal literature is hardly more complete. Despite the constant stream of articles on antitrust questions, only three or four have dealt in any detail with the task of

---

[153] See, *e.g.*, the Court of Appeals' opinion, 276 F.2d 766 (6th Cir. 1960).

[154] For a discussion of some of the problems involved in the Court's disposition of the market problem, see Note, 75 HARV. L. REV. 40,196 (1961).

[155] Perhaps the most helpful work is Stocking & Mueller, *The Cellophane Case*, 45 AM. ECON. REV. 29 (1955). The best example of undiluted criticism is Adelman, *Economic Aspects of the Bethlehem Opinion*, 45 VA. L. REV. 684 (1959).

defining a relevant product market.[156] Almost all of these are student works which are helpful but throw no more than a wavering light upon the problems involved. Still greater darkness envelops the question of geographic markets, for there has been little more than a portion of a student's comment to light the way.[157]

In the face of such deficiencies as these, it is hard to escape the feeling that of all the agencies that affect the development of antitrust law, legal criticism has fallen farthest short of realizing its potentialities. From any serious standpoint, however, this is a conclusion that calls for rejoicing rather than despair, for without such unused capabilities there could be little possibility for reform. As it is, the potentialities of legal criticism, together with those of the Federal Trade Commission, seem ample to undertake the process of doctrinal refinement, and though these capacities may never be realized, it is at least a good omen that both institutions just mentioned have exhibited marked progress over the course of the past twenty years.

The recent history of legal commentary and the experience of the Trade Commission deserve re-emphasis in an era in which it has become commonplace to worry over the crisis of our legal institutions. Certainly, the narrow study attempted here suggests that none of the agencies concerned with antitrust law has suffered a decline in performance, and some have quite clearly improved. The difficulties encountered in this field, therefore, appear to have resulted not so much from some flaw in our institutions as from our wholehearted acceptance of the pleas of earlier critics to study the effects of law on society and to shape legal doctrine in accordance therewith.[158] If the course of the law seems confused and erratic, it is simply that the affairs of men have turned out to be far more puzzling and intricate than those jurists were wont to admit.

---

156 Turner, *Antitrust Policy and the Cellophane Case*, 70 HARV. L. REV. 281 (1956); MacDonald, *Product Competition in the Relevant Market under the Sherman Act*, 53 MICH. L. REV. 69 (1954); Comment, 58 COLUM. L. REV. 1269, 1272–77 (1958); Note, 54 COLUM. L. REV. 580, 585–94 (1954).

157 Comment, *"Substantially to Lessen Competition ...": Current Problems of Horizontal Mergers*, 68 YALE L. J. 1627, 1630–36 (1959).

158 For a discussion of the ideas, forces, and writers instrumental in this shift in the purpose and function of law, see CAHILL, JUDICIAL LEGISLATION: A STUDY IN AMERICAN LEGAL THEORY (1952).

GEORGE J. STIGLER

UNITED STATES v. LOEW'S INC.:

A NOTE ON BLOCK-BOOKING

The phenomenon of block-booking of movies—the offer of only a combined assortment of movies to an exhibitor—has been the subject of several antitrust cases. In the most recent case, *United States v. Loew's Inc.*,[1] Mr. Justice Goldberg, speaking for the Court, again struck down the practice, stating flatly: "The antitrust laws do not permit a compounding of the statutorily conferred monopoly."

The explanation of the practice of block-booking is not explicit in the decision, but a fair interpretation is this: The owner of two films uses the popularity of one to compel the exhibitor to purchase the other as well. This is not a full explanation, however, for it does not explain why the seller should wish to sell the inferior film.

Consider the following simple example. One film, Justice Goldberg cited *Gone with the Wind*, is worth $10,000 to the buyer, while a second film, the Justice cited *Getting Gertie's Garter*, is worthless to him. The seller could sell the one for $10,000, and throw away the second, for no matter what its cost, bygones are forever bygones. Instead the seller compels the buyer to take both. But surely he can obtain no more than $10,000, since by hypothesis this

---

George J. Stigler is Charles R. Walgreen Distinguished Service Professor of American Institutions, The University of Chicago.

[1] 371 U.S. 38, 52 (1962).

is the value of both films to the buyer. Why not, in short, use his monopoly power directly on the desirable film? It seems no more sensible, on this logic, to block-book the two films than it would be to compel the exhibitor to buy *Gone with the Wind* and seven Ouija boards, again for $10,000.

The explanation of the practice must lie elsewhere. The simplest plausible explanation is that some buyers would prize one film much more relative to the other. Consider the two buyers:

A would pay $8,000 for film X and $2,500 for film Y.
B would pay $7,000 for film X and $3,000 for film Y.

If the seller were to price the two films separately, he would receive:

1. $5,000 from the sale of Y, at $2,500 per buyer. A higher price would exclude A and reduce receipts.
2. $14,000 from the sale of X, at $7,000 per buyer, on the same logic.

The total received is $19,000. But with block-booking, a single price of $10,000 can be set for the pair of films, and $20,000 will be received.[2]

On this approach, block-booking is a method of selling calculated to extract larger sums than otherwise would be possible. The value of ten films will be the same for two TV stations with comparable markets and advertising rates, but the relative values of the individual films will vary from city to city. These differences cannot be gauged as closely by the seller as by the buyer, so a block price is used to capture a larger return.[3]

---

[2] Of course a price of $10,500 could have been set for buyer A, but this degree of precision of measurement of demand may be impossible. If it is possible, then clearly there is no need for block-booking, on the present explanation.

[3] The formal theory may be sketched; it was suggested to me by Milton Friedman. Let p_{1a} be the maximum price buyer 1 would pay for film a, and similarly with other subscripts. With separate prices,

$$p_a = \min (p_{1a}, p_{2a}) ,$$
$$p_b = \min (p_{1b}, p_{2b}) .$$

With block-booking,

$$p = \min (p_{1a} + p_{1b}, p_{2a} + p_{2b}).$$

The latter will be larger than the sum of the former if $p_{1a} > p_{2a}$, $p_{1b} < p_{2b}$ (or the converse). The argument is incomplete in that $2p_a$ may be less than p_{1a} or

This is a logical explanation for block-booking, but is it the correct explanation? Several empirical tests may be specified:

1. From *Variety*, in olden days one could look up the receipts from the exhibition of movies in various cities. If the relative appeal of movies in different cities varied substantially, the theory is plausible; if the relative appeal is much the same in most cities, the theory is false.

2. Again from trade sources, one can determine whether the average receipts (per year) of a theater were determined by attendance, income, etc. If there was a good relationship, the block rate could be established with some precision and would not forfeit large gains from discriminating among individual theaters.

3. From the record, one can perhaps determine whether the sales prices of given blocks of films were closely related to objective criteria of stations' ability to pay (chiefly advertising rates). If so, again the possibility of personal discrimination in price must be ruled out.

No systematic testing has been carried out, but a few suggestive, and supporting, pieces in evidence are given in the Appendix.

Whether this simple hypothesis survives or not, clearly the Court's assertion that monopoly must not be compounded is futile. Let a man own two patents on related products, say a gas turbine engine and a diesel engine, or two copyrights, on *Gone with the Wind* and *Leaving with the Gale*. They are substitutes and in setting the price of one, he must take account of its effect on the sales of the other: the monopolies will be compounded.

The decision to outlaw block-booking is not objectionable because it rests on an incomplete analysis. The effect of the decision, if it is effective, is to reduce the receipts of the owners of the films, and to increase the receipts of another set of monopolists, the owners of TV licenses. If the TV licenses were sold by the government, the redistribution would be beneficial; as it stands, no clear judgment seems possible.

---

p_{2a}, but the argument could be extended to cover no sales to one buyer by using expressions such as max $(2 \min [p_{1a}, p_{2a}], p_{1a}, p_{2a})$, etc.

APPENDIX

Two separate studies shed some light on the plausibility of the hypothesis that block-booking is essentially a price discrimination technique.

1.   The first week, first-run attendance receipts of a series of movies in large American cities were tabulated. A period before the major onslaught of television was chosen. The underlying data are reported in Table 1.

TABLE 1

RECEIPTS FROM FIRST-WEEK EXHIBITION OF MOVIES, 1946–47*
(Thousands of Dollars)

CITY	Movie†											
	A	B	C	D	E	F	G	H	I	J	K	L
Washington, D.C.........	31.0	28.0	33.0	25.0	24.0	26.0	29.0	20.0	25.0	26.0	23.0	29.0
Indianapolis....	27.0	22.0	19.0	21.0	17.0	14.0	20.0	13.0	12.0	13.0	18.0	15.0
Los Angeles.....	62.5	65.7	111.0	75.6	80.0	66.0	23.0	74.9	65.2	67.0	73.8	62.0
Minneapolis....	38.0	22.0	21.0	23.0	15.0	11.0	27.0	15.0	14.0	20.0	26.0	17.0
Montreal.......	17.0	22.5	16.0	16.0	14.5	13.0	18.0	14.2	14.0	15.0	13.0	14.5
Philadelphia....	52.0	47.5	50.0	53.5	31.5	37.0	53.0	32.0	33.0	32.0	35.0	45.0
Pittsburgh......	40.0	27.0	26.1	28.0	24.0	20.0	32.5	13.0	19.5	24.0	22.0	22.0
Buffalo........	31.0	28.0	24.0	29.5	24.0	16.0	27.0	....	....	....	....	....
Cincinnati......	36.0	30.5	29.5	18.0	16.0	13.0	26.0	....	....	....	....	....
Seattle.........	27.3	16.0	26.0	16.0	16.8	13.2	27.0	....	....	....	....	....
San Francisco...	45.0	23.0	46.0	37.5	24.5	30.0	45.0	....	....	....	....	....
St. Louis.......	24.0	30.0	21.0	32.0	24.0	19.0	24.0	....	....	....	....	....
Omaha.........	23.0	9.3	18.0	15.3	12.2	8.5	17.2	....	....	....	....	....

* Source: *Variety*, Nov. 6, 1946, through May 7, 1947.

† See below for key to movie titles.

For each city a receipts figure (say, r_e) was calculated for each film on the assumption that this film had obtained the same share of receipts in this city as it did in all cities combined. The expected receipts (r_e) are compared with actual receipts (r_a), by the formula

$$\frac{|r_a - r_e|}{r_e},$$

taking absolute values since we are not interested in the sign of the relative deviation.

The mean absolute relative deviation, to give the average of this expression its formidable title, is 14.4 per cent for 12 pictures in 7 cities, and 14.9 per cent for 7 pictures in 13 cities. Thus if the seller (actually lessor) of a picture to the theater in a particular city assumed that it would have the same appeal (relative to other pictures) as in other cities, he would on average be making a 14 per cent over- or underestimate. This is indeed an underestimate of the variation among cities, since our procedure excluded pictures appearing in certain cities in double features or with stage shows.

TABLE 2

NUMBER OF WEEKS OF FIRST RUN OF MOVIES, 1946–47*

CITY†	MOVIE‡											
	A	B	C	D	E	F	G	H	I	J	K	L
Washington, D.C..........	2	2	5	2	3	2	2	1	2	5	3	2
Indianapolis....	3	4	2	2	2	2	3	3	1	1	2	2
Minneapolis....	5	8	5	3	2	1	4	2	4	6	6	4
Montreal........	4	7	2	1	2	1	2	2	2	1	2	2
Philadelphia....	9	8	5	4	3	3	4	4	4	4	4	3
Pittsburgh......	4	7	6	4	3	3	2	3	3	4	4	3
Buffalo........	3	5	3	4	2	2	3	......	......	......	......	......
Cincinnati......	4	6	4	4	3	3	3	......	......	......	......	......
Seattle.........	7	15	6	3	2	3	5	......	......	......	......	......
San Francisco...	3	3	4	3	2	3	5	......	......	......	......	......
St. Louis.......	7	8	4	4	3	3	3	......	......	......	......	......
Omaha.........	2	3	3	2	1	1	2	......	......	......	......	......

* Source: same as Table 1.

† Los Angeles excluded from weeks of first-run analysis because of multiple first runs.

‡ See below for key to movie titles.

KEY TO MOVIE CODE IN TABLES 1 AND 2

A. *Blue Skies*
B. *Jolson Story*
C. *Razor's Edge*
D. *Till the Clouds Roll By*
E. *Undercurrent*
F. *Humoresque*
G. *Two Years before the Mast*
H. *Dark Mirror*
I. *Deception*
J. *It's a Wonderful Life*
K. *Margie*
L. *The Time, the Place, and the Girl*

A related aspect of this difference among cities in tastes for particular shows is the length of the first run (Table 2). A summary number corresponding to that used for Table 1 would indicate a larger relative difference among cities, chiefly because the unit of time (a week) is rather lumpy.

2. The aggregate value of all films to a television station is, on our hypothesis, tolerably well explained by the power of the station, characteristics of the population it serves, etc. If this be true, block-booking does not forego appreciable revenue relative to higgling over individual pictures.

A forthcoming study by Professor Harvey Levin[4] gives some support to this view. He made a statistical analysis of the excess of the sales price of thirty-one television stations over the replacement costs of their tangible assets in 1956–59, as a measure of their franchise values. The explanatory variables were:

> Retail sales in the station's market
> Buying income in the market
> TV homes per TV station
> Network hourly rate of the station
> National minute spot rate of the station
> Age of station
> Network affiliation
> Percentage of market population that is urbanized

He obtained a coefficient of multiple correlation of .935.

---

[4] LEVIN, THE VALUE OF BROADCAST LICENSES. Most of the explanatory variables were not very helpful: buying income and national minute spot rate explained most of the franchise values.

G. E. HALE
ROSEMARY D. HALE

POTENTIAL COMPETITION UNDER SECTION 7: THE SUPREME COURT'S CRYSTAL BALL

The Supreme Court's dislike for corporate mergers reached new heights in three cases decided during the 1963 Term. In *United States v. Continental Can Co.*,[1] *United States v. Penn-Olin Chemical Co.*,[2] and *United States v. El Paso Natural Gas Co.*[3] the Court made it pellucidly clear that the proscriptions of § 7 of the Clayton Act[4] extend to situations in which the parties to the proposed merger might become competitors as well as those in which the parties

---

G. E. Hale is a member of the Illinois Bar.
Rosemary D. Hale is Lecturer in Economics, Lake Forest College.

[1] 378 U.S. 441 (1964).

[2] 378 U.S. 158 (1964).   [3] 376 U.S. 651 (1964).

[4] 38 Stat. 731, as amended, 15 U.S.C. § 18 (1958). Its relevant language: "No corporation engaged in commerce shall acquire, directly or indirectly, the whole or any part of the stock or other share capital and no corporation subject to the jurisdiction of the Federal Trade Commission shall acquire the whole or any part of the assets of another corporation engaged also in commerce, where in any line of commerce in any section of the country, the effect of such acquisition may be substantially to lessen competition, or to tend to create a monopoly."

actually are in competition. This paper is concerned with the possible scope to be given the concept of "potential competition" in merger cases under the antitrust laws.[5]

I. WHAT "POTENTIAL COMPETITION" IS NOT

First it is important to distinguish the closely related notion of ease of entry from the concept of potential competition. It is orthodox theory that if entry into a market is sufficiently easy, mergers and monopolies in that area of business are not matters of public concern because the threat of entry will make even monopolists behave like competitors.[6] The meat-packing industry of a generation ago, for example, presented a situation in which any trend toward competition could be at least partially offset by ease of entry. A maxim of the trade was that "a rope and a knife are all you need to go into this business."[7] In situations of this order, the courts recognized that no degree of monopoly power could be dangerous whether the problem arose in merger cases or in other types of litigation under the antitrust laws.[8] By contrast, where entry was difficult, the courts utilized this factor so that the antitrust laws bit more readily.[9]

---

[5] Cf. Webster, *The Clayton Act Today: Merging and Marketing*, in NEW YORK STATE BAR ASS'N ANTITRUST LAW SYMPOSIUM: HOW TO COMPLY WITH THE CLAYTON ACT 74, 81 (1959). See also the concept of potential competition expressed in *Penn-Olin* in the district court. 217 F. Supp. 110, 127 n.20 (D. Del. 1963).

[6] Brown Shoe Co. v. United States, 370 U.S. 294, 322 (1962); REPORT OF ATTORNEY GENERAL'S COMMITTEE TO STUDY THE ANTITRUST LAWS 326-37 (1955).

[7] WHITNEY, 1 ANTITRUST POLICIES 66 (1958).

[8] United States v. Standard Oil Co. of New Jersey, 47 F.2d 288, 313 (E.D. Mo. 1931); United States v. Columbia Pictures Corp., 189 F. Supp. 153, 200 (S.D. N.Y. 1960); United States v. Gimbel Bros., Inc., 202 F. Supp. 779, 780 (E.D. Wis. 1962); United States v. Crocker-Anglo National Bank, 223 F. Supp. 849, 854 (N.D. Cal. 1963); United States v. Aluminum Co. of America, 214 F. Supp. 501, 513 (N.D. N.Y. 1963), *rev'd*, 377 U.S. 271 (1964); HALE & HALE, MARKET POWER § 3.12 (1958). In United States v. Bliss & Laughlin, Inc., 202 F. Supp. 334, (S.D. Cal. 1962), *vacated*, 371 U.S. 70 (1962), the district court there said: "The record in this case shows an abundance of capacity and of competing sellers, a wide choice of suppliers among which the purchasers may choose, a lack of obstacles restraining new entrants into the business, and a lack of power in the defendant to control prices, supply or entry. All of these factors tend to insure vigorous competition." 202 F. Supp. at 335.

[9] American Crystal Sugar Co. v. Cuban-American Sugar Co., 259 F.2d 524, 530 (2d Cir. 1958); Scott Paper Company v. FTC, 57 F.T.C. 1415, 1438 (1960), *re-*

Ease of entry, however, is an idea differing somewhat from that of potential competition. For when we speak of ease of entry, we mean that any entrepreneur might go into the field of business endeavor. We do not confine our attention to existing firms in related types of business. Nor is ease of entry a quantitative notion. Potential competition, on the other hand, is concerned with specified existing companies that are considered prospective competitors and the effect of their removal by merger is taken into account in determining the changed competitive situation.

It is also important to distinguish the concept of potential competition from that of the hazard of potential injury to competition. Potential injury to competition might be found, for example, in a situation wherein a merger creates an enterprise so much larger than others in its industry as to suggest the possibility of predatory practices. By such practices the merged firm might drive its smaller rivals from the field.[10] Potential competition relates to the structure of an industry rather than to the possibility of destructive tactics. It is well to keep in mind, however, that the hazards of potential injury to competition have played a large role in recent merger cases in which the courts have displayed a highly protectionist point of view.[11]

---

manded, 301 F.2d 579 (3d Cir. 1962); Pillsbury Mills, Inc., 57 F.T.C. 1274, 1403 (1960). On the other hand, it has been argued that ease of entry should be disregarded in merger cases. Bok, *Section 7 of the Clayton Act and the Merging of Law and Economics*, 74 HARV. L. REV. 226, 261 (1960).

[10] *But cf.* New Grant-Patten Milk Co., Inc. v. Happy Valley Farms, Inc., 222 F. Supp. 319, 320 (E.D. Tenn. 1963). In that case the court said: "There is a total absence of either allegations or evidence as to how the acquisition of non-competing properties or companies located outside the relevant market area could be a direct and proximate cause of injury to the plaintiff. That such acquisition increased the size, resources, and ability of Sealtest to compete in the relevant market area could at most be only a remote and indirect cause of the plaintiff's damages. . . ."
Fears have been expressed that the formation of a joint subsidiary might enable the parents to collude with respect to other products. See the district court opinion in *Penn-Olin*, 217 F. Supp. at 133–34. Note also that the larger firm need not engage in predatory practices in order to drive competitors from the field. It might enjoy economies of scale sufficient to reduce costs significantly and hence lower prices generally.

[11] Reynolds Metals Co. v. FTC, 309 F.2d 223 (D.C. Cir. 1962); Pacific Intermountain Express Co., 57 M.C.C. 341, 362–78 (1950); Auclair Transportation, Inc., 57 M.C.C. 262, 265 (1950); Commercial Carriers, Inc., 75 M.C.C. 215, 222, 224 (1958); Comment, *Diversification and the Public Interest: Administrative Responsibility*

II. The Decisions of the 1963 Term

The three cases decided last Term by the United States Supreme Court moved a long distance toward giving crucial weight to potential competition as a bar to merger. In *United States v. Continental Can Co.*, Continental Can had acquired Hazel-Atlas Glass Company. The products of the two companies were dissimilar and, in general, not destined for the same end uses. Continental, for example, made beer cans, but Hazel-Atlas did not make beer bottles. The Court nevertheless found that Hazel-Atlas was a potential manufacturer of beer bottles and hence that the merger tended to reduce competition between the parties. On that subject the Court wrote:[12]

> In these [beer bottle, etc.] industries the District Court found that the glass container and metal container manufacturers were each seeking to promote their lines of containers at the expense of the other lines. . . . We think it quite clear that Continental and Hazel-Atlas were set off directly against one another in this process and that the merger therefore carries with it the probability of foreclosing actual and potential competition between these two concerns.

In the *Penn-Olin* case,[13] involving the creation of a joint subsidiary by two companies that had not been in competition, the Court

---

of the FCC, 66 YALE L. J. 365, 367 (1957). *Cf.* United States v. Ingersoll Rand Co., 320 F.2d 509 (3d Cir. 1963), where the potential ability of a merged firm to practice reciprocity was held to bring the merger within the statute.

Another factor to be taken into account is the potential exercise of regulatory power. When regulation supplants competition, a delicate question may arise whether the regulatory powers have in fact been exercised sufficiently to create an antitrust exemption. United States v. Borden Co., 308 U.S. 188 (1939); United States v. Philadelphia National Bank, 374 U.S. 321, 368 (1963); FTC v. National Casualty Co., 357 U.S. 560, 564 (1958); Travelers Health Assn. v. FTC, 298 F.2d 820 (8th Cir. 1962); In re Aviation Insurance Industry, 188 F. Supp. 374, 379–80 (1960). *Cf.* also the notion of potential competition in trademark cases. RESTATEMENT, TORTS § 371(b) (tentative draft No. 8, 1963).

[12] 378 U.S. at 462–63. Recognition of the competition between beer cans and beer bottles, for example, is consistent with concepts of market definition urged by economists. HALE & HALE, *op. cit. supra* note 8, at § 3.5. Such recognition, however, does not carry with it the implication that Hazel-Atlas would necessarily have gone into the beer bottle business.

[13] In addition to *Penn-Olin*, see Vanadium Corp. of America v. Susquehanna Corp. 203 F. Supp. 686, 697 (D. Del. 1962); Scott Paper Co., 57 F.T.C. 1415, 1431, 1433,

reversed a finding that the transaction did not violate § 7 of the Clayton Act. In so doing the Court said:[14]

> Certainly the formation of a joint venture and purchase by the organizers of its stock would substantially lessen competition—indeed foreclose it—as between them, both being engaged in commerce. This would be true whether they were in actual or potential competition with each other. . . .

A similar rule was applied when the parties to a merger were operating at a great distance from each other. *El Paso Natural Gas* involved the acquisition of Northwest, a pipeline company, by El Paso, another pipeline company that distributed gas in California. Northwest had never sold gas in California. The Court, holding that § 7 of the Clayton Act applied and that the merger must be enjoined, did so on the sole basis that Northwest was a potential competitor in the California market. That result was reached despite findings by the trial court that Northwest could not have sold gas in California, could not have secured supplies of gas for those sales, could not have secured regulatory authority, and could not have financed a pipeline into California. Such findings were said to be "irrelevant."[15] In the face of such a holding it is difficult to envisage a situation in which potential competition should not be taken into account.

Potential competition can be and has been recognized in two other dimensions. In the first place, one may take account of potential competition of third parties in appraising the effects of a merger. For example, in the *Continental Can* case, the Court found that Continental Can and Hazel-Atlas, although not in competition, were potential competitors and hence that the merger was unlawful. It could have gone further and looked at all the other firms which might have gone into the business of making beer cans or beer bottles. If it had done so, the market shares of the merged firms

---

1441 (1960), *remanded,* 301 F.2d 579 (3d Cir. 1962); Procter & Gamble Co., 63 F.T.C. No. 6901 (Nov. 26, 1963); United States v. Standard Oil Co. of New Jersey, 47 F.2d 288, 309 (E.D. Mo. 1931).

[14] 378 U.S. at 168.

[15] 376 U.S. at 657–58. *Accord,* American Fuel & Power Co., 122 F.2d 223, 225–26, 228–29 (6th Cir. 1941), Columbia Gas & Electric Corp. v. United States, 151 F.2d 461 (6th Cir. 1945), *modification denied,* 153 F.2d 101 (6th Cir. 1946), *cert. den.,* 329 U.S. 737 (1946).

would have shrunk rapidly as the denominator of the fraction was increased by all potential competitors. In *Continental Can*, the Court failed to take that step although in other cases courts—including the Supreme Court—have been alive to the existence of potential competition as a factor tending to minimize as well as to exacerbate the adverse effects of a merger.[16]

Again a merger might be found unlawful because of a prospective injury to potential competition. In the *Continental Can* case, the Court might very well have thought—although it did not say so—that the merged firm was so large that it would have a deterrent effect upon companies not yet in the field but potentially capable of making one or more competitive products. To date the cases give little recognition to injury to potential competition[17] but it is a concept embodied in many suits instituted by the Attorney General.[18]

In the older cases, presumably now overruled, the courts frequently refused to take account of potential competition in adjudicating the legality of mergers. The notion that the relevant market should be broadened because the parties could easily make products other than those currently sold was usually rejected. The question was discussed at some length in terms of those precedents in both the *Penn-Olin* and *Continental Can* cases at the trial level. In *Penn-Olin* the district court said that the mere fact that two parents of a joint subsidiary might have entered into competition did not render creation of the joint subsidiary invalid under § 7.[19] Relying on earlier precedents, the district court wrote:[20]

---

[16] See United States v. Columbia Steel Co., 334 U.S. 495, 528 (1948); Erie Sand & Gravel Co. v. FTC, 291 F.2d 279, 281 (3d Cir. 1961); United States v. Standard Oil Co. of New Jersey, 47 F.2d 288, 317 (E.D. Mo. 1931); United States v. Columbia Pictures Corp., 189 F. Supp. 153, 199 (S.D. N.Y. 1960). *Cf.* United States v. Aluminum Co. of America, 214 F. Supp. 501, 512 (N.D. N.Y. 1963), *rev'd*, 377 U.S. 271 (1964).

[17] Handler, *A Study of the Construction and Enforcement of the Federal Antitrust Laws*, 38 TEMP. NAT'L ECON. COMM. 1 (1941).

[18] Rahl, *Applicability of the Clayton Act to Potential Competition*, 12 A.B.A. ANTITRUST REP. 128, 131 (1958).

[19] 217 F. Supp. at 123–24.

[20] *Id.* at 135. In the *Continental Can* case the Attorney General argued to the trial court that Hazel-Atlas might have gone into the beer bottle business. The Court, however, 217 F. Supp. at 796, disregarded that contention, saying there was no showing of reasonable probability that Hazel-Atlas would enter the beer

The concept of potential competition is, to say the least, a flexible one, and is subject to almost unlimited gradations in meaning. The degree of likelihood of competition may cover a broad range. In point of time its prospect may be remote or imminent. Involved may be companies which are financially weak or strong or both. The problem may concern companies with experience in manufacturing and selling the same product in other relevant markets or companies which are newcomers to the industry. The potential market may be one occupied by other competitors, or one ripe for exploitation because of the absence of competition. A whole gamut of other environmental factors may be envisioned which will bear upon the significance of the so-called potential to compete. Only if the "potential competition" is analyzed and defined in the light of the evidence can the concept be meaningful in the solution of an antitrust problem. To simply describe companies as potential competitors is not enough.

A striking case in which potential competition was disregarded is *United States v. Lever Brothers.*[21] In that case Monsanto Company had sold a detergent known as "All" to Lever Brothers. "All" was a low-sudsing detergent and hence desirable for use in household washing machines. Previously Lever Brothers had marketed such a detergent called "Vim" and lost a lot of money on it. "Vim" was withdrawn from the market in 1956 and negotiations started for the purchase of "All" in January 1957.[22] Despite the fact that Lever Brothers had recently been in the low-sudsing detergent business and obviously was a potential competitor in that market, the Court found no adverse impact upon competition in the transaction. The Court wrote:[23]

---

bottle business. A similar view was expressed by the trial court in United States v. Aluminum Co. of America, 214 F. Supp. 501, 517–18 (N.D. N.Y. 1963), *rev'd*, 377 U.S. 271 (1964).

[21] 216 F. Supp. 887 (S.D. N.Y. 1963).

[22] *Id.* at 897.

[23] *Id.* at 898. The Court went on to say: "It would make the Clayton Act a means of suppressing rather than promoting competition, for it would mean that in the future a company with a failing brand could never transfer that brand to another company ready and able to market and distribute it in true competitive fashion. The brand would die, and competition would be diminished. Certainly such was not the intention of Congress in passing the Act. Congress undoubtedly intended, as the Supreme Court indicated, that the court should look to the reality of the situation. The reality of the situation in 1956 was that Lever, which had no low-

This product was chemically different from other heavy duty detergents. It was separately marketed, separately advertised and used for a distinctive purpose. There had been active competition in this sub-market. The effect of the competition was that Monsanto had determined to withdraw from the distribution of "All." If it had simply done this the effect would have been undoubtedly to reduce competition in this important sub-market. Instead, it transferred the business to Lever Brothers which had previously had a low sudsing detergent which had failed and gone out of business. Lever was in a position to promote actively the sale and distribution of this important product. If this transfer had not been made the entire market in low sudsing detergents would have been concentrated in Procter & Gamble and Colgate. By transferring the product to Lever the product remained available and remained in active competition with the products of Procter & Gamble and Colgate. . . .

We have in this case a situation where an acquisition by one company of the particular brand of another preserved the competitive business of the other company and promoted a more active competition than if the acquisition had not been made.

Potential competition between Lever Brothers and Monsanto was not even mentioned in the opinion.

Until recently it had been orthodox doctrine that potential competition was to be disregarded when the parties were separated by great distance. In other words, the fact that one of the parties to a merger might invade the territory of another was disregarded. Thus, in *United States v. Crocker-Anglo National Bank*[24] two banks which were parties to the merger were found to be geographically sepa-

---

sudsing detergent, acquired a low-sudsing detergent from a company which was no longer an effective competitor in that submarket. By so doing the brand remained an active brand in a competitive market. The product remained available for the housewife. The acquisition aided, rather than impeded, competition." *id.* at 899. The fact that Lever Brothers had failed to make a success of its low-sudsing detergent may have been relevant to the decision.

Other cases disregarding potential competition are United States v. Columbia Pictures Corp., 189 F. Supp. 153, 178, 202 (S.D. N.Y. 1960); FTC v. Thatcher Mfg. Co., 5 F.2d 615, 622 (3d Cir. 1925), *rev'd*, 272 U.S. 554 (1926); United States v. Associated Press, 326 U.S. 1 (1945).

[24] United States v. Crocker-Anglo National Bank, 223 F. Supp. 849, 856–57 (N.D. Cal. 1963).

rated. On the subject of potential competition the trial court wrote: [25]

> We think it is plain that before a merger may be condemned merely because its effect may be to lessen *potential* competition it must be ascertained that the potential competition is a reality, that is to say, that there is a reasonable probability of such potential competition.

Similarly, it had been customary to disregard potential competition of non-parties. *United States v. First National Bank & Trust Co.*[26] involved the merger of two banks in Fayette County, Kentucky. In defining the geographic area that was relevant for the consideration of market shares, the Court said that it would take no account of banks outside Fayette County. Those banks were said to do a negligible business within the county and hence their activities were not used in determining the denominator of the fraction used to calculate market shares of the merged institution. In so calculating shares the court, of course, disregarded the fact that banks outside Fayette County were potential competitors of those inside the county. Banking may be somewhat unusual in that branch banking is frequently prohibited, but the holding is nevertheless plain that market shares of the defendants were not to be diminished by consideration of potential competitors in distant areas. As Professor Bok recently wrote: [27]

> . . . [P]otential firms are no substitute for actual companies in preserving such non-economic advantages as the independence of small business, local initiative, and maximum career oppor-

---

[25] *Id.* at 855–56. *Accord,* United States v. Bliss & Laughlin, Inc., 202 F. Supp. 334 (S.D. Cal. 1962), *vacated and remanded,* 371 U.S. 70 (1962). See Rahl, *supra* note 18, at 136; Handler, *Emerging Antitrust Issues: Reciprocity, Diversification and Joint Ventures,* 49 VA. L. REV. 433, 444–45 (1963); BOCK, MERGERS & MARKETS 18 (1960).

[26] 208 F. Supp. 457 (E.D. Ky. 1962), *rev'd,* 376 U.S. 665 (1964). Refusal to acknowledge potential competition may be sound insofar as small borrowers are concerned but plainly is not applicable to larger ones. It may be significant that the opinion in United States v. Philadelphia National Bank, 374 U.S. 321 (1963), did not mention potential competition. In accord with the *Lexington Bank* case are Reynolds Metals Co. v. FTC, 309 F.2d 223, 225, 227, 228 (D.C. Cir. 1962); A. G. Spalding & Bros. Inc. v. FTC, 301 F.2d 585, 616 (3d Cir. 1962).

[27] Bok, note 9 *supra.*

tunity. Even from a strictly economic standpoint, there is no reason to assume that the market performance of a dominant firm will always be tempered in a satisfactory manner by low entry barriers.

In *Crown Zellerbach*,[28] involving the acquisition of St. Helen's by Crown Zellerbach, both in the paper business, Crown Zellerbach asserted that its factories could readily be adjusted to the production of paper products theretofore never produced therein, that paper-making machines can, with relatively small changes, produce anything from sanitary tissues to corrugated boxing. Therefore, Crown Zellerbach argued, the entire field of paper products should be considered in determining the market share of the merged concern. The court refused to accept that argument on what appears to be the sound ground that ability to manufacture does not imply the ability to sell. Crown Zellerbach might well have been able to produce other paper products but it might not equally have been able to market them. The other products might have been purchased by totally different types of customers and have required a wholly different sales organization. On the other hand, in the famous *Brown Shoe* case,[29] the Supreme Court intimated that the convertibility of plants should be taken into account in considering the validity of a vertical merger.

III. ASSESSING THE POTENTIAL

Since the Court has ruled that account must be taken of potential competition, it is important to determine how to proceed. Plainly, not every existing firm or firm yet to be created is to be considered a potential competitor. What, then, are the rational limits to the circle of potential competitors?

It is not even wholly clear precisely how the concept of potential competition is worked into the language of § 7. Normally the first step in testing the legality of a merger is to define the relevant

---

[28] Crown Zellerbach Corp. v. FTC, 296 F.2d 800, 805, 812 (9th Cir. 1961). *Accord,* United States v. Bethlehem Steel Corp., 168 F. Supp. 576, 592 (S.D. N.Y. 1958); Mann & Lewyn, *The Relevant Market under § 7 of the Clayton Act: Two New Cases—Two Different Views,* 47 VA. L. REV. 1014, 1018–19 (1961).

[29] Brown Shoe Co. v. United States, 370 U.S. 294, 325 n.42 (1962). See Harlan, J., concurring, *id.* at 367.

product and geographic markets.[30] After defining the applicable commodity and the territory in which the transaction is to be tested, the market shares can then be computed. The inclusion of potential competition can be said to amount to a modification of a hitherto held notion with respect to the proper method of delineating the applicable product and geographic markets; or, in the alternative, it can be said that the commodity and territory remain defined as before but new heads are to be counted in computing market shares. So far as potential competition between the parties to a merger is concerned (as in the *Continental Can* case), the Court seems to be redefining the commodity in which competition is to be lessened. When it comes to a question of the potential competition of third parties, however, perhaps the change amounts to adding figures to the denominator of the fraction by which market share is determined.

However that may be, a real question arises as to how the potential competitor should be identified. In that connection the first step is easy: the fact that one of two parties to a merger is willing to engage in that transaction does not indicate that it is a potential competitor. True, the party to the merger desires to enter into the field of business in which the other party is engaged. That desire, however, sheds no light on the feasibility of the first party's entry apart from the merger. Any other rule would make every merger unlawful. The test cannot be whether one of the parties would like to be in the other party's field but whether, taking into account all economic factors, there is a likelihood that it would have gone into that field apart from the merger.[31]

The question then is whether one of the parties (or a third party) would have been likely to enter into competition apart from the merger. In a free enterprise system the inducement to going into business is profit. The situation must be examined with a view to determining whether the alleged potential competitor would be

---

[30] United States v. E. I. duPont de Nemours & Co., 353 U.S. 586, 593 (1957); United States v. Lever Bros. Co., 216 F. Supp. 887, 890 (S.D. N.Y. 1963).

[31] As noted above, see text at note 28, the ability to manufacture products by making minor adjustments in productive equipment is not determinative of the existence of potential competition. It must further be shown that a product could be marketed. *But cf.* Adelman, *Economic Aspects of the Bethlehem Opinion*, 45 VA. L. REV. 684, 690 (1959).

lured into a new field of operation because it expected higher returns therein.[32] Here the conduct of the grocery chains affords an interesting example.[33] Many of them have recently entered into the field of non-food items, particularly products customarily sold in drugstores. It is widely known that the retail "mark-up" on drugs is far higher than on groceries, which may well account for the movement into that field. There must, in short, be a gap between unit cost and price: the entrepreneur must see an opportunity for returns in excess of those available from safe securities. Opportunity cost, in other words, is a floor in determining whether an enterprise will enter into a given field of competition. There is no reason to incur all the risks and uncertainties involved unless the return promises to be substantially greater than that available on highly rated bonds.

In the last analysis high profits will probably be found to result either from an element of innovation or from a factor of indivisibility. Innovation, of course, though fraught with uncertainty, may

---

[32] Entering a new field is commonly called diversification. HALE & HALE, *op. cit. supra* note 8, at §§ 6.5–6.10. One study indicated that about one merger in four took that form. F.T.C., REPORT ON CORPORATE MERGERS AND ACQUISITIONS 7 (1955). As to the lure of high profits Mrs. Penrose wrote: "There is no need to deny that other 'objectives' are often important—power, prestige, public approval, or the mere love of the game—it need only be recognized that the attainment of these ends more often than not is associated directly with the ability to make profits. There surely can be little doubt that the rate and direction of the growth of the firm depend on the extent to which it is alert to act upon opportunities for profitable investment. It follows that lack of enterprise in a firm will preclude or substantially retard its growth, although 'enterprise' is by no means a homogeneous quality. . . ." PENROSE, THE THEORY OF THE GROWTH OF THE FIRM 30 (1959). *Cf.* Ansoff & Weston, *Merger Objectives and Organization Structure*, 2 Q. REV. OF ECON. & BUSINESS 49, 52 (Aug. 1962). Some recent examples: Bell and Howell, a manufacturer of photographic equipment, purchased Micro Photo, Inc., Ditto, Inc., and Southern Business Forms Corp. Wall Street Journal, Feb. 25, 1963, p. 8, col. 5 (Midwest ed.). International Silver Co. purchased W. H. Hutchinson & Sons, Inc., makers of bottle caps for brewers and soft drinks. *Id.* Oct. 10, 1962, p. 24, col. 4.

[33] Wall Street Journal, Nov. 16, 1962, p. 6, col. 5 (Midwest ed.). JEWEL TEA COMPANY ANNUAL REPORT 5, 6 (1961). Other examples: Dean Milk Company bought Green Bay Food Company, a processor of pickles, relishes, and dressings. *Id.* Nov. 12, 1962, p. 4, col. 3. Stone and Webster, Inc., acquired Commercial Cold Storage, Inc., of Atlanta. *Id.* Jan. 21, 1963, p. 6, col. 2. Congoleum-Nairn, a maker of floor and wall coverings, acquired Mersman Bros. Corp., a table maker. *Id.* Mar. 5, 1963, p. 11, col. 3. *Cf.* EMMET & JEUCK, CATALOGUES AND COUNTERS 442 (1950) (entry of Sears, Roebuck into banking business).

offer large opportunities for profit because of the time lag involved in creating conditions of active competition.[34] Indivisibility, however, is important only on the cost side.[35] Suppose, for example, a situation in which a manufacturer of glass has a far-flung system of distribution that could easily handle other products. That manufacturer may enter into the paint business simply because the sales cost already incurred in the glass enterprise can be spread over a higher sales volume when paint is added to the product line. Vertical expansion, for example, is typically motivated by some saving in cost, such as that of reheating steel ingot to put it through a rolling mill.[36]

Professor Chandler's study of many prominent corporations and their growth has indicated that the strategy of product diversification is often a direct response to the threat of unused resources.[37] This, perhaps, is a supplement to the factors of indivisibility men-

---

[34] E.g., acquisition of National Research Corporation by Norton Co. It's No Longer Just Grind, Grind at Norton, 68 FORTUNE, 118, 121 (Aug. 1963).

[35] An elaboration of the thesis of the text will be found in Ansoff & Weston, supra note 32, at 51. That study contains an elaborate analysis of cost relationship focusing on the concept "concentric." "Concentric mergers involve a common thread in the relationships between firms." A "concentric" merger is said to "fit" if the joint firm has an ability to develop new products which neither partner could produce alone. The authors conclude: "There is an optimal degree of integration, control, and centralization related to the nature of the merger. Where there is little fit between firms in a merger, the optimal degree of integration is low, and exceeding this optimum will lead to failure of the merger. However, where the degree of carryover is great, the optimal degree of integration is large. Here the danger is failure to marshal effectively the independent potential contributions that the constituent members of the merger have available and which might react in a highly favorable fashion if the potential carryover is effectively exploited." Id. at 58. Cf. PENROSE, op. cit. supra note 32, at 5.

[36] HALE & HALE, op. cit supra note 8, at § 5.18. Uncertainty with respect to the salability of products fabricated from aluminum led Alcoa into doing the fabricating itself, others being unwilling. Id. at 476. The merger of Sunray with Mid-Continent Petroleum Company allowed Sunray, a refiner, to utilize Mid-Continent's marketing facilities. 3 DE CHAZEAU & KAHN, INTEGRATION AND COMPETITION IN THE PETROLEUM INDUSTRY 534 n.5 (1959). Vertical integration may, of course, increase rather than decrease costs. HALE & HALE, op. cit. supra note 8, at § 5.18. It has also been contended that vertical integration is a means of exploiting a monopoly. Burstein, A Theory of Full-Line Forcing, 55 Nw. U. L. REV. 62, 81–82 (1960).

[37] CHANDLER, STRATEGY AND STRUCTURE 90 (1962). See also id. at 82; PENROSE, op. cit. supra note 32, at 67–71.

tioned above.[38] On the other hand, unless some such factors can be identified the venture may well result in disaster. In 1955 the Singer Sewing Machine Company went into the business of manufacturing pulp in Canada. The venture was not profitable; a Singer executive was quoted as saying: ". . . we forgot we didn't know how to run a chemical business."[39]

While the basic reason for moving into a new field is always the attraction of prospective profits, the fact that the existing business is encountering difficulties may prod management into more rapid action. Diversification, for example, is a tactic frequently employed by firms in an industry facing obsolescence.[40] Note, for example, the case of Studebaker Corporation. Floundering in the automobile business, it started in 1959 a vigorous program of diversification into air carriage, household appliances, and other products. In late 1963 it abandoned domestic manufacture of automobiles altogether.[41]

---

[38] Note also the situation in which a manufacturer of one product (razor blades) finds it desirable to push the sale of another (razors) in order to promote the sale of its principal product. HALE & HALE, *op. cit. supra* note 8, at 477 (Appendix B); Rieser, *National Homes' Big Roof*, 60 FORTUNE 129, 131 (Sept. 1959). *Cf.* the notion of a market definition in which all forms of athletic goods were lumped together because they were distributed through the same channels. A. G. Spalding & Bros. v. FTC, 301 F.2d 585, 604–05 (3d Cir. 1962). Stability may be considered another factor or simply an aspect of indivisibility. Ansoff & Weston, *supra* note 32, at 50.

[39] Faltermayer, *It's a Spryer Singer*, 68 FORTUNE 145, 160 (Dec. 1963). Note the amusing account of Rapid-American Company under the guidance of Mr. Riklis, showing that mere diversification is not necessarily profitable. Brown, *Who's to Blame for Riklis?–Riklis?* 68 FORTUNE 136 (Oct. 1963). In 60 NEW YORKER 140 (June 18, 1960) there appeared a clipping from the *New York Herald Tribune* as follows: "I. Rokeach & Sons, Inc., makers of gefilte fish, frozen blintzes and other Kosher foods, said it is discussing a possible merger with Exquisite Form Brassiere, Inc." Sears, Roebuck has had a varied experience in the insurance field. See EMMETT & JEUCK, *op. cit. supra* note 33, at 439.

The courts have recognized the factor of indivisibility in a negative fashion. Union Leader Corp. v. Newspapers of New England, Inc., 284 F. 2d 582, 590 (1st Cir. 1960), *cert. den.*, 365 U.S. 833 (1961). In that case the court found it unlikely that the defendant would purchase additional newspapers because of the fact that each community only had one and there was room for no more.

In purely horizontal expansion (additional production of the same commodity) uncertainty is always a factor. While economies of scale may permit reduction of unit costs as output is increased, the slope of the demand curve is usually unknown and hence the effect upon profits is difficult to predict.

[40] Ansoff & Weston, *supra* note 32; PENROSE, *op. cit. supra* note 32, at 36–37.

[41] Wall Street Journal, Oct. 10, 1963, p. 8, col. 2.

Again, the fact that competitors have expanded in a particular way, principally by way of vertical integration either forward or backward, may suggest the advisability of similar moves as a defensive measure. Such tactics mean that the firm is taking out insurance against monopoly prices that might someday be asked for commodities that it must buy, or for retail outlets to which it must have access.[42] Similarly, the firm may be tempted into the making of a product which constitutes a close substitute for its present output.[43] Soft-drink makers, for example, have gone into the dietetic beverage field because of the possibility that demand may shift heavily in that direction. Stabilization, too, properly seen as an aspect of indivisibility, may suggest the desirability of broader product lines.[44]

Geographic dispersion[45]—entry of a firm into new territories—is governed by the same basic principles. It is, however, often considered in somewhat different terms. Whether to build an auxiliary factory in California is often thought of as nothing but a nice calculation of raw material, production, and finished product shipping costs. Actually, the ultimate criterion is prospective profit. Of course, there is some difference in the fact that in the short run a manufactured product may be shipped almost anywhere provided transportation costs are not excessive. Since freight tariffs are known factors, it is frequently possible to calculate the radius of profitable sales with an accuracy unavailable to other types of expansion.

The pull of high profits is the rational motivation for entry into competition. Account must, however, be taken of obstacles to such expansion. We have already adverted to the fact that the test of

---

[42] See United States v. Standard Oil Co. of New Jersey, 47 F. 2d 288, 310 (E.D. Mo. 1931); CHANDLER, *op. cit. supra* note 37, at 88, 228; EMMET & JEUCK, *op. cit. supra* note 33, at 241. Such integration may remove valuable checks on wasteful activities. HALE & HALE, *op. cit. supra* note 8, at § 5.18.

[43] *In Packaging, Everybody Merges,* BUSINESS WEEK 128 (July 13, 1957); McKIE, TIN CANS AND TIN PLATE 95 (1959). Regulated industry, of course, presents a problem of governmental barriers to expansion. *Cf.* United States v. Philadelphia Nat'l Bank, 374 U.S. 321, 354 (1963); United States v. Crocker-Anglo Nat'l Bank, 223 F. Supp. 849, 859 (N.D. Cal. 1963); Averch & Johnson, *The Behavior of the Firm under Regulatory Constraint,* 52 AM. EC. REV. 1052, 1057–58 (1962). In United States v. El Paso Natural Gas Co., 376 U.S. 651 (1964), the Supreme Court inexplicably appears to have ignored that factor.

[44] HALE & HALE, *op. cit. supra* note 8, at § 6.13.

[45] F.T.C., *op. cit. supra* note 32, at 7.

possibility does not lie in manufacturing alone: the potential competitor must be able to foresee a profit arising after sales expense has been covered as well as other costs.[46] Another obstacle, of course, lies in the capacity of management. Unless the managers of the firm are endowed with sufficient and specialized abilities they cannot successfully enter a new market.[47] Furthermore, capital of a substantial character may well be required. Other things being equal, a wealthy firm can more easily expand in a new market than a firm which enjoys only small resources. The large, established organization has more ready access to capital markets and there are fewer imperfections to overcome in order to raise funds necessary for expansion.[48] Finally, account must be taken of the factor of time. A firm with capacity and resources to go into another field of endeavor may find that the time required for successful penetration is so long that success is imperiled.[49] It is for that reason that mergers have often taken the place of internal growth.[50]

IV. Evidence of Potential

For a court to determine that a company is a potential competitor is obviously a larger order. The factors mentioned above

---

[46] United States v. Crocker-Anglo Nat'l Bank, 223 F. Supp. 849, 855, 858–59 (N.D. Cal. 1963).

[47] Penrose, *op. cit. supra* note 32, at 34–35. Mrs. Penrose also wrote: "[I]t is not necessarily capital that prevents the expansion of the small firms often found on the fringes of an industry; it may just as well be that the organization and execution of an expansion on the required scale is only possible for firms already large. The small firms may survive because of some small advantage in some special market, but they will not in such circumstances become large producers in the industry. New entrants to the industry, if any, will consist of large firms, usually from related industries, which are able to undertake the necessary expansion." *Id.* at 99.

[48] *Id.* at 43.

[49] de Chazeau & Kahn, *op. cit. supra* note 36, at 164. There is some evidence, however, that while small firms may be slower to adopt innovations, they are at least as quick to substitute new techniques for old ones. Mansfield, *Intrafirm Rates of Diffusion of an Innovation,* 45 Rev. of Economics & Stat. 348, 358 (1963). Expansion, of course, may take the form of another merger as well as internal growth.

[50] Mace & Montgomery, Management Problems of Corporate Acquisitions 21 (1962); United States v. Aluminum Co. of America, 214 F. Supp. 501, 512 (N.D. N.Y. 1963), *rev'd,* 377 U.S. 271 (1964). Another name for time is experience. Mace & Montgomery, *op. cit. supra,* at 17; Chandler, *op. cit. supra* note 37, at 88; Emmet &

may be soundly conceived. It will be much more difficult, however, to determine whether they exist in an actual situation. How, for example, can a court determine that a product is sufficiently new that its manufacture and sale will reap the profits of innovation? A few suggestions can be offered regarding the type of evidence that may be relevant in such situations. For example, the fact that others had or had not been able to enter into competition from a comparable base of wealth should be important in determining whether resources are adequate.[51] If plants are physically convertible into the manufacture of the new product then at least one hurdle can be cleared. If the prospective competitor has been able to raise capital easily in the past, that fact too will be suggestive. On the other hand, if a firm has not for a considerable period of time actually entered into competition in a field which might well prove attractive to it, one may surmise that factors are in operation that make it unlikely that it will ever enter.

In the case of an expansion of a geographic market the fact that a prospective competitor has actually shipped into the area from time to time will, of course, be highly suggestive.[52] If, on the contrary, it has acquired facilities in distant areas in the past in order to enter into such territories, that fact will indicate that considerable capital investment is required before the territorial expansion can be completed.[53]

JEUCK, *op. cit. supra* note 33, at 652. When Red Owl Stores bought Snyder's Drug Stores, Inc., the financial vice-president of the purchaser commented, "Primarily we were buying management." Wall Street Journal, Aug. 1, 1962, p. 22, col. 2.

[51] Brown Shoe Co. v. United States, 370 U.S. 294 (1962).

[52] *Cf.* United States v. Bliss & Laughlin, Inc., 202 F. Supp. 334, 335 (S.D. Cal. 1962), *vacated and remanded*, 371 U.S. 70 (1962). When the business in question is retail in character, it will almost always be necessary to acquire local facilities. See, *e.g.*, Wall Street Journal, Nov. 12, 1962, p. 17, col. 2 (Midwest ed.) (Hart, Schaffner & Marx expansion in Arizona).

[53] Interchemical Corp. purchased an Italian firm engaged in the same line of business in Italy. Wall Street Journal, Sept. 21, 1962, p. 22, col. 4. Beatrice Foods bought a Belgian producer of dairy products. *Id.* Sept. 28, 1962, p. 15, col. 3. A cement manufacturer purchased the assets of two other cement makers, resulting in the addition of eleven new states to its marketing area. MARQUETTE CEMENT MANUFACTURING CO., 1960 ANNUAL REPORT 5 (1961); Crescent Petroleum Company bought Permalab Equipment Company, a corporation operating a factory in California, to avoid shipping goods from its existing plant in Hicksville, New York, to the west coast. Wall Street Journal, Mar. 6, 1962, p. 24, col. 4.

In other words, what the firm under consideration has been able to do in the past may well be indicative of its role as a potential competitor in the future. Likewise, the experience of other similarly situated firms in the past may prove suggestive. It cannot be expected, however, that evidence immediately and directly relevant to the problem of potential competition can be brought before any tribunal.[54]

V. CONCLUSION

As indicated above, in the past it has usually been thought unwise to take account of potential competition. The difficulties involved have been regarded as insuperable and the boundary lines too difficult for demarcation. Several years ago, Professor Rahl wrote:[55]

> If the theory is that the statute has been violated by elimination of potential competition, it should be a necessary part of the burden of proof to show that the potential element about which complaint is made possessed positive substantial competitive force of such degree as to rank with actual competition, and further that this positive force was great enough in and of itself to qualify for statutory protection.

On the other hand, the mere difficulty of determining whether potential competition exists would not seem to dispose of the question. Many antitrust problems are difficult of solution. Perhaps the existence of potential competition is no more elusive than several other determinations which must be made under the antitrust laws.

Whatever may be the desirability of taking account of potential competition, the United States Supreme Court has now ruled that it must be done. Indeed, it has gone to great lengths to find the

---

[54] An interesting controversy has arisen over whether it is permissible in a merger case to examine evidence of post-acquisition market conditions. Scott Paper Company, 57 F.T.C. 1415, 1420, 1425–26 (1960), *remanded*, 301 F.2d 579 (3d Cir. 1962); Comment, *The New Law of Mergers*, 56 Nw. U. L. Rev. 630, 631 (1961).

[55] Rahl, *supra* note 18, at 128, 133. Professor Rahl went on to say: "Anyone who takes the position that the elimination of competition not in being is as serious as elimination of actual competition must assume a heavy burden of proof." *Id.* at 136. *But cf.* Markham, *Merger Policy under the New Section 7: A Six-Year Appraisal* 43 Va. L. Rev. 489, 496 (1957). Professor Markham expressed the view that merger of potential rivals should fall within § 7, but that a different standard of injury to competition should be adopted.

existence of potential competition. More scientific proof of the existence of potential competition requires the subordinate resolution of many of the basic factors involved in the larger question of the validity of a merger. Economies of scale (indivisibility) may be invoked. The savings in cost to be realized through different types of business structure are involved. On the other hand, there is a limit to the concept of potential competition. If the notion of potential competition is to be carried to its logical conclusion, it might compel consideration of every possible restructuring of all markets and present wholly impossible tasks.[56] Furthermore, the notion of "submarkets" recently developed by the Court[57] would seem to present some kind of a curb upon the limits of recognizing potential competition.

Because potential competition works in both directions, the courts should not shut their eyes to potential competition when it will aid a defendant. If, as may be the case, the Court is determined to block all mergers at whatever cost in efficiency—a position that is not wholly without merit on political grounds—then it would be preferable for the Court candidly to say so. Manipulation of the concept of potential competition so that plaintiffs invariably prevail can only lead to confusion.

---

[56] *Cf.* A. G. Spalding & Bros., Inc., v. FTC, 301 F.2d 585, 603–05 (3d Cir. 1962).

[57] Brown Shoe Co. v. United States, 370 U.S. 294, 325 (1962).

EDMUND W. KITCH

GRAHAM V. JOHN DEERE CO.: NEW STANDARDS FOR PATENTS

In the 1964 Term, it was news of importance to the patent bar, though of little note elsewhere, that the Supreme Court had, for the first time in fifteen years,[1] undertaken to review some patent cases turning on the issue of invention.[2] The Court had granted certiorari to consider the effect of the standard of non-obviousness imposed by § 103 of the Patent Act of 1952[3] on theretofore judicially developed tests of invention.

The interest of the patent bar derived from a widespread concern that the Court might use § 103 as a basis for promulgating more rigorous standards of invention than had yet been utilized. Indeed, after the Court had granted certiorari in *Graham v. John*

Edmund W. Kitch is Assistant Professor of Law, The University of Chicago.

[1] The Court last considered the issue in Great Atl. & Pac. Tea Co. v. Supermarket Equip. Corp., 340 U.S. 147 (1950).

[2] Graham v. John Deere Co., 379 U.S. 956 (1965); United States v. Adams, 380 U.S. 949 (1965); Calmar, Inc. v. Cook Chemical Co., 380 U.S. 949 (1965); Colgate-Palmolive Co. v. Cook Chemical Co., 380 U.S. 949 (1965).

[3] 35 U.S.C. § 103 (1964): "A patent may not be obtained though the invention is not identically disclosed or described as set forth in section 102 of this title, if the differences between the subject matter sought to be patented and the prior art are such that the subject matter as a whole would have been obvious at the time the invention was made to a person having ordinary skill in the art to which said subject matter pertains. Patentability shall not be negatived by the manner in which the invention was made."

Deere Co.,[4] in order to resolve a conflict between the Fifth[5] and Eighth[6] Circuits, the Solicitor General had invited the Court "to consider pressing problems relating to the administration of the patent laws in a variety of contexts and in broad perspective."[7] This language took on an ominous sound when the Court accepted the invitation and granted certiorari in *United States v. Adams*[8] and the twin cases of *Calmar, Inc. v. Cook Chemical Co.* and *Colgate-Palmolive Co. v. Cook Chemical Co.*[9]

The Court was inundated with a shower of amicus curiae briefs revealing an apprehension that the Court would utilize the new statutory language as a valve to cut down the flow of patents that pour forth from the Patent Office each year.[10] The worry of the patent bar was perhaps expressed most frankly in an amicus brief filed by Professors E. Ernest Goldstein and Page Keeton of the University of Texas patronizingly entitled "Brief Amicus Curiae in Support of 35 USC 103." Such a brief was necessary, wrote these self-appointed defenders of the statute, "because some writings by some Justices of this Court[11] and the opinions by the Court of Appeals in this case, appear to put the practical operating life of the patent system at stake, and to put the whole socio-economic functioning of the entire patent system at issue."[12]

The decisions that the Court has rendered may assuage this fear. They expressly purport to follow the earlier decisions and to turn

---

[4] 383 U.S. 1 (1966).

[5] The Fifth Circuit had found the patent valid in Graham v. Cockshutt Farm Equip. Co., 256 F.2d 358 (5th Cir. 1958), and Jeoffroy Mfg. Inc. v. Graham, 219 F.2d 511 (5th Cir. 1955).

[6] The Eighth Circuit had held the patent invalid. John Deere Co. v. Graham, 333 F.2d 529 (8th Cir. 1964).

[7] Petition for Certiorari, pp. 15–16, United States v. Adams.

[8] 383 U.S. 39 (1966).   [9] 383 U.S. 1 (1966).

[10] The amicus curiae briefs were filed by the American Bar Association, the New York Patent Law Association, the Illinois State Bar Association, the State Bar of Texas, and the School of Law of the University of Texas.

[11] In a concurring opinion in the *Supermarket* case, note 1 *supra*, Mr. Justice Douglas, joined by Mr. Justice Black, had observed "how far our patent system frequently departs from the constitutional standards" and accused the Patent Office of having "placed a host of gadgets under the armor of patents." 340 U.S. at 154, 158.

[12] Amicus Curiae Brief of the School of Law of the University of Texas, pp. 1–2, Graham v. John Deere Co.

toward neither leniency nor harshness. "We believe," wrote Mr. Justice Clark for the Court, "that the revision [in 1952] was not intended by Congress to change the general level of patentable invention."[13] And, if actions speak louder than words, the Court held a patent valid for the first time in twenty-two years.[14] The opinions leave the impression that the decisions represent a mere ripple in the long stream of the law of invention and that the Court will now leave that complicated and hopelessly technical subject to the care of the courts of appeals for another fifteen years. But in fact the cases may, indeed, foreshadow an important doctrinal clarification of what has been a needlessly confused concept.

The petitioner in *Deere* eschewed the arguments offered by the amici curiae and asserted instead that "there can be no doubt that Congress has spoken and has defined for the first time a statutory requirement for patentable invention. The wording of the statute is clear and should be followed."[15] In essence, he argued that the Court of Appeals for the Eighth Circuit had erroneously used a standard of invention that required proof of a new or different result in order to sustain the validity of the patent. The patent involved in *Deere* was on an improved clamp whose structure is difficult to describe but simple to understand from a diagram. The clamp was designed to provide a strong connection between the shank of a plow and the implement frame. The important feature of the clamp was that it permitted the shank to pivot upward when the plow point struck rocks, preventing damage. The patented clamp was an improvement on an earlier clamp that functioned in the same way and was also developed and patented by Graham. By having the shank pass under instead of over the pivot point and providing a rigid connection between the end of the shank and the clamp, Graham had designed a clamp that would perform better because of less wear and because it offered minutely greater freedom of movement along the whole length of the shank.

The Eighth Circuit had rejected this as a ground of patentability because "the inversion of the parts so as to allow the

---

[13] 383 U.S. at 17.

[14] United States v. Adams, 383 U.S. 39 (1966) (8-1). The Court last held a patent valid in Goodyear Tire & Rubber Co. v. Ray-O-Vac Co., 321 U.S. 275 (1944) (5-4).

[15] Brief of Petitioner Graham, p. 25, Graham v. John Deere Co.

shank to flex downwardly away from the plate above it did not bring about a significantly new or different result."[16] On this issue it differed from the Fifth Circuit, which had found the patent valid because of the rule "long recognized by this Court, that an improvement combination is patentable even though its constituent elements are singly revealed by the prior art, where, as here, it produces an old result in a cheaper and otherwise more advantageous way."[17] A concern with "result" as a test for invention has venerable origins in American patent law, but the petitioners in *Deere* argued with complete persuasiveness that "nowhere in [the] . . . statute is there any requirement that to be patentable an invention must produce a new result."[18] The Court agreed, concluding "that neither Circuit applied the correct test."[19]

By rejecting the "result test" of invention, the Court brought to an end a standard of patentability that has created confusion for far too many years. Even more important is the implication that in the future § 103 can be used to eliminate other historic tests of invention that have no rational relationship to the non-obviousness inquiry required by § 103. It is thus that the approach adopted by the Court in *Deere* may make it an important turning point in the history of American patent law. But to understand this possibility it is necessary first to understand the history.

The generally received history seems to be that the non-obviousness test of § 103 was articulated in the very first patentability case before the Supreme Court, *Hotchkiss v. Greenwood*,[20] and has remained the test of invention ever since, with the possible exception of certain "hostile" Supreme Court decisions after 1930.[21] Thus, the Supreme Court concluded in *Deere* that § 103 "was intended to codify judicial precedents embracing the principle long ago an-

---

[16] 333 F.2d at 534.

[17] 219 F.2d at 519.

[18] *Supra* note 15, at 26.

[19] 383 U.S. at 4.

[20] 11 How. 248 (1851).

[21] Discussion of this thesis generally centers on Great Atl. & Pac. Tea Co. v. Supermarket Equip. Corp., 340 U.S. 147 (1950), and Cuno Eng'r Corp. v. Automatic Devices Corp., 314 U.S. 84 (1941), as the most hostile. But under the non-obviousness test, the *Supermarket* case was clearly right on its facts and *Cuno* arguably so. General Elec. Co. v. Jewel Incandescent Lamp Co., 326 U.S. 242 (1945), discussed below, appears really to be the most hostile: wrong both on its facts and its law. But two Terms earlier the Court had held a doubtful patent valid. Goodyear Tire & Rubber Co. v. Ray-O-Vac Co., 321 U.S. 275 (1944).

nounced by this Court in *Hotchkiss*."[22] And at oral argument all counsel appeared to agree that the test of invention is the same today as it was a century ago.[23]

The idea that the history of a test for invention has so stable a continuity, however, is simply misleading. The history of invention in American patent law only begins to make sense if it is first understood that there have been not one but three different tests which, during the twentieth century, have existed side by side in the decisions of the courts. Section 103 can properly be construed as a selection of one of those three tests and a rejection of the other two. If it is so construed, the law based on the other two tests should now be rejected. Until *Deere*, however, the lower federal courts were not dealing with § 103 in this way. Rather they seemed to assume that since § 103 dealt with invention, all prior law dealing with invention was relevant in applying the section to particular cases. For example, even though Judge Hand recognized that § 103 had changed the prior law, his decision in *Lyon v. Bausch & Lomb Optical Co.*[24] apparently would preserve as relevant all earlier tests of invention no matter what their doctrinal underpinnings.

This incorporative approach is apparent in the history of the *Graham* patent litigation. The Fifth and Eighth Circuits turned to the issue of "result" because they were dealing with a problem of "invention," and the case law on "invention" is full of talk about result. But result is a subject of inquiry related to one of the two tests rejected by § 103. The Supreme Court properly rejected its use as a focus of inquiry. Similar treatment should be afforded other subjects of inquiry based on the tests rejected by *Deere*. For they, too, can no longer be relevant.

I. The Three Tests

The three distinct tests of patentability can be denominated, in the order of their historic development, the "novelty" test, the "genius" test, and the "non-obviousness" test. It is the thesis of this paper that only the last survives the decision in *Deere*.

· [22] 383 U.S. at 3–4.

[23] 34 U.S.L. Week 3125 (1965).

[24] 224 F.2d 530 (2d Cir. 1955).

A. THE NOVELTY TEST

The novelty test focuses inquiry on a simple question: Is the device new? If the device is new, then it is patentable. This was the test of the Statute of Monopolies[25] and of the American patent acts of 1793,[26] 1836,[27] and 1870.[28]

In its simple, natural law form, the rationale can be stated as follows. In the specification of his patent the inventor has given to society something that is, by definition, new, something that society did not have before. Because he has given this to society, it is only natural justice that society should give him the exclusive right to its commercial development.

If one prefers an economic justification to one based on "natural right," an argument can also be made that the test of patentability should be "newness." In this view, the purpose of the patent system is not only to encourage invention but to encourage the production and marketing of new products. A new process or product that would be of marginal entrepreneurial interest when facing free entry might become an attractive investment proposition if the right to commercial development were exclusive. Thus, in 1837 Willard Phillips wrote in his *Law of Patents for Inventions:*[29]

> [W]ithout some encouragement and hope of indemnity for expenses, held out by the law, many inventions, after being made, would not be rendered practically useful. . . . Now without the encouragement of a patent, how is any man to engage in a novel and expensive process, if the moment he succeeds, at the cost of all this outlay, he must be sure that his neighbors, who were cautious enough to shun all chances of loss, will come into competition with him, and make the remuneration of all this outlay impossible?

In 1942, Judge Frank stated this rationale at some length:[30]

> [T]here seems still to be room for some kind of patent monopoly which, through hope of rewards to be gained through such a monopoly, will induce venturesome investors to risk large sums needed to bring to the commercially useful stage those new ideas which require immense expenditures for that pur-

[25] 21 James I c.3 (1623).

[26] 1 Stat. 318 (1793).

[27] 5 Stat. 117 (1836).

[28] 16 Stat. 198 (1870).

[29] PHILLIPS, THE LAW OF PATENTS FOR INVENTIONS 12–14 (1837).

[30] Picard v. United Aircraft Corp., 128 F.2d 632, 642 (2d Cir. 1942) (concurring).

pose. . . . [I]f we never needed, or do not now need, patents as bait for inventors, we may still need them, in some instances, as a lure to investors.

Judge Frank recognized the argument against this position. "Some persons, to be sure, argue that the too rapid obsolescence of plant and equipment through new developments is socially undesirable."[31] His response was both unanswerable and unresponsive. "[R]etardation of our nation's technology now seems of doubtful value since it weakens preparedness for war with another country which has not similarly, in pre-war days, retarded its technology."[32]

This same reasoning controls important governmental policies at the present time. In 1965, the Administrator of the National Aeronautics and Space Administration informed a committee of the United States Senate, with obvious satisfaction, that patents developed on NASA research contracts at government expense would be available for only two years on a non-exclusive, royalty-free basis. But "after the 2-year period, if the benefits of the invention have not been brought to the public, NASA will grant an exclusive license to exploit the invention."[33]

This is either sloppy or bad economics. It is sloppy because there is no effort to clarify whether the costs of commercial development that investors should be induced to meet are costs that must be borne by any entrant into the field, or whether they are costs of innovation that must be borne by only the first entrant. If they are of the latter kind, the point is reasonably sound. But it can be taken care of either by granting patents for the first innovation—the one to be developed—or by granting patents for the additional innovations that are necessary before commercial exploitation is achieved. An advocate of the non-obviousness test—to jump ahead for a moment—would argue that if commercial development requires only the exercise of the ordinary skill of the art, it hardly requires a patent to call it forth. In addition, it should be noted that the whole issue is in part a false one since the development work that concerned Judge Frank and the director NASA (nylon is commonly given as the great example) will usually involve processes and

---

[31] *Id.* at 645.   [32] *Ibid.*

[33] *Hearings on S. 789, S. 1809 and S. 1899 before the Subcommittee on Patents, Trademarks, and Copyrights of the Senate Committee on the Judiciary,* 89th Cong., 1st Sess., pt. 1, 149, 155 (1965) (statement of James E. Webb).

technical know-how that can probably be kept secret for a substantial period of time.

If the costs that concerned Frank and the director of NASA are of a kind that must be borne by every entrant into the field, costs such as investment in production and marketing facilities, then the argument is bad economics. Neither Frank nor the director of NASA seems to realize that there is no a priori principle dictating that the development of the new is the best use of capital resources. If capital can earn a higher return elsewhere absent the prospect of monopoly for the new product, it may well be because that capital is better applied to the alternative use. But that is a point directly contrary to the very existence of NASA, an existence which can be rationalized only by means of an appeal to national defense or national honor, the same unanswerable and yet unresponsive argument that Frank offered. But again, both NASA and Frank make the same error by assuming that "retardation" of commercial exploitation is the same thing as "retardation" of technology. They are not necessarily the same. An adequate military or space technology potential is not assured by incentives for commercial innovation. And, conversely, the costs of developing and maintaining this technological potential are not reduced by the grant of monopoly incentives to include "spinoff" in the civilian economy.

B. THE GENIUS TEST

The genius test is an extension of the natural law argument for the novelty test. But it is based on a negative economic premise about patents. A patent monopoly is costly to the consumer and should not be granted without good reason. It is a reward that should be given only for worthy achievements, for the achievements of genius. The history of this test has been the unfolding of an effort to define this achievement, the true inventive act, as a certain kind of mental process.[34] One inevitable result of this approach has been the economically absurd conclusion that organized, plodding, group research does not produce patentable discoveries because a group does not have genius.[35] Section 103 of the 1952 Act provides that "pat-

---

[34] This effort received its fullest exposition in ROBINSON, THE LAW OF PATENTS FOR USEFUL INVENTIONS (1890).

[35] Potts v. Coe, 145 F.2d 27, 28 (D.C. Cir. 1944) (Arnold, J.): "A discovery which is the result of step-by-step experimentation does not rise to the level of invention." Cf. Picard v. United Aircraft Corp., 128 F.2d 632, 636 (2d Cir. 1942) (Hand, J.). Arnold went on to observe that "the research laboratory has gradually raised the

entability shall not be negatived by the manner in which the invention was made,"[36] thereby eliminating the test of "genius" from the patent law.[37]

C. THE NON-OBVIOUSNESS TEST

The non-obviousness test shares the economic premises of both the novelty and genius tests. With the novelty test it shares the premise that innovation should be encouraged. With the genius test it shares the premise that patent monopolies represent a substantial cost to the consumer. These two premises are accommodated by the basic principle on which the non-obviousness test is based: a patent should not be granted for an innovation unless the innovation would have been unlikely to have been developed absent the prospect of a patent. Unlike the novelty test, it does not view the inducement of investment in production and marketing facilities, after the innovation has been developed, as an appropriate function of the patent system. These are costs that must be borne by everyone who wishes to market the innovation and if, in the face of competition, investors do not find the innovation an attractive prospect, that is because there are better uses for their capital elsewhere, not because the competitive situation should be altered. The non-obviousness test makes an effort, necessarily an awkward one, to sort out those innovations that would not be developed absent a patent system. Through the years the test has been variously phrased, but the focus has always been on the question whether the innovation could have been achieved by one of ordinary skill in the art, or whether its achievement is of a greater degree of difficulty.

If an innovator must bear costs that need not be borne equally by his competitors (because they will have the advantage of his work) and that he cannot recoup, he will not make the expenditures to innovate. But in a competitive system some non-recurring costs

---

level of industrial art until discoveries by ordinary skilled men, which would have seemed miraculous in the last century, are definitely predictable if money is available for organized research." 145 F.2d at 30. But why will the money be expended if it cannot be recovered by means of a patent monopoly?

[36] 35 U.S.C. § 103 (1964).

[37] In response to the suggestion of the amicus curiae brief of the State Bar of Texas, the Court expressly noted the demise of the "flash of genius" test in *Deere*. 383 U.S. at 15.

can be recouped because the innovator has the advantage of the lead time inherent in his position. Even in the case of products that can be easily imitated the innovator has the advantage of the good will and additional experience inherent in the position of being first in the field. The argument that the innovator can reasonably expect to recoup his costs simply by being first has been seriously offered as an argument against any patent system at all.[38] The difficulty is that as a matter of empirical fact it is not known to what extent the position of innovator gives one an advantage in a competitive situation, nor is it possible to determine the magnitude of a particular innovator's costs to determine whether he can recoup them without an exclusive grant. But what the economic argument does underline is that much innovation will occur in a competitive system with no patent rights. Only the costlier kinds of innovation will be retarded by the absence of patents. That these innovations will probably be the socially and economically more important only underlines the importance of the patent system. But the central point is that not every innovation needs the patent system to induce its appearance. In fact in many cases, the desire to obtain a superior competitive position by being known as "advanced" and first on the market will induce the appearance of the new product or process. An innovation obvious to one of ordinary skill in the art may indeed be new, in the sense that it did not exist before, and the costs may indeed be substantial if it takes a long time to perfect. But it is the implied judgment of the test that the cost of innovation of this order of difficulty can probably be recouped in a competitive situation while the costs of innovation of a greater difficulty cannot.

The argument has to be made somewhat differently in relation to processes that can be commercially exploited in secrecy. Innovations in this area would occur absent the patent system so long as there was reasonable assurance that the techniques involved could be kept secret. Here the function of the patent system is to induce disclosure of innovations that would otherwise be kept secret. This is desirable, not only because at the expiration of the patent the innovation becomes freely available, but also because during the period of the patent the nature of the innovation is dis-

---

[38] Plant, *The Economic Theory concerning Patents for Inventions*, ECONOMICA No. 1, 30, 43–44 (1934).

closed on the public record, and this knowledge may make it possible for others to make further innovations in the same or related fields. But since the patent grant is not to be given lightly, it should be given only to obtain the disclosure of innovations that would otherwise be unlikely to become known. If one of ordinary skill in the art could develop the innovation, it is likely to become known with reasonable ease. Only the non-obvious innovation has any prospect of remaining secret for long and therefore justifies the award of a patent to induce its disclosure.

II. The History

These three tests, then, are the components of the history of the idea of invention in the patent law. But for the first eighty-five years there was one basic test, the test of novelty. The Act of 1793 provided that a patent should issue for the invention of any "machine, manufacture, or composition of matter" which was "new and useful."[39] (The earlier Act of 1790 had provided that a patent should issue if the invention was "sufficiently useful and important."[40] It has no significance in the history of the requirement of patentability.) The text of the Act of 1793 makes it clear that new as used in the Act means new and no more. But the drafters felt constrained to add that "simply changing the form or the proportions of any machine, or composition of matter, in any degree, shall not be deemed a discovery."[41]

For the next eighty-two years American patent law followed the process of working out rules designed to prevent trivial advances from falling within the concept of patentable novelty. The problem was to distinguish between changes that were merely changes of form and changes that were changes of substance. "The sufficiency of the invention," Phillips wrote in 1837, "depends not upon the labor, skill, study, or expense applied or bestowed upon it, but upon its being diverse and distinguishable from what

---

[39] 1 Stat. 318–19 (1793).

[40] 1 Stat. 110 (1790). Section 7 of the 1836 Act, 5 Stat. 119–20 (1836), provided that "if the Commissioner shall deem it to be sufficiently useful and important, it shall be his duty to issue a patent therefor," but the courts never treated this language as legally significant. This provision was continued in § 31 of the 1870 Act, 16 Stat. 202 (1870), but it has no counterpart in the present law.

[41] 1 Stat. at 321.

is familiar and well known, and also substantially and materially, not slightly and trivially so. This requisite of an invention is sometimes expressed to be a difference in principle."[42] These distinctions have the ring of metaphysical debate and indeed the efforts of the courts to distinguish between the new and the really new were to lead them to distinctions that sound metaphysical and were meaningless. To quote Justice Story, "The doctrine of patents may truly be said to constitute the metaphysics of law."[43]

The pressures that led to this line of development are not difficult to identify. On the one hand, the courts were bound by the conceptual framework of a statute whose only requirement was that the invention be "new." On the other hand, they were confronted by a quickening pace of technological advance, particularly after the Civil War, that threatened to bring every commodity within a private patent grant. This pressure was revealed and its consequences described in an 1826 opinion:[44]

> The most frivolous and useless alterations in articles in common use are denominated improvements, and made pretexts for increasing their prices, while all complaint and remonstrance are effectually resisted by an exhibition of the great seal. Implements and utensils, as old as the civilization of man, are daily, by means of some ingenious artifice, converted into subjects for patents. If they have usually been made straight, some man of genius will have them made crooked, and, in the phraseology of the privileged order, will swear out a patent. If, from time immemorial, their form has been circular, some distinguished artisan will make them triangular, and he will swear out a patent, relying upon combinations among themselves, and that love of novelty which pervades the human race, and is the besetting sin of our own people, to exclude the old and introduce the new article into use, with an enhanced price for the pretended improvement. . . . More than three thousand patents have been granted since the year 1790. The number obtained for the same or similar objects is well worthy of observation. Eighty are for improvements on the steam engine and on steam boats; more than a hundred for different modes of manufacturing nails; from sixty to seventy for washing machines; from forty to fifty for threshing machines; sixty for pumps; fifty for churns; and a still greater number for stoves. The demand for

---

[42] Phillips, *op. cit. supra* note 29, at 127.

[43] Barrett v. Hall, 2 Fed. Cas. 914, 923 (No. 1,047) (C.C. D. Mass. 1818).

[44] Thompson v. Haight, 23 Fed. Cas. 1040, 41 (No. 13,957) (C.C. S.D. N.Y. 1826).

this article has called forth much ingenuity and competition. There are now not less than sixty patents for stoves, pretended to be constructed upon different principles. Some are patented, as it is called, because they have ten plates; some, because they have eleven; some because the smoke is permitted to escape at one side, and some because it is let out at the other. Some indefatigable projectors have contrived them with a door on each side, and others, still more acute and profound, make them with a door on one side. . . . The contribution levied upon the community, in the sale of these articles, is enormous, and would be sufficient to satisfy the most inordinate avarice, if it were not distributed among so many men of merit.

The point thus made by Judge Van Ness is that as the pace of obsolescence in a society quickens, the standard of invention must be raised lest every common product be the subject of a patent monopoly. Thus it was logical for Judge Van Ness to raise the specter of no "barriers against the growth and introduction of all the evils that distinguished the ancient system of monopolies," when "all trade and commerce, whether foreign or domestic, was appropriated by monopolists."[45] Much of Judge Van Ness's complaint was directed to the absence of an examination system under the statute of 1793, a complaint to which Congress finally responded in 1836. But a necessary implication of his remarks is that the substantive law should be more demanding. For at least some of his parade of horribles, such as changes in the chimneys of stoves, were properly patentable under the law of his own day.

The central influence on the development of the law of inventive novelty was nascent American legal scholarship. By the year 1850, American patent law had been the subject of three different treatises: Fessenden,[46] Phillips,[47] and Curtis.[48] No other area received so much special attention, and the tradition of ponderous treatises on patent law extended into the first decade of this century before finally expiring.[49] Reasons readily suggest themselves. First, patent

---

[45] *Id.* at 1042.

[46] Fessenden, An Essay on the Law of Patents for New Inventions (1810) (2d ed. 1822).

[47] Phillips, *op. cit. supra* note 29.

[48] Curtis, The Law of Patents for Useful Inventions (1849) (2d ed. 1854; 3d ed. 1867; 4th ed. 1873).

[49] The "death bed" efforts seem to be Macomber, The Fixed Law of Patents (1909), and Rogers, The Law of Patents (1914) .

law, designed to induce technological innovation, had great appeal to scholars of a young country that prided itself on modernity and progress. Second, systematic English concern with the problem was relatively recent,[50] and thus the Americans were less likely to be overawed in this area. Third, American patent law was a creature of statute and English cases could be dismissed as irrelevant.[51] Fessenden, Phillips, and Curtis—together with the omniscient and omnipresent Story on circuit—laid the foundations.

Viewing the complexities of patent law from the perspective of the 1960's, it is difficult to return to the spirit of the law of the first half of the nineteenth century. The pace of technological innovation was slower and the pressure of commercial activity less constant. The first relevant reported decision indicates the difference. The case is *Park v. Little*,[52] decided by Justice Bushrod Washington on circuit in 1813. The plaintiff complained of an infringement of his patent. The plaintiff, Park, a member of a company of volunteer firemen in Philadelphia, was an enterprising fellow who undertook to improve the efficiency of his comrades. Many of the fires that were the objects of the regular ministrations of this company occurred at night. The custom was that when the cry of fire was raised, the engine would proceed directly to the scene. It was the duty of the members of the company to leave their homes and join the engine there. But this could be the occasion of delay, for the members of the company might become confused and, hearing the sound of another engine, join up with the wrong company. Park undertook to remedy this situation by placing a bell on the engine. But it was not an ordinary bell. He mounted the bell on the end of a horizonal arm attached to the top of a flexible upright. On top of the upright was a ball weighing four or five pounds. As the horses pulled the engine through the streets, this arrangement would become agitated and the bell would ring. The device was a great success until the defendants, members of another company, copied the idea—they varied the details—and

---

[50] The first systematic English treatment of patent law appears to be RANKIN, AN ANALYSIS OF THE LAW OF PATENTS (1824).

[51] But see FESSENDEN, *op. cit. supra* note 46, at 41–42. That English decisions under the Statute of Monopolies would be consulted was established in Pennock v. Dialogue, 2 Pet. 1 (1829).

[52] 18 Fed. Cas. 1107 (No. 10,715) (C.C. D. Pa. 1813).

set a similar bell upon their engine. This caused no end of confusion to the members of the complainant's company, who could never be sure that they were pursuing the sound of their own bell rather than that of the interlopers. Park brought his patent to court to eliminate this difficulty. "Whether this is a new and a useful invention, you must decide," Justice Washington instructed the jury. "But the question is not, whether bells to give alarm or notice are new, but whether the use and application of them to fire engines, to be rung, not by manual action, but by the motion of the carriage, for the purpose of alarm or notice, is a new invention, or improvement of an old one? The power of steam is not new, and yet its application for propelling boats would be considered as such."[53] The jury, displaying more wisdom than fidelity to these instructions, found for the defendant.

The principles were equally clear for Justice Story. In *Earle v. Sawyer*[54] the jury had found against the defendant for infringement and awarded $300 damages. The defendant moved for a new trial, contending that the plaintiff's patent was invalid. The patent related to a device known as a shingle mill, apparently an apparatus for cutting lumber into shingles. The particular patent, issued in 1822, was an improvement on an earlier patent issued to the plaintiff in 1813. The improvement of the first machine over the second was "to admit the use and application in said machine of the circular saw, instead of the perpendicular saw heretofore used, and the substitution of such other parts as are rendered necessary by these alterations."[55] The defendant's counsel argued in prescient terms that the patent was invalid:[56]

> It is not sufficient, that a thing is new and useful, to entitle the author of it to a patent. He must do more. He must find out by mental labor and intellectual creation. If the result of accident, it must be what would not occur to all persons skilled in the art, who wished to produce the same result. There must be some addition to the common stock of knowledge, and not merely the first use of what was known before. The patent act gives a reward for the communication of that, which might be otherwise withholden. An invention is the finding out by some effort of the understanding. The mere putting of two things together, although never done before, is no invention.

[53] *Id*. at 1108.

[54] 8 Fed. Cas. 254 (No. 4,247) (C.C. D. Mass. 1825).

[55] *Id*. at 254.

[56] *Id*. at 255.

Story's answer was unequivocal. "It . . . does not appear to me now, that this mode of reasoning upon the metaphysical nature, or the abstract definition of an invention, can justly be applied to cases under the patent act."[57] And he added, "It is of no consequence, whether the thing be simple or complicated; whether it be by accident, or by long, laborious thought, or by an instantaneous flash of mind, that it is first done. The law looks to the fact, and not to the process by which it is accomplished."[58] It must be new, and it must be useful, and that is all.

But *Earle v. Sawyer* is not evidence that the judges were not capable of using the test of inventive novelty to strike down patents. *Earle v. Sawyer* was an unusual case on its facts. The patent claimed exactly what was concededly new, and no more. But if the patent claimed more than the inventor's exact contribution, which was usually the case, the patentee faced a more exacting standard. Thus, in the case of *Woodcock v. Parker*,[59] involving a patent on a machine for splitting leather, Justice Story instructed the jury that:[60]

> [I]f the machine, for which the plaintiff obtained a patent, substantially existed before, and the plaintiff made an improvement only therein, he is entitled to a patent for such improvement only, and not for the whole machine; and under such circumstances, as this present patent is admitted to comprehend the whole machine, it is too broad, and therefore void. . . . If he claim a patent for a whole machine, it must in substance be a new machine; that is, it must be a new mode, method or application of mechanism, to produce some new effect, or to produce an old effect in a new way.

Justice Story groped for words and the test of invention was born. "A new mode, method or application of mechanism, to produce some new effect, or to produce an old effect in a new way." In 1818, the judges began to speak of changes in principle, as opposed to changes in form.[61] "The question for your determination,"

---

[57] *Ibid.*

[58] *Id.* at 256.

[59] 30 Fed. Cas. 491 (No. 17,971) (C.C. D. Mass. 1813).

[60] *Id.* at 492.

[61] Barrett v. Hall, 2 Fed. Cas. 914 (No. 1,047) (C.C. D. Mass. 1818) (Story, J.); Pettibone v. Derringer, 19 Fed. Cas. 387 (No. 11,043) (C.C. D. Pa. 1818) (Washington, J.). In so doing, they adopted the language of the English decisions. See Boulton v. Bull, 2 H. Bl. 463, 126 Eng. Rep. 651 (C.P. 1795). This change may have resulted from the language of the Supreme Court in Evans v. Eaton, 3 Wheat. 454 (1818), and the extensive note on the English patent case to be found *id.* at Appendix, p. 13.

Washington explained, is "whether it is an improvement on the principle [of the prior art] . . . or whether it is merely a change in the form, or proportions."[62] But although the concept of a "principle" was later to be the subject of learned exposition, the courts first used it as a shorthand way of stating Justice Story's earlier instruction. The issue of novelty, said Story, "in the present improved state of mechanics, . . . is often a point of intrinsic difficulty."[63]

This remained the law of invention until 1875, so far as the Supreme Court Justices were concerned. *Hotchkiss v. Greenwood*,[64] decided in the 1850 Term, can be understood only against this background. For an examination of that opinion reveals that despite all the significance that has been attributed to it, it merely re-affirmed the law as it then existed, adding only a minor wrinkle that in context liberalized the standard of invention still further. This addition, the non-obviousness test, was understood as a specialized doctrine applicable in a narrow situation, and it was only later that the case became a "leading" case.

The patent in the *Hotchkiss* case was for an improved method of making knobs for "locks, doors, cabinet furniture, and for all other purposes for which wood and metal or other material knobs are used."[65] "This improvement consists," explained the specifications of the patent, "in making said knobs of potter's clay, such as is used in any species of pottery; also of porcelain."[66] The key passage in the specifications stated:[67]

> [T]he modes of fitting them for their application to doors, locks, furniture, and other uses will be as various as the uses to which they may be applied, but chiefly predicated on one principle, that of having the cavity in which the screw or shank is inserted, by which they are fastened, largest at the bottom of its depth, in form of a dovetail, and a screw formed therein by pouring in metal in a fused state.

The evidence at trial developed two important facts. First, the defendant was unable to adduce any evidence that knobs of clay had ever been made before. Second, it had been common to fasten

---

[62] 19 Fed. Cas. at 390.

[63] Lowell v. Lewis, 15 Fed. Cas. 1018, 1019 (No. 8,568) (C.C. D. Mass. 1817).

[64] 11 How. 248 (1850).   [66] *Ibid.*

[65] *Id.* at 249.   [67] *Ibid.*

knobs made of other materials to their spindles by means of the dovetail fastening described in the plaintiff's specifications. The significance of these uncontroverted facts was the legal issue of the case.

The plaintiff had requested an instruction that the patent was valid "if such shank and spindle had never before been attached in this mode to a knob of potter's clay, and it required skill and invention to attach the same to a knob of this description, so that they would be firmly united, and make a strong and substantial article, and which, when thus made, would become an article much better and cheaper than the knobs made of metal or other materials."[68] This was in substance a request for a directed verdict for the plaintiff, for as the trial court correctly observed, "it requires skill and thought to attach a spindle to any kind of knob."[69] Indeed, it requires skill and thought to do any kind of mechanical work. The trial court rejected the instruction because it failed to take account of the requirement that the knob, to be patentable, must embody a new principle. And, insisted the trial court, improved quality and economy did not mean that the article embodied a new principle. (This was an issue that was still agitating the courts of appeals in the Deere case and that provoked a dissent from Justice Woodbury in Hotchkiss.) The trial court took the position that if the material was old and the mode of fastening the material to the spindle was old, there was no new principle in the operation of the knob and gave the jury an instruction that amounted to a directed verdict for the defendant. The patent was therefore void, added the court, because the material was in common use, and no other ingenuity or skill was necessary to construct the knob than that of an ordinary mechanic acquainted with the business.[70] This implied that a patent might still be valid even if it did not embody a new principle if it required more than mechanical skill for its development. But what is more important, it took the issue away from the jury and held that the knobs had not required more than mechanical skill for their construction. The jury had no choice but to find for the defendant.

In his argument before the Supreme Court, this was the point the defendant raised. The lower court had taken "upon themselves

---

[68] Id. at 263–64.

[69] 12 Fed. Cas. 551, 552 (No. 6,718) (C.C. D. Ohio 1848).   [70] Id. at 553.

to determine in the negative the question whether 'it required skill and thought and invention to attach the knob of clay to the metal shank and spindle, so that they would unite firmly, and make a solid, substantial article of manufacture,' instead of submitting it to the jury. It was a question of fact . . . depending upon evidence, and ought to have been submitted to the jury."[71] The argument fell on unsympathetic ears, for in his opinion Justice Nelson misunderstood the instruction as having put to the jury the issue whether the construction of the device had required more than mechanical skill, and the dissent accepted this interpretation. It is important to note, however, that in his argument plaintiff continued to insist on the language of his requested instruction. "Skill, thought and invention," under the principle of *ejusdem generis*, seems to mean that invention is simply the exercise of skill and thought. One possible interpretation of Justice Nelson's opinion is that he understood the objection to the instructions to be that a requirement of "more than mechanical skill" was too severe and he simply rejected that ground. For it could have been argued under the law prior to *Hotchkiss v. Greenwood* that if an innovation did not incorporate a new principle it was not patentable, even if the innovation required more than mechanical skill, because it would still not be new.

The invasion of the competence of the jury was not, however, the principal argument of the plaintiff. He quoted Curtis: "The mere substitution of one metal for another in a particular manufacture might be the subject of a patent, if the new article were better, more useful, or cheaper than the old."[72] Clay and porcelain knobs, he argued, were better than the earlier knobs of wood and metal:[73]

> It is indeed an invention of much more than common importance and merit. It is the combination of two materials, metal and earth, never before united in this manner, so as to give to the new manufacture the strength of iron with the durability and beauty of the clay or porcelain; its exemption from the corrosive action of acids and other chemical agents, and its consequent freedom from tarnish.

---

[71] 11 How. at 253.

[72] *Id.* at 255, quoting CURTIS, *op. cit. supra* note 48, at 27.

[73] *Id.* at 257.

The defendant based his argument on two alternative constructions of the patent. "Does the patent . . . confine its claim to a mere right to use clay or porcelain for the purpose of making . . . knobs, or does it claim to cover the manufacturing [of] knobs of clay and porcelain in the manner . . . set forth in the specification?"[74] He argued for the latter construction. He favored this construction because if the patent covered knobs of clay attached to spindles by means of the dovetail fastening, then the patent covered both old and new matter. He, too, relied on Curtis: "[I]f it turns out that any thing claimed is not new, the patent is void, however small or unimportant such asserted invention may be."[75] This had the ironic result of making the narrower construction of the claim the invalid one. If the patent covered all clay knobs, it might be valid; if it covered only clay knobs of this type, it might be invalid. The argument, however, was a literal application of the controlling law.

The case was more difficult for the defendant if the patent was construed as simply claiming knobs of clay and porcelain. His argument on this contingency required a creative analogy. A number of earlier circuit court decisions had decided that a new use for an old machine did not entitle one to a patent for the machine, since the machine, after all, was not new.[76] Clay and porcelain, the defendant pointed out, were old materials and the patent was simply for a new use of an old material.[77] Therefore it was not new, and not patentable.

Writing for the Court, Justice Nelson first answered the plaintiff's contention that the knobs were patentable because they were better. That they are better "is doubtless true," he said, "but the peculiar effect . . . is not distinguishable from that which would exist in the case of the wood knob, or one of bone or ivory, or of other materials that might be mentioned."[78] Justice Woodbury, citing *Earle v. Sawyer*, dissented on this point.[79] For an article that is better, he reasoned, must surely be new.

Nelson went on in his opinion to admit of an exception. The knob might be patentable, even though there was no new principle or effect, if "more ingenuity and skill in applying the old method

---

[74] *Ibid.*   [75] *Id.* at 259, quoting CURTIS, *op. cit. supra* note 48, at 133.

[76] Bean v. Smallwood, 2 Fed. Cas. 1142 (No. 1,173) (C.C. D. Mass. 1843); Howe v. Abbott, 12 Fed. Cas. 656 (No. 6,766) (C.C. D. Mass. 1842).

[77] 11 How. at 261.   [78] *Id.* at 266.   [79] *Id.* at 266–71.

of fastening the shank and the knob were required in the application of it to the clay or porcelain knob than were possessed by an ordinary mechanic acquainted with the business."[80] But since in this case the jury had found that no such skill was exercised, a conclusion Nelson reached because of his misunderstanding of the instruction, "there was an absence of that degree of skill and ingenuity which constitute essential elements of every invention."[81] It was this phrase that presaged wider application of the test. For its time, the rule of *Hotchkiss v. Greenwood* was that a change of materials is not of itself patentable even if it results in an improvement, unless the application of the material to the use requires more than mechanical skill. In his 1854 edition Curtis added a special section on *Hotchkiss*. He could accommodate it without difficulty:[82]

> [T]he end, effect, or result attained must be new; and ... if the same end, effect, or result has been attained before, it is not new, and there has been no invention. ... So, too the substitution of one material for another, in a particular manufacture, if the inventive faculty has not been at work, has been held by the Supreme Court of the United States not to be sufficient to support a patent. ... But on the other hand, if the end, effect, or result is new, although the same means may previously have been used to produce a different effect, and for a different purpose, there may be a patent for the application of the materials to produce the new effect or result.

In 1850 Curtis' was the leading treatise on patent law. The first edition of *Treatise on the Law of Patents for Useful Inventions* had appeared the year before and, as the summary of the arguments of counsel in *Hotchkiss* makes clear, it was already regarded as authoritative. It was shortly completely to supersede an older and better work: Phillips' *Treatise* of 1837.[83] Phillips' was a fine and careful book. Fessenden's, which preceded it, was largely a collection of cases followed by a sketchy and badly organized "synthetical view of the Law of Patents for New Inventions, together with such rules as may appear best calculated to prevent, as far as possible, future disputes on the subject."[84] Phillips was

---

[80] *Id*. at 266.   [81] *Ibid*.

[82] CURTIS, *op. cit. supra* note 48, at 45–49 (2d ed.).

[83] PHILLIPS, *op. cit. supra* note 29.

[84] FESSENDEN, *op cit. supra* note 46, at 186–89 (1st ed.); 362–89 (2d ed.).

the first to pursue the implications of the general approach adopted by the courts. The general problem was: when is a patent covering a change that is not entirely new valid? Since every innovation will build on existing technology, this is a question that must be answered in relation to every patent. The general answer preferred was that the innovation is patentable if it is an application of a new principle or if it produces a new effect or result. Phillips began to divide this general problem into subcategories. These were: improvement; new use; combination; and change of form, proportions, or materials. By dealing separately with the different classes of innovation, Phillips hoped to add precision to the application of the ambiguous generality of the controlling rule. But he was aware that the categories were treacherous:[85]

> [W]e are without the usual help to satisfactory speculation, that is, clear language, intelligible to every one, which proves, in this, as in other cases, a double hindrance, first to clear and discriminate thinking, and second, to the ready and perspicuous communication of thought. As the different expressions used in describing patentable subjects are very analogous to each other in signification, and are mutually blended and implicated together in their meaning, and in the application made of them in the cases, the most convenient mode of treating of them, at least the most concise, will be to enumerate them all, and examine them successively.

If later writers had remained as sensitive to these difficulties, perhaps these categories would not have been raised to the dogmas they have become. But Phillips had one basic limitation. He saw himself as expositor of the law, not as commentator on it. The categories were useful, not for analytic purposes, but in order to set out the law with greater precision.

Of the four categories, improvement was the most general. On this Phillips said that either a new effect or a new method of obtaining an old effect was patentable.[86] But what of an improvement which applies known apparatus to achieve a new effect? Not patentable said Phillips: "There is no instance in which it has been held that a mere new effect of the use of a machine already known, without any new combination, machinery, or process, is the subject of a valid patent."[87] But what of the problem of combinations?

---

[85] PHILLIPS, *op. cit. supra* note 29, at 77.

[86] *Id.* at 122–23.   [87] *Id.* at 109.

"It is sufficient . . . that the combination is new, though the separate things combined may have been before in use and well known."[88] But then is a change of materials patentable? For a change of materials, after all, is a combination of an old device with a different material. "The substitution of one material for another is not, at least ordinarily, an invention for which a patent can be claimed."[89] The upshot of these inconsistencies was that it made a great deal of difference under which category an innovation was subsumed. The argument in *Hotchkiss v. Greenwood* was an argument for competing categories. "Our invention," argued the plaintiff, "is a combination of dissimilar materials."[90] "[W]e ‚maintain," responded the defendant, "that they cannot obtain a patent for a new use, or double use, of the article of clay."[91]

In 1849, Curtis did not give these categories the same prominence. He re-emphasized the general rule that the "line of demarkation between invention and a mere application to a new use" is "that the end, effect, or result attained must be new"[92] and, unlike Phillips, he seemed to assume that this rule applied to combinations as much as to any other kind of innovation.[93] But after Phillips the important thing is that the conceptual structure he created began to dominate the cases.

Cases before the Supreme Court raising issues of patentable novelty after *Hotchkiss* were infrequent. The small number, a characteristic of the entire period from 1793 to 1870, certainly cannot be explained by the ease with which the controlling rules could be applied. The concept of change of "principle" was ambiguous and the text writers' categories were inconsistent. The simplest explanation lies in the small number of patents issued each year prior to the Civil War.[94] But even when computed as a percentage of the patent cases litigated, there appears to have been a marked rise in the incidence of the patentability issue after 1870. The rules as applied resulted in the validation of most patents and, except in the unusual case, the issue of patentability did not represent a fruitful avenue of attack for defendants. So long as

---

[88] *Id*. at 115.

[89] *Id*. at 133.

[90] 11 How. at 256.

[91] *Id*. at 261.

[92] CURTIS, *op. cit. supra* note 48, at 45.

[93] *Id*. at 41–44.

[94] 1840: 458; 1850: 883; 1860: 4,357. U.S. DEPT. OF COMMERCE, THE STORY OF THE U.S. PATENT OFFICE 34 (1965).

the controlling approach was that anything new was patentable, only the most trivial innovations would pose a serious problem. After 1836 many of these were screened out by the Patent Office examining procedure with which the Court seems to have been satisfied. "It is evident," the Court said in 1854, "that a patent . . . issued, after an inquisition of examination made by skillful and sworn public officers, appointed for the purpose of protecting the public against false claims or useless inventions, is entitled to much more respect, as evidence of novelty and utility, than those formerly issued without any such investigation."[95] The few cases decided by the Court on the issue address themselves to the problem of working out the categories suggested by the early circuit decisions and organized by Phillips. There are so few of them that they can be catalogued.

The first case after *Hotchkiss* was *Winans v. Denmead*,[96] a change-of-form case. The plaintiff had patented an improvement of cars for transporting coal. The Court without difficulty concluded that the car was patentable: "[B]y means of this change of form, the patentee has introduced a mode of operation not before employed in burden cars."[97] *Phillips v. Page*,[98] was both a new-use and change-of-size case. The patent was on a saw mill. The plaintiff's saw was larger than the earlier saws in use and was meant to be used on full-sized saw logs instead of small blocks. The Court said the enlargement of the machine was no ground for a patent. Using the language of the non-obviousness test, the Court observed that enlarging a machine is "done every day by the ordinary mechanic in making a working machine from the patent model." But it then concluded that novelty rather than non-obviousness was the appropriate standard by adding that "in order to reach invention," the patentee "must contrive the means of adapting the enlarged old organization to the new use."[99] Neither a change of size nor a new use made the saw a patentable device.

The pace accelerated in 1870. *Stimpson v. Woodman*[100] was an improvement case. The patent was for a machine for ornamenting leather by means of a figured roller. Previously a figured roller had been applied by hand for the same purpose, but the same

---

[95] Corning v. Burden, 15 How. 252, 270 (1854).

[96] 15 How. 329 (1854).

[97] *Id.* at 338.

[98] 24 How. 164 (1861).

[99] *Id.* at 167.

[100] 10 Wall. 117 (1870).

machine had existed using a smooth roller. The Court reversed the trial court for refusing to give a requested instruction that "if they should find that the form of the surface of the rollers in the plaintiff's machine is not material to the mechanical action of the roller in combination with the other devices and their arrangements, by which the roller is moved, the leather supported, and the pressure made,"[101] the patent is invalid. The Court added that the improvement "required no invention; the change with the existing knowledge in the art involved simply mechanical skill, which is not patentable."[102] Although the approved instruction said nothing about mechanical skill, this sentence was apparently thought to justify the instruction, not to constitute an independent test of invention. *Seymour v. Osborne*,[103] was also an improvement case and was explicit in ruling that non-obviousness did not constitute an independent ground of invalidity. "Improvements for which a patent may be granted," explained the Court, "must be new and useful, within the meaning of the patent law, or the patent will be void, but the requirement of the patent act in that respect is satisfied if the combination is new and the machine is capable of being beneficially used for the purpose for which it was designed."[104] *Tucker v. Spalding*,[105] held that a new use of an old device was not patentable, leaving to the jury the question whether the patented device was identical to an earlier device or not. *Hicks v. Kelsey*,[106] held a change of materials unpatentable, and represented the first time in twenty-three years that *Hotchkiss* was cited in an opinion of the Court.[107]

Hailes v. Van Wormer[108] was a combination case in which Justice Strong pompously gave forth the doctrine of aggregation. The doctrine managed to combine the appearance of complex significance with the substance, if not the grace, of a nonsense rhyme:[109]

> [T]he results must be a product of the combination, and not a mere aggregate of several results each the complete product of

---

[101] *Id.* at 119.

[102] *Id.* at 121.

[103] 11 Wall. 516 (1871).

[104] *Id.* at 548–49.

[105] 13 Wall. 453 (1872).

[106] 18 Wall. 670 (1874).

[107] *Hotchkiss* had been cited by Justice Campbell, dissenting, in *Winans v. Denmead*, arguing that a patent on a change of form should be held invalid as equivalent to a patent on a change of material. 15 How. at 344.

[108] 20 Wall. 353 (1874).

[109] *Id.* at 368.

one of the combined elements. Combined results are not necessarily a novel result, nor are they an old result obtained in a new and improved manner. Merely bringing old devices into juxtaposition, and there allowing each to work out its own effect without the production of something novel, is not invention. No one by bringing together several old devices without producing a new and useful result, the joint product of the elements of the combination and something more than an aggregate of old results, can acquire a right to prevent others from using the same devices, either singly or in other combinations.

Rubber Tip Pencil Co. v. Howard,[110] held invalid a patent for placing an eraser on the end of a pencil. It was a good idea, the Court conceded, but the device itself incorporated nothing new.

The 1874 Term brought a change. It was a silent change, unacknowledged by the Court. It first appeared in *Smith v. Nichols*,[111] involving a patent for an improved fabric. The Court held the patent invalid, although it conceded that the cloth was better, because the improvements were only improvements in degree. "Doing substantially the same thing in the same way by substantially the same means with better results, is not such invention as will sustain a patent."[112] This holding suggests that novelty alone is not enough but was not very different from *Hotchkiss v. Greenwood*. The Court added a phrase, however, suggestive of a new approach. "A patentable invention is a mental result."[113] For the first time the Court did not speak of an invention, a thing, which must be new and useful. Now it spoke of invention, an act, something that must be done, and implied that this too was a requirement of patentability.

Less than two months after *Nichols*, the Court decided *Collar Company v. Van Dusen*.[114] The patent was for a shirt "collar made of long-fibre paper."[115] The contribution of the patentee was to find a quality of paper suitable for making paper collars which, prior to his innovation, had always been found unsatisfactory. Collars already existed. The paper already existed. The Court might easily have disposed of the case as a change of materials case. But it did not:[116]

---

110 20 Wall. 498 (1874).

111 21 Wall. 112 (1875).   114 23 Wall. 530 (1875).

112 *Id*. at 119.   115 *Id*. at 542.

113 *Id*. at 118.   116 *Id*. at 563.

Articles of manufacture may be new in the commercial sense when they are not new in the sense of patent law. New articles of commerce are not patentable as new manufactures, unless it appears in the given case that the production of the new article involved the exercise of invention or discovery beyond what was necessary to construct the apparatus for its manufacture or production.

For the first time *Hotchkiss v. Greenwood* was cited as a case of general application, standing for the proposition that "nothing short of invention or discovery will support a patent."[117] Invention became a third requirement for patentability.

This was a change of ultimate significance but of little immediate effect. The Court had recognized a new requirement, invention, but it still had no idea what it was. The Court simply fell back on older patent cases and their tests of novelty. At first, the cases experimented with language about genius and what it means to invent;[118] only slowly does the non-obviousness test come to the forefront.[119] Indeed, the change may have been at the time imperceptible to both the Court and its bar.[120] Not until 1885, in *Thompson v. Boisselier*, did the Court take pains to point out that "it is not enough that a thing shall be new, in the sense that in the shape or form in which it is produced it shall not have been before known, and that it shall be useful, but it must, under the Constitution and the statute, amount to an invention or discovery."[121]

---

117 *Ibid.*

118 See, *e.g.*, Densmore v. Scofield, 102 U.S. 375, 378 (1880): "It does not appear . . . that there was a 'flash of thought' by which such a result . . . was reached, or that there was any exercise of the inventive faculty, more or less thoughtful, whereby anything entitled to the protection of a patent was produced."

119 The non-obviousness test predominated after 1880. But it never became the exclusive test.

120 The lower federal courts never recognized the *Paper Collar* case as a turning point. *Hotchkiss*, which eventually came to be cited as the leading case establishing the requirement of invention, was not even cited by the lower federal courts of general jurisdiction until 1882. Scott v. Evans, 11 Fed. 726, 727 (C.C. W.D. Pa. 1882). It was there cited as a change of material case. (It was cited in review of a Patent Office decision in *In re* Maynard, MacArthur's Patent Cases 536, 537–38 (C.C. Dist. Col. 1857).) It was first cited for the general proposition that "not every trifling device, nor any obvious improvement in the material already possessed is intended to be rewarded" by the patent laws, in Leonard v. Lovell, 29 Fed. 310, 314 (C.C. W.D. Mich. 1886).

121 114 U.S. 1, 11 (1885).

Perhaps the reference to the Constitution was felt necessary to validate the pronounced change. But, in spite of this strong position, the Court was confronted the next Term with the argument that "the statute makes novelty and utility the only tests of patentability."[122] "It is sufficient answer to these suggestions," Justice Blatchford wrote, "to say that the questions presented are not open ones in this court."[123]

It was fortuitous that the Court's change of position took place when it did. The 1836 statute had always been susceptible of two different readings. The statute provided that "any person or persons [who] discovered or invented any new and useful" device was eligible for a patent.[124] The problem was how to read "discovered or invented." Was it the equivalent of "found," if what is found is "new and useful?" Or did "discovered or invented" connote some additional requirement? The original interpretation posited two requirements for patentability: novelty and utility. The new reading posited three: novelty, utility, and invention. As early as 1856, a district judge had read the statute in the second way, instructing a jury that "it is required that there should be an invention, that the invention should be new, and that it should be useful. In other words, before a patent can be issued, the thing patented must appear to be of such a character, as to involve or require 'invention' for its production—require the exercise of the genius of an inventor as contradistinguished from the ordinary skill of a mechanic in construction."[125]

A satisfactory explanation of the Court's shift can only be found in non-legal forces at work in the country after the Civil War. First and foremost is the sharp rise in the number of patents issued immediately after the cessation of hostilities. In 1860, 4,357 original patents were issued on inventions.[126] After a decline during the war, the number jumped to 8,863 in 1866. In 1867 the number jumped again to 12,277. The number of patents issued annually

---

[122] Gardner v. Herz, 118 U.S. 180, 191 (1886).   [123] *Ibid*.

[124] § 6, 5 Stat. 117, 119 (1836). The 1793 Act had provided simply that the person must have "invented." § 1, 1 Stat. 318 (1793). The 1870 statute said "any person who has invented or discovered. . . ." § 24, 16 Stat. 198, 201 (1870).

[125] Ransom v. New York, 20 Fed. Cas. 286, 288 (No. 11,573) (C.C. S.D. N.Y.) 1856.

[126] U.S. DEPT. OF COMMERCE, *op. cit. supra* note 94, at 34.

remained at about this level until 1880, when it rose to an annual level of about 20,000. This is in striking contrast to the 883 patents issued the year *Hotchkiss* was decided. This increase was reflected in a rapidly expanding volume of patent litigation before the courts. At the same time, the patent abolition controversy in England and on the Continent[127] exacerbated worry about the threat of the patent system to a competitive economy. During the debate on the codification of 1870, one senator put the question "whether our whole patent system is not founded in an error" and quoted from an abolitionist a statement "that patents are injurious alike to the inventor, the public, and the manufacturer."[128] Although the patent abolition position never gained substantial support in the United States, it gave impetus to the drive to limit patents. "The time is not yet ripe for the propagation of this idea [of the abolition of patents] in the United States," explained an editorial writer in the *New York Times* in 1870, but "another phase of it, which will in due time lead up to the great issue, is the tendency . . . [in official American circles] not, indeed to repress the introduction of inventions, but to confine the period and chances of their reward to narrower limits."[129]

By the 1870's the Patent Office had lost the prestige it had once enjoyed. During the Civil War charges of misappropriation of funds had been made against the commissioner. An investigating committee of the House found no evidence of misappropriation, but ample evidence of mismanagement.[130] During the debate on the codification of 1870 some of the speakers suggested corruption in the Patent Office,[131] and a new provision was put in the patent laws to prevent employees of the office from taking a personal interest in patents issued.[132]

The quickening pace of innovation also made patents seem less necessary. In 1872, an engineer and inventor suggested that the art

---

[127] Assorted documents related to this controversy may be found in RECENT DISCUSSIONS ON THE ABOLITION OF PATENTS FOR INVENTIONS (1869) and 2 COPYRIGHT AND PATENTS FOR INVENTIONS (Macfie ed. 1883).

[128] CONG. GLOBE, 41st Cong., 2d Sess. 4827 (1870).

[129] N.Y. Times, March 20, 1870, p. 4, col. 4.

[130] H.R. REP. No. 48, 37th Cong., 3d Sess. (1863).

[131] CONG. GLOBE, 41st Cong., 2d Sess. 2874, 4825 (1870).

[132] 16 Stat. 200 (1870), 35 U.S.C. § 4 (1964).

of inventing had advanced to the point where "bribes for discovery" were no longer necessary:[133]

> We no longer need the incentive of personal right in invention or demonstration to develop our arts, and the writer, from his own observation, both in England and America, finds that the better class of engineers and mechanics have come already to look with disfavor upon patents, a question of fact which will be confirmed by as many as have noticed the matter, and one that can be determined by searching the records of the patent office for the names of our best engineers.

Only once, however, did the Court take notice of all this in its opinions. In 1882 the Court observed:[134]

> It was never the object of . . . [the patent] laws to grant a monopoly for every trifling device, every shadow of a shade of an idea, which would naturally and spontaneously occur to any skilled mechanic or operator in the ordinary progress of manufactures. Such an indiscriminate creation of exclusive privileges tends rather to obstruct than to stimulate invention. It creates a class of speculative schemers who make it their business to watch the advancing wave of improvement, and gather its foam in the form of patented monopolies, which enable them to lay a heavy tax upon the industry of the country, without contributing anything to the real advancement of the arts. It embarrasses the honest pursuit of business with fears and apprehensions of concealed liens and unknown liabilities to lawsuits and vexatious accountings for profits made in good faith.

The story of the Court's efforts after 1874 to delimit the boundaries of the concept of invention is the story of failure. The non-obvious test predominated; yet in 1892 the Court upheld the barbed-wire patent without a mention of non-obviousness, observing tersely that "in the law of patents it is the last step that wins."[135] In the preceding Term the Court had apparently despaired of ever defining invention:[136]

> The truth is the word cannot be defined in such manner as to afford any substantial aid in determining whether a particular device involves an exercise of the inventive faculty or not. In a

---

[133] Richards, *Patent Invention*, 63 J. FRANKLIN INST. 17, 21 (1872).

[134] Atlantic Works v. Brady, 107 U.S. 192, 200 (1883).

[135] The Barbed Wire Patent, 143 U.S. 275, 283 (1892).

[136] McClain v. Ortmayer, 141 U.S. 419, 427 (1891).

given case we may be able to say that there is present invention of a very high order. In another we can see that there is lacking that impalpable something which distinguishes invention from simple mechanical skill.

Novelty, genius, and non-obviousness are all part of the requirement. In the infamous *Cuno* case of 1941,[137] Mr. Justice Douglas referred to all three in almost the same breath:[138]

> [T]he new device, however useful it may be, must reveal the flash of creative genius not merely the skill of the calling. . . . Tested by that principle Mead's device was not patentable. We cannot conclude that his skill in making this contribution reached the level of inventive genius. . . . A new application of an old device may not be patented if the "result claimed as new is the same in character as the original result. . . ."

The reason for the Court's inability to settle on the non-obviousness test as the controlling one may be due to the fact that it was never acknowledged to be a new test, but rather a continuation of an old one always required by the statute. This myth, largely the myth of *Hotchkiss v. Greenwood*, meant that the Court continued to treat the earlier cases as good law, and forced the concept of non-obviousness into an unhappy marriage with a concept of novelty and its doctrines of "new principle," "new result," or "new function." In one case, the Court attempted to accommodate these quite different notions by propounding a rule of evidence. "It may be laid down as a general rule, though perhaps not an invariable one, that if a new combination and arrangement of known elements produce a new and beneficial result, never attained before, it is evidence of invention."[139] But the irrelevance of "new result" to "non-obviousness" made this a hopeless solution. The inherent instability was only increased by the additional test of genius, and the Court's actions became erratic and unpredictable. Ironically, in the 1940's the inventive novelty tests, originally favorable to patents, were used by the Court to invalidate patents on substantial technical advances.[140]

The analytic dilemma was clearly revealed in the secondary lit-

---

[137] Cuno Eng'r Corp. v. Automatic Devices Corp., 314 U.S. 84 (1941).

[138] *Id.* at 91.

[139] Loom Co. v. Higgins, 105 U.S. 580, 591 (1882).

[140] See General Elec. Co. v. Jewel Incandescent Lamp Co., 326 U.S. 242 (1945); Cuno Eng'r Corp. v. Automatic Devices Corp., 314 U.S. 84 (1941).

erature of the last quarter of the nineteenth century. In 1883, Henry Merwin attempted to resolve the problem by creating two categories.[141] Turning to the language of the statute, he made the original observation that it did not say "invented," but "invented or discovered." For Merwin this perception put everything in place. A patent was valid if it was either invented or discovered. Some cases dealt with one category, some cases with the other. In his introductory essay he wrote that "Most patents are granted for inventions strictly."[142] But there is another class, where "the patentee has discovered a new principle, and if he makes some practical application thereof . . . he may obtain a valid patent."[143] Merwin went on to explain that in the case of a discovery "no inquiry need be made into the mental process by which a knowledge of the principle was attained. It is sufficient that the principle upon which the patent is based should be new, *i.e.*, that it should not have been known till the patentee revealed it."[144] This division made it possible for Merwin to accommodate the old novelty (discovery) cases with the new invention cases. Merwin lavished his warmest attention on the description of invention: "Invention is imagination; it is the very opposite of reasoning or inference; it is a single act of the mind; rather an instantaneous operation than a process. It has no stages; the essence of it is that it dispenses with them."[145] But the discussion was a failure. And with a sigh of resignation, he admitted that his was "a distinction which has not, in terms, been taken by the courts."[146]

A far more comprehensive work than Merwin's, a three-volume work by William C. Robinson of the Yale law faculty, appeared in 1890.[147] Robinson did not look for an easy way out. For Robinson, it was the nature of the inventive act that would furnish "a correct and definite apprehension of the attributes which must be found in every true invention."[148] Each inventive act consists of two ele-

---

[141] MERWIN, THE PATENTABILITY OF INVENTIONS (1883).

[142] *Id.* at 3.　　　　　　　[144] *Ibid.*

[143] *Ibid.*　　　　　[145] *Id.* at 22.　　　　　[146] *Id.* at 557.

[147] ROBINSON, THE LAW OF PATENTS FOR USEFUL INVENTIONS (1890). It was described in Davis, *Proposed Modifications in the Patent System,* 12 LAW & CONTEMP. PROB. 796, 806 (1947), as "perhaps the most profound study of our patent system ever made."

[148] ROBINSON, *op. cit. supra* note 147, at 115.

ments: "(1) An idea conceived by the inventor; (2) An application of that idea to the production of a practical result."[140] This second element incorporated the traditional idea that there must be a reduction to practice. Most interesting was Robinson's definition of the necessary mental element: "an exercise of the creative faculties, generating an idea which is clearly recognized and comprehended by the inventor, and is both complete in itself and capable of application to a practical result."[150] Thus he was able to transform the old novelty doctrine into a test of the inventive act and thereby harmonize the old cases with the new. His solution has three fundamental defects. First, it involves tests that have little relation to reality, or to the extent they are based on reality, that reality is exclusively one of mechanical improvements. Second, the tests are derived inductively from a given concept of invention without any reference to the economic functions a patent system might or should perform. And, third, it is discriminatory because it suggests that of two people who discover the same thing, only one might have invented it. Only the person who understands the "idea" is worthy of a patent. Robinson extended the metaphysics of invention begun in Story's early opinions. He was the last scholar to attempt to move directly from "invention" to a test of patentability on the basis of inductive logic. It is as if the thoroughness of his attempt proved once and for all the futility of the approach.

Walker's *Text-Book of the Patent Laws*, published in 1883, is much different from the works of both Merwin and Robinson. Merwin and Robinson conceived of themselves as walking among the inventors of genius they so laboriously describe. Walker, on the other hand, plods through the cases. This is both the weakness of his analysis and the source of the book's endurance for more than eighty years. Walker does not solve the analytic dilemma, he encapsulates it. And fossilized in Walker, the dilemma has been treated as the law down to the *Deere* decision. Walker is quick to acknowledge that "invention" is not defined. "There is no affirmative rule by which to determine the presence or absence of invention in every case."[151] But Walker does have something to offer: "negative rules of invention" derived from the cases in which patents have been held invalid. For the most part these are the old novelty

---

[149] *Id*. at 116.   [150] *Id*. at 132.

[151] WALKER, TEXT-BOOK OF THE PATENT LAWS 18 (1883).

tests put into the negative. For instance, Walker announces that "aggregation is not invention."[152] The negative novelty tests are supplemented by a negative non-obviousness test: "It is not invention to produce a device or process which any skillful mechanic or chemist would produce whenever required."[153] Commercial success is used to resolve borderline cases: "When the other facts in a case leave the question of invention in doubt, the fact that the device has gone into general use, and has displaced other devices which had previously been employed for analogous uses, is sufficient to turn the scale in favor of the existence of invention."[154]

The use of the negative form was a rhetorical device that eased the tension between the old novelty tests and the new requirement of invention. When the Court said that a new result is evidence of invention, that left the basic problem what is invention if its presence can be proved by a new result. But if one says that aggregation is not invention, there is no such problem because the rule in form does not claim to say anything about what invention is. Thus Walker's contribution was to give the new requirement of invention and the old tests of novelty a framework in which they could coexist in an uneasy but apparently permanent peace. The 1937 edition,[155] the sixth version of the book to appear, contains these same tests, illustrated in greater detail by cases that relied on earlier editions. And if the structure of the 1964 edition is substantially affected by the 1952 statute, the negative novelty tests are still given a prominent role,[156] in spite of the fact that they find no basis in § 103.

Walker captured the inconsistencies of the law of his day as well as anyone could. But having structured the analytic dilemma, he

---

152 *Id.* at 24.

153 *Id.* at 18.

154 *Id.* at 30.

155 DELLER, WALKER ON PATENTS (1937).

156 DELLER, WALKER ON PATENTS (3d ed. 1964). The negative tests were summarized as follows: "(1) mere exercise of skill expected of a person having ordinary skill in the art; (2) substitution of materials or elements; (3) change of location, size, degree and form; (4) reversal of parts; (5) unification or multiplication of parts; (6) making old devices adjustable, durable, portable or moveable; (7) change of proportion; (8) duplication of parts; (9) omission of parts with a corresponding omission of function; (10) substitution of equivalents; (11) new use for a new and analogous purpose; (12) conversion of manual to a mechanical operation; (13) superior or excellent workmanship; and (14) aggregation." 2 *id.* at 75. This framework treats non-obviousness as one of many tests rather than as the controlling test of invention.

made it harder for the Court to move away from it. In 1962 Congress explicitly legislated that non-obviousness was the controlling test of invention and thus eliminated any basis for the old novelty tests. In *Deere*, the Court applied the non-obviousness test and rejected new result as a relevant subject for inquiry. Now that new result has fallen, all tests of invention, whether negative or affirmative, based on a test of novelty should quickly follow. Patent law has too long suffered under the confusing concepts of "combination," "aggregation," "new effect," and "new use." These tests only complicate the inquiry into non-obviousness that is required by § 103.

III. Novelty and Inventive Novelty: Adams

This conclusion may bury tests based on inventive novelty before their demise. Their past durability suggests that they will not fall simply on the basis of the Court's action in the *Deere* case. Section 101 provides that "whoever invents or discovers any new and useful process, machine, manufacture, or composition of matter, or any new and useful improvement thereof, may obtain a patent therefor, subject to the conditions and requirements of this title."[157] This is the language of § 24 of the 1870 codification, the very language on which Walker based his negative tests. Some courts consider the inventive novelty tests to derive from § 101 rather than § 103.[158]

The answer to this position must be that in a statute that contains § 103, "new" in § 101 should be interpreted as it was in *Earle v. Sawyer*.[159] The whole metaphysical apparatus that developed to distinguish the new from the trivially new would never have been necessary in a statute that contained a non-obviousness test. Now that the statute does contain such a test, the apparatus can be dispensed with and new can once again be interpreted as meaning new. The only good reason for inserting § 103 in the statute was to choose one of the three competing tests of invention. If tests implicitly rejected by § 103 are to reappear in § 101, these statutory changes will prove fruitless. Several of the nineteenth-century cases clearly imply that the Court then thought that a finding of non-

---

[157] 35 U.S.C. § 101 (1964).

[158] See, *e.g.*, Gould-Nat'l Batteries, Inc. v. Gulton Indus. Inc., 150 U.S. P.Q. 77 (3d Cir. 1966), applying the doctrine of aggregation under § 101 rather than § 103.

[159] See text *supra*, at notes 54–58.

obviousness would override a finding of lack of inventive novelty.[160] This was the case in *Hotchkiss* itself where Justice Nelson went on to discuss the non-obviousness issue after he had already found no new effect.

The decision of the Court in *United States v. Adams*[161] can be read, if with some difficulty, as confronting this issue. The record in *Adams* made the non-obviousness issue a simple one. In 1939 Adams had found, after considerable experimentation, that a battery with unusual properties could be made from a positive electrode of magnesium, a negative electrode of cuprous chloride, and an electrolyte of water with a carbon catalyst. The battery was light in weight relative to its output. It could be activated in the field with impure water, even salt water. It produced a constant voltage and current throughout the period of its life. Once activated, the battery produced heat, which meant that it would continue to operate in extremely low temperatures. That a battery with these characteristics could be constructed was not suggested by anything previously known to the art. In fact, the scientists of the Army Signal Corps whom Adams tried to interest in his discovery at first thought it was not workable. Adams' battery was clearly non-obvious.

The Government, defendant in the infringement action in the Court of Claims, nevertheless argued for the invalidity of the patent. Not because anything in the prior art suggested that a battery with these characteristics could be built. But because the prior art suggested that a battery made of these materials was not new. The Government's brief spelled this out:[162]

> [I]f, as we submit, the combination of magnesium and cuprous chloride in the Adams battery was not patentable because it represented either no change or an insignificant change as compared to prior battery designs, the fact that, wholly unexpectedly, the battery showed certain valuable operating advantages over other batteries would certainly not justify a patent on the essentially old formula.

---

[160] *E.g.*, Ansonia Brass & Copper Co. v. Electrical Supply Co., 144 U.S. 11, 18 (1892); "[I]f an old device or process be put to a new use which is not analogous to the old one, and the adaption of such process to the new use is of such a character as to require the exercise of inventive skill to produce it, such new use will not be denied the merit of patentability."

[161] 383 U.S. 39 (1966).   [162] Brief for the United States, pp. 21–22.

Although the Government did not cite it,[163] the strongest case in support of the Government position was *General Electric Co. v. Jewel Incandescent Lamp Co.*[164] The Court in that case held a patent for an inside-frosted light bulb invalid. Earlier frosted light bulbs had either been frosted on the outside so that dirt collected in the crevices or on the inside which made them weak and easily broken. The patent in issue taught that if a bulb was frosted on the inside twice, the second etching treatment would increase the strength of the bulb because the angular crevices formed by the first frosting would be smoothed into saucer-shaped pits. Before this discovery, it was not known that a second treatment would strengthen the bulb, and the Court practically conceded that this characteristic was non-obvious. But the Court held the patent invalid on grounds of lack of novelty even though theretofore "electric bulbs had [not] been frosted on the interior with rounded rather than sharp angular crevices or pits."[165] The Court's reason was that the prior art revealed both the inside-frosted bulb and that double etching would affect the surface of the glass, although for decorative and light-diffusing purposes, not for strengthening purposes. A patent is invalid when "the prior art discloses the method of making an article having the characteristics of the patented product, though all the advantageous properties of the product had not been fully appreciated."[166]

The facts in the *Adams* case could easily have brought the patent within this rule. Not only would an elementary table of electrochemical characteristics have suggested a battery of magnesium and cuprous chloride, but a British patent of 1880 showed a battery with magnesium and cuprous chloride electrodes in a liquid electrolyte. The chief difference between the two batteries seems to be that the British patent showed the carbon in the cuprous chloride

---

163 The Government placed its chief reliance on Sinclair & Carroll Corp. v. Interchemical Co., 325 U.S. 327 (1945). That case held a patent on a printing ink invalid. The ink was developed through the use of solvents whose relevant characteristics could be obtained from the manufacturer's catalogue. Thus, unlike the battery in *Adams,* the properties of the ink were obvious to one skilled in the art. The Court distinguished the case on this ground. But it also said that "here [unlike *Sinclair*] . . . the Adams battery is shown to embrace elements having an interdependent functional relationship." 383 U.S. at 50. This language suggests that the Court was using the doctrine of aggregation to distinguish the cases, although one would have thought that the solvents in *Sinclair* also had such a relationship with the ink.

164 326 U.S. 242 (1945).   165 *Id.* at 248.   166 *Ibid.*

electrode rather than in the electrolyte. It was perfectly possible for the Court again to hold that lack of inventive novelty made the patent invalid even in the face of non-obviousness.

The Court did not do so. It found the patent valid. But not on the ground that simple novelty was enough. The Court dismissed the British patent on the ground that it had been shown to be inoperable, although there was no explanation of why the British patent was inoperable and the Adams patent highly useful. And it dismissed the contention that the Adams discovery simply involved the substitution of known electrochemical equivalents, and therefore was not new, on the ground that its characteristics were wholly unexpected. This seems to be the Court's way of saying that simple novelty is enough where non-obviousness is present. The *Adams* decision can and should be read as overruling the *General Electric Co.* case and holding that simple novelty is enough under § 101. If it is so read, the inventive novelty tests have no place under either § 101 or § 103.

IV. COMMERCIAL SUCCESS: THE COOK CASES

The elimination of the inventive novelty tests cannot be effected by a simple declaration. Tests based on inventive novelty so permeate the patent cases that it is necessary to analyze each test in terms of its relation to non-obviousness. That much work remains to be done was revealed in the *Cook Chemical Co.*[167] cases, which turned on the role to be assigned to commercial success and long-felt need in a determination of non-obviousness. The patent was for a hold-down cap on the pump-type sprayers so familiar to every American housewife. Before the development of the patented cap, it had been necessary to distribute the fluids in bottles with regular caps and the sprayer separately attached to the package. After purchase, the customer had to remove the cap and put the sprayer on the bottle. The sprayer, thus exposed, was subject to loss and breakage. The patented cap holds the pump in retracted position and provides a seal effective against even low viscosity insecticides, making it possible to ship the fluids with the sprayer on the bottle forming a compact, break-resistant unit. The cap is, as the description should indicate, a simple device. The district

---

[167] Decided together with Graham v. John Deere Co., 383 U.S. 1 (1966).

court found it patentable on the basis of evidence that for at least five years the industry had been aware of the need for a sprayer that could be shipped on the bottle and that once the patented device was developed, it was a commercial success. Citing the *Barbed Wire Patent* case, the court concluded that "the last step is the one that wins and he who takes it when others could not, is entitled to patent protection."[168] The Court of Appeals affirmed, observing that "instantaneous industry, as well as public acceptance of the device in issue, confirms our belief invention was produced."[169]

The Supreme Court held the patent invalid, answering that in this case factors such as commercial success and long-felt need did not "tip the scales of patentability."[170] The Court added, however, that "such inquiries may lend a helping hand to the judiciary which, as Mr. Justice Frankfurter observed, is most ill-fitted to discharge the technological duties cast upon it by patent legislation. . . . They may also serve to 'guard against slipping into hindsight,' . . . and to resist the temptation to read into the prior art the teachings of the invention in issue."[171] The effect of this language is to leave commercial success the role it has traditionally enjoyed. Even when rejecting commercial success in a particular case, the Court has almost always conceded that "commercial success may be decisive where invention is in doubt."[172]

But how is commercial success relevant to non-obviousness? The argument for commercial success is set out in a law review comment cited with apparent approval by the Court in *Cook*:[173]

> The possibility of market success attendant upon the solution of an existing problem may induce innovators to attempt a solution. If in fact a product attains a high degree of commercial success, there is a basis for inferring that such attempts have been made and have failed. Thus the rationale is similar to that

[168] 220 F. Supp. 414, 421 (W.D. Mo. 1963).

[169] 336 F.2d 110, 114 (8th Cir. 1964).   [170] 383 U.S. at 36.

[171] *Ibid.*, citing Marconi Wireless Co. v. United States, 320 U.S. 1, 60 (1943), and Monroe Auto Equip. Co. v. Heckethorn Mfg. & Supply Co., 332 F.2d 406, 412 (6th Cir. 1964).

[172] Textile Mach. Works v. Louis Hirsch Textile Mach., Inc., 302 U.S. 490, 498 (1938).

[173] *Subtests of "Nonobviousness": A Nontechnical Approach to Patent Validity*, 112 U. PA. L. REV. 1169, 1175 (1964).

of longfelt demand and is for the same reasons a legitimate test of invention.

This argument involves four inferences. First, that the commercial success is due to the innovation. Second, that if an improvement has in fact become commercially successful, it is likely that this potential commercial success was perceived before its development. Third, the potential commercial success having been perceived, it is likely that efforts were made to develop the improvement. Fourth, the efforts having been made by men of skill in the art, they failed because the patentee was the first to reduce his development to practice. Since men of skill in the art tried but failed, the improvement is clearly non-obvious.

Each inference is weak. The commercial success might not be due to the innovation but rather, as the petitioners in *Cook* argued, to "sales promotion ability, manufacturing technique, ready access to markets, consumer appeal design factors, and advertising budget."[174] But given the commercial success of the innovation, why is it likely that the commercial potential was perceived in advance? And why is it likely that because the commercial potential was perceived, men of skill began to work on the problems of that innovation as opposed to other potential improvements? And if men of skill start to work on the improvement, why does the fact that the patentee was first to perfect the improvement mean the others failed? Perhaps they were only a little slower. This seems a fragile thread on which to hang a conclusion of non-obviousness, particularly in a case where the patentee shows only commercial success but does not show that the commercial potential was perceived or that attempts actually were made that failed. How, then, does commercial success constitute a helping hand? The Court said that "these legal inferences or subtests do focus attention on economic and motivational rather than technical issues and are, therefore, more susceptible of judicial treatment than are the highly technical facts often present in patent litigation."[175] Perhaps commercial success is a familiar distraction for judges confused by the facts.

It is not difficult to see why lawyers for patent owners are eager to introduce evidence of commercial success. By introducing evidence of commercial success the lawyer is telling the judge that his client's patent is very valuable and that if the judge holds the patent

---

[174] Brief for Petitioner Calmar, p. 30.   [175] 383 U.S. at 35–36.

invalid he is destroying expectations of great value. This is not an argument without persuasiveness. The Supreme Court itself was once led to recognize an exclusive right simply because the plaintiff's right was valuable and he had created it.[176] When Walker suggested to the courts that they should resolve borderline cases on the basis of commercial success, he was really saying, "Decide all of the borderline cases where the patent is worth something in favor of the patentee, decide all the other borderline cases against the patentee." Since it is unlikely that patents that are not commercially successful will be brought to litigation, this amounts to a suggestion that borderline cases be decided in favor of patentees. In fact, if one is willing to infer from the litigation itself that the patent is valuable because it is worth litigating, and that since it is valuable it must be commercially successful, one ends up with the rule that all patents that are litigated should be held valid.[177]

If commercial success is a relevant "economic issue," then one can argue that it should be a factor weighing against patentability in borderline cases. Commercially successful patents are the ones that truly impose a monopoly tax on the market, and therefore courts should be even more cautious in holding them valid. Furthermore, it is in the area of innovations that quickly meet consumer acceptance that the innovator has the best chance of recovering his special costs without a patent monopoly. The chances of doing this in any particular case depend, of course, on the good-will advantages of being first and the speed with which potential competitors can enter. But the more quickly a substantial market can be developed and its profit returns enjoyed, the greater (as a general rule) would seem to be the advantages accruing to the innovator who enters the market first. He will not need extensive market development that will alert potential competitors before the profits begin. Thus, in the area of the commercially successful improvement quickly recognized by the market, a patent is less likely to

---

176 See International News Service v. Associated Press, 248 U.S. 215 (1918). Use of commercial success as a basis for validity in patent cases reached its peak in Temco Elec. Motor Co. v. Apco Mfg. Co., 275 U.S. 319, 328 (1928), where the Court reversed a holding of invalidity because the patent's "usefulness was demonstrated by ten years' use in such large numbers and by such profitable business."

177 Cf. Diamond Rubber Co. v. Consolidated Rubber Tire Co., 220 U.S. 428, 441 (1911): ". . . the utility of a device may be attested by the litigation over it, as litigation 'shows and measures the existence of the public demand for its use.'" See also Eames v. Andrews, 122 U.S. 40, 47 (1887).

be necessary to evoke the improvement. The argument assumes, of course, that the commercial potential is perceived in advance by the innovator so that it can affect his decision to develop the innovation. This is not necessarily so, but the same assumption is made by the traditional argument for commercial success as a factor favoring a finding of invention. At the very least, these two arguments should cancel each other and leave commercial success with no role to play in a non-obviousness inquiry.

Commercial success entered the picture because it was relevant to the issue of inventive novelty.[178] If an innovation is received by the commercial community as a substantial improvement, it is hardly for the courts to hold that it is only a trivial advance. "[I]f there be anything material and new," said an often quoted English judge in 1785, "which is an improvement of the trade, that will be sufficient to support a patent."[179] In 1849, a federal district judge explained to a jury that the higher the degree of utility, the stronger the evidence that "some new principle, or mechanical power, or mode of operation, producing a new kind of result, has been introduced."[180] "It is said," reported Curtis, "that whenever utility is proved to exist in a very great degree a sufficiency of invention to support a patent must be presumed."[181] The Supreme Court, citing the same authority as Curtis—an essay by an English writer[182] —recognized the doctrine in 1877.

In *Smith v. Goodyear Dental Vulcanite Co.*[183] the defendants contended that the plaintiff's patent for denture plates of hard rubber was invalid because it simply involved a change of materials. Justice Strong rejected this contention, writing of the merits of the plaintiff's teeth as if he himself had acquired a pair: "It was capable of being perfectly fitted to the roof and alveolar processes of the mouth. It was easy for the wearer, and favorable for perfect

---

178 This relationship was spelled out in Strobridge v. Lindsay, Sterritt & Co., 2 Fed. 692 (C.C. W.D. Pa. 1880). The case was decided at a time when the federal trial courts were still applying the test of inventive novelty alone.

179 Rex v. Arkwright, 1 Webs. Pat. Cas. 64, 71 (K.B. 1785) (Buller, J.).

180 Many v. Sizer, 16 Fed. Cas. 684, 688 (No. 9,056) (C.C. D. Mass. 1849).

181 Curtis, *op. cit. supra* note 48, at 37.

182 Webster, *On the Subject Matter of Letters-Patent for Inventions,* reprinted as an appendix to Curtis, *op. cit. supra* note 48, at 521 (2d ed.).

183 93 U.S. 486 (1877).

articulation. It was light and elastic, yet sufficiently strong and firm for purposes of mastication."[184] Observing that many thousands of "operators" were using the new improvement in preference to older devices, he concluded that "all this is sufficient . . . to justify the inference that what Cummings [the inventor] accomplished was more than substitution of one material for another; more than the exercise of mechanical judgment and taste [sic];—that it was, in truth, invention."[185]

Fifteen years later, the Court reversed its position and rejected commercial success: "If the generality of sales were made the test of patentability, it would result that a person by securing a patent upon some trifling variation from previously known methods might, by energy in pushing sales or by superiority in finishing or decorating his goods, drive competitors out of the market and secure a practical monopoly, without in fact having made the slightest contribution of value to the useful arts."[186] But when the Court upheld the barbed wire patent, it laid heavy emphasis on the widespread use of the improvement covered by the patent.[187] Although commercial success has often been rejected in particular cases, its general relevance has never again been questioned.

Like new result, commercial success passed into the potpourri of the law of invention without any attempt to relate it to non-obviousness. If the Court is going to follow the logical implications of its approach in *Deere*, it will be necessary to reject commercial success as a standard, not only in particular cases but generally. It only distracts judges from the issue of validity and draws their attention to the value of the patent. Unlike actual proof of long-felt need or efforts that failed, it is not a relevant "motivational or economic" issue.

V. PROBLEMS FOR THE FUTURE: THE PRIOR ART

Should the Court be willing to pursue the implications of *Deere* and focus the issue of invention on an inquiry into non-obviousness, subsidiary tests of invention unrelated to non-obviousness must be rejected. Tests so old and so familiar will not disappear

---

[184] *Id.* at 494.   [185] *Id.* at 495.

[186] McClain v. Ortmayer, 141 U.S. 419, 428 (1891).

[187] The Barbed Wire Patent, 143 U.S. 275, 282–84 (1892).

unless the Court subjects each one to the inquiry: what does this test have to do with non-obviousness?

Given the present state of the law on invention, this will constitute a substantial departure. But it is, in fact, only a beginning not an end. It should help the courts to concentrate on the resolution of the factual issues instead of relying on inherited, irrelevant doctrinal crutches. But the test of non-obviousness is not without its own difficulties. The Court said in *Deere:* "Under § 103, the scope and content of the prior art are to be determined; differences between the prior art and the claims at issue are to be ascertained; and the level of ordinary skill in the pertinent art resolved."[188] Although the resolution of these factual issues is often difficult, the issues themselves are reasonably clear. But underlying each of the three steps there is one central problem that has never really been faced: the meaning of the "pertinent art." This is a crucial issue because it plays a double role: it determines both the relevant prior subject matter and relevant level of skill. Nevertheless, it has barely been touched on in the cases or the secondary literature.

There are, at least, two possible approaches. One is to define the "pertinent art" as the art of the industry for which the innovation is designed. This can be called the "product-function" approach. The second is to define the "pertinent art" as the art of dealing with the kind of problem which the innovation is designed to solve. This is the "problem-solving" approach.

To illustrate. In *Cook* the basic, unarticulated premise of the patentee-respondent was that the relevant art was the "shipper-sprayer" industry. Since Calmar, an important member of this industry, had worked unsuccessfully for ten years to produce an integrated breakage-resistant sprayer, it was beyond argument, the patentee contended, that the development of such a successful device was non-obvious. "Either the technicians employed by Calmar to solve the problem did not possess ordinary skill in the art or the subject matter of the Scoggin patent was not obvious at the time the invention was made to persons possessing such skill."[189] The patentee dismissed the first possibility facetiously, citing the testimony of the president that the company had "'for a good many years a number of good, clever people' engaged in research

---

[188] 383 U.S. at 17.

[189] Brief for Respondent, pp. 33–34.

efforts."[190] Indeed, this conception of the pertinent art was so narrow that he argued that a patent for a seal on a cover for a pouring spout "had nothing to do with a sprayer."[191]

Colgate argued for a somewhat broader art, but gave the same kind of definition: "the art of making dispensers for liquids in containers for household use."[192] Rejecting the contention that a patent relating to a pouring spout was not pertinent art, the Court offered a definition of the pertinent art different from that advanced by either side. "The problems confronting Scoggin and the insecticide industry were not insecticide problems; they were mechanical closure problems."[193] The Court defined the pertinent art, not in terms of the industry or the type of product, but in terms of the kind of problem that the patent was designed to solve.

The product-function approach to the prior art is compatible with the inventive novelty test. If the issue is whether the device is new, the sensible place to look for anticipation is in the industry where it is used. It is also the implicit concept of the art that lies behind the commercial success test. If the innovation was commercially successful in the industry it must be new to the industry, and since the industry is the relevant "art" it is patentable. It is the concept of the art that lies behind the Patent Office classification system: "[T]he characteristic selected as the basis of classification is that of essential function or effect. Arts or instruments having like functions, producing like products, or achieving like effects are brought together."[194]

There is a basic difficulty with the product-function approach to the definition of the art when it is used in conjunction with the non-obviousness test. It can be called the problem of the dumb art. The respondent in *Cook* raised this problem when he facetiously suggested that Calmar's technicians might not have possessed ordinary skill in the art. The respondent could flippantly dismiss this possibility because Calmar was such an important part of the consumer pump-sprayer industry. But suppose Calmar's technicians were in fact incompetent to develop a satisfactory breakage-resistant sprayer? Should the innovation be patentable because the industry is staffed by unskilled men? The product-function ap-

---

[190] *Id.* at 34.

[191] *Id.* at 25.

[192] Brief for Petitioner Colgate, p. 4.

[193] 383 U.S. at 35.

[194] U.S. Patent Office, Manual of Classification 1 (1964).

proach would suggest that it should be. But if patents are viewed in relation to their economic function this is an unsettling result. In terms of economic purpose, the idea behind the non-obviousness test is to evaluate the magnitude of the costs involved in a given innovation. What are the costs of a development that is non-obvious only to the dumb industry? They are the costs of hiring the personnel with the skill to deal with the problems in need of solution. If the solution to the problems is indeed obvious to the person with skill in the art concerned with solving them, these costs should not be very great. A patent hardly seems necessary in order to enable the innovator to recover his costs.

A recent example of a case where the traditional approach to the definition of the pertinent art was carried to its logical extreme is *Abington Textile Machinery Works v. Carding Specialists Ltd.*[195] The patent in suit was for an improvement in cotton-carding machinery. The improvement consisted of an addition to the machine of a pair of rollers that would crush impurities in the cotton, causing the impurities to fall out at later stages in the processing. A professor in the School of Textiles at North Carolina State College testified for the parties attacking the patent that at the time the invention was made it would have been obvious to him. The district court dismissed this testimony on the grounds the professor was a man of extraordinary skill in the art. The question, said the district court, was whether the improvement would "have been obvious in 1957 to a person having ordinary skill in the art, namely, a typical card operator in a fine cotton processing mill."[196] Clearly, there is a great deal of difference between the "art" of the men who actually operate the machines and the "art" of the men who concern themselves with the design and effective operation of textile-processing machinery. If the "pertinent art" is the first, then the Court was clearly right in dismissing the professor's testimony. But if the art is the art of solving problems in textile processing, then perhaps the professor really was a man of ordinary skill in that art. The crucial issue in the case was whether similar crushing rollers used in different processing systems—woolen, worsted, and cotton-condenser systems—made the use of the rollers

---

[195] 249 F. Supp. 823 (D. D.C. 1965). An older example is *In re* Peddrick, 48 F.2d 415 (C. C. P. A. 1931).

[196] 249 F. Supp. at 829.

in a fine cotton-processing system obvious. The chief difference between the other uses of crushing rollers and the use in the patent in suit was that the earlier uses put the crushing rollers in place before further carding operations. The parties attacking the validity of the patent argued that "since the conventional single cylinder cotton carding machine used in fine cotton mills provides a web at only one location,"[197] and since the crushing rollers had to be applied to a web, it was obvious to locate them where the innovation in issue did. The court dismissed this on the grounds that it was obvious only after one had decided to use crushing rollers in such a machine. The court assumed that the innovation must be obvious, not to one trying to improve cotton processing, but to the day-to-day operator of the machinery.

Defining the art in terms of the problem to be solved also has its difficulties. If the relevant art is the art of inventing, all inventions become obvious because the improvement was obvious to its inventor. This definitional quandary clearly appears in the design-patent cases. Design patents are an archaic survival of the nineteenth-century view that copyright did not provide a basis for design protection. They do, however, provide some examples of the problems of the non-obviousness test. So long as the only requirement was that the design be new, the concept of an inventive design patent was not inherently absurd.[198] But it is impossible to apply the non-obviousness test. In desperation the courts have fallen back on distinguishing between the designs of genius and designs not of genius,[199] which reduces to an attempt to discriminate between good art and bad art. The application of the test requires that there be a craft with norms of problem solving whose skills are reasonably widely known and which are directed to the solution of the type of problems the innovation in question is designed to solve. To advance a tentative definition of the "pertinent art," it is the art to which one can reasonably be expected to look for a solution to the problem which the patented device attempts to solve.

[197] *Id.* at 834.

[198] See, *e.g.,* Untermeyer v. Freund, 37 Fed. 342 (C.C. S.D. N.Y. 1889); Smith v. Stewart, 55 Fed. 481 (C.C. E.D. Pa. 1893).

[199] General Time Instruments Corp. v. United States Time Corp., 165 F.2d 853, 854 (2d Cir. 1948); "In short, the test is whether the design involved a step beyond the prior art requiring what is termed 'inventive genius.' "

This is the definition of the pertinent art that the Supreme Court adopted in *Cook*.

This definition raises two issues. First, what of the device that solves no problem? Is it non-obvious? Second, what of the innovation where the solution was obvious but the existence of the problem was not?

The first difficulty is only of theoretical curiosity. And there is no need to confront this rhetorically plausible problem. The device is not patentable for lack of utility. The Court only recently reaffirmed the requirement that utility is necessary for patentability,[200] so that every patentable device must respond, with some degree of success, to some need.

The second difficulty is an important one. The case that provides the most useful example of the problem is *Great Atlantic & Pacific Tea Co. v. Supermarket Equipment Corp.*[201] That case turned on the validity of a patent for a counter extension and frame used to pull groceries along a checkout counter. The frame was simplicity itself, made of three pieces of wood fastened together and a handle to enable the cash register operator to pull it forward along the counter. The evidence in the record showed that the patentee, a district supervisor for a supermarket chain, had developed it in a short period of time after being confronted with the need to be able to handle more customers in one of his stores that lacked adequate space to install an additional checkout counter.[202] The Court chose to speak in terms of inventive novelty and found the device lacked invention on the grounds that it was an aggregation that performed no new function. This conclusion was contrary to the facts. But the conclusion of the Court that the device lacked invention is nonetheless proper. Surely the device was an obvious solution to the problem of speeding up the flow of customers through the checkout lane. But the evidence also suggested that what had not been obvious to the industry was

---

200 Brenner v. Manson, 383 U.S. 519 (1966).

201 340 U.S. 147 (1950), *reversing* 179 F.2d 636 (6th Cir. 1950).

202 The Court did not note this fact. The Court of Appeals described the patentee as an employee "who was assigned the task of solving the problem" of speeding up the flow of customers in the checkout lane. 179 F.2d at 636. This gives the impression that the development was the result of a concerted effort to solve a perceived problem. In fact, the patentee-employee was assigned to solve the "problem" of an unhappy store manager, if necessary by the installation of an additional counter. Record, p. 55.

the problem about the rate of flow through checkout lanes, or that it might be possible to improve it. The contribution of the patentee was the recognition of the need to improve the flow and a willingness to investigate the problem. The problem was surely non-obvious to an industry that had ignored it for years. And if the problem was non-obvious, why was its solution not also non-obvious, since there can be no solution without a problem? A traditional verbal answer to this contention in patent law has been that the patent is on the solution, not the problem, and therefore the solution must contain the "invention" or the non-obvious element.[203] But there is a serious economic argument for this position as well. The patent law is designed to induce innovations that would not otherwise appear in a competitive system. The prospect of a patent gives the innovator the assurance that if he is successful he will make profits, and this prospect of profits makes the expenditures on experimentation, whether they be expenditures of time or money or both, a reasonable investment. But before the prospect of a patent can begin to operate in this fashion, the person must have been confronted with the decision whether to innovate or not. If he has no knowledge that there is a problem to be solved, he is hardly in a position to decide whether or not to try solving it. Once he has a perception that there is a problem, no matter how general that perception may be, he is then in a position to decide whether to expend time and money to solve it. And only if he is confronted with such a decision, can the prospect of a patent have any role to play. So when an innovation results merely from the perception of a problem, rather than the working-out of a non-obvious solution, no patent should issue. That seems a sensible way to state the holding of the *Supermarket Equipment Corp.* case. And if that is so, the situation creates no difficulty for the tendered definition of the "pertinent art," because every patentable innovation must be responsive to a problem.

VI. THE COURT'S RESPONSIBILITY

Deere, Adams, and *Cook* are hopeful signs that the courts will begin to work out the implications of the non-obviousness test that have been ignored. If the courts begin to face and solve

---

[203] Robinson stated that the idea generated by the mental part of the inventive act must be "an idea of means as distinguished from an idea of end." ROBINSON, *op. cit. supra* note 34, at 155.

these analytic issues, the administration of § 103 should be made easier. But the Supreme Court did not think the problem of § 103 was one for the courts at all. "[I]t must be remembered," said the Court, "that the primary responsibility for sifting out unpatentable material lies in the Patent Office. To wait litigation is—for all practical purposes—to debilitate the patent system. We have observed a notorious difference between the standards applied by the Patent Office and by the courts."[204] Although gentler in language, this criticism of the Patent Office is in the tradition of the attack on the office made by Mr. Justice Douglas in his concurring opinion in the *Supermarket Equipment Corp.* case.[205] This attack accuses the Patent Office of ruining the patent system because of its failure to apply the invention requirement with sufficient rigor. The problem with this statement is not that it is untrue but that it is unwise. The Court should be more sensitive to the roots of its power even in so small a matter. Can the Court seriously expect men who have dedicated themselves to the operation of the Patent Office and the patent system to respond warmly to the charge that they have debilitated the patent system? Yet the co-operation of these men is essential if there is going to be any change in Patent Office practice.

The usual complaint is that the Patent Office issues many patents that are invalid under § 103. This appears to be true, but how does it debilitate the system? The explanation offered is that each of the invalid patents issued is a "license to litigate" which can be used as a "threat" to "coerce" weaker competitiors into submission. The problem is presently receiving serious attention from the Antitrust Division, which has filed a suit against the Minnesota Mining and Manufacturing Company charging abuse of patents in this manner.[206] But if the patents are invalid, how are they such an effective threat? The answer is that the defense of an infringement suit, even if the patent is held invalid, is expensive and that the patentee can always offer a settlement cheaper than the litigation costs. A leading patent lawyer has estimated the costs for

---

[204] 383 U.S. at 18.   [205] 340 U.S. at 154.

[206] United States v. Minnesota Mining & Mfg. Co., Civ. No. 66C627 (N.D. Ill. April 7, 1966). "According to the suit, the company has attempted to control the industries by systematic coercion of competitors, through suits or threatened suits for patent infringement, to accept illegal patent license agreements." 5 TRADE REG. REP. ¶ 45,066 (1966).

each side in a patent infringement suit at a minimum of $50,000.[207] Invalid patents, in the hands of unscrupulous and powerful men, are worth money. This debilitates the patent system because it makes patents the vehicles for suppression of competition rather than the reward for invention.

But why is it so expensive to defend a patent suit? The answer is twofold. First, there are endless procedural devices in the hands of a patent holder willing to use them. And, second, the factual issues in patent cases are made unnecessarily complex by the doctrinal difficulties of the invention requirement. These are not the fault of the Patent Office. If fault is the appropriate word, surely Congress and the Supreme Court must share the blame.

A determined patent holder is in a position to keep relitigating the validity of his patent against the infringing manufacturer and his customers. These suits can be brought in every part of the country.[208] Motions under § 1404(a) for transfer and consolidation can be made, ruled on, and taken to the courts of appeals.[209] The factual issues are "complicated" and summary judgment is seldom available. Discovery procedures can be used to increase the costs that a patent-infringement action inflicts on the defendant. The Supreme Court must bear some responsibility for failing to keep these abuses in check.

For fifteen years the Supreme Court failed to take cases raising the issue of non-obviousness. Differences have arisen among the circuits, encouraging litigants to engage in complex maneuvering to get in the "right" court. It is traditionally said that the facts in patent cases are extremely complicated. This is not true. The facts in patent cases, as in any other class of cases, are sometimes com-

---

[207] Statement of Tom Arnold, Chairman, Section on Patent, Trademark, and Copyright Law, The American Bar Association, *Hearings before the Subcommittee on Patents, Trademarks, and Copyrights of the Senate Committee on the Judiciary on S.789, S.1809 and S.1899,* 89th Cong., 1st Sess., pt. 1, 268, 271 (1965): "Patent infringement suits cost at a minimum on the order of $50,000, and they go up from there. They go away up from there."

[208] 28 U.S.C. § 1400 provides for venue where "the defendant has committed acts of infringement and has a regular and established place of business." In the case of an infringing product sold throughout the country, the provision permits suit to be brought almost anywhere.

[209] I have discussed these problems elsewhere. Kitch, *Section 1404(a) of the Judicial Code: In the Interest of Justice or Injustice,* 40 IND. L.J. 99 (1965). They are particularly troublesome in patent cases.

plicated and sometimes simple. *Deere, Adams,* and *Cook* are examples of cases in which the facts themselves are simple and easily understood. But even simple facts become complicated if there are no controlling legal principles around which they can be organized. In a case as simple as *Deere* two circuits differed on the validity of the patent, not because they differed on the facts, but because they differed regarding the law. These failures of the Court are perhaps minor when one considers the heavy responsibilities that it has in other more important areas. But it ill becomes the Court, whose own performance in the area has suffered from lack of interest, to castigate the Patent Office for "debilitating" the patent system.

The Patent Office has remained insensitive to the requirement that invention must be shown for patentability because it applies the "inventive novelty" law that was in force prior to 1875. The basic question for a Patent Office examination is whether the device is new. The primary effort of the examiner is to have the claims narrowed so that they only read on what is new in the development. There seem to be two important reasons for this apparent disregard of the invention requirement. The first lies in the history of the Patent Office and the law. The Patent Office as presently organized has been an on-going institution since 1836. During the first thirty-nine years of its life, it quite appropriately applied the controlling law of inventive novelty. Since that time its internal traditions have perpetuated the approach. This tendency has been condoned by the Supreme Court, which never, until *Deere,* suggested that the inventive novelty approach was inconsistent with non-obviousness. The second reason is the organization of the Patent Office itself. Because of the heavy backlog of applications there is pressure on examiners to dispose of them. If an examiner approves the application, the matter is closed. If he denies it, the applicant has a right of appeal up through the Patent Office to the Court of Customs and Patent Appeals and now to the Supreme Court.[210] Such an appeal places additional burdens on the office. At the very least, it is considered undesirable for an examiner to be reversed once an appeal is taken.[211] In this situation even a

[210] Brenner v. Manson, 383 U.S. 519 (1966), established the existence of certiorari jurisdiction over the Court of Customs and Patent Appeals.

[211] See Stedman, *The U.S. Patent System and Its Current Problems,* 42 TEXAS L. REV. 450, 463–64 (1964).

conscientious examiner is unlikely to reject an application unless he is sure of his ground. A rejection for lack of novelty is relatively stable ground. If something is not new, it is hard for the applicant to argue that it is. But a rejection on grounds of non-obviousness is shakier because it may involve differences in judgment between the examiner and the review board.

It is even possible to argue that it is not the duty of the Patent Office to screen out non-obvious patents. Why should not the Patent Office concentrate on weeding out those applications that do not involve new developments? When a patent is granted on an innovation, it assures that information about it is placed on the public record. At the Patent Office stage in the proceedings it is difficult to predict whether the patent will ever be important or the subject of controversy. The *ex parte* proceeding of the Patent Office is not the best forum in which fully to ventilate the validity issue.[212] If the validity issue is determined negatively, the information about the innovation is never placed on the public record. Why should the resources necessary to make the non-obviousness determination be expended unless the validity of the patent actually matters? Once it matters, the courts can provide a forum in which the validity issue can be litigated. Although this is not the system contemplated by the statute, it has long been the *de facto* system in American patent law.[213] And it would work, if the courts provided a reasonably efficient and conclusive forum

---

[212] In Walker Process Equip., Inc. v. Food Mach. & Chem. Co., 382 U.S. 172 (1965), the Court held that the enforcement of a patent obtained by fraud on the Patent Office is actionable under the Sherman Act. If "fraud" is interpreted to include negligent failures to cite prior art, the decision should have an impact on the amount of prior art brought to the examiner's attention. But it may not be wise to reform Patent Office procedure by using the threat of a punitive statute to force the applicant to be his own adversary.

[213] The Court of Customs and Patent Appeals and the Patent Office recognize this in the "rule of doubt." This rule is that in cases of doubt concerning patentability, the doubt should be resolved in favor of the applicant. "There are very sound policy reasons underlying the rule applied in this court, and supposedly in the Patent Office, that doubts are to be resolved in favor of applicants. Several of the factors properly taken into account in determining patentability, especially unobviousness and utility, are often not known at the time when the application is being prosecuted in the Patent Office but are developed later, perhaps even after the patent is issued. It therefore is proper that doubt should be resolved in favor of applicants so that they shall not be denied patents which later events may show them entitled to." *In re* Hofstetter, 150 U.S.P.Q. 105, 109 (C. C. P. A. 1966).

for the adjudication of validity. The present statutory framework makes this difficult for the courts, but they have not done their best to maximize their effectiveness even within this framework.

Deere points in the direction of removing complicating doctrinal irrelevancies and returning patent law to the relative simplicity of the statute. It is a significant step toward the improvement of the patent system if the courts are willing to insist that the inquiry be focused on the statutory test of non-obviousness. It is perfectly possible for the tradition-minded reader to interpret the opinions in *Deere*, *Adams*, and *Cook* as simply continuing past doctrine.[214] The myth of *Hotchkiss v. Greenwood* seems to be part of an even larger myth in patent law—the myth that invention decisions differ only on the "facts" or the "attitude" of the court, but that they all embody the same law. The courts ought not permit this myth to overtake *Deere*.

---

[214] See Brumbaugh, *The Standard of Patentability Now*, 21 RECORD 291 (1966). Brumbaugh reads *Adams* as continuing the inventive novelty tests under § 101 and views § 103 as simply an additional negative test. This is, of course, the scheme of the Walker treatise.

KENNETH W. DAM

FORTNER ENTERPRISES v.

UNITED STATES STEEL:

"NEITHER A BORROWER,

NOR A LENDER BE"

The Supreme Court handed down an impressive number of important antitrust decisions in its 1968–69 Term. Some, such as the *Container* case,[1] will be remembered as major contributions to steadily evolving antitrust doctrine. *Fortner Enterprises, Inc. v. United States Steel Corp.*,[2] in contrast, was merely bizarre. But bizarre cases can be important.

The importance of *Fortner* rests more in the reasoning of the majority than in any positive contributions to antitrust doctrine. This reasoning permitted conventional legal principles to be used to reach an unexpected result. The decision cast a legal shadow on a practice that had not hitherto been thought subject to antitrust challenge—the provision of credit by a supplier on condition that

Kenneth W. Dam is Professor of Law, The University of Chicago.

[1] United States v. Container Corp. of America, 393 U.S. 333 (1969). The decision represents a further evolution of the rule against horizontal price-fixing and price-tampering agreements. The broadest reading of *Container* is that the exchange of current price information among competitors is illegal per se. Whether Mr. Justice Douglas' majority opinion announces a per se rule is an issue on which other Supreme Court Justices are divided. Compare Mr. Justice Fortas' concurring opinion with Mr. Justice Marshall's dissent.

[2] 394 U.S. 495 (1969).

the credit be used to purchase the supplier's goods. Not only the antitrust bar but the lower courts in the *Fortner* case were surprised by the Supreme Court disposition. The district court had decided for the defendant in an unhesitant, straightforward opinion. The court of appeals, affirming, had not even bothered to write an opinion. But Mr. Justice Black, speaking for a five-man majority, saw nothing unusual about the case. All that he found necessary to support reversal was the application of a short list of well-established antitrust principles.

Perhaps the most interesting question posed by *Fortner* is why the Supreme Court decision engendered surprise. Is it to be explained by the inability of the bar and the lower federal courts to reason logically from principle to result? Or is *Fortner* an example, par excellence, of a Supreme Court tendency to spawn simplistic rules—rules that increasingly permit a court so inclined to find antitrust violations at will in complex business arrangements, without the need to consider economic consequences?

If the second interpretation is correct, a number of implications command attention. When the courts have enough per se principles available to them to find both anticompetitive and procompetitive practices illegal, it is unlikely that all courts will readily use those principles on all occasions. Some judges will choose not to find illegality in arrangements that, to them, make sense for the economy as a whole. Decisions will thus become less predictable.

The Antitrust Division and the Federal Trade Commission will also have increased discretion. They will not be able to prosecute in every case, or indeed in any significant percentage of the cases, where illegality might be found. Such expanded prosecutorial discretion might be welcomed. Those who think that the purpose of the antitrust laws is to promote competition might be prepared to rely on the government (or at least the Antitrust Division) to prosecute only where a threat to competition actually exists.

So sanguine a view overlooks the rapidly expanding institution of the treble-damage antitrust action. A legal system that relies on prosecutorial discretion for the sensible application of overly stringent, undiscriminating prohibitions cannot function well when private attorneys-general are accorded massive financial incentives for not exercising equal restraint. The private treble-damage plaintiff has no interest in determining the impact on competition of the practices challenged. Indeed, where, as in the usual case, the defendant is a competitor or supplier, the plaintiff will often be seeking through litigation to offset the consequences of competition. Moreover, since the treble-damage plaintiff's transactions may be de minimis when viewed in the context of an industry as a whole, he will often have every incentive to direct the court's attention away from the underlying economic questions.

I. A Look at the Record

It is no coincidence that *Fortner* was a treble-damage action. The facts of the case throw light on the incentives of private plaintiffs and provide an essential background for an appreciation of how, as in *Fortner*, per se rules operate in private antitrust litigation.

The United States Steel Corporation had entered the business of manufacturing prefabricated houses. Through its Homes Division it sold house components in "home packages" to real estate builders and developers, who erected the houses on the home site for resale to the general public. In order to promote sales, like the vendors of many other products in the modern economy, U.S. Steel found it necessary to offer credit to purchasers. To that end in 1954 it created a wholly owned subsidiary, U.S. Steel Homes Credit Corporation. Since houses are located on land and the typical developer has to seek financing for the land during the period of construction, the Credit Corporation introduced the practice of financing not only the houses but also the land, pending sale of each house and lot.

U.S. Steel's venture into the housing market did not achieve unlimited success. For example, one of the markets where it was interested in establishing itself was Louisville, Kentucky, strategically located just across the Ohio River from the Homes Division plant in New Albany, Indiana. Despite the transportation cost advantages that such proximity might afford, however, the Homes Division had been singularly unsuccessful in penetrating the Louisville market. Although in 1957 it had succeeded in selling thirteen houses in Jefferson County (an area which included Louisville and environs), it had sold only two in 1958 and none at all in 1959.[3]

What the Homes Division obviously needed was a first-rate real estate developer in the Louisville area who could make a success

---

[3] Record, pp. 149a, 184a.

of a U.S. Steel homes subdivision. In late 1959 they thought they had located their man—A. B. Fortner, Jr., the president of Zettwoch Fortner Corporation and a successful real estate developer who had been in the business in Louisville since 1939.[4] Fortner not only had ability, but he also had the land on which to construct the homes. He held this land with a partner in another corporation, Iroquois Development, Inc. After negotiations between Homes Division salesmen and Fortner, it was decided that an appeal would be made to the Credit Corporation to finance the buying out of the partner's one-half interest in the land. Such financing would also help Fortner to realize, prior to sale of the completed homes to the public, at least part of the considerable increase in the value of the land in the five years since its purchase.[5]

Another Fortner corporation was to be the recipient of the loan and would use the proceeds to buy the land from Iroquois Development. This third Fortner corporation, Fortner Enterprises, Inc., was well suited to the purpose because it had an accumulated deficit for tax purposes of about $16,000.[6] Under the proposal made by the Homes Division sales department to the Credit Corporation, the latter would advance $151,950 of which $111,900 would be used to buy the land from Iroquois Development. Of the additional $96,000 that would be required to develop the yet undeveloped lots, the loan proceeds would cover $40,050 and the remaining $55,950 would be Fortner's equity in the land during the construction period.[7] This arrangement, in which the Credit Corporation would provide $151,950 of the $207,900 of the total purchase and development cost of the land, was somewhat in excess, but still within reach, of the 60 percent that was, under the Credit Corporation's announced policy, the maximum it would normally finance.[8]

---

[4] *Id.* at 385a–388a.

[5] The land had been purchased as farmland some five years previously at $1,100 an acre, but in the meantime the surrounding area had been partially built up by other developers, and utilities had been made available. Consequently, the still undeveloped land was now worth $1,100 a lot. The development averaged nearly four lots per acre. *Id.* at 313a–314a, 386a–387a, 392a.

[6] *Id.* at 295a. Fortner Enterprises, Inc., was inactive. The custom in the industry was to use a new corporation for each new subdivision, thereby limiting liability in the event of an unsuccessful project. *Id.* at 379a.

[7] Memorandum dated December 22, 1959. *Id.* at 385a–389a.

[8] *Id.* at 373a–379a.

Following the Homes Division recommendation on December 22, 1959, a meeting was scheduled for January 8, 1960, at which Fortner, Homes Division representatives, and Credit Corporation representatives were to discuss the loan. Fortner came to the meeting, however, with a totally new proposal. Whereas the original proposal had covered only 99 lots, Fortner's new proposal covered 186 lots, again all property of Iroquois Development. Fortner stated that he was prepared to proceed only if the Credit Corporation would finance the full cost of the 155 lots that were undeveloped ($170,500) plus the cost of their development ($139,500) and that, as his equity, he would put up 31 developed lots (valued at $62,000). In this version, as in the December version, it was assumed that the Credit Corporation would in addition finance Fortner's purchase of the home packages themselves.

Since Fortner's demands far exceeded the 60 percent guideline, Credit Corporation executives were unhappy. No final arrangements were made.[9] In March, moreover, Fortner demanded that the proposed land note bear a two-year maturity rather than the twelve-to-eighteen-month maturity theretofore discussed. When the Credit Corporation urged as an alternative a reduction of the number of lots to be covered by the financing, Fortner refused.[10] Further complications developed when Fortner's partner decided that the proposed transaction was too attractive for him to bow out. That hurdle was eventually surmounted, but the negotiations continued until September when the Credit Corporation finally agreed "to provide 100% financing for the purchase and development of the land in question."[11]

In October, 1960, the loan agreement was signed. It called for

---

[9] *Id*. at 634a. The president of the Credit Corporation complained to a subordinate that "the Fortner loan on the new basis is an extreme" and reminded him of the dangers involved: "With all our money out front, he has very little incentive to finish off a project. . . . In making this statement, it is not the financial risk aspects which are referred to, but rather the fact that the loan will not produce house sales. The worst thing that can happen is an unsuccessful development. This precludes, in most cases, any other house sales in that area, because the one we have there has been unsuccessful." Memorandum dated January 12, 1960. *Ibid*.

[10] *Id*. at 393a–394a.

[11] *Id*. at 290a. The language is the characterization given the transaction by Fortner in an affidavit.

land notes for $88,000 and $231,920 bearing 6 percent interest.[12] The loan agreement also called for construction notes for $373,200 and $1,362,180, also bearing interest at 6 percent.[13] Apparently neither of the latter two notes, which were to finance purchase of the house components from the Home Division and their subsequent erection on the land, represented "100% financing."

The following May, Fortner, having already sold at least 35 homes and having acquired additional land through his Iroquois Development corporation, sought an additional land loan for $54,000, to acquire 32 additional lots, and an additional construction loan of $462,000.[14] Since some $30,000 of the requested land loan was to be used to replenish working capital, the Credit Corporation representative explained to Fortner that "expenditures of this nature are normally borne by all builders and in many instances represents [sic] about the only risk capital a builder provides."[15] The Credit Corporation representative sought "to determine if there was a more conservative basis upon which we would provide financing on the lots in question and still be of assistance to him." But "Mr. Fortner's position was that he needed the financing as requested and felt that a loan similar to that which [the Credit Corporation] originally made was justified."[16] By August, 1961, the parties had agreed on a land loan of $59,000 (a total construction loan commitment of $403,400), again at a 6 percent rate.[17]

Fortner soon began to complain about the quality of the housing components delivered to him. Whether the frequency of complaints became significant before or after the second land loan is the subject of some ambiguity in the documents and affidavits,[18] but in

---

[12] The due dates were December 31, 1961, and December 31, 1962, respectively. Fortner thus got the better part of what he had asked with respect to his demand for a two-year maturity. *Id.* at 27a–37a, 47a–50a.

[13] *Id.* at 25a–26a, 50a–53a.

[14] *Id.* at 399a–401a, 407a–413a. The land had previously been sold by Iroquois Development but was reacquired. *Id.* at 408.

[15] *Id.* at 411a.

[16] The quotations are from a contemporaneous memorandum by the Credit Corporation representative. *Id.* at 409a.

[17] *Id.* at 243a–268a. All advances under both the 1960 and 1961 loan agreements were secured by mortgages.

[18] Plaintiff claimed that all of the 70 houses that had been delivered were defective. Many had been delivered prior to the completion of negotiations on the second loan agreement. *Id.* at 117a–118a.

any case the trickle of complaints soon became a flood. Windows leaked, exterior panels did not align, closet doors did not fit, and nails popped out. A contemporaneous Homes Division document suggests that Fortner's complaints were not exaggerated.[19]

Several meetings were held in late April and early May between Homes Division representatives and Fortner to discuss the complaints. It was apparently about this time that Fortner consulted his attorneys. A meeting was arranged with Homes Division and Credit Corporation representatives in the attorneys' offices on May 31, 1962. At that meeting Fortner or his attorneys proposed that the loans could be paid off if he were to complete the project with conventional housing. The representative of the Credit Corporation explained that so long as the loans were outstanding, Fortner had an obligation to construct only Homes Division housing on the land and that if Fortner wanted to construct other housing, he should first pay off the Credit Corporation. Fortner unsuccessfully requested the deletion of a loan agreement provision requiring the borrower "to complete the development of the Premises and to erect on each of said Lots . . . a prefabricated dwelling house manufactured by United States Steel Homes Division."[20]

Until this meeting the controversy between Fortner and U.S. Steel was a typical commercial dispute over the quality of goods, not greatly different from thousands of other disputes that are erupting and being resolved in the economy at any given time. Most lawyers consulted would probably have thought of the dispute in terms of warranties and other sales law concepts. But the explicit demand for the deletion of the clause in question suggested that Fortner had consulted uncommonly resourceful lawyers. Just how resourceful they were became clear a few weeks later when Fortner Enterprises filed an action under §§ 1 and 2 of the Sherman Act, alleging that the Homes Division and the Credit Corporation had conspired "to force corporations and individuals, including the plaintiff, as a condition to availing themselves of the services of United States Steel Homes Credit Corporation, to purchase at artificially high prices only United States Steel Homes."[21] The complaint further alleged that, after the construction of 70 houses,

---

[19] *Id*. at 116a–127a, 418a–422a.

[20] *Id*. at 26a, 292a–294a. This clause was somewhat reformulated in the second loan agreement. *Id*. at 245a.

[21] *Id*. at 21a.

Fortner Enterprises had not been able to complete the project because of the "faulty and defective" housing packages and that the defendants were effectuating the conspiracy by threatening to foreclose on the mortgage.[22] The plaintiff's principal theory was that the defendants had conspired to make a tie-in sale. In order to obtain the loan, the plaintiff had been compelled to take Homes Division houses. In the jargon of antitrust, the money was the tying product and the houses were the tied product.

After extensive interrogatories, depositions, and other pretrial proceedings lasting some four years (in the course of which the mortgages were foreclosed),[23] defendants moved for summary judgment. The motion was granted.

II. The Majority Opinion

Mr. Justice Black, writing for the majority, viewed the case as elementary. He had no doubt that the defendants had imposed a tying arrangement. It was, in fact, a "tying arrangement of the traditional kind."[24] Tie-ins are illegal per se. It suffices to bring a tie-in within the sphere of per se illegality that a significant volume of commerce is foreclosed in the tied product and that the seller has "sufficient market power" in the market for the tying product.[25] As to the foreclosure requirement, Mr. Justice Black could not say that the annual volume of sales of housing to the plaintiff, almost $200,000, "is paltry or 'insubstantial' " and, in any case, one must look to the volume of commerce foreclosed from all of the defendants' tie-in sales, not merely from sales to the plaintiff.[26] Sufficient market power is established whenever "the seller has the power to raise prices, or impose other burdensome terms such as a tie-in, with respect to any appreciable number of buyers within the market."[27] The implication left by Mr. Justice Black was that since the tie-in had been imposed, the defendants must have had the power to impose it. But he did not consider it necessary to state explicitly

---

[22] *Id*. at 21a–22a.

[23] The Credit Corporation's counterclaim sought foreclosure of the mortgages. Summary judgment for the Credit Corporation on the counterclaim was granted. The mortgages were foreclosed, and the secured property was sold. *Id*. at 52a–81a, 192a–200a, 229a–236a.

[24] 394 U.S. at 498.

[25] *Id*. at 498–99.

[26] *Id*. at 502.

[27] *Id*. at 504.

that the existence of the tie-in established the power to impose it since, in view of plaintiff's affidavits, the fundamental error had been to grant summary judgment.

Moreover, even if foreclosure and market power were not present, those two "standards are necessary only to bring into play the doctrine of *per se* illegality."[28] Even if plaintiff might fail to establish one or both of those two requisites, he "can still prevail on the merits whenever he can prove, on the basis of a more thorough examination of the purposes and effects of the practices involved, that the general standards of the Sherman Act have been violated."[29] Therefore, a trial would in any event be necessary on the plaintiff's "general allegations that respondents conspired together for the purpose of restraining competition and acquiring a monopoly in the market for prefabricated houses."[30]

The concluding paragraphs of the majority opinion are devoted to the rebuttal of several arguments made by the defendants and in the dissenting opinions of Justices White (with Harlan joining) and Fortas (with Stewart joining). Mr. Justice Black rejected the argument that the transaction should be treated as merely the "usual sale on credit" in which "the entire transaction could be considered to involve only a single product."[31] In the arrangement under challenge "the credit is provided by one corporation on condition that a product be purchased from a separate corporation" and "the borrower contracts to obtain a large sum of money over and above that needed to pay the seller for the physical products purchased."[32] Nor can credit be distinguished, ruled Mr. Justice Black, "from other kinds of goods and services, all of which may, when used as tying products, extend the seller's economic power to new markets and foreclose competition in the tied product."[33] Not only might credit tie-ins involve the same evils as other tie-ins but credit tie-ins might raise barriers to entry into the market for the tied product. An entrant into that market would have to have "sufficient financial strength to offer credit comparable to that provided by larger competitors under tying arrangements."[34] The argument of the majority opinion concludes with the observation that "it is easy to see how a big company with vast sums of money in its treasury could wield very substantial power in a credit market."[35]

---

[28] *Id.* at 499–500.   [30] *Ibid.*   [32] *Ibid.*   [34] *Id.* at 509.

[29] *Id.* at 500.   [31] *Id.* at 507.   [33] *Id.* at 508.   [35] *Ibid.*

On its face, Mr. Justice Black's opinion does not purport to bring anything fresh to the law on tie-ins. The standards are unchanged, he says, and credit tie-ins are not only subject to those standards but are tie-ins of the "traditional kind," creating dangers at least as grave as tie-ins involving two tangible products. That being so, there is no basis for summary judgment for the defendants where the plaintiff has any substantial evidence on the crucial issues of foreclosure and market power.

III. The Standards for Summary Judgment

In considering the importance of the *Fortner Enterprises* decision, it is worth asking whether this case can be viewed as dealing primarily with the standards for summary judgment in antitrust cases. Certainly every antitrust lawyer knows that the probability of a grant of certiorari following summary judgment against the plaintiff is high, whatever the importance to the economy or to antitrust doctrine of the case. *Fortner* may stand primarily for the proposition that it is per se erroneous to grant summary judgment against a plaintiff in any treble-damage action. The grant of certiorari and per curiam reversal without oral argument in a case decided only a few weeks after *Fortner* supports that view.[36]

The consequences of such a rule would be substantial. Although what little evidence is available suggests that juries can usually detect a meritless case,[37] a jury trial may be of considerable value to an antitrust plaintiff, if only because it improves his position in settlement negotiations. A rule guaranteeing every antitrust plaintiff the right to a jury trial, however groundless his case, would thus influence settlement practices, thereby increasing the cost of practices that engender litigation and, at the margin, altering the economic behavior of firms. The only matter for debate is the importance of this effect.

The fundamental case on the use of summary judgment in antitrust cases is *Poller v. Columbia Broadcasting Co.*[38] That decision

---

[36] Norfolk Monument Co. v. Woodlawn Memorial Gardens, Inc., 394 U.S. 700 (1969).

[37] KALVEN & ZEISEL, THE AMERICAN JURY 149–62 (1966). This product of the University of Chicago jury study was concerned with criminal cases only.

[38] 368 U.S. 464 (1962).

has frequently been cited for the language that Mr. Justice Black quoted in *Fortner Enterprises:*[39]

> We believe that summary procedures should be used sparingly in complex antitrust litigation where motive and intent play leading roles, the proof is largely in the hands of alleged conspirators, and hostile witnesses thicken the plot. It is only when the witnesses are present and subject to cross-examination that their credibility and the weight to be given their testimony can be appraised. Trial by affidavit is no substitute for trial by jury which so long has been the hallmark of "even handed justice."

Although the Supreme Court has put a good deal of energy into the enforcement of this procedural rule, it has on occasion, as in the 1967 Term's *Cities Service* decision,[40] conceded that not every complaint automatically entitles its draftsman to a jury trial. But Mr. Justice Black had heatedly dissented in the aberrational *Cities Service* case, arguing that "the best service that could be rendered in this field would be to abolish summary judgment procedures, root and branch."[41] In that dissent, in which Justices Warren and Brennan joined, he sought to make clear that his objection to summary judgment is that it "tempts judges to take over the jury trial of cases, thus depriving parties of their constitutional right to trial by jury."[42]

One may seriously doubt that the result in *Fortner* and similar antitrust cases is, as the *Cities Service* dissent suggests, compelled by the Constitution. Certainly the proliferation of per se rules militates against that view, for a per se rule has the effect and even the purpose of eliminating a trial in whole or in part. Mr. Justice Black made that very point in *Fortner,* where he observed that in the two principal Supreme Court tie-in precedents, *Northern Pacific*[43]

---

[39] *Id.* at 473, quoted 394 U.S. at 500.

[40] First National Bank of Arizona v. Cities Service Co., 391 U.S. 253 (1968).

[41] *Id.* at 304.

[42] *Ibid.* This dislike of summary judgment extends well beyond the antitrust area. Cases decided under the Federal Employees Liability Act are the leading example. The *Fortner* case thus provides an answer to Judge Aldrich's query in Dehydrating Process Co. v. A. O. Smith Corp., 292 F.2d 653, 656 n. 6 (1st Cir. 1961), whether FELA cases are to be considered "on their own bottom" or apply also to tie-in and other antitrust cases.

[43] Northern Pacific Railway Co. v. United States, 356 U.S. 1 (1958).

and *International Salt*,[44] the Court had "approved summary judgment against the defendants" because the standards "necessary . . . to bring into play the doctrine of *per se* illegality" had been satisfied.[45] Thus, the antitrust rule against summary judgment is a one-way street, benefiting plaintiffs but not available to defendants. No one has explained why the Constitution protects plaintiffs but not defendants. Since the coercive power of the state is brought to bear in a more direct manner when a defendant is ordered to pay than when the coercive resources of the judicial system are withheld from a plaintiff,[46] one might have thought that any constitutional bias would run the other way.

On a non-constitutional level, one might read some non-neutral principles of procedure into the Clayton Act's provision in § 5 for private actions. The Court did just that in *Radovich v. National Football League*[47] where, speaking of the standards for judging the sufficiency of a complaint, it condemned "technical objections" to a complaint on the ground that, in view of the general congressional policy embodied in the treble-damage provision of the antitrust laws, "this Court should not add requirements to burden the private litigant beyond what is specifically set forth by Congress in those laws."[48] That the Court reads this injunction to mean even more than that every plaintiff must have his day before a jury is suggested by the recent *Albrecht* case[49] where the Supreme Court set aside a jury verdict for the defendant and ordered not a new trial but rather judgment notwithstanding the verdict for plaintiff.

Whatever the doctrinal justification for this pro-plaintiff bias in treble-damage actions, one cannot put aside *Fortner* as no more than a further manifestation of it. If the Court wanted to leave the substantive reach of the Sherman Act undisturbed, it could merely have reversed on the authority of *Poller*. Although Mr. Justice Black's opinion does not purport to extend the substantive law on tie-ins, the opinion certainly calls into question a large number of

---

[44] International Salt Co. v. United States, 332 U.S. 392 (1947).

[45] 394 U.S. at 499–500.

[46] *Cf.* Shelley v. Kraemer, 334 U.S. 1 (1948).

[47] 352 U.S. 445 (1957).

[48] *Id.* at 454.

[49] Albrecht v. Herald Co., 390 U.S. 145 (1968).

credit practices not formerly thought subject to the Sherman Act. The summary judgment aspect of the case, although revealing the motivations of the Court, is a bit like the breakfast menu theory of jurisprudence. It may tell you why a particular judge decided as he did but it does not tell you what the precedent thus created will mean to cerebrally oriented lower-court judges in the future. It is not inappropriate, therefore, to turn to the implications of the discussion of the law on tie-ins in order to assess the full meaning of *Fortner*.

IV. What Is a Tie-In?

More complicated than the question whether the tying arrangement found in *Fortner* was illegal is the question whether there was any tie-in at all. A person untutored in antitrust law might find absurd the notion that a sale on credit was a tie-in. It warrants discussion whether, even assuming some sophistication in the mysteries of antitrust, that notion is not, at the very least, curious.

Mr. Justice Black had, as we have seen, no difficulty in finding a tie-in. As he quite properly observed, what was involved was technically more than a mere credit sale. The Credit Corporation had financed not only the home packages but also the land, which Fortner Enterprises bought from another Fortner venture. It is, of course, on such technical distinctions that antitrust law is built. But one may fairly ask whether the distinction does not distort the factual situation. The bulk of the advances (about $1,700,000 of the total of about $2,000,000) was to be disbursed against purchase and installation of the houses.[50] Financing exceeding the cost of the goods themselves is not at all unusual. As Mr. Justice Fortas observed, "It is common in our economy for a seller to extend financing to a distributor or franchisee to enable him to purchase and handle the seller's goods at retail, to rent retail facilities, to acquire fixtures or machinery for service to customers in connection with distribution of the seller's goods."[51] Where prefabricated houses are involved, the real estate builder is perhaps more in the retailing than the construction business. As a matter of fact, at the very outset of his relations with U.S. Steel, Fortner signed a "fran-

---

[50] 394 U.S. at 522.   [51] *Id*. at 524.

chise agreement."[52] But perhaps Mr. Justice Black sees such arrangements as tie-ins, too.[53]

Mr. Justice Black strongly suggests that credit would be a separate product even if it did not exceed the price of the goods. The methodology of this part of the opinion is particularly interesting for the light it throws on his judicial technique. He starts by conceding what would appear to be the decisive point, namely, that in the usual credit sale only a single product can be found because the so-called tying by the seller is nothing other than an "agreement determining when and how much he will be paid for his product."[54] But then he ominously adds a formula sometimes used by law-extending judges for distinguishing, while throwing a baleful shadow upon, a practice theretofore clearly legal: "It will be time enough to pass on the issue of credit sales when a case involving it actually arises."[55] After reminding his readers that *Fortner* did not involve the usual credit sale, he then waxes warm on the dangers of credit sales in the hands of large and competitively unscrupulous companies, concluding with a populist warning about the evils that may be perpetrated by "a big company with vast sums of money."[56] One is led to conclude that, so far as Mr. Justice Black is concerned, the usual credit sale, at least in the hands of big companies with vast sums of money, stands at the front lines of advancing per se illegality.

Whatever future tie-in battles may be fought in the Supreme Court, it is worth pondering whether the *Fortner* arrangement was a tie-in in the sense that the other practices condemned as tie-ins by the Supreme Court have been. To be sure, there is nothing special about credit as such. For example, a refusal to sell automobiles to dealers who would not utilize the manufacturer's credit facilities,

---

[52] Record, pp. 922a–926a.

[53] One Federal Trade Commissioner immediately took the public position that the importance of *Fortner* lies precisely in its invalidation of "those franchise situations where a franchisor finances the purchaser of its franchisees on the condition that they purchase from suppliers approved by the franchisor." Address by Commissioner Everette MacIntyre, 5 CCH TRADE REG. REP. ¶ 50240, at p. 55489 (May 8, 1969). And Commissioner James M. Nicholson announced that under *Fortner* "the extension of valuable financial or management assistance on the condition that the franchisee agree to buy inferior ingredients at exhorbitant prices may establish . . . a tie." 5 CCH TRADE REG. REP. ¶ 50238, at p. 55481 n. 10 (April 26, 1969).

[54] 394 U.S. at 507.   [55] *Ibid.*   [56] *Id.* at 509.

as in the *GMAC* case,[57] can readily be said to be a tie-in of two products. *GMAC* was, of course, the opposite of *Fortner*, since in the former case, credit was the tied, not the tying product. But if the test is whether there are two products, then surely credit can be a product. Let us assume for the purposes of discussion therefore that, in this mechanical sense, two products can be said to be involved. The policy question still remains whether it makes antitrust sense to view the practice involved as a tie-in.

The relationship between the two products is different in *Fortner* than in the principal Supreme Court tie-in cases, *International Salt* and *Northern Pacific*. In both of those cases the tied product —salt and transportation—was purchased in quantities bearing no particular relation to the quantities of the tying product—salt machines and land. In the *Fortner* case, in contrast, the so-called tied and tying products were used in fixed proportions. A one-to-one relation existed between the provision of financing and the sale of houses. Not only was this true in the case of the construction loans that financed the purchase and erection of the houses, but it was also true in substance with respect to the land. Although the land was not acquired lot by lot, the total advance was calculated to equal the aggregate value of the lots. That was what was meant by "100% financing."

Moreover, unlike *International Salt* and *Northern Pacific*, the tied product was not used continuously following the purchase of the tying product. The proceeds of that portion of the loans represented by construction notes were disbursed as needed to purchase the houses and then to erect them.[58] Similarly, the advances under the land notes were to be made available as needed, first to acquire the land and later to improve it.[59]

The importance of these differences is not to be found in the mechanics of the present law on tie-ins but rather in the motives leading to different practices that the present law lumps together as tie-ins. Let us take the case where the two products are used in variable proportions, and particularly where sale of one unit of the tying product is followed by sale over time of a number of units

---

[57] United States v. General Motors Corp., 121 F.2d 376 (7th Cir. 1941).

[58] Record, pp. 34a–35a, 249a–251a.

[59] *Id.* at 30a–33a, 248a.

of the tied product. The tying arrangement in that situation serves as a counting device permitting a seller of the tying product to measure the intensity of its use. If the seller has some monopoly power in the tying product, price discrimination on sales of that product is facilitated by means of the tie-in. Price discrimination permits a monopolist to earn a greater return than he could earn by charging a uniform price. Differential pricing may take the form either of non-uniform prices for the tying product (based on marketing information obtained through prior tie-ins) or, if a uniform price is charged for the tying product, by a supracompetitive price for the tied product.[60] In *International Salt* the intensity of use for the salt machines could be measured by the volume of purchases of salt. It is less clear that this theory explains the tie-in in *Northern Pacific*, but the volume of transportation service required may be a measure of the intensity of use of land. If that was not the effect of the *Northern Pacific* tie-in, then its effect can be dismissed as de minimis.

Where, however, as in *Fortner*, the products are used in fixed proportions (and particularly where they are sold simultaneously), the purpose of any tie-in must be much different. Even if the seller had a monopoly in the tying product, he could achieve no greater supracompetitive profit through the tying arrangement than he could by selling the products separately.[61]

Two points should be observed. First, to assimilate the arrangement in *Fortner* to that in *International Salt* and *Northern Pacific* is to treat two economically different situations identically because, at a high level of abstraction, both involve "two products." Such mechanistic reasoning by a busy Court may be excused but hardly commended. Second, the evil involved in the price discrimination

---

[60] This explanation assumes that intensity of use provides a rough measurement of elasticity of demand. The use of a tie-in as a counting device to facilitate discrimination is considered in Bowman, *Tying Arrangements and the Leverage Problem*, 67 YALE L.J. 19 (1957). Bowman credits Professor Aaron Director with first formulating this explanation. In his dissent, Mr. Justice White picked up this point as part of a compendium of learning on tie-ins but apparently did not see its immediate relevance to the law on tie-ins. 394 U.S. at 515. This explanation, it should be noted, has nothing to do with popular leverage notions under which a monopoly in the tying product is supposedly extended to the tied product.

[61] See Bowman, note 60 *supra*, at 20–23. As Bowman points out, a tie-in in such a situation could be a technique for avoiding price regulation in the monopolized product.

explanation, if it is an evil,[62] is dependent upon monopoly power in the tying product. Although an economist would not be satisfied, a court might be justified in inferring that monopoly power in the tying product exists where the two products are used in variable proportions and hence the price discrimination explanation seems a priori plausible. On this ground, the determination concerning market power in the tying product in *International Salt* and *Northern Pacific* might be defended. But where, as in *Fortner*, no such explanation is possible, a deeper economic inquiry into the existence of market power in the tying product is essential, even if one believes that market power can somehow be transferred from the tying to the tied product. In the absence of market power in the tying product, there is nothing to transfer. Such a use of leverage is, of course, the evil that the courts have seen in tie-ins[63] and was decried by Mr. Justice Black once again in *Fortner* under the rubric of "barriers to entry": "[E]conomies in financing should not, any more than economies in other lines for business, be used to exert *economic power over other products* that the company produces no more efficiently than its competitors."[64]

The foregoing analysis suggests that the weakness of the "two products" approach is that it tends to sweep within the category of tie-ins many arrangements that are competitively benign. Mr. Justice Fortas suggested a technique for remedying this weakness in certain cases. He argued that no tie existed in *Fortner* because the "financing which [U.S. Steel] agrees to provide is solely and entirely ancillary to its sale of houses."[65] Mr. Justice Fortas' approach has much to recommend it. It affords the possibility of building on the ancillary restraints doctrine, which condemns only

---

[62] The output of the price discriminating monopolist may in certain circumstances exceed that of the monopolist charging a uniform price. Where that is so, the principal economic objection to monopoly—that it reduces output—becomes less forceful. ROBINSON, THE ECONOMICS OF IMPERFECT COMPETITION 188–95 (1933).

[63] "[T]he essence of illegality in tying agreements is the wielding of monopolistic leverage; a seller exploits his dominant position in one market to expand his empire into the next." Times-Picayune Publishing Co. v. United States, 345 U.S. 594, 611 (1953). "A tie-in contract may have . . . undesirable effects when the seller, by virtue of his position in the market for the tying product, has economic leverage sufficient to induce his customers to take the tied product along with the tying item." United States v. Loew's, Inc., 371 U.S. 38, 45 (1962). See Northern Pacific Railway Co. v. United States, 356 U.S. 1, 6 (1958).

[64] 394 U.S. at 509. (Emphasis supplied.)   [65] *Id.* at 521–22.

those restraints that are not ancillary to a lawful main transaction. Such a line of inquiry would permit more economic analysis than the intellectually sterile per se approach since a court would be forced to seek the purpose of the putative tie-in. Moreover, the ancillary doctrine would fit the facts of cases like *Fortner* well. As Mr. Justice Fortas observed, U.S. Steel was not "selling credit in any general sense."[66] All parties were agreed that the Credit Corporation made credit available only to purchasers of houses from the Homes Division.[67] Hence, the ancillarity approach expresses well the common-sense feeling that there is something wrong with saying that U.S. Steel was tying its credit to sales when the only purpose of making credit available at all was to promote the sale of houses. Finally, the ancillary restraints doctrine would distinguish most of the earlier tie-in cases, since, for example, it would be difficult to say that the lease of the patented salt machines was purely ancillary to the sale of salt in *International Salt*.

Although the ancillary restraints doctrine would thus provide a useful approach to the issue whether two products were tied, the underlying significance of the Credit Corporation's self-imposed restriction on the range of its money market activities is once more the light thrown on the issue of market power. It is difficult to believe that U.S. Steel could have any market power over an item so widely useful as credit if it made it available only in connection with sales of prefabricated homes. Whatever leverage advantages in the housing market it might be thought to gain through a tie-in could surely never compensate for the foregone supracompetitive profits it could secure, assuming it really had market power over credit, by making credit generally available to the public. When the point is put in those terms, the specter of U.S. Steel's market power in credit stemming from its "vast sums of money" dissolves. However "imperfect" credit markets may be, it is, Mr. Justice Black notwithstanding, far from "easy to see how a big company with vast sums of money in its treasury could wield very substantial power in a credit market."[68] If U.S. Steel had such power over credit, it could and surely would use it outside the narrow field of financing prefabricated houses.

---

[66] *Id.* at 521.

[67] The plaintiff's attorney went out of his way to establish this fact in the course of the depositions. *E.g.,* Record, pp. 838a–840a.

[68] 394 U.S. at 509.

Here again one is led to the conclusion that the definitional question is hard to separate from the question when tie-ins are harmful. Yet the decisions, in adopting the per se rule, have attempted to flee from that economic question by ruling that tying arrangements are presumptively harmful, at least whenever certain nominal threshold standards on power and foreclosure are met. The weakness of the per se methodology is that it places crucial importance on the definition of the practice. Once an arrangement falls within the defined limits, no justification will be heard. But a per se rule gives no economic standards for defining the practice. To treat the definitional question as an abstract inquiry into whether one or two products is involved is thus to compound the weakness of the per se approach.

V. The Requirement of Economic Power

As the foregoing discussion has suggested at several points, any harm that can arise from a tie-in, whether as envisaged by the Court's leverage theory or through monopolistic price discrimination, requires market power in the market for the tying product. Aside from the cloud that *Fortner* throws on many financing arrangements in the economy, the practical importance of the case lies primarily in the further attenuation of the requirement of market power as a prerequisite to per se illegality.

A. ECONOMIC POWER FROM INTERNATIONAL SALT TO FORTNER

The attenuation of the market power requirement has been in process for some time. The Court has usually tended to view the market power requirement as a technicality to be manipulated in the particular case in such a way as to sweep the challenged practice within the sphere of the per se rule.

In *International Salt* the tying product, the salt machines, was patented. The Court, observing that patents confer "a limited monopoly of the invention they reward,"[69] failed to consider the possibility that legal monopoly might not correspond to an economic monopoly. In *Standard Stations*,[70] Justice Frankfurter noted that it had not been established in *International Salt* "that equivalent machines were unobtainable" or "what proportion of the business

---

[69] 332 U.S. at 395.

[70] Standard Oil Co. v. United States, 337 U.S. 293 (1949).

of supplying such machines was controlled by defendant."[71] But, he reasoned, a "patent, . . . although in fact there may be many competing substitutes for the patented article, is at least *prima facie* evidence of [market] control."[72] The *Times-Picayune* case[73] made clear that patents could indeed be taken, "on their face" and without further evidence, as conferring "monopolistic, albeit lawful, market control."[74] Whatever empirical justification there might be for assuming that economic monopoly was associated with patents, a line of patent cases treating tie-in clauses in patent licenses as a misuse of the patents made clear that a patent did not justify a tie-in.[75] *International Salt* might at the time have been read as saying that patent misuse was an antitrust violation whenever a substantial volume of commerce was involved.

The practice challenged in *Times-Picayune*, however, was a unit contract requiring advertisers in the city's sole morning paper to advertise in the same publisher's evening paper, which faced competition. No patent or copyright was involved. The question of requisite market power in the tying product therefore had to be faced, but the answer had two levels. Since advertising was not a "commodity" and hence the unit contract did not fall within the ambit of § 3 of the Clayton Act,[76] the Court treated that contract as subject only to the stricter standards of § 1 of the Sherman Act:[77]

> From the "tying" cases a perceptible pattern of illegality emerges: When the seller enjoys a monopolistic position in the market for the "tying" product, *or* if a substantial volume of commerce in the "tied" product is restrained, a tying arrangement violates the narrower standards expressed in § 3 of the

---

[71] *Id.* at 305.   [72] *Id.* at 307.

[73] Times-Picayune Publishing Co. v. United States, 345 U.S. 594 (1953).

[74] *Id.* at 608. See also *id.* at 611 n. 30.

[75] Morton Salt Co. v. G. S. Suppiger Co., 314 U.S. 488 (1942); Mercoid Corp. v. Mid-Continent Investment Co., 320 U.S. 661 (1944); Mercoid Corp. v. Minneapolis-Honeywell Regulator Co., 320 U.S. 680 (1944).

[76] Section 3 applies to leases and sales of "goods, wares, merchandise, machinery, supplies or *other commodities* . . . on the condition, agreement or understanding that the lessee or purchaser thereof shall not use or deal in the goods, wares, merchandise, machinery, supplies or *other commodities* of a competitor or competitors of the lessor or seller, where the effect . . . may be to substantially lessen competition or tend to create a monopoly in any line of commerce." 38 Stat. 731 (1944), 15 U.S.C. § 14 (1964). (Emphasis supplied.)

[77] 345 U.S. at 608–09.

Clayton Act because from either factor the requisite potential lessening of competition is inferred. And because for even a lawful monopolist it is "unreasonable *per se*, to foreclose competitors from any substantial market," a tying arrangement is banned by § 1 whenever *both* conditions are met.

In measuring control over the tying products, patent and copyright cases were to be distinguished: "Unlike other 'tying' cases where patents or copyrights supplied the requisite market control, any equivalent market 'dominance' in this case must rest on comparative marketing data."[78] The Court therefore examined the facts and found that the defendants did not have the market dominance required for a § 1 tie-in violation. Forty percent of the market did not in the circumstances confer the requisite dominance.[79]

Whether or not this disparity between Clayton and Sherman Act standards in *Times-Picayune* could be justified by the precedents, the gap was soon narrowed in the *Northern Pacific* case. Since neither the land nor the transportation service was a "commodity," the tie-in was again tested under the Sherman Act standards. In the hands of Mr. Justice Black, writing for the majority, the "monopolistic position" prerequisite to liability was watered down to "sufficient economic power": tie-ins "are unreasonable in and of themselves whenever a party has sufficient economic power with respect to the tying product to appreciably restrain free competition in the market for the tied product and a 'not insubstantial' amount of interstate commerce is affected."[80] The finding of "sufficient economic power" over the tying product was predicated not on "comparative marketing data" as in *Times-Picayune* but merely on the qualitative observations that the land was "strategically located," "within economic distance of transportation facilities," and "often prized by those who purchased or leased it and frequently essential to their business activities."[81] The only quantitative measurement was that "several million acres" were subject to the tie-in. No attempt was made to define any relevant market within which one could judge whether such an area could give rise to any market power in fact. Mr. Justice Black came close to saying that the

---

[78] *Id.* at 611.

[79] The percentage control of the market for the tying product was probably improperly defined. See Turner, *The Validity of Tying Arrangements under the Antitrust Laws*, 72 Harv. L. Rev. 50, 55 n. 21 (1958).

[80] 356 U.S. at 6. See also *id.* at 11.   [81] *Id.* at 7.

requisite power was shown by the tie-in itself, particularly if many contracts contained the tying clauses: "The very existence of this host of tying arrangements is itself compelling evidence of the defendant's great power, at least where, as here, no other explanation has been offered for the existence of these restraints."[82] Mr. Justice Black made clear that he did not think it necessary to make a serious inquiry into the actual degree of market power in the tying product. After all, no such inquiry had been made in *International Salt*. And, *Times-Picayune* (in which Mr. Justice Black had dissented) to the contrary notwithstanding, the tie-in in *International Salt* was illegal "*despite* the fact that the tying item was patented, not because of it."[83]

The next step in the attenuation of the requirement of market power over the tying product was taken in 1962 in the *Loew's* case.[84] The Court there held block booking of copyrighted motion picture films for television exhibition to constitute an illegal tying practice. Again, since films are not "commodities," only the Sherman Act standards were in question. "Market dominance," in the sense of power in a significant economic market—that is, "some power to control price and to exclude competition"—became only one species of the "requisite economic power." Such power might also be "inferred from the tying product's desirability to consumers or from uniqueness in its attributes."[85] To emphasize that "uniqueness or consumer appeal" might be found in the absence of any power over price in the market for the tying product, Mr. Justice Goldberg added that "it should seldom be necessary in a tie-in sale case to embark upon a full-scale factual inquiry into the scope of the relevant market for the tying product and into the corollary problem of the seller's percentage share in that market."[86] And since, unlike *Northern Pacific*, industrial property rights were once

---

[82] *Id.* at 7–8. As the dissenting opinion of Mr. Justice Harlan pointed out, no substantial inference of power would be drawn from the existence of the clauses, since purchasers of the land were permitted to purchase transport service from other rail carriers "when offered either lower rates *or* lower rates or superior service." *Id.* at 13, 17. (Emphasis in original.)

[83] *Id.* at 9. The Government had argued that land could be analogized to patents or copyrights because it was unique. The Court did not fully accept that argument, but the idea had enough vitality to reappear in Justice Fortas' dissent in *Fortner*. 394 U.S. at 520, 523.

[84] United States v. Loew's, Inc., 371 U.S. 38 (1962).

[85] *Id.* at 45.   [86] *Id.* at 45 n. 4.

again involved, the Court stated that it would be appropriate to presume "sufficiency of economic power" from the fact that "the tying product is patented or copyrighted."[87] Moreover, with "uniqueness" now the test, the presumption could be reformulated. Just as the purpose of patents was to "reward uniqueness," so too was a copyrighted film unique. It did not matter that films might be "reasonably interchangeable"; they "varied in theme, in artistic performance, in stars, in audience appeal, etc.," and a copyright was by definition a species of monopoly.[88]

B. THE UNIQUENESS TEST APPLIED

Since even U.S. Steel has no patent or copyright on money, some ambiguity concerning the proper standard still remained in *Fortner*. To understand how the issue was treated by the Court, it is essential to understand the contention made by the plaintiff. On the motion for summary judgment, the plaintiff based its case on the economic power issue on two sentences in Fortner's affidavit:[89]

> Affiant states that to his knowledge no [100%] financial assistance was available to Fortner Enterprises, Inc. in 1959–1962 on the terms offered by the Credit Corporation from any other source. The offered financial assistance, particularly in terms of the 100% financing feature, was so unusual, unique as far as the Plaintiff was concerned, and attractive that the Plaintiff because of economic circumstances accepted the assistance offered, including conditions imposed by the Credit Corporation that prefabricated homes manufactured by the Homes Division would be built in the subdivision.

This affidavit was supplemented by the affidavit of the president of Louisville Mortgage Service Company, a local institutional lender, who stated that the Credit Corporation "financing package . . . was unusual and unique during the period from 1959 to 1962 in Jefferson County, Kentucky" and that "such a financing plan was not available to Fortner Enterprises or any other potential borrower from or through Louisville Mortgage Service Company or

---

[87] *Ibid.*

[88] The Court did not consider whether the difference between the legal rights accorded by a patent and a copyright might require a different result. A patent grants a monopoly in the sense of a right to exclude others even though they may independently have subsequently discovered the product. A copyright protects only against copying.

[89] Record, p. 290a.

from any lending institution or mortgage company to this affiant's knowledge during this period."[90]

In considering the plaintiff's theory of uniqueness, it is important to recognize the relationship between the amount advanced (measured as a percentage of value of the collateral) and the interest rate. The essential difference between the Credit Corporation's credit and institutional lenders' credit was that the Credit Corporation would advance Fortner more than institutional lenders against a given amount of collateral.[91] No assertion was made that the Credit Corporation charged a higher interest rate. The interest rate, however, tends to be an inverse function of the amount advanced (measured in terms of the collateral). Moreover, many institutional lenders make unsecured loans at a higher interest rate than secured loans. In view of this trade-off between the interest rate and the ampleness of the security, Mr. Justice White was surely correct in viewing the sole uniqueness of the Credit Corporation's loans as being their "low cost" to Fortner Enterprises.[92] U.S. Steel credit was unique because it was cheap.

The alternative theory of uniqueness, suggested by Mr. Justice Black but not argued by plaintiff, was that U.S. Steel may have had a legal advantage (presumably analogous to a patent or a copyright) because institutional lenders "may have been prohibited from offering 100% financing by state or federal law."[93] This theory is imaginative but questionable. The very affidavit of the mortgage company president relied upon by Mr. Justice Black states in the immediately following paragraph that after the Fortner transactions, Louisville institutional lenders "have been forced to offer their customers similar 100% financing for purchase and development of land."[94] In short, the amount of security required, like the interest rate, is determined by competition. Local Louisville lenders,

---

[90] *Id.* at 294a–295a, partially quoted, 394 U.S. at 504–05.

[91] This was not denied by defendants. On the contrary, it was explicitly stated to be against Credit Corporation policy to grant credit where institutional loans were available. Record, p. 857a.

[92] 394 U.S. at 515. Plaintiff's affidavits did not directly address themselves to the terms of credits made available by competing suppliers. The record suggests that the Credit Corporation's service fee of one-half point (that is, one-half percent of the loan) may have been less than that charged by other suppliers (Record, p. 377a), but the discounting of loan proceeds by such points is generally regarded as merely an adjustment of the interest rate.

[93] 394 U.S. at 506.   [94] Record, p. 295a.

perhaps in the face of competition from suppliers like U.S. Steel, found themselves willing to make equally "unique" loans when they found it in their self-interest to do so.

The district court, faced with the contention that the amount of the loan in relation to the amount of the collateral made the loan "unique" under the *Loew's* case, responded with two separate lines of argument. First, anyone could have provided "100% financing"; the Credit Corporation's generosity was thus not tantamount to economic power. Second, the test is not uniqueness for a particular customer; rather, the "test is universal compulsion not a peculiar attraction for one corporation as here."[95]

Mr. Justice Black opened his discussion of the economic power issue by attacking the latter argument. The earlier tie-in cases, he argued, "have made unmistakably clear that the economic power over the tying product can be sufficient even though the power falls far short of dominance and even though the power exists only with respect to some of the buyers in the market."[96] Then, perhaps lest it might appear that his definition of the relevant market was merely narrower than that of the court below, he quoted the language from *Loew's* permitting an inference of power "from the tying product's desirability to consumers or from uniqueness of its attributes."[97]

Thereafter, following an intricate discussion of the meaning of market power, he concluded that "the proper focus of concern is whether the seller has the power to raise prices *or* impose other burdensome terms such as a tie-in, with respect to any appreciable number of buyers within the market."[98] One important question in interpreting the *Fortner* decision is the meaning of this language. Taken out of context, it might be thought to mean that, just as the "host of tying arrangements" was "compelling evidence" of "great power" in *Northern Pacific*,[99] so the inclusion of tie-in clauses in contracts with "any appreciable numbers of buyers" establishes market power. But the passage read in context does not warrant this interpretation. For the immediately preceding sentence makes clear that market power in the sense of power over price must still

---

[95] *Id.* at 306a; 1968 Trade Cases ¶ 72576, at p. 85996.

[96] 394 U.S. at 502–03.

[97] *Id.* at 503, quoting from 371 U.S. at 45.

[98] *Id.* at 504.   [99] 356 U.S. at 8.

exist.[100] If the price could have been raised but the tie-in was demanded in lieu of the higher price, then—and presumably only then—would the requisite economic power exist. Thus, despite the broad language available for quotation in later cases, the treatment of the law on market power is on close reading not only consonant with the precedents but in some ways less far-reaching than *Northern Pacific* and *Loew's*, which could be read to make actual market power irrelevant.

The interesting methodological question is therefore how Mr. Justice Black, with a traditional reading of the law, could find the requisite economic power here. There was no showing of any power to raise price, that is, to charge higher interest rates or, the functional equivalent, to demand greater security. U.S. Steel had rather reduced its price on the credit. One might have thought such evidence showed that U.S. Steel, which was using the Fortner transaction to break into the Louisville market, had no power over price in either homes or credit.

Mr. Justice Black's response to this difficulty was technically careful and imaginative but, in part, hard to square with any traditional purpose of the antitrust laws. After observing that the procedural issue was whether the affidavits entitled the plaintiff to "its day in court," he noted that the affidavit of a construction company president that U.S. Steel's prices exceeded those of competitors by at least $400.[101] This affidavit, which was apparently offered in support of the complaint allegation that the Homes Division and the Credit Corporation had conspired to cause the plaintiff "[t]o purchase United States Steel Homes at unreasonably high prices"[102] and in support of plaintiff's damage theory, was relied on by Mr. Justice Black as tending to prove power over credit: "Since in a

---

[100] The preceding sentence reads: "In both instances [that is, 'regardless of whether the seller has the greatest economic power possible or merely some lesser degree of appreciable economic power'], despite the freedom of some or many buyers from the seller's power, other buyers—whether few or many, whether scattered throughout the market or part of some group within the market—can be forced to accept the higher price because of their stronger preferences for the product, and the seller could therefore choose instead to force them to accept a tying arrangement that would prevent free competition for their patronage in the market for the tied product." 394 U.S. at 503–04.

[101] 394 U.S. at 504. This "construction company president" was Fortner's general contractor on the U.S. Steel project (Record, p. 349a) and was a former owner of the land financed under the 1961 loan agreement. Record, pp. 638a–639a.

[102] Record, p. 22a.

freely competitive situation buyers would not accept a tying arrangement obligating them to buy a tied product at a price higher than the going market rate, this substantial price difference with respect to the tied product . . . in itself may suggest that respondents had some special economic power in the credit market."[103] Since on motion for summary judgment such an affidavit must be taken at face value, this portion of the opinion would be convincing, were it not for Mr. Justice White's point that the plaintiff had not in fact made any "offer of proof that the seller has any market power in the credit market."[104] Rather, as plaintiff's Supreme Court brief indicates and as stated in unmistakable terms in oral argument, the plaintiff relied solely on "the general uniqueness of the special financing plans offered by the Credit Corporation." That, argued the plaintiff, under *Loew's* was all that it had to show.[105]

After this resourceful use of the construction company executive's affidavit, Mr. Justice Black adopted as the second part of his reasoning the plaintiff's principal argument—that the terms of the credit were unique. But he carefully explained that he was not accepting the argument as made to the Court:[106]

> We do not mean to accept petitioner's apparent argument that market power can be inferred simply because the kind of financing terms offered by a lending company are "unique and unusual." We do mean, however, that uniquely and unusually advantageous terms can reflect a creditor's unique economic advantages over his competitors.

The unique terms alone would not give rise to an inference of economic power. In the absence of a patent or copyright where competitors are "prevented from offering the distinctive product themselves," economic uniqueness could only prevent competitors from offering the product if the seller had a "cost advantage in producing it."[107] Thus, it is not unique terms themselves but rather "unique economic advantages" that, if present, would constitute the "sufficient economic power" that *Northern Pacific* made the prerequisite to illegality. The plaintiff's affidavits could, and on motion for summary judgment should, be construed to mean that the Credit Corporation "had a unique economic ability to provide 100% financing at cheap rates."[108] The unwillingness of local lenders to offer com-

---

103 394 U.S. at 504.

104 *Id.* at 510.

105 Petitioner's Brief, p. 29.

106 394 U.S. at 505.

107 *Id.* at 505 n. 2.

108 *Id.* at 505.

petitive terms "probably reflects their feeling that they could not profitably lend money on the risks involved."[109] U.S. Steel's ability to offer better terms might stem, speculates Mr. Justice Black, from "economies resulting from the nationwide character of their operations" or from legal prohibitions placed on institutional competitors.[110]

C. ECONOMIES AND COMPETITION "ON THE MERITS"

In suggesting that "economies" constitute a "competitive advantage" rendering conduct illegal that would otherwise be legal, the majority opinion returned to a theme that has appeared in a number of recent merger decisions.[111] No doubt cost advantages stemming from patents or economies of scale may lead to monopoly power and, if one adopts the leverage theory, one might be concerned with the transfer of that monopoly power in the market for the tying product to the market for the tied product. But despite Mr. Justice Black's language about market power permitting the seller to charge a higher price,[112] a reading of his opinion as a whole suggests that he was concerned more with U.S. Steel's competitive tactics than with the possibility that U.S. Steel had actual market power in the money market. It is surely difficult to see how evidence that U.S. Steel had to underbid its competitors in the credit market to get Fortner's business indicates that it had the economic power, even with respect to Fortner himself, to impose a supracompetitive price for U.S. Steel money and had merely traded off that possibility for the tying clause.

---

[109] *Ibid.* Mr. Justice Black did not consider the construction company president's statement that those lenders thereafter began to offer "100% financing." Surely it is equally plausible to infer that they could have offered such financing in the earlier period. In the absence of a study of competitive conditions in the Louisville area in the earlier period, it is difficult to make any inference. But it seems unlikely that Mr. Justice Black's conclusion would have been altered, even if he had considered this alternative inference to be drawn from the plaintiff's own affidavits, since on summary judgment a plaintiff's "claims . . . should be read in a light most favorable to [him]." *Ibid.*

[110] *Id.* at 506. Here, again, the fact that institutional lenders rather promptly began offering "100% financing" suggests that those legal impediments were minor or nonexistent.

[111] Brown Shoe Co. v. United States, 370 U.S. 294, 344 (1962); United States v. Aluminum Co. of America, 233 F. Supp. 718 (E.D. Mo. 1964), *aff'd per curiam*, 382 U.S. 12 (1965); *cf.* F.T.C. v. Procter & Gamble Co., 386 U.S. 568, 578 (1967).

[112] 394 U.S. 503–04. See text *supra*, at notes 97–103.

Far more likely, if one reads the affidavits and depositions as a whole, is that U.S. Steel had no such power but was merely competing vigorously.[113] The depositions and documents submitted by the plaintiff indicate that U.S. Steel began to give credit in order to meet terms offered by competitiors in the prefabricated and conventional housing markets. The Credit Corporation's policy was to provide credit when not available to the purchaser from institutional sources in order to make sales that would otherwise be lost to Homes Division competitors who did provide such credit.[114] The terms for such credit were dictated by commercial rather than strictly financial considerations. Thus it would be at least as plausible to infer that softer terms on credit were a reflection of intense competition in the housing market than that they were indicia of market power in the money market. Lower-priced credit was an alternative to lower-priced houses,[115] and U.S. Steel's competitive desire to establish itself in the Louisville market made it necessary to improve its original offer in the protracted negotiations with a hard-bargaining, sophisticated real estate operator like Fortner.

Mr. Justice Black appeared to recognize that soft credit terms were a competitive measure, particularly in the passage where he observed that "advantageous credit terms may be viewed as a form of price competition in the tied product."[116] Perhaps that is why he used "market power" and "competitive advantage" interchangeably.[117] Although he paid lip service to the leverage theory, he did not appear to be so concerned that U.S. Steel would trade market power in money for market power in goods as he was that U.S.

---

[113] Record, pp. 756a–758a, 828a, 851a–852a.

[114] *Id*. at 853a–854a.

[115] It is not clear why U.S. Steel preferred to cut the price of credit rather than the price of houses. If there had been a cartel in housing, offering better terms on credit might have been a means of covertly cheating on the cartel. But in view of the vast number of competitors and the nonstandardized form of the product in the housing market, this rationale is implausible. Another possibility is that the Robinson-Patman Act's prohibition against differential pricing made it legally risky to cut the price of housing components selectively to obtain new business.

[116] 394 U.S. at 508. The Court had previously, in *Brown Shoe*, recognized that the per se rule would not invalidate a tie-in when used "by a small company . . . to break into a market." 370 U.S. at 330. And see United States v. Jerrold Electronics Corp., 187 F. Supp. 545 (E.D. Pa. 1960), *aff'd per curiam*, 365 U.S. 567 (1961). It is not clear why, if a small company may use a tie-in for competitive purposes, a large company in similar circumstances should be encouraged not to compete.

[117] *Compare* 394 U.S. at 503 *with id*. at 506.

Steel would have an unfair advantage over competing sellers of housing who did not provide credit. He was particularly concerned that U.S. Steel, with "economies resulting from the nationwide character of its operations" and with "vast sums of money in its treasury" would be able to take business away from local competitors who did not have the same "financial strength."[118]

One might well ask whether it is not precisely the purpose of competition to provide what the buyer needs, which in cases like *Fortner* appears to be not only houses but also extensive credit. Under this view, if it is true that "larger companies have achieved economies of scale in their credit operations,"[119] then the passing of such credit economies on to buyers of those larger companies' products, such as Fortner Enterprises, is a sign that competition is working.

That view of competition is not, however, shared by Mr. Justice Black. For him there can be competition only where each product sells on its own merits. Houses must compete only against houses, credit only against credit. That "economies" can be achieved through provision of credit by suppliers or through the packaging of diverse products is irrelevant in Mr. Justice Black's view of competition. This atomistic view of competition is a strong theme in recent Supreme Court antitrust decisions. It is related to, but distinct from, the leverage theory. The latter requires economic power, whereas the atomistic view is that competition is distorted if each product does not have its price.

The attraction of the atomistic view explains not only the attenuation of the market power requirement in tie-in cases where Mr. Justice Black has twice stated that the vice of the tie-ins is that "competition *on the merits* with respect to the tied product is inevitably curbed."[120] This notion is at the heart of the block-book-

---

[118] *Id*. at 506, 509. Some basis for skepticism about the "vast sums of money" is to be found in the record. The Credit Corporation's total paid-in capital was $2 million and the sums generated (including bank borrowings) apparently never exceeded $20 million for the country as a whole. Record, pp. 753a–759a. The district judge found that the funds available in Louisville, Kentucky, from local sources alone exceeded $160 million in 1960 and that in that year over $130 million in real estate mortgages had been recorded in Jefferson County, Kentucky. Record, pp. 311a–312a; 1968 Trade Cases ¶ 72576, at p. 85993.

[119] 394 U.S. at 509.

[120] *Northern Pacific*, 356 U.S. at 6, quoted in *Fortner Enterprises*, 394 U.S. at 508.

ing cases.[121] That reciprocal trading does not permit competition solely on the basis of "price, quality and service" appears to be the primary ground for challenging that practice.[122]

The atomistic view seems to be based on a dream of an ideal economy, filled with tiny firms, each selling a different product.[123] Whatever the legislative justification for this social objective,[124] it has little to do with competition in the economic sense. And at the doctrinal level, the weakness of this predominantly social view of antitrust when applied to tie-ins is that it presupposes that we know what a single product is. It is not readily apparent why in the ideal universe of small firms, each should not extend credit to purchasers.

D. THE SINCLAIR CASE

One residual doctrinal question created by the majority's treatment of price reduction as evidence of economic power is what effect the *Fortner* decision will have on the continued vitality of *F.T.C. v. Sinclair Refining Co.*,[125] a case relied upon by the defendants but ignored in the Court's opinion. The parallels between *Sinclair* and *Fortner* are striking. In *Sinclair* the defendant oil company provided gas pumps and storage tanks to service stations on condition that only defendant's gas be used in them. The terms in *Sinclair* were even better than in *Fortner;* the pumps and tanks were provided "at nominal prices."[126] In neither case was there any

---

[121] In *Loew's*, Justice Goldberg was concerned that competition for "Gone With the Wind" would be distorted if that film was sold together with "Getting Gertie's Garter." See Stigler, *United States v. Loew's Inc.: A Note on Block-Booking,* 1963 SUPREME COURT REVIEW 152. In United States v. Paramount Pictures, Inc., 334 U.S. 131, 158 (1948), Mr. Justice Douglas argued that when films are block-booked, "[e]ach stands not on its own footing but in whole or in part on the appeal which another film may have."

[122] F.T.C. v. Consolidated Foods Corp., 380 U.S. 592, 599 (1965) (quoting from F.T.C. opinion). One detects the same theme, somewhat muted, in the *TBA* cases: "The nonsponsored brands [of tires, batteries, and accessories] do not compete on even terms of price and quality competition; they must overcome, in addition, the influence of the dominant oil compan[ies]." F.T.C. v. Texaco, Inc., 393 U.S. 223, 230 (1968). See also Atlantic Refining Co. v. F.T.C., 381 U.S. 357 (1965).

[123] *Cf.* Mr. Justice Black's attack on the disappearance of the family firm, in United States v. Von's Grocery Co., 384 U.S. 270 (1966).

[124] *Compare* United States v. Aluminum Co. of America, 148 F.2d 416, 427–29 (2d Cir. 1945) *with* Bork, *Legislative Intent and the Policy of the Sherman Act,* 9 J. LAW & ECON. 7 (1966).

[125] 261 U.S. 463 (1923).   [126] *Id.* at 465.

exclusive dealing provision. The service stations in *Sinclair* could accept additional pumps from other suppliers, and so also, according to the finding of the district court, could Fortner Enterprises deal freely with other purveyors of homes and credit.[127]

The *Sinclair* decision is often explained by saying that since the oil company was only in effect providing free financing for its distributors, it would be inappropriate to condemn the arrangement as a tie-in. Now, in *Fortner*, the provision of financing on favorable terms is treated as a suspect tie-in. Whether *Sinclair* can be distinguished as involving equipment rather than credit is questionable. Mr. Justice Fortas' analogy between extension of credit and "ancillary services," such as "delivery, installation, fixturing, servicing, training of the customer's personnel in use of the material sold, [and] furnishing display material and sales aids," suggests that such a distinction is not inevitable.[128]

The financing justification was more implicit than explicit in *Sinclair*. Emphasis was placed by Justice McReynolds on the importance of the practice to "preserving the integrity of . . . brands," to safety, and to the prevention of fraud. These and other distinctions between *Sinclair* and *Fortner* must be authoritatively rejected before it can be concluded that *Sinclair* has been overruled.

VI. The Two-Hurdle Doctrine

Although *Fortner* does not purport to introduce any new concepts into the law on the per se illegality of tie-ins, one more general portion of the opinion might be interpreted to introduce new dimensions into the use of the per se doctrine. Until *Fortner* the general understanding had been that once a particular practice became subject to the per se doctrine, the judicially announced prerequisite for per se illegality set forth the sole standards of illegality. Under that view, for example, a tie-in imposed by a firm not having economic power in the tying product not only would not be illegal per se but also could not be found to be unreasonable under the rule of reason.

The traditional interpretation is supported by *Northern Pacific* itself. Mr. Justice Black there explained that although § 1 of the Sherman Act "preclud[es] only those contracts or combinations

---

[127] Record, p. 313a; 1968 Trade Cases ¶ 72576, at p. 85994.

[128] 394 U.S. at 525.

which 'unreasonably' restrain competition," certain practices are "presumed to be unreasonable and therefore illegal without elaborate inquiry as to the precise harm they have caused or the business excuse for their use."[129] This presumption of unreasonableness was justified, he explained, on both substantive and procedural grounds. The "pernicious effect on competition and lack of any redeeming virtue of certain practices" warranted such out-of-hand condemnation.[130] And use of the per se doctrine "avoids the necessity for an incredibly complicated and prolonged economic investigation into the entire history of the industry involved, as well as related industries, in an effort to determine at large whether a particular restraint has been unreasonable—an inquiry so often wholly fruitless when undertaken."[131]

Language near the beginning of the *Fortner* opinion appears to reintroduce the possibility of such a thoroughgoing investigation where a tie-in is alleged but either the economic power or the foreclosure prerequisite is not established: "A preliminary error that should not pass unnoticed is the District Court's assumption that two prerequisites mentioned in *Northern Pacific* are standards that petitioner must meet in order to prevail on the merits. On the contrary, these standards are necessary only to bring into play the doctrine of *per se* illegality."[132] Although the presence of the two prerequisites justified summary judgment for plaintiff in *Northern Pacific* and *International Salt*, those decisions "by no means implied that inability to satisfy these standards would be fatal to a plaintiff's case," since the "general standards of the Sherman Act" remain.[133]

The conclusion that a challenged practice must clear two hurdles successively—first the per se and then the reasonableness test—cannot be said to be illogical. The basic test of § 1 is reasonableness, and the fact that a practice in some circumstances may be patently unreasonable does not mean that in other circumstances it may not prove to be, on close analysis, an unreasonable restraint.

Two practical objections to what might be called the "two-hurdle doctrine" may, however, be interposed. First, if the firm imposing a tie-in does not have economic power in the market for the tying product or if the foreclosure in the market for the

---

[129] 356 U.S. at 5.   [131] *Ibid.*

[130] *Id.* at 5.   [132] 394 U.S. at 499–500.   [133] *Id.* at 500.

tied product is not substantial, then surely one can conclude that the effect of the tie-in is de minimis. Since the rule-of-reason test is whether the restraint, and not merely the practice itself, is unreasonable, the Sherman Act should not be construed to invalidate a practice that has a negligible effect. Even under the now discredited "quantitative substantiality" test of *Standard Stations*,[134] for example, exclusive dealing practices are not illegal where the foreclosure is not substantial.

The second practical objection is that the two-hurdle doctrine is likely, wherever the trial court is unwilling to grant summary judgment for the plaintiff, to turn the trial into just that "so often wholly fruitless" and "incredibly complicated and prolonged economic investigation" that Mr. Justice Black decried in *Northern Pacific*. If there is a sufficient issue of fact about the economic power or foreclosure issues to warrant a trial, then the plaintiff will be inclined to introduce his evidence on the reasonableness of the restraint lest he abandon that second string in his antitrust bow. Although one could conceive of a bifurcated trial in which the per se prerequisite issue was tried first, and then, if necessary, the reasonableness issue was tried, such an alternative would involve covering much of the same ground twice. Not only would such a split trial be wastefully repetitious, but it would also not necessarily be justified under the existing patent infringement and negligence precedents, where the split is between liability and damages.[135]

If these practical objections to the two-hurdle doctrine are persuasive reasons for staying with the "per se or nothing" approach, then comfort may be found in the possibility that Mr. Justice Black did not mean to announce any such new doctrine. When the entire passage is read in context, particularly in the light of the complaint and the briefs, one may conclude that it is unlikely that Mr. Justice Black meant what the passages just discussed would appear on their face to say. After the language just discussed comes a sentence that suggests he was talking about applying a reasonableness test not to the tie-in allegation but rather to the conspiracy allegation: "[E]ven if we could agree with the District Court that the *Northern Pacific*

---

[134] Standard Oil Co. v. United States, 337 U.S. 293 (1949). And see Tampa Electric Co. v. Nashville Coal Co., 365 U.S. 320, 327 (1961).

[135] Cases permitting separate trials on affirmative defenses are also distinguishable. See generally 5 MOORE'S FEDERAL PRACTICE ¶ 42.03 (1968).

standards were not satisfied here, the summary judgment against petitioner still could not be entered without further examination of petitioner's general allegations that respondents conspired together for the purpose of restraining competition and acquiring a monopoly in the market for prefabricated houses."[136] The complaint, it may be noted, does not refer to the challenged clause as a tying arrangement. Rather it charges that the two defendants conspired to restrain trade under § 1 and to monopolize under § 2.[137] In the light of its defeat in both lower courts, the plaintiff made its principal point at the Supreme Court level that whatever the law on tie-ins might be, the two defendants had conspired with each other.[138] The defendants' brief led off with contention that the conspiracy theory was "a new theory . . . not urged below,"[139] a contention hotly denied in the reply brief.[140] This aspect of *Fortner* is largely ignored in the opinions, except for the passage here under consideration and Mr. Justice Black's statement that no conventional credit sale was involved, since one corporation provided the credit and the other sold the product. In the light of the complaint and the briefs, it may thus be concluded that Mr. Justice Black simply meant to say that even if the defendants should win on the tie-in issue, the plaintiff would still be entitled to a jury trial on the "general allegations that respondents conspired together for the purpose of restraining competition and acquiring a monopoly in the market for prefabricated houses."[141]

This attempt to explain away the two-hurdle doctrine may, however, render the passage subject to even more strenuous objection. Even if one ignores the special difficulties posed by this invocation of the intra-enterprise conspiracy doctrine,[142] one can nonetheless be surprised by the suggestion that two firms can conspire in violation of § 2 to commit an act which, if committed, is not illegal.[143]

---

[136] 394 U.S. at 500.

[137] Record, pp. 21a–22a.

[138] Petitioner's Brief, pp. 14–25.

[139] Respondent's Brief, p. 33.

[140] Petitioner's Reply Brief, pp. 4–6.

[141] 394 U.S. at 500.

[142] By citing the intra-enterprise conspiracy cases, 394 U.S. at 507 n. 4, Mr. Justice Black made *Fortner* an additional authority for that form-over-substance doctrine.

[143] The § 2 conspiracy-to-monopolize theory may also be subject to the somewhat different objection that the plaintiff did not offer to prove the existence of a dangerous probability that, if the conspiracy were successful, a monopoly would have resulted. American Tobacco Co. v. United States, 328 U.S. 781, 785 (1946). But see United States v. Consolidated Laundries Corp., 291 F.2d 563, 572–73 (2d Cir. 1961).

The intra-enterprise conspiracy cases to date have involved situations where related corporations were engaged in activity that would be illegal if engaged in by unrelated corporations. Among the practices thus potentially unlawful when engaged in by related corporations have been price-fixing[144] and allocation of territories.[145] Those are practices which are not illegal when only a single trader is involved. Therefore, a finding of multiplicity of actors via the intra-enterprise conspiracy doctrine is often the sine qua non of liability. A tie-in, on the other hand, is in substance a single-trader offense, the jurisdictional agreement being the agreement of sale itself. But if a credit sale does not constitute an illegal tie-in when imposed by a single firm, it is not clear why it should be illegal when two firms are involved, particularly if those two firms are not competitors. And if such a sale is an unlawful restraint of trade, then surely it is unlawful whether or not the defendants are related. One hesitates to conclude that Mr. Justice Black meant to suggest that independent lenders taking security in goods may not pass on the source of those goods.[146]

Thus, although the two-hurdle language in *Fortner* may be explained away as referring only to the intra-enterprise conspiracy doctrine, such an explanation would create new doctrinal difficulties not touched on by Mr. Justice Black.

VII. FORTNER AND THE PRIVATE ACTION

Although *Fortner* expresses great concern for U.S. Steel's competitors, who are said to be at a competitive disadvantage because they do not have its "vast sums of money," the ruling redounds directly to the benefit of one of the purchasers of U.S. Steel's products, Fortner Enterprises. Such a consequence is not surprising. In *Northern Pacific* Mr. Justice Black argued that tying arrangements harmed both competitiors and buyers. Tie-ins, he

---

[144] *E.g.*, Keifer-Stewart Co. v. Joseph E. Seagram & Sons, Inc., 340 U.S. 211 (1951).

[145] Timken Roller Bearing Co. v. United States, 341 U.S. 593 (1951).

[146] Certain facts in the record might distinguish the Credit Corporation's position from that of the typical independent lender. Certain Credit Corporation loans were guaranteed by the Homes Division pursuant to an underwriting agreement. Record, pp. 439a–442a, 764a. And although some residual control over source might be essential to assure the value of the collateral, the Credit Corporation insisted on Homes Division products in all cases. Thus, a conspiracy is easier to infer in *Fortner* than would ordinarily be true with independent lenders.

said, "deny competitors free access to the market for its tied product," and, at the same time, "buyers are forced to forego their free choice between competing products."[147] A paradox in *Fortner* is that Mr. Justice Black ignores the buyer justification in reaching a result directly benefiting a buyer while emphasizing at great length the competitor justification in a case where any harm to competitors is totally speculative.

Perhaps one of the explanations for this paradox is that when the market power criterion is watered down as far as it has been in *Fortner* and applied to as unusual a transaction as a credit sale, the buyer justification is hardly applicable. Certainly it is hard to believe that Fortner Enterprises was injured by accepting the tie-in. To be sure, it would have been better off with both the Credit Corporation credit and the right to pick and choose suppliers, but that choice would never have existed even if the result of the *Fortner* litigation had been known in advance. The Credit Corporation was not a bank. Furthermore, the Credit Corporation was only one of a great many sources of credit. The advantageous terms were not imposed on the plaintiff. It was Fortner himself who, throughout the extended negotiations, demanded easier terms than the Credit Corporation was offering. Moreover, having compromised his own freedom to buy competing products to the extent of the loan, Fortner sought a further loan on identical terms.[148] Certainly the plaintiff's assertion that it was only through "economic necessity" that Fortner accepted the tie-in is difficult to square with the history of the negotiations.[149]

Perma Life Mufflers suggests that Mr. Justice Black would see no anomaly in granting treble damages to one who had actively solicited the illegal transaction. In that case he sought to read the *in pari delicto* doctrine out of the antitrust laws on pragmatic law enforcement grounds:[150]

> The plaintiff who reaps the reward of treble damages may
> be no less morally reprehensible than the defendant, but the

---

[147] 356 U.S. at 6. The enchancement of freedom of choice of distributors through antitrust policy is an important theme in Supreme Court decisions, particularly in resale price-maintenance cases. See Albrecht v. Herald Co., 390 U.S. 145, 152–53 (1968); Kiefer-Stewart Co. v. Seagram & Sons, Inc., 340 U.S. 211, 213 (1951).

[148] See text *supra*, at notes 14–17.

[149] Petitioner's Brief, pp. 16–20; Record, p. 290a.

[150] Perma Life Mufflers, Inc. v. International Parts Corp., 392 U.S. 135, 139 (1968).

law encourages his suit to further the overriding public policy in favor of competition. A more fastidious regard for the relative moral worth of the parties would only result in seriously undermining the usefulness of the private action as a bulwark of antitrust enforcement.

Thus, even though Fortner aggressively sought precisely the contractual arrangement he obtained, his recourse to the court system is to be encouraged as a "bulwark of antitrust enforcement."[151]

The enthusiasm of the Supreme Court for the private action has been manifested in a number of decisions of procedural antitrust issues. The Supreme Court has uniformly decided these cases for plaintiffs, candidly offering the justification that private actions are to be encouraged. The cases on the standards for summary judgment, of which *Fortner* is one, are examples.[152] *Perma Life*, the *in pari delicto* decision, is another. Others include decisions limiting the "passing on" defense,[153] eliminating the public injury requirement,[154] and expanding the scope of the provision tolling limitations in § 5(b) of the Clayton Act.[155]

One can hardly deny that the private action plays a major, perhaps indispensable, role in the enforcement of the antitrust laws. The resources of the Antitrust Division are severely limited. So long as fines for criminal antitrust violations are subject to the present absurdly low maximum,[156] large corporations have more to fear from the private litigant than from the government.

---

[151] It is doubtful that an *in pari delicto* defense would have been available even before *Perma Life*, if for no other reason than that Fortner had not sought the tying clause itself. A motion to amend the answer to set forth an *in pari delicto* defense was held by the district court to have been filed too late. Record, pp. 320a, 927a.

A touch of irony may be detected in the Court's holding in a case decided only a few months after *Fortner* that a licensee may not challenge a package patent license (which bears a close analytical resemblance to a tying contract) where he did not demand individual patent licenses at the time of the original negotiations. Zenith Radio Corp. v. Hazeltine Research, Inc., 395 U.S. 100 (1969).

[152] See text *supra*, at notes 42–49.

[153] Hanover Shoe, Inc. v. United Shoe Machinery Corp., 392 U.S. 481 (1968).

[154] Klor's, Inc. v. Broadway & Hale Stores, Inc., 359 U.S. 207 (1959); Radiant Burners, Inc. v. People's Gas Light & Coke Co., 364 U.S. 656 (1961).

[155] Leh v. General Petroleum Corp., 382 U.S. 54 (1965); Minnesota Mining & Mfg. Co. v. New Jersey Wood Finishing Co., 381 U.S. 311 (1965).

[156] Violations of the Sherman Act are subject to a maximum fine of $50,000. 15 U.S.C. § 1. See discussion in the *Stigler Task Force Report*, 5 CCH Trade Reg. Rep. ¶ 50250, at pp. 55521–22 (1969).

Fortner suggests, however, that enthusiasm for the private suit should not be unbounded. In the first place, it is far from clear that the case would have been brought by a rational enforcement agency. Certainly the odds are extremely slim that the Antitrust Division would have brought the case, even if its resources had been multiplied. U.S. Steel's attempt to establish itself in the Louisville market intensified competition in the housing market there and, insofar as one can judge from the record, in the local money market as well.[157] Any harm to competitors of the Homes Division is totally undocumented. And in this particular point in our national history, with mounting concern over the spiraling costs of housing, it might be thought to be in the public interest to encourage the introduction of factory-built houses in markets dominated by conventional construction methods.

Quite aside from doubts about the effect on competition of this species of private action, one may also have qualms about the relation between the antitrust laws and private law in the resolution of commercial disputes. This dispute was over the quality of goods. The plaintiff was not concerned about the effect of the loan agreement on competition until the deal went sour.[158] On the contrary, he sought an additional loan on identical terms some months after the first loan and after delivery of a number of houses. The private action was in *Fortner* simply what it has become with increasing frequency, an ace in the hand of a distributor in commercial disagreements with his manufacturer. Instead of being limited to the sales law measure of damages, the plaintiff was enabled to sue for three times its prospective profits plus attorney's fees and costs. The question of who was responsible for the failure of the housing project need never be litigated, except possibly in assessing the amount of damages.[159]

---

[157] See text *supra*, at notes 89–94.

[158] The record suggests that a slump in the Louisville new homes market may have contributed significantly to the plaintiff's difficulties. The rate of single-family dwelling completions in 1960–61 averaged less than 75 percent of the rate in the 1958–59 and 1963–65 periods. Record, p. 277a.

[159] The amended complaint sought "treble the sum of $249,837.31 . . . , a reasonable fee for the services of its attorneys in prosecuting this action, and its costs herein expended." Seventy houses were delivered at a price of about $3,000–$4,500 each plus tax and prepaid freight. Record, pp. 22a, 457a–632a. Sixty-two of the seventy houses had been sold to the public. *Id.* at 116a–118a.

The potential conflict between antitrust and private law policies has been considered by the Supreme Court in the context of antitrust defenses to actions for the price of goods sold. Such a defense was held improper on the ground that "the courts are to be guided by the overriding general policy, as Justice Holmes put it, 'of preventing people from getting other people's property for nothing when they purport to be buying it.' "[160] Although the contract defense cases can be distinguished, the treble-damage action nonetheless affords the purchaser the analogous possibility of waiting to see whether a transaction is profitable before deciding whether to pay or to sue.

It is probably no exaggeration to say that the private antitrust action has come to outweigh the Federal Trade Commission proceeding and the Antitrust Division action in practical importance.[161] The reasons for this development are complex, but surely one of the reasons is the steady expansion of the substantive law. In the area of manufacturer-distributor relations the trend of decisions has been toward protecting the distributor against unfair acts of the manufacturer rather than toward improving the allocation of resources and lowering prices to consumers, which are the economic *raisons d'être* of competition.[162] The emphasis on fairness suggests that the antitrust laws on vertical arrangements are coming increasingly to play for distribution agreements the role that the private law on contracts of adhesion has played for the insurance contract. The *Fortner* decision, while paradoxically relying solely on supposed harm to competitors, furthers this trend. Not only does it give franchisees and other distributors a new theory by which to challenge manufacturers wherever financing or other services are provided, but it also assures them a chance to appeal to the sympathy of a jury regardless of the substantiality of their offer of proof.

---

[160] Kelly v. Kosuga, 358 U.S. 516, 520–21 (1959).

[161] See A.B.A. Section on Antitrust Law, Antitrust Developments 1955–1968 274–75 (1968).

[162] See generally Bork, *The Rule of Reason and the Per Se Concept: Price Fixing and Market Division,* 74 Yale L.J. 775 (1965); 75 Yale L.J. 373 (1966).

G. E. HALE and ROSEMARY D. HALE

THE OTTER TAIL POWER CASE:

REGULATION BY COMMISSION OR

ANTITRUST LAWS

Over a decade ago we surveyed a number of regulated industries to determine whether it was unnecessary and undesirable that the industries be subject to the antitrust laws.[1] Our conclusion, in a nutshell, was that a "pervasively" regulated industry should be exempt from antitrust regulation.

There have been important developments in the intervening years. Courts have handed down scores of decisions. Technological changes have taken place, increasing the possibility of competition in what was once regarded as the public utility sector of the economy.[2] A microwave system operating between St. Louis and Chicago opens the door to competition in the telephone industry. CATV systems are growing despite FCC opposition. Another important development is the concept of Total Energy that envisions

---

G. E. Hale is a member of the Illinois Bar. Rosemary D. Hale is Professor of Economics, Lake Forest College.

[1] Hale & Hale, *Competition or Control VI: Application of Antitrust Laws to Regulated Industries*, 111 U. PA. L. REV. 46 (1962); Hale & Hale, *Mergers in Regulated Industries*, 59 Nw. U. L. REV. 49 (1964).

[2] Gies, *The Need for New Concepts in Public Utility Regulation*, in SHEPHERD & GIES, eds., UTILITY REGULATION: NEW DIRECTIONS IN THEORY AND POLICY 88–111 (1966); Kestenbaum, *Competition in Communications*, 16 ANTITRUST BULL. 679, 773 (1971); Trebing, *Common Carrier Regulation—the Silent Crisis*, 34 LAW & CONTEMP. PROB. 299 (1969); Rosan, *Comment*, in TREBING, ed., PERFORMANCE UNDER REGULATION 128–30 (1968).

an arrangement whereby the proprietors of a shopping plaza or an office building generate their own electricity and use the exhaust for heating and cooling. Obviously such a system competes with regulated electric utilities.

With such developments in mind we propose, first, to ascertain from the new decisions the degree to which regulated industries are exempt from the antitrust laws, and, second, whether there are conflicts between regulation by commission and by the antitrust laws and how they might be reconciled.

I. Cases Applying Antitrust Principles to Utilities

It would be easy to make a case that the antitrust laws are now fully applicable to all public utilities and that commission regulation is no impediment thereto. A vivid illustration of that trend is found in the very recent decision of the United States Supreme Court in *Otter Tail Power Co. v. United States*.[3] Otter Tail is an electric utility regulated by both state and federal authorities. Under federal statutes the Federal Power Commission was expressly authorized to require Otter Tail to supply wholesale power to municipally owned distribution systems.[4] The FPC did not act and suit was brought under the antitrust laws against Otter Tail by the United States for refusing to sell at wholesale to the municipal distribution system. The United States Supreme Court, in a four-to-three decision, approved a decree requiring such an interstate connection. The opinion for the majority by Mr. Justice Douglas brushed aside the possibility of conflict with the jurisdiction of the Federal Power Commission, saying:[5]

> [The decree] . . . contemplates that future disputes over interconnections . . . will be subject to Federal Power Commission perusal. It will be time enough to consider whether the antitrust remedy may override the power of the Commission . . . as, if and when the Commission denies the interconnection and the District Court nevertheless undertakes to direct it.

In the concurring and dissenting opinion by Mr. Justice Stewart a more complex view was taken of the conflict between the two forms of regulation:[6]

---

[3] 410 U.S. 366 (1973).

[4] *Id*. at 373.

[5] *Id*. at 376–77.

[6] *Id*. at 394–95.

The Court goes on vaguely to suggest that there will be time to cope with the problem of a Commission refusal to order interconnection which conflicts with this antitrust decree when such a conflict arises.

But the basic conflict between the Commission's authority and the decree entered in the District Court cannot be so easily wished away. . . . The Court's decree plainly ignores the Commission's authority to decide *whether* the involuntary interconnection is warranted. . . . Unless the decree is modified, its future implementation will starkly conflict with the explicit statutory mandate of the Federal Power Commission.

Otter Tail is far from the only decision of its kind. Another devastating blow was dealt to regulation in *Cascade Natural Gas Corp. v. El Paso Gas Co.*[7] That prolonged litigation involved the acquisition by El Paso Natural Gas Company of another corporation also operating a gas pipeline. The two pipelines were not in competition since they did not traverse the same territory. They did, however, form a connection on an end-to-end basis. Here again, the jurisdiction of the state and federal regulatory agencies was ignored and the Supreme Court ruled that full divestiture of the acquired pipeline must be accomplished despite a lower court settlement of the matter to the contrary.

Numerous other cases can be cited to the same effect. Stockyards subject to the powers of the Secretary of Agriculture have also been subjected to the antitrust laws.[8] The New York Stock Exchange, regulated in detail by the SEC, was held liable in damages under antitrust principles.[9] The jurisdiction of the Federal Maritime Commission was not sufficient to prevent antitrust applications to the corporations it regulated.[10]

This trend is not new. For decades the antitrust laws have been

---

[7] 386 U.S. 129 (1967).

[8] Denver Union Stockyard Co. v. Denver Live Stock Commission Company, 404 F.2d 1055 (10th Cir. 1968).

[9] Silver v. New York Stock Exchange, 373 U.S. 341 (1963).

[10] Federal Maritime Comm'n v. Seatrain Lines, Inc., 411 U.S. 726, 732–33 (1973): "The Commission vigorously argues that such agreements can be interpreted as falling within the third category—which concerns agreements 'controlling, regulating, preventing, or destroying competition.' Without more, we might be inclined to agree that many merger agreements probably fit within this category. But a broad reading of the third category would conflict with our frequently expressed view that exemptions from antitrust laws are strictly construed, . . ." See also Deaktor v. L. D. Schreiber & Co., 479 F.2d 529 (7th Cir. 1973).

applied to the railroads despite the regulatory powers of the Inter-state Commerce Commission.[11] And in some instances the regula-tory commissions have themselves been directed by the courts to consider alleged antitrust issues in proceedings before them. Thus in *Gulf States Utilities Co. v. F.P.C.*,[12] it was said:

> This power clearly carries with it the responsibility to con-sider, in appropriate circumstances, the anticompetitive effects of regulated aspects of interstate utility operations pursuant to §§ 202 and 203, and under like directives contained in §§ 205, 206, and 207. The Act did not render antitrust policy irrele-vant to the Commission's regulation of the electric power industry. Indeed, within the confines of a basic natural mo-nopoly structure, limited competition of the sort protected by the antitrust laws seems to have been anticipated. . . .
>
> Nothing in the Act suggests that the "public interest" stan-dard of § 204 contains any less broad directive than that con-tained in the other similarly worded and adjacent sections. Under the express language of § 204 the public interest is stressed as a governing factor. There is nothing that indicates that the meaning of that term is to be restricted to financial considerations, with every other aspect of the public interest ignored. Further, there is the section's requirement that the object of the issue be lawful. The Commission is directed to in-quire into and to evaluate the purpose of the issue and the use to which its proceeds will be put. Without a more definite indication of contrary legislative purpose, we shall not read out of § 204 the requirement that the Commission consider matters relating to both the broad purposes of the Act and the fundamental national economic policy expressed in the anti-trust laws. . . .

This direction, of course, is at variance with the decision in the natural gas pipeline cases where the implication was that the com-mission had no role whatsoever in such matters.

II. On the Other Hand

Despite the authorities just cited, a good many cases have gone in the other direction. Hence it is far from clear that the fact of regulation will not provide at least some degree of shelter from the application of the antitrust laws.

---

[11] See United States v. Trans-Missouri Freight Ass'n, 166 U.S. 290 (1897).

[12] 411 U.S. 747, 758–59 (1973); cf. Utility Users League v. F.P.C., 394 F.2d 16 (7th Cir. 1968).

First there is the doctrine of primary jurisdiction that requires submission of an antitrust issue to the regulatory commission in advance of court determination. The basic theory is that the regulatory body with its vast expertise will guide the court in the resolution of the antitrust issue. One might think in the light of cases such as *Otter Tail Power*, that no role was left for the application of that doctrine. To the contrary, the United States Supreme Court, in the 1972 Term, also handed down its opinion in *Ricci v. Chicago Mercantile Exchange*,[13] applying the doctrine of primary jurisdiction.

In that case the plaintiff had challenged the membership rules of the Chicago Mercantile Exchange. The Court coolly announced that the Commodities Exchange Act contemplated that the exchange and its members could engage in restraints of trade which might otherwise be held unreasonable.[14] Accordingly, the membership rules of the exchange fell under the jurisdiction of the Commodities Exchange Commission, and the case was referred to the commission to resolve issues with respect to the facts and to evaluate them. After such evaluation, the Court announced in a five-to-four decision, it would then be time to decide whether the antitrust suit would be barred.[15]

Other decisions invoking the doctrine of primary jurisdiction in recent years have involved REA Express,[16] Executive Airlines,[17] Monsanto Company,[18] and Macom Products Co.[19] The dissent in the *Otter Tail* case expressly referred to these matters and pointed out the seeming contradiction among them.[20]

The courts, however, have gone farther than to apply the doctrine of primary jurisdiction. In several important decisions they have found that the regulated industry was wholly exempt from the operation of the antitrust law. Perhaps the most startling decision was that in *Hughes Tool Co. v. T.W.A.*[21] After years of litigation in the lower courts, Trans World Airlines secured an enor-

---

[13] 409 U.S. 289 (1973).

[14] *Id.* at 303–04.   [15] *Id.* at 307–08.

[16] REA Express, Inc. v. Alabama Great Southern Railroad, 412 U.S. 934 (1973).

[17] Executive Airlines v. Air New England, 357 F. Supp. 345 (D. Mass. 1973).

[18] Monsanto Co. v. United Gas Pipe Line Co., 360 F. Supp. 1054 (D.D.C. 1973).

[19] Macom Products Corp. v. A.T.&T., 359 F. Supp. 973 (C.D. Cal. 1973). See also Price v. T.W.A., 481 F.2d 844 (9th Cir. 1973).

[20] 410 U.S. at 391.   [21] 409 U.S. 363 (1973).

mous judgment against Hughes Tool. That judgment was upset by the United States Supreme Court on the ground that transactions authorized by the Civil Aeronautics Board could not be the subject of antitrust attacks. Competition was also given short shrift in approving the merger of the New York Central and Pennsylvania railroads.[22] Other cases to the same effect can be found in recent years.[23]

In the lower courts several decisions have involved clashes between gas and electric utilities. Typically, the gas companies have attacked rates offered by the electric utilities. Here again, the courts have found an exemption from the antitrust laws in the existence of state regulatory approval. Even inaction by the regulatory commission has been held sufficient to confer an exemption from antitrust liability.[24]

Thus despite the vigorous language of the *Otter Tail* decision it is far from clear that regulated utility companies are fully subject to the antitrust laws. The resulting confusion has no doubt led in some measure to disillusionment of the bar and the public utility enterprises.[25]

III. Failure of Regulation

One factor bearing upon this problem is the tidal wave of adverse comment that has descended upon the regulatory agencies in recent years. Disillusionment with regulation is rampant. Professor George J. Stigler, characteristically more vigorous than other economists, has asserted:[26]

> Regulation may be actively sought by an industry, or it may be thrust upon it. A central thesis of this paper is that, as

---

[22] Penn Central Merger Cases, 389 U.S. 486, 499–500 (1968).

[23] See Northern Natural Gas Co. v. F.P.C., 399 F.2d 953 (D.C. Cir. 1968). In *Pan American Airways, Inc. v. United States*, 371 U.S. 296 (1963), the exemption from the antitrust laws was expressly founded on the existence of regulation.

[24] Gas Light Co. of Columbus v. Georgia Power Co., 440 F.2d 1135, 1137–38, 1140 (5th Cir. 1971); Washington Gas Light Co. v. Virginia Electric Co., 438 F.2d 248, 252 (4th Cir. 1971); cf. Business Aides, Inc. v. Chesapeake & Potomac Tel. Co., 480 F.2d 754 (4th Cir. 1973); Utility Users League, note 12 *supra;* Mathews v. Jersey Central Power & Light Co., CCH ¶ 50,176 (21 June 1973), see also Allstate Insurance Co. v. Lanier, 361 F.2d 870 (4th Cir. 1966).

[25] Kauper, *The "Warren Court" and the Antitrust Laws*, 67 Mich. L. Rev. 325 (1968).

[26] Stigler, *The Theory of Economic Regulation*, 2 Bell J. Econ. & Manag. 3, 5 (1971).

a rule, regulation is acquired by the industry and is designed and operated primarily for its benefit.

.   .   .   .

The second major public resource commonly sought by an industry is control over entry by new rivals. There is considerable, not to say excessive, discussion in economic literature of the rise of peculiar price policies (limit prices), vertical integration, and similar devices to retard the rate of entry of new firms into oligopolistic industries. Such devices are vastly less efficacious (economical) than the certificate of convenience and necessity (which includes, of course, the import and production quotas of the oil and tobacco industries).

Professor Stigler went on to suggest that regulated industry does not try to extract money directly from government. Instead, it seeks to bar new entrance into competition through governmental machinery.[27]

We propose the general hypothesis: every industry or occupation that has enough political power to utilize the state will seek to control entry. In addition, the regulatory policy will often be so fashioned as to retard the rate of growth of new firms.

After an industry has achieved entry control it will often, according to Professor Stigler, want price controls administered by a body with coercive power. This control is desired in order to obtain more than a competitive rate of return. It will also, by statute or otherwise, seek to control or eliminate the production of substitutes.[28]

An important factor for consideration is the cost of administrative proceedings. One student found that the price of gas sold in interstate commerce was 5 to 6 percent higher than that sold in intrastate commerce because of the expense of proceedings before the Federal Power Commission.[29] This is a not insignificant matter when one

---

[27] *Id.* at 5.   [28] *Id.* at 6.

[29] *Id.* at 7. Professor Stigler further noted: "The idealistic view of public regulation is deeply imbedded in professional economic thought. So many economists, for example, have denounced the ICC for its pro-railroad policies that this has become a cliché of the literature. This criticism seems to me exactly as appropriate as a criticism of the Great Atlantic and Pacific Tea Company for selling groceries, or as a criticism of a politician for currying popular support. The fundamental vice of such criticism is that it misdirects attention: it suggests that the way to get an ICC which is not subservient to the carriers is to preach to the commissioners or to the people who appoint the commissioners. The only way to get a different commission would be to change the political support for the

considers that assets of public utilities may constitute almost a fifth of total industrial capacity.[30]

Another student who takes a dim view of regulatory commissions is Professor Ronald Coase:[31]

> What I have in mind is a feature which, with the best will in the world, it seems to me very difficult to eliminate. However fluid an organization may be in its beginning, it must inevitably adopt certain policies and organizational forms which condition its thinking and limit the range of its policies. . . . It is difficult to operate closely with an industry without coming to look at its problems in industry terms. The result is that the commission, although thinking of itself as apart from and with different aims from the industry, will nonetheless be incapable of conceiving of or bringing about any radical changes in industry practices or structure.
>
> This opposition [to pay television] comes, as Dr. Frank Stanton of CBS told us, not because the industry has any "economic axe to grind," but because it would not be in the best interests of the public. It is, I think, a universal rule that businessmen never act from higher motives than when they are engaged in restricting potential competition.

Other observers are equally disillusioned about public utility control. Professor Massel is a good example:

> Public utility regulation in the United States is enveloped in a legalistic framework which provides few positive pressures for greater efficiency, more innovation or substantial cost reduction. The regulatory process has been evolved through the

---

Commission, and reward commissioners on a basis unrelated to their services to the carriers.

"Until the basic logic of political life is developed, reformers will be ill-equipped to use the state for their reforms, and victims of the pervasive use of the state's support of special groups will be helpless to protect themselves. Economists should quickly establish the license to practice on the rational theory of political behavior." *Id.* at 17–18.

[30] Daniel, *The Regulation of Private Enterprises as Public Utilities*, 34 Soc. Res. 347 (1967); Stigler, *The Process of Economic Regulation*, 17 Antitrust Bull. 207 (1972): "The specialized agency [regulatory commission], however, is as welcome to the regulated activity as it is necessary to the legislature: by constant association and pressure the regulator is brought to a cooperative and even complaisant attitude toward the regulated group."

[31] Coase, *The Economics of Broadcasting and Government Policy*, 56 Am. Ec. Rev. 440, 442, 446 (1966). See also Loevinger, *Regulation and Competition as Alternatives*, 11 Antitrust Bull. 101 (1966).

inherited superstitions of generations of lawyers, who have usually looked upon regulation as an exercise in legal procedures.[32]

In his view the commissions are constantly seeking a magic mechanical formula which can be applied to all situations. They refuse to consider the effects of their price policy on consumption or demand.[33]

Many other observers have called for a review of regulatory policies. They seek to find what the actual effects of regulations have been. The old complaint about combining legislative, executive, and judicial functions in one agency is by no means dead. It has been pointed out that the effort to "judicialize" the conduct of the agencies has led to many problems including inordinate delays.[34] Recurrent, however, is the theme that regulation is actually protective rather than regulatory in character:[35]

. . . without regulation the firm would face competition from neighboring firms which might encroach on its territory. To

---

[32] Massel, *The Regulatory Process and Public Utility Performance*, in TREBING, note 2 *supra*, at 113. He continued: ". . . the regulatory problems have been left largely in the hands of the lawyers with some help from the accountants. The legal profession has dominated the regulatory process in the companies, the legislatures, the commissions and the courts. Counsel for the companies and the regulatory agencies have had to carry on their battles with small assistance from other professions. Public considerations of the problems of regulation have usually been regarded as the domain of the lawyers, who have pursued their natural bent for improving procedures while issues of substance have fallen between the chairs." *Id*. at 114.

[33] *Id*. at 115–16. He complained further: "A natural result of the dearth of economic analysis has been a disregard of experience. Despite the many thousands of decisions which have been made, there has been little interest in examining the consequences of these rulings. Virtually no attention has been paid to the effects of the past proceedings on rate levels, volume of activity, efficiency, costs, and innovation. When a decision is made, the job is done."

[34] See, *e.g.*, Trebing, *Government Regulation and Modern Capitalism*, 3 J. ECON. ISSUES 94 (March 1969); PHILLIPS, THE ECONOMICS OF REGULATION: THEORY AND PRACTICE IN THE TRANSPORTATION AND PUBLIC UTILITY INDUSTRIES 712–13 (1965): "The independent regulatory commission combines in the same body legislative, judicial, and executive functions in regulation of an industry. A number of advantages were assumed to accrue to regulatory commissions, including continuity of policy, expertise, impartiality, experimentation, and flexibility in procedures. And independence was designed to gain for commissions the isolation from politics enjoyed by the judiciary. Today, however, all these supposed virtues have been challenged." He referred also to the inordinate delays in deciding cases. *Id*. at 730.

[35] Moore, *The Effectiveness of Regulation of Electric Utility Prices*, 36 SOUTHERN ECON. J. 365, 374 (1970).

the extent that this type of competition is possible, any removal of regulation would increase the elasticity of demand
faced by a single firm above the elasticity of the market and
so lead to lower prices.

It has been argued further that deregulation would not necessarily
require the establishment of "pure" competition. Some degree of
"workable" competition would suffice.[36]

In terms of specific regulatory agencies the Federal Power Commission has frequently borne the brunt of the attack. Professor
MacAvoy's study of the effect of its regulation of the price of the
gas at the well-head is devastating. He found that the result of the
regulation was to divert the gas to unregulated consumers at the
expense of domestic and commercial patrons.[37] Another calculation
indicated that the cost of regulation of the price of natural gas ran
to about 7 percent of the base price.[38] This is indeed a high expense
for achieving a negative benefit.

The pioneer study of this type, and still one of the most important studies, was that carried out by Professor Stigler and
Mrs. Friedland with respect to the rates of electric utilities. The
public utility commission controls were found to be almost totally
ineffective.[39] Here again, the consumer is the victim, both of regulation and of its expense.

Although somewhat rehabilitated from the iniquitous reputation
it enjoyed a few years ago, the Federal Communications Commission has likewise come in for a large share of blame. Professor Ronald Coase declared that the task imposed on the commission could
not be handled efficiently by any organization, however competent.
He found that the principal reason for the FCC's poor performance
was its method of allocating frequencies.[40] Other observers have

---

[36] Gies, note 2 *supra*, at 96; Lerner, *Toward an Improved Decision Framework for
Public Utility Regulation*, 44 LAND ECON. 403 (1968).

[37] MacAvoy, *The Regulation-Induced Shortage of Natural Gas*, 14 J. LAW & ECON.
167 (1971).

[38] Gerwig, *Natural Gas Production: A Study of the Costs of Regulation*, 5 J. LAW &
ECON. 69, 91 (1962).

[39] Stigler & Friedland, *What Can Regulators Regulate? The Case of Electricity*, 5 J. LAW
& ECON. 1 (1962); see Stathas, *Some Future Considerations and Implications for Regulated
Industries and Regulatory Agencies*, in THE ECONOMICS OF REGULATION OF PUBLIC UTILITIES
172, 173, 184, 185 (1969); Moore, note 35 *supra*, at 374.

[40] Coase, *Evaluation of Public Policy Relating to Radio and Television Broadcasting: Social
and Economic Issues*, 41 LAND ECON. 161 (1965); ". . . it is my considered opinion that

condemned the FCC for its attempt to obstruct the so-called CATV industry in order to protect television licensees already in the market.[41] Many other uncomplimentary comments have been made about the Communications Commission, perhaps the most important being that it gave only minor attention to the vital questions of prices and costs.[42] The activities of the same commission in the television industry have also met with unfavorable response.[43] One student enumerated the following fundamental mistakes made by the commission:[44]

1. It has not solved the standard of subsidization.
2. Its studies have been inadequate to solve its problems.
3. It has not attacked the cost-benefit problem or established adequate guidelines for spectrum use.
4. Its case-by-case approach to various market problems is unlikely to constitute an effective method of coping with its tasks.

Professor Cramton raised the question whether regulation really did anything other than enrich lawyers and create vested property interests.[45]

Even the Interstate Commerce Commission, long the revered

---

the task imposed on the FCC could not be handled efficiently by any organization, however competent." Professor Coase wrote further: "The task of charting a sensible future for the broadcasting industry is not one which can be left to the industry, which has its own interests to protect. It cannot be left to the Federal Communications Commission, which cannot conceive of any future which is not essentially a repetition of the past. Who, therefore, is to perform this task? I suggest that it has to be assumed by academic economists. . . . I would not argue that academic economists are technically the best qualified to investigate what government policy should be toward the broadcasting industry. But unless they do it, no one else will." *Id.* at 446–47. Cf. Frech, *Institutions for Allocating the Radio-TV Spectrum and the Vested Interests*, 4 J. ECON. ISSUES 23, 30–36 (Dec. 1970).

[41] Barnett & Greenberg, *Regulating CATV Systems: An Analysis of FCC Policy and an Alternative*, 34 LAW & CONTEMP. PROB. 562 (1969); Park, *Cable Television, UHF Broadcasting and FCC Regulatory Policy*, 15 J. LAW & ECON. 207 (1972).

[42] Comanor & Mitchell, *The Costs of Planning: The FCC and Cable Television*, 15 J. LAW & ECON. 177, 180 (1972).

[43] Frech, *More on Efficiency in the Allocation of Radio-TV Spectrum*, 5 J. ECON. ISSUES 100 (1971).

[44] TREBING, note 2 *supra*, at 315, 317, 325. Arbitrary allocation of joint costs is another FCC mistake. *Id.* at 315. The list of mistakes is long. *Id.* at 314.

[45] Cramton, *The Effectiveness of Economic Regulation: A Legal View*, 54 AM. ECON. REV. 182 (1964).

object of adoration by advocates of intervention,[46] has been the subject of bitter abuse. In the eyes of Professor (as he then was) Felix Frankfurter, the Interstate Commerce Commission, with its long record of integrity, constituted the ideal method of coping with economic problems.[47] Today scarcely anyone has a good word to say about it.[48] One of the kinder comments is that of Professor Cramton, who wrote:[49]

> The Commission, understandably, concentrates its energies on the most manageable and specific of the tasks assigned to it by the legislature: protecting interests created in the past and moderating the effects of undesirable change. The Commission's attempts to prevent or ameliorate departures from the existing rate structure and traffic pattern—a kind of soft-hearted and backward-looking cartelism—indicate its true purpose and function as a conservative body fighting a rear guard action against the inevitable forces of change.

Professor Harper was more specific in his accusations:[50]

> Restrictions on the freedom to compete that are found in entry control, rate regulation, and other aspects of regulation can be a cause of economic inefficiency in our transportation system, since they can have the effect of slowing down decision making, making it difficult for carriers to adapt quickly to changes in their environment, misallocating traffic among modes, forcing empty back hauls in some situations, providing protection to the inefficient carrier, making rates higher than they would be without regulation, making single-carrier service over long hauls difficult, discouraging initiative, preserving excess capacity, and so on. The degree of inefficiency caused by regulation is, of course, not equally distributed among the several modes. And, in addition to the problem of inefficiency, it also appears that the goals of regulation have been lost sight of in the tangle of laws and commission and court decisions that have accumulated over the past eighty years.

---

[46] See 4 SHARFMAN, THE INTERSTATE COMMERCE COMMISSION 342 (1937).

[47] See also Frankfurter, *The Interstate Commerce Commission*, in OF LAW AND LIFE AND OTHER THINGS THAT MATTER 235 (Kurland, ed., 1967).

[48] See Huntington, *The Marasmus of the ICC*, 61 YALE L. J. 467 (1952).

[49] Cramton, note 45 *supra*, at 189.

[50] Harper, *Transportation and the Public Utilities: Discussion*, 59 AM. ECON. REV. 270, 271 (1969).

Other observers have pointed out that the notion of a "fair return on fair value" is misplaced when an industry is declining but that the ICC continues to utilize it.[51] It continues to adhere to cost formulas that inhibit the use of the market as a gauge for economic pricing when numerous competitors of different kinds are seeking the same traffic.[52]

More fundamentally, the critics claim that the ICC does not have a carefully reasoned and consistently applied philosophy of the meaning of "inherent advantage"—the statutory precept applicable to its activity. Furthermore, it pays little attention to matters not presented to it by carriers and shippers, disregarding the public's viewpoint insofar as it differs from those of the mentioned adversaries.[53] It is now said that we should recognize the fact that the commission was never designed to protect the public but rather to bring order to an industry by enforced cartelization.[54] Frequent comments are made to the effect that the regulators find it convenient and comfortable to be on cozy terms with the industries which they are supposed to regulate.[55]

IV. DISTORTION OF ECONOMIC ALLOCATIONS

In general terms the argument is that all regulatory activity induces a higher than optimal level of investment and thus fails to minimize cost. In more familiar language this might be termed "inflating the rate base" so as to justify higher prices.[56] Professor West-

---

[51] Hilton, *The Basic Behavior of Regulatory Commissions*, 62 AM. ECON. REV. 47 (1972). Hilton complained that ICC regulation misallocated resources in two ways. First, it promoted monopoly, and second, it insisted on producing services not desired by patrons. *Id.* at 47.

[52] Pegrum, *Should the I.C.C. Be Abolished?* 11 TRANSP. J. 5, 10 (1971). Pegrum complained that ICC regulation had lacked flexibility, adaptability, and imagination. It was so enmeshed in detail that it had become a vast bureaucracy, usurping the functions of both management and the market.

[53] Sampson, *Inherent Advantages under Regulation*, 62 AM. ECON. REV. 55, 57 (1972).

[54] Carson, *Ralph Nader Discovers the ICC*, 5 J. ECON. ISSUES 93, 97 (June 1971). Carson draws attention to the 1935 legislation curbing motor carriers to protect the railroads.

[55] Stigler, note 30 *supra*. Journalists recently reported that state regulation of insurance companies was a farce. Blundell & Meyer, *Toothless Tigers?*, WALL ST. J. p. 1, col. 6, 2 Aug. 1973.

[56] Sheshinski, *Welfare Aspects of a Regulatory Constraint*, 61 AM. ECON. REV. 175 (1971); Takayama, *Behavior of the Firm under Regulatory Constraint*, 59 AM. ECON. REV. 255 (1969).

field declared he had demonstrated that it could be in the interests of a regulated industry to pay a higher rather than a lower price for its plant and equipment.[57] Others have avoided adverse criticism of the structure of the regulated industries, particularly the railroads. But they would prefer to apply the strict anti-merger standards of the antitrust laws.[58] Still others refer to the "static character of the regulatory structure" and suggest that it has a stultifying effect.[59] The regulated monopolist may be even less efficient than the unregulated and, in any event, there is always a fringe area in which the regulated firms compete against those without constraints with attendant ill results. Optimum service is not achieved and minimum costs are neglected.[60]

Professor Demsetz, one of those who has found much fault with regulation, has suggested an interesting alternative:[61]

> At this juncture, it should be emphasized that I have argued, not that regulatory commissions are undesirable, but that economic theory does not, at present, provide a justification for commissions insofar as they are based on the belief that observed concentration and monopoly price bear any necessary relationship.

His suggestion is that the privilege of operating the public utilities be sold to the highest bidder and thus avoid the necessity for regu-

---

[57] Westfield, *Regulation and Conspiracy*, 55 Am. Econ. Rev. 424 (1965). Professor Westfield's demonstration appears to require an inelastic demand for the utility's services. *Quaere*, whether this is always a sound assumption. He also argues that regulation creates an environment conducive to conspiratorial practices. *Id.* at 442–43. This argument is difficult to follow since, under regulation, the utility companies rarely encounter competition.

[58] Pegrum, note 52 *supra*, at 10.

[59] Shepherd, *Utility Growth and Profits under Regulation*, in Shepherd & Gies, note 2 *supra*, at 3; Cross, *Incentive Pricing and Utility Regulation*, 84 Q. J. Econ. 236 (1970); cf. Trebing, note 2 *supra*, at 7–8. A differing view is presented in Rosoff, *The Application of Traditional Theory to a Regulated Firm*, 4 Bus. Econ. 77, 80 (1969).

[60] Wilson, *The Effect of Rate Regulation on Resource Allocation in Transportation*, 54 Am. Econ. Rev. 160, 170 (1964); Daniel, note 30 *supra*, at 351–52, 354; cf. Hilton, note 51 *supra*, at 50–51. Professor Gies has questioned the basic notion that public utility services are necessities rather than luxuries. Gies, note 2 *supra*, at 93, 94. In economic theory it is axiomatic that luxuries will sell at competitive prices. But cf. United States v. Container Corp., 393 U.S. 333, 336 (1969).

[61] Demsetz, *Why Regulate Utilities?* 11 J. Law & Econ. 55, 61 (1968).

lation at all. In that way the heavy hand of regulation would be lifted and replaced by a form of taxation, but at the same time forces of competition would discipline the managements of the utility companies:[62]

> In the case of utility industries, resort to the rivalry of the market place would relieve companies of the discomforts of commission regulation. But it would also relieve them of the comfort of legally protected market areas. It is my belief that the rivalry of the open market place disciplines more effectively than do the regulatory processes of the commission. If the managements of utility companies doubt this belief, I suggest that they re-examine the history of their industry to discover just who it was that provided most of the force behind the regulatory movement.

V. A HANDFUL OF LOYALISTS

Not everyone is ready to abandon regulation. In the first place, even those who find much fault with the present system sometimes say that it is better than deregulation. Thus Professor Cramton wrote:[63]

> The record of performance in the transportation industries justifies the assertion that the present halfway house, despite its deficiencies, is superior to the more effective protectionism that would be the only likely result of centralized control and broader authority over the transportation industries, the proposal that is concealed under slogans of the need for increased "coordination" and integration in the transportation.

Professor Phillips is another student who has found that the growth rates of the regulated industries have been good and their prices lower, although he admits that enterprises in the transportation sector do not fully sustain his point of view.[64]

---

[62] *Id.* at 65. Cf. Frenkel & Pashigian, *Regulation and Excess Demand: A General Equilibrium Approach*, 45 J. Bus. 379 (1972).

[63] Cramton, note 45 *supra*, at 190. See also Telser, *On the Regulation of Industry*, 77 J. Pol. Econ. 937, 950 (1969). An imaginative defense of regulation has been presented by Professor Sheshinski. Note 56 *supra*.

[64] PHILLIPS, note 34 *supra*, at 735–36; cf. Daniel, note 30 *supra*, at 348; Irwin, *Computers and Communications: The Economics of Interdependence*, 34 LAW & CONTEMP. PROB. 360, 386 (1969); Sherman, *The Design of Public Utility Institutions*, 46 LAND ECON. 51, 52 (1970).

Other students cling to the idea of regulation while voicing strong disapproval of the manner in which the various commissions have acted. One stalwart supporter of regulation is Professor Lewis, who wrote:[65]

> I believe firmly in the institution of public utility regulation but, along with many others, I have little enthusiasm for its performance. Public-utility regulation has not lived up' to its early-twentieth-century promise, and if that promise continues to fade, both regulation and private ownership in the utility industries are in deep trouble.

He went on to say that the United States Supreme Court was largely to blame for the sad state of regulation. His complaint is that the Court gave the commissions too much leeway and did not eliminate the cumbersome, inefficient, and cluttered methods employed by the regulatory bodies.[66] In a somewhat similar vein, Professor Parker found that the commissions were not adequate as a substitute for competition. Nevertheless, he found no reason to eliminate them.[67] One commentator, however, advised the regulatory agencies to employ better planning and to exercise a broader vision. While his view, of course, is tenable, it amounts to a counsel of perfection. He finds several reasons for the continuance of regulation but none of them is new.[68]

Finally, as one might imagine, some observers have published more sophisticated views of the effects and possibilities of regulation. For example, it is argued that nobody knows the exact cost of capital at any particular moment in time and, therefore, it is impossible to fix rates based thereon. On the other hand, the existence of rate controls may motivate the firm to increase its output and to take other steps beneficial to the economy as a whole.[69]

---

[65] Lewis, *Emphasis and Misemphasis in Regulatory Policy*, in SHEPHERD & GIES, note 2 *supra*, at 212, 213.

[66] *Id.* at 229.

[67] Parker, *The Regulation of Public Utilities*, 10 NAT. RES. J. 827 (1970); Pegrum, note 52 *supra*, at 12; Harper, note 50 *supra*; Sampson, note 53 *supra*. Specific suggestions are, however, meager.

[68] Trebing, *Government Regulation and Modern Capitalism*, 3 J. ECON. ISSUES 87, 103 (1969); Trebing, note 2 *supra*, at 300.

[69] Rosoff, note 59 *supra*, at 79; Frenkel & Pashigian, note 62 *supra*, at 384; Westfield, *Methodology of Evaluating Economic Regulation*, 61 AM. ECON. REV. 211, 214 (1971).

VI. Some Problems of Conflicts between the Two Concepts

Let us suppose that Mr. Justice Douglas's opinion in *Otter Tail* becomes accepted law. All public utilities then are subject to the constraints of the antitrust laws. In addition, of course, they are subject to the various state, federal, and municipal regulative statutes which control their rates, service, and financing.

A convenient starting point is the prohibition of monopoly by § 2 of the Sherman Act. It will be recalled that in the *Otter Tail* case the regulated public utility which refused to sell at wholesale to municipal power systems was held, over a dissent, to be in violation of that statute.[70] Several decisions dealing with nonregulated enterprises indicate that a defendant may be found guilty of enjoying monopoly power in violation of § 2 if he has 89 percent of a defined market.[71] It would be interesting to observe how few public utilities enjoyed less than 89 percent of the business in their geographic areas.[72] It would seem to follow, therefore, that most public utility companies, like Otter Tail Power, are in violation of § 2 of the Sherman Act. Hence they could be subjected to the civil and criminal penalties provided in the Sherman and Clayton Acts, including an injunction. But how would such an injunction be framed? Could the public utility company be dismembered? Such a suggestion leads to the old argument about duplicate and triplicate gas, water, and electric lines in the streets and the difficulties inherent therein. Such duplication of facilities would undoubtedly prove expensive as well as inconvenient.[73] It is hard to conceive of widespread public support for any such ruling.

Closely allied to the monopoly problem is that of division of territory. Most public utilities operate in a defined geographical

[70] Mr. Justice Stewart wrote: "With respect to decisions by regulated electric utilities as to whether or not to provide nonretail services, I think that in the absence of horizontal conspiracy, the teaching of the 'primary jurisdiction' cases argues for leaving governmental regulation to the Commission instead of the invariably less sensitive and less specifically expert process of anti-trust litigation." 410 U.S. at 391.

[71] United States v. Grinnell Corp., 384 U.S. 563 (1966); Denver Union Stockyard v. Denver Live Stock Commission Company, 404 F.2d 1055 (10th Cir. 1968).

[72] But cf. Illinois Motor Carrier of Property Law, Ill. Rev. Stat. c. 95.5, §§ 18–301 (existence of one carrier not a bar to issuance of certificate to another).

[73] Demsetz, note 61 *supra*.

area and do not attempt to invade the neighboring area of another utility company. We know from the famous *Sealy* case[74] that any agreement so to divide territories would be illegal and even in the case of public utilities the United States Supreme Court has insisted that natural gas pipelines must operate in the same areas and compete.[75] This, of course, is all at odds with the general theory of public utility regulation whereby, for example, the certificate issued to a common carrier must specify the routes and termini or territory which it will serve.[76] The carrier is not allowed to operate in other areas. Again, the question is whether problems of indivisibility and perhaps aesthetic considerations will indicate that only a single utility should serve in any one area. The only solution which has been offered for this dilemma is the suggestion of Professor Demsetz that the right to serve any territory should be auctioned off periodically and awarded to the highest bidder. This solution would not remove the element of monopoly but would presumably recapture monopoly profit.

Moving back to § 1 of the Sherman Act, we observe the familiar rule that price-fixing is unlawful thereunder. Indeed, in the *Container Corporation* case,[77] the mere exchange of price information, absent any agreement with respect thereto, was found to be illegal under the Sherman Act. This rule is directly at war with the common provision of public utility statutes that common carrier rates must be "established," filed, published, and posted. Even contract carrier rates must be filed with the regulatory commission.[78] Hence the prices of those utilities are public information available to competitors in direct contravention of the rule laid down in the *Container* case. A careful comment on this problem reached the conclusion that dual controls were not feasible:[79]

---

[74] United States v. Sealy, Inc. 388 U.S. 350 (1967).

[75] Cascade Natural Gas Corp. v. El Paso Gas Co., 386 U.S. 129, 135 (1967); see Shenefield, *Antitrust Policy within the Electric Utility Industry*, 16 ANTITRUST BULL. 681, 686, 693 (1971).

[76] Illinois Motor Carrier of Property Law, Ill. Rev. Stat. c. 95.5, § 18–301(d).

[77] United States v. Container Corp., 393 U.S. 333 (1969); see Hale, *Communication among Competitors*, 14 ANTITRUST BULL. 63 (1969).

[78] Illinois Motor Carrier of Property Law, Ill. Rev. Stat. c. 95.5, § 18–310, –501, –505.

[79] Pegrum, note 52 *supra*, at 12.

One proposal is to abolish the Commission [ICC] and transfer the responsibility for regulation to the Sherman and Clayton Acts with enforcement in the hands of the Antitrust Division and the Federal Trade Commission. This approach assumes separate and completely independent action by all the individual enterprises. This ignores the unique problems of transport, which have already been discussed, but it also ignores the fact that antitrust has had no experience whatsoever in dealing with transport problems.

Rate-making in transport requires cooperation on joint rates, through rates, joint routes, division of rates, interchange of traffic and equipment as well as cooperative use of facilities such as terminals. All this requires agreements that would find an inhospitable home under current interpretation of antitrust. Discrimination in pricing would impose a hopeless task on antitrust authorities under the present interpretation of the Robinson-Patman Act, and could not be dealt with in any case under concepts applicable to industry in general. Common carrier obligations and arrangements do not fall within the antitrust laws. Consolidation, at least among railroads, would face even greater barriers than it does today. The mergers that have been approved to date have been possible only because the I.C.C. does not have to meet the standards of the Clayton Act, and the Antitrust Division has been unsuccessful in imposing its concepts of the application of the Sherman Act.

In short, transportation does not fit into antitrust interpretation, even though in some areas the I.C.C. could bring its policies more into line with the philosophy of antitrust. Transportation is a mixture of public utility and competitive economics that is not amenable to antitrust jurisdiction alone.

Tying arrangements have been the subject of vigorous condemnation under the antitrust laws. Perhaps the most striking decision is *Fortner v. United States Steel Corporation*.[80] In that opinion it was declared that U.S. Steel had unlawfully "tied" the sale of its prefabricated houses to the extension of credit for the purchase thereof. The logic of this holding would appear to prohibit any seller from extending credit to any customer. As in the case of other esoteric decisions, extrapolation apparently has not taken place. Nevertheless, the principle of the decision would appear to prohibit a grocer from providing both vegetables and meats. Carried far enough, perhaps a railroad could not haul more than a single commodity;

---

[80] 394 U.S. 495 (1969). See Dam, *Fortner Enterprises v. United States Steel: "Neither a Borrower, Nor a Lender Be,"* 1969 SUPREME COURT REVIEW 1.

and an electric utility could be forbidden to offer 220 volt service in addition to 110 volt service. It seems unlikely that any such determination would be acceptable to public opinion.

Another vicious practice forbidden under the antitrust laws is that of reciprocity. A manufacturer is not allowed to purchase his supplies from persons who happen to be his customers.[81] As applied to public utilities, such a holding might prohibit an electric generating company from purchasing wire from a patron whose plant it served. This problem could probably be obviated by finding another source of supply in a more distant area but it would also add to the costs of the public utility.

In fairly recent years we thought that an acquisition by a firm in the free market sector could only be attacked if some anticompetitive effect resulted therefrom. Recent decisions, including the famous *Procter & Gamble* case,[82] appear to have altered that view in some degree. If applied to an electric utility company, therefore, *Procter & Gamble* might suggest that the company should divest itself of water, gas, or other services it may be providing. On the other hand, a recent empirical study indicates that there is no demonstrable adverse effect on rates when the public utility supplies both electricity and gas.[83]

A few years ago no one saw harm in vertical mergers—and some still don't. The courts, however, have found them to be vicious instruments of "foreclosure."[84] We have mentioned above the last phase of the *Northwest Pipeline*[85] case which forbade vertical integration by a public utility. Now we find that despite state regulation and possibly Civil Aeronautics Board regulation, a merger of airlines can be attacked under § 7 of the Clayton Act.[86] A logical extrapolation of these holdings would require one public utility company to generate electricity and a separate one to distribute it to consumers. Here again the cost of breaking up a public utility system may seem high in comparison with whatever benefits may possibly be derived therefrom.

---

[81] F.T.C. v. Consolidated Foods Corp., 380 U.S. 592 (1965).

[82] F.T.C. v. Proctor & Gamble Co., 386 U.S. 568 (1967).

[83] Pace, *The Relative Performance of Combination Gas-Electric Utilities*, 17 ANTITRUST BULL. 519 (1972).

[84] Ford Motor Co. v. United States, 405 U.S. 562 (1972).

[85] Cascade Natural Gas Corp., note 75 *supra*.

[86] United States v. Pacific Southwest Airlines, 358 F. Supp. 1224 (C.D. Calif. 1973).

Closely allied to the subject of merger is that of joint ventures. They, too, have been found to be in violation of § 7 of the Clayton Act.[87] Hence, it is not surprising to find that § 7 was also applied to a joint venture by gas distributing companies to build a common pipeline to producing areas. Further, we have learned that § 7 of the Clayton Act must be applied to joint ventures among utilities such as the operation of a common electric generating plant.[88] Here again the cost of competition may soon seem excessive.

In the private sector of the economy a seller may stop doing business with one distributor and take on another so long as he does not enter into a conspiracy.[89] Public utility firms, however, are obliged by law to serve any responsible patron. Here is an application of the antitrust laws which would work a result contrary to the import of those described above. It seems unlikely that the courts are ready to abandon the doctrine that a public utility must serve any patron within its territory.

We have saved to the last the most glaring example of the clash between the commands of the antitrust laws and those of public utility regulation. We are referring, of course, to enforcement of § 2 of the Clayton Act, commonly referred to as the Robinson-Patman Act. In a recent Supreme Court decision a Robinson-Patman Act claim was sustained on the ground that the defendant was selling pies at lower prices in some areas than in others.[90] If applied to a public utility this might mean that the nearby patrons would be compelled to subsidize extension of mains or lines to a distant patron. In the *Utah Pie* case, again the court claimed that the defendant had failed to "cost justify" its prices.[91] Public utility rate structures with their separate schedules for interruptible and firm service, their demand charges for larger customers, and their sharp reduction of charges with volume of use would require wholesale revision to fit into the mysteries of Robinson-Patman compliance. We know from a recent case, for example, that § 2 of the Clayton Act reaches

---

[87] United States v. Penn-Olin Chemical Co., 378 U.S. 158 (1964).

[88] Northern Natural Gas Co. v. F.P.C., 399 F.2d 953 (D.C. Cir. 1968); Municipal Electric Ass'n v. S.E.C., 413 F.2d 1052, 1057–59 (D.C. Cir. 1969); cf. Shenefield, note 75 *supra*, at 714.

[89] Joseph E. Seagram & Sons, Inc. v. Hawaiian Oke, Ltd., 416 F.2d 71 (9th Cir. 1969); cf. United States v. Arnold, Schwinn & Company, 388 U.S. 365 (1967).

[90] Utah Pie Co. v. Continental Baking Co., 386 U.S. 685 (1967).

[91] *Id.* at 694–95.

discrimination against a plaintiff who received deliveries of lumber more slowly than other customers.[92] *Quaere*, how this could be applied to distant patrons of public utility companies. Furthermore, the entire rate structure administered by the Interstate Commerce Commission is known to discriminate against high value commodities. Coal moves for much less per ton than jewels. Here again the system of regulation is wholly different from that imposed by § 2 of the Clayton Act. For that reason, presumably, one court has declared the quantity discounts of an electric utility to be exempt from antitrust controls.[93]

A final specter is the possibility that suits against public utilities might result in huge treble damage awards. In private litigation, judgments running into the millions are no longer uncommon.[94] As applied to a public utility such a judgment might constitute a discrimination against the nonfavored patrons; they would, in effect be compelled to pay higher rates in order to keep the utility solvent. This very idea was expressed many years ago by the United States Supreme Court in the *Keogh* case[95] in which damages under the antitrust laws were refused in a suit against railroads. The court expressly referred to the possibility that such damages could constitute an illegal rebate.[96]

VII. Conclusion

Application of the antitrust laws to regulated industries presents many promising possibilities. As noted above, many observers are weary of direct controls and would prefer pushing the utilities into the free market.[97] The case against regulation has been so con-

---

[92] Centex-Winston Corp. v. Edw. Hines Lumber Co., 447 F.2d 585 (7th Cir. 1971).

[93] Gas Light Co. of Columbus v. Georgia Power Co., 440 F.2d 1135, 1137–38, 1140 (5th Cir. 1971).

[94] Philadelphia Electric Co. v. Westinghouse Electric Co., CCH Trade Cases ¶ 71, 123 (E.D. Pa. 1964); cf. Simpson v. Union Oil Co., 377 U.S. 13 (1964), 396 U.S. 13 (1969).

[95] Keogh v. Chicago & North Western Railway, 260 U.S. 156 (1922).

[96] *Id*. at 162.

[97] Shenefield, note 75 *supra*, reviews cases applying antitrust law to electric utilities and finds no objection unless increase of costs, etc., are shown. Owen, *Monopoly Pricing in Combined Gas and Electric Utilities*, 15 Antitrust Bull. 713, 722 (1970); Daniel, note 30 *supra*; Irwin, note 64 *supra*, at 381; Park, note 41 *supra*, at 230.

vincingly stated that only a handful of students continue to place faith in interventionist regulation. Moreover, technological developments, as mentioned above, possibly are working in the direction of market freedom.[98] Even if the only savings were to relieve the utilities and their patrons of the burden of filing and examining thousands upon thousands of tariff schedules, there would seem to be a net benefit.

One is, of course, attracted to the solution suggested by Professor Demsetz. As indicated above, he has proposed a system of bidding for the right of supplying utility service in situations wherein duplication of facilities would be onerous. Thus, there would remain only one distributor of gas in any area and only one set of gas mains in the streets, but the identity of the proprietor of the system might change from time to time depending on who would pay the highest price for the privilege of becoming the sole supplier.[99] On the other hand, there are some problems with respect to Professor Demsetz's suggestion, one being that it may not be the right remedy for a decreasing cost industry.[100]

The bland assumption that antitrust laws can be applied to utility companies while interventionist controls remain in effect seems naive.[101] There is always the danger that application of the antitrust laws to pervasively regulated industries might turn into a protectionist program designed to shelter existing firms.[102]

As pointed out above, many conflicts occur between the commands of public utility commissions and their organic laws, on the one hand, and the antitrust statutes, on the other. The uncertainty over which set of controls might be applicable to any given situation would be costly and time-consuming. Almost any move by a public utility firm could be questioned under both means of control. This is scarcely a time—if ever there was one—to add needless costs to public utility service. Long periods of uncertainty, possibly

---

[98] Trebing, note 2 supra, at 308–09.

[99] Demsetz, note 61 supra, at 65.

[100] Telser, note 63 supra, at 939, 950; Pace, Relevant Markets and the Nature of Competition in the Electric Utility Industry, 16 ANTITRUST BULL. 725, 729 (1971).

[101] Northern Natural Gas Co. v. Federal Power Comm'n, 399 F.2d 953, 959 (D.C. Cir. 1968).

[102] Hale & Hale, note 1 supra, at 52; Hale & Hale, Regulation: A Defense to Anti-Merger Litigation? 54 KY. L. J. 683, 715 ff. (1966).

extending for five or more decades, might be required to ascertain what activities of the utilities remained under interventionist regulation and which would be attacked under the antitrust laws. In short, the utility companies can scarcely be expected to serve two masters. Hence the issue should be put to the legislative branch of government for resolution. If the Congress were to abolish the federal system of utility regulation—and we think it should—state legislators should also act. In a word, the cry is: Repeal!

PAUL GOLDSTEIN

KEWANEE OIL CO. v. BICRON

CORP.: NOTES ON A

CLOSING CIRCLE

With its decision last Term in *Kewanee Oil Co. v. Bicron Corp.*,[1] the Burger Court closed a circle of decision initiated by the Warren Court a decade earlier in the *Sears* and *Compco* cases.[2] Renewing the major premise endorsed in *Sears* and *Compco*, that the national commitment to a competitive economy is in part effected by the congressional provision for patent and copyright monopolies, the Court implicitly rejected the decisions' minor premise, that "because of the federal patent laws a State may not, when the article is unpatented and uncopyrighted, prohibit the copying of the article itself or award damages for such copying."[3] Indeed, the Court approved the operation of state law in precisely the circumstances its predecessor had condemned. The Court overrode the two precedents with that most effective vehicle of judicial restraint, benign neglect.[4] Where *Sears* and *Compco*, because they spoke in broad

---

Paul Goldstein is Professor of Law, State University of New York at Buffalo.

[1] 94 S. Ct. 1879 (1974).

[2] Sears, Roebuck & Co. v. Stiffel Co., 376 U.S. 225 (1964); Compco Corp. v. Day-Brite Lighting, Inc., 376 U.S. 234 (1964).

[3] 376 U.S. at 232–33.

[4] See Dershowitz & Ely, *Harris v. New York: Some Anxious Observations on the Candor and Logic of the Emerging Nixon Majority*, 80 YALE L. J. 1198 (1971).

preemptive terms, were widely seen to revolutionize state and federal relations in the regulation of economic activity,[5] the counter-revolution worked by *Kewanee* has gone unheralded.[6]

In *Sears*, the Court had reversed a lower court decision enjoining as unfair competition defendant's sale of "substantially exact" copies of plaintiff's pole lamp. The unfair competition count had been joined to a count for infringement of mechanical and design patents on the pole lamp, but these had been invalidated by the district court because of the lamp's failure to meet one of the patent statute's standards of invention. Asserting that a state "could not, consistently with the Supremacy Clause of the Constitution, extend the life of a patent beyond its expiration date or give a patent on an article which lacked the level of invention required for federal patents," the Court concluded that a state could not "under some other law, such as that forbidding unfair competition, give protection of a kind that clashes with the objectives of the federal patent laws."[7]

The facts of *Kewanee* were not materially different. The subject matter in suit, plaintiff's processes for the production of synthetic crystals useful in the detection of ionizing radiation, though of a type protectable under the Patent Act, was, because it had been in commercial use for over a year, disqualified from protection under the novelty standards of § 102(b).[8] Like the injunction in *Sears*, the district court injunction prohibiting plaintiff's former employees from using these secret processes restricted the copying of subject matter that, otherwise patentable, failed to meet one of the patent law's standards. Consequently, though holding that the district court had properly applied Ohio's trade secret law, the Sixth Circuit Court of Appeals reversed on the ground that, under *Sears*, the state law conflicted with the federal patent law.

Reversing the Court of Appeals, but without attempting to distinguish *Sears* or to come to grips with its preemptive logic, the Supreme Court in *Kewanee* rested its decision on an analysis of the

---

[5] See, *e.g.*, Symposium, *Product Simulation: A Right or a Wrong?* 64 COLUM. L. REV. 1178 (1964).

[6] Remarks at one panel discussion, conducted shortly after the decision was rendered, 17 PATENT, TRADEMARK & COPYRIGHT J. 5–6 (23 May 1974), evidence the view that the decision's import does not extend beyond the immediate confines of state trade secret law.

[7] 376 U.S. at 231.   [8] 35 U.S.C. § 102(b) (1970).

discrete roles played by patent and trade secret law. Recognizing that federal power in the area of intellectual property is not exclusive, that the "patent law does not explicitly endorse or forbid the operation of trade secret law," and that the "only limitation on the States is that in regulating the area of patents and copyrights they do not conflict with the operation of the laws in this area passed by Congress,"[9] the Court observed that the objectives of the patent law—inducing investment in innovation and its disclosure through the reward of a seventeen-year monopoly—and those of trade secret law—"maintenance of standards of commercial ethics and the encouragement of invention"[10]—do not necessarily conflict. One specific possible conflict, between the secrecy permitted under state law and the patent law's objective of disclosure, gave the Court greater pause.[11] But, after an extensive analysis of probable firm behavior in the circumstances, it concluded that "[i]n the case of trade secret law no reasonable risk of deterrence from patent application by those who can reasonably expect to be granted patents exists."[12]

What is perhaps most remarkable about the ruling in *Kewanee* is that it was necessary at all. Why should the centuries' old systems of monopoly subsidy—trade secret, common law copyright, unfair competition—ever be thought to occupy other than a legitimate place in a nation whose political structure predicates a federal system and whose economic structure predicates competitive markets? The decision was necessary, however, because the Court in *Sears* and *Compco* had mistaken a superficial syllogism for an economic fact. It had overlooked the point, long appreciated by practitioners in the field, that state systems of monopoly subsidy, no less than their federal law counterparts—patent, copyright, trademark—contribute to efficiency in the allocation of resources and that each "has its own particular role to play, and the operation of one does not take away from the need for the other."[13]

On their facts, *Sears* and *Kewanee* form a perfectly matched pair. In their approach and result, however, the two are diametrically

---

[9] 94 S. Ct. at 1885.   [10] 94 S. Ct. at 1886.

[11] "If a State, through a system of protection, were to cause a substantial risk that holders of patentable inventions would not seek patents, but rather would rely on the state protection, we would be compelled to hold that such a system could not constitutionally continue to exist." 94 S. Ct. at 1890.

[12] *Ibid.*   [13] 94 S. Ct. at 1892.

opposed. The approach taken in *Kewanee* seems to me clearly correct, as I have argued elsewhere and will not closely detail here.[14] Because the Court's abrogation of the *Sears* rule was accomplished so covertly, I think it more useful to demonstrate here that the result was neither aberrant nor unintended but was rather the product of a careful delimiting process begun shortly after *Sears*. Because the new approach was announced in such modest terms, it may also be helpful to chart two of its more critical, far-ranging implications.

I. Sears on a Slippery Slope

Postulating a broad, affirmative mandate for a competitive economy, the Court in *Sears* and *Compco* devised for the mandate's implementation an essentially negative preemptive rule. If the subject matter for which state protection is sought falls within the congressional power under Art. I, § 1, cl. 8, of the Constitution, yet fails to qualify for protection under the federal patent or copyright statutes, either because it is not of a type protected by these statutes or because it does not meet the statutes' qualitative standards, state protection is to be denied.

On their facts, *Sears* and *Compco* addressed only the second question, whether state law could protect statutorily protectable subject matter that fails to qualify under the federal statute's standards.[15] The logic of the opinions, captured in Justice Black's statement of the question for decision—"whether a State's unfair competition law can, consistently with the federal patent laws, impose liability for or prohibit the copying of an article which is protected by neither a federal patent nor a copyright"[16]—leaves no doubt that state protection of subject matter in both classes was to be preempted. Even under subsequent decisions of the Warren Court, the preemptive formula gradually contracted, first, through Justice Harlan's exemplification of an alternative approach in *Lear, Inc. v. Adkins;*[17] second, through the decision in *Goldstein v. California,*[18]

---

[14] Goldstein, *The Competitive Mandate: From Sears to Lear,* 59 Calif. L. Rev. 873 (1971).

[15] The subject matter in each case, a pole lamp in *Sears,* a lamp reflector in *Compco,* was clearly of a protectable type. Indeed, mechanical and design patents had been issued in the first case, and a design patent in the second.

[16] 376 U.S. at 225.

[17] 395 U.S. 653 (1969).   [18] 412 U.S. 546 (1973).

that state protection could reach subject matter that did not qualify as to type; and finally, in *Kewanee*, that state protection could reach subject matter that, though qualifying as to type, did not meet the statute's qualitative standards. The original negative presumption of *Sears* and *Compco* was thus gradually converted to an affirmative one that generally endorsed state systems of monopoly subsidy.

Brulotte v. Thys Co.,[19] rendered only eight months after *Sears* and *Compco*, indicated some early inconsistency in the Court's views. The Court held that defendants, who had purchased hop-picking machines from plaintiff who held patents to several of the devices incorporated in the machines under a contract requiring them to pay plaintiff royalties based on the amount of crops they harvested, were excused from paying royalties accruing after the expiration of the life of the patents. To hold otherwise, Mr. Justice Douglas wrote, would subject "the free market visualized for the post-expiration period . . . to monopoly influences that have no proper place there."[20] To plaintiff's astute question, whether the Court would also refuse to enforce a similar contract involving unpatented subject matter, Mr. Justice Douglas answered that such arrangements "seldom rise to the level of a federal question."[21] Yet, that answer implied a profound betrayal of *Sears*, for state protection in the hypothesized circumstances, no less than in *Sears*, would extend to subject matter failing to meet the federal statute's requirements as to type or standard.

One possible ground for distinguishing *Sears* from *Brulotte*, the difference between the state doctrines of unfair competition and contract, was ostensibly removed in *Lear, Inc. v. Adkins*, where the Court overruled the doctrine of licensee estoppel. That doctrine, last endorsed in *Automatic Radio Manufacturing Co. v. Hazeltine Research Inc.*,[22] was that so long as a licensee is operating under a license agreement, in a suit for royalties under the agreement the licensee is estopped to deny the validity of his licensor's patent. Recognizing that contract enforcement, no less than unfair competition injunctions, exerts a cloistering effect, Justice Harlan perceived the conflict to lie between, "the law of contracts [which] forbids a purchaser to repudiate his promises simply because he later becomes dissatisfied with the bargain he has made," and "federal law [which] requires that all ideas in general circulation be dedicated

---

[19] 379 U.S. 29 (1964).

[20] *Id*. at 32–33.

[21] *Id*. at 32.

[22] 339 U.S. at 827 (1950).

to the common good unless they are protected by a valid patent."
Relying on *Sears* and *Compco*, and their emphasis on "the strong
federal policy favoring free competition in ideas which do not
merit patent protection,"[23] the Court struck the balance for the
second interest.

Brulotte and *Lear* both involved state contract law and, while
they depart from the Court's earlier and subsequent concern with
state systems of monopoly subsidy—unfair competition in *Sears*,
trade secrets in *Kewanee*—they are nonetheless important to the
evolution of the approach taken in *Kewanee*. *Brulotte* should be
read simply as an application of orthodox patent misuse doctrine,
forbiding the extension by contract of the prescribed seventeen-
year patent term. Justice Harlan's opinion in *Lear*, particularly
when taken together with his dissent in *Brulotte*,[24] must, however,
be read as a shrewd appreciation that misuse doctrine, peremptorily
negating contract claims, arose in the period before *Erie R. R v.
Tompkins*[25] imbued state law with independent vigor. State contract law, Harlan seems to have been saying, no less than other state
laws, represents a diverse expression of state interests, interests that
ought to be carefully evaluated when state law is measured against
federal command.

That this perspective animated Justice Harlan's opinion in *Lear*
seems evident from his disposition of the second phase of the case
in which Adkins sought to recover contract royalties that had ac-
crued before the patent in question was issued, royalties to have
been paid in consideration for his confidential disclosure to Lear of
the subject matter in suit. In approaching the estoppel issue in the
first phase of the case, Justice Harlan had endorsed as much of
Sears as dealt with patented subject matter that arguably failed in
some respect to meet the patent law's standards. In the second phase
of the case, he carefully avoided examining the extent of *Sears*'s
impact, specifically, "the difficult question whether federal patent
policy bars a State from enforcing a contract regulating access to
an unpatented secret idea":[26]

> Our decision today will, of course, require the state courts
> to reconsider the theoretical basis of their decisions enforcing
> the contractual rights of inventors and it is impossible to pre-

---

23 395 U.S. at 656.

24 379 U.S. at 34–39.

25 304 U.S. 64 (1938).

26 395 U.S. at 672, 675.

dict the extent to which this re-evaluation may revolutionize the law of any particular State in this regard. Consequently, we have concluded, after much consideration, that even though an important question of federal law underlies this phase of the controversy, we should not now attempt to define in even a limited way the extent, if any, to which the States may properly act to enforce the contractual rights of inventors of unpatented secret ideas.

This question, which Justice Black, dissenting, contended had already been answered in the affirmative by *Sears* and *Compco*,[27] was essentially the one to be confronted, and answered in the negative, in *Kewanee.*

Two contradictory hints of the Court's attitude toward preemption of state doctrines protecting subject matter that fails to meet the federal statute's standards came in *Goldstein v. California*,[28] which dealt with the question, impliedly resolved in the affirmative by *Sears*, whether federal law preempts state protection of subject matter not qualified as to type for protection under the federal statute. The specific question was whether a California criminal statute proscribing the piracy of recorded performances contravened the federal copyright law, which at the time excluded sound recordings from its categories of copyrightable subject matter. The Court's decision, that because federal law nowhere expressly prohibited state protection in the area, and that, because it would not necessarily conflict with federal interests, state protection of this uncopyrightable class of subject matter should be permitted, intimated a favorable attitude toward the operation of state systems of monopoly subsidy generally.

At the same time, the ground that Chief Justice Burger, writing for the Court, employed to distinguish *Sears* and *Compco* suggested that, where failure to meet federal statutory standards is involved, the Court would not be so generously disposed. *Sears* and *Compco*, he declared, dealt only with state protection of subject matter failing to meet the statutory standard:[29]

> In regard to mechanical configurations, Congress had balanced the need to encourage innovation and originality of invention against the need to insure competition in the sale of identical or substantially identical products. The standards

---

[27] *Id.* at 676–77.

[28] 412 U.S. 546 (1973).

[29] *Id.* at 569–70.

established for granting federal patent protection to machines thus indicated not only which articles in this particular category Congress wished to protect, but which configurations it wished to remain free. The application of state law in these cases to prevent the copying of articles which did not meet the requirements for federal protection disturbed the careful balance which Congress had drawn and thereby necessarily gave way under the Supremacy Clause of the Constitution.

By restricting *Sear*'s and *Compco*'s preemptive rule to state laws protecting subject matter not meeting federal standards—an interpretation probably inconsistent with the intended sweep of the two earlier opinions—the Chief Justice not only saved the California legislation but appeared, too, to have strengthened the thrust of the preemptive rule within the area to which he confined it.

Had Chief Justice Burger chosen to renew in *Kewanee* the distinction employed in *Goldstein*, the decision would necessarily have gone the other way, for the processes involved were of a kind subject to patent protection and, having been in commercial use for over a year, were undeniably disqualified from protection for failure to meet the novelty standard set by § 102(b) of the Patent Law. In the terms established by *Sears* and confirmed by *Goldstein* no clearer case can be imagined in which the "application of state law . . . to prevent the copying of articles which do not meet the requirements for federal protection disturbed the careful balance which Congress had drawn and thereby necessarily gave way under the Supremacy Clause of the Constitution."

Sears and *Compco* were, of course, indistinguishable from *Kewanee*, and this explains the short shrift the decisions received. Rather than pursue the process of distinction, the Chief Justice turned instead to the spirit of *Goldstein* in support of the Court's decision. "Certainly," he reasoned, "the patent policy of encouraging invention is not disturbed by the existence of another form of incentive to invention. In this respect the two systems are not and never would be in conflict."[30] Moreover, "[t]rade secret law provides far weaker protection in many respects than the patent law."[31] Both points, the first positing that state and federal systems of monopoly subsidy have the shared purpose of advancing market processes in a competitive economy, the second, that counterpart federal and state doctrines can helpfully be compared, seem emi-

[30] 94 S. Ct. at 1887.   [31] *Id.* at 1890.

nently sound. Both are, however, to use the phrase of Mr. Justice Douglas, dissenting, "at war with the philosophy of *Sears* . . . and *Compco*."[32]

Kewanee, particularly when read together with *Goldstein*, stands for the proposition that states are not necessarily foreclosed from acting to protect subject matter that, though constitutionally protectable by Congress, fails to qualify under a federal statute's prescription either of classes or standards for protection. The decision probably stands for much more: that, at least where not expressly preempted by federal law, state systems of monopoly subsidy—trade secrets, common law copyright, and unfair competition—like their federal statutory counterparts—patent, copyright, and trademark—enjoy a legitimate, and important, place in a federal system that is rooted in a competitive economy.[33]

II. The Meaning of Kewanee

Sears and *Compco* were cited four times in the *Kewanee* opinion, thrice for the principle that "when state law touches upon the area of federal statutes enacted pursuant to constitutional authority, 'it is "familiar doctrine" that the federal policy "may not be set at naught, or its benefits denied" by the state law' ";[34] and once for the *non sequitur*, "that which is in the public domain cannot be removed therefrom by action of the states."[35] The Court's failure to explicate the two precedents suggests that it was taking an approach in *Kewanee*, first definitively sketched in *Goldstein v. California*, that differed markedly from the one that preoccupied the Warren Court. This approach postulates a broad power in the states to stimulate economic activity through means consistent with the nation's commitment to competition and recognizes the need for close practical judgments on the economic effects of the means employed.

The commitment to competition to which the Court subscribed

---

[32] *Id.* at 1892.

[33] At the same time, this interpretation is not inconsistent with the continued vitality of *Brulotte* and *Lear*, for it was contract doctrines of general application, not counterpart state systems of monopoly subsidy, that were involved there.

[34] 94 S. Ct. at 1885, quoting Sola Elec. Co. v. Jefferson Elec. Co., 317 U.S. 173, 176 (1942).

[35] 94 S. Ct. at 1886.

predicates that the national interest in technological advance and in the dedication of resources to their most productive possible uses will most effectively be advanced by a market economy.[36] The doctrinal fabric in which this commitment is expressed consists in part of explicit competitive instruments, antitrust law and the Constitution's copyright and patent clause, and, in more substantial part, of instruments implicitly aimed at competitive objectives, state and federal laws that, for example, specify the conditions for the private ownership and use of land and personalty, and the form and management of business enterprise. Of the several observations that can be made about the commitment adhered to, two are immediately pertinent: Essentially economic in its bearing, this commitment requires that the state doctrine under review be evaluated for its implications for economic behavior. Catholic in its operation, the commitment may require that this examination for economic effects extend to state rules that are noneconomic in motive no less than to state rules that are economically motivated.

A. ECONOMICS OF INCENTIVES TO INVENTION

For its determination that state trade secret law does not substantially conflict with the patent law's objective of disclosure, the Court drew heavily on Judge Friendly's analysis of the point in *Painton & Co. v. Bourns, Inc.*,[37] decided three years earlier. The Court's reliance on *Painton*, a diversity case, together with its unusually extensive reference to other lower federal and state decisions in the area, amply reflects a concern for the intricacies of the state doctrine involved and of its implications for federal competitive policy, a concern distinctly alien to *Sears* and *Compco*.

Following *Painton's* analysis of whether the availability of trade secret protection will deter patent applications and disclosure, the Court distinguished three classes of trade secrets: (1) The trade secret believed by its owner to constitute a validly patentable invention. (2) The trade secret known to its owner not to be so patentable. (3) The trade secret whose valid patentability is considered dubious.[38] With respect to the second class, the Court concluded that very little in the way of disclosure would be ac-

---

[36] For a more complete development of this position and its doctrinal expression, see Goldstein, note 14 *supra*, at 875–80.

[37] 442 F.2d 216 (2d Cir. 1971).   [38] 94 S. Ct. at 1887.

complished by abolishing trade secret protection, for "the patent alternative would not reasonably be available to the inventor."[39] As to the third class, the Court said, "the potential rewards of patent protection are so far superior to those accruing to holders of trade secrets, that the holders of such inventions will seek patent protection, ignoring the trade secret route."[40] Considerations underlying the judgment about the third class press even more forcefully with regard to the first. Because trade secret law "provides far weaker protection in many respects than the patent law," the "possibility that an inventor who believes his invention meets the standards of patentability will sit back, rely on trade secret law, and after one year of use forfeit any right to patent protection, 35 U.S.C. § 102(b), is remote indeed."[41]

The Court may be faulted for accepting as an accomplished fact the patent law's objective of disclosure. Artfully drafted specifications may defeat the disclosure objective. In any event the extent to which the scientific and engineering communities rely on these documents for instruction is speculative at best. At the same time, the Court was properly alert to other practical limitations on the comparable benefits to be yielded by disclosure. Secrecy is a function only of time, and competitors are free under state law to "reverse engineer" the secret subject matter and replicate the processes and ingredients secretly employed in production through analysis of the marketed product itself. And, even where the product is not marketed, so that no opportunity for reverse engineering exists, as for example, "were an inventor to keep his discovery completely to himself . . . there is a high probability that it will be soon independently developed."[42]

A more striking and welcome point of analysis in the Court's opinion lies in its appreciation of a behavioral principle frequently ignored, sometimes even by the Court itself.[43] The critical locus of the patent system's operation is in the pre-invention period where the level of investment in innovation can be expected to correspond,

---

[39] *Id.* at 1888.   [41] *Id.* at 1890.

[40] *Id.* at 1889.

[42] *Ibid.* Interestingly, the Court did not explore the difficult, related question, whether the costs that attend reverse and independent engineering, or licensing under the trade secret, will contribute to a more or less desirable result than those attending free disclosure and licensing under the patent monopoly.

[43] See Gottschalk v. Benson, 409 U.S. 63 (1972).

however roughly, with the inducement offered. A rule that subject matter of a certain class is unpatentable can be expected to deter private investment in research and development for this class. Because cases do not arise until a patent has authoritatively been granted or withheld, courts have naturally fallen into a habit of truncated consideration. They decide, for example, that the public would be injured by patent awards to innovations that are somehow too significant, that constitute "the basic tools of scientific and technological work,"[44] ignoring entirely that to withhold a patent in these circumstances will, absent direct subsidy, likely deter investment in innovations of this class.

This appreciation of the nature of investment behavior was especially critical to the immediate decision in *Kewanee*, for it illumines the integral relationship between the federal patent system and state trade secret systems. During most of the period over which investment is committed to innovation the firm has little idea whether the end product—if there is one—will qualify under the patent law's standards of nonobviousness, novelty, and utility or, if it qualifies, whether the patent will withstand judicial review. Consequently, to eliminate the trade secret system, the Court appeared to recognize, would not produce the salutary effect of stimulating investment only in patentable invention. The research and development process is incapable of discrimination along these nice lines of legal conclusion. Rather, a rule reducing the probability that the values of the investor's innovation could be privately appropriated under any scheme of monopoly subsidy might instead curtail overall investment in innovation, with resulting losses to the development of both unpatentable and patentable subject matter.

B. ECONOMIC AND NONECONOMIC OBJECTIVES OF STATE LAWS

As the Court recognized, the state trade secret law accredited in *Kewanee* possessed objectives that were both economic and noneconomic. Designed to encourage investment in innovation, the law was also intended to advance local ethical and personal values. In the Court's view, "there is the inevitable cost to the basic decency of society when one firm steals from another. A most fundamental human right, that of privacy, is threatened."[45] Trade secret law is not unique in this dualism. Other state doctrines, unfair competition

---

[44] *Id*. at 67.   [45] 94 S. Ct. at 1889.

and common law copyright, and federal laws, patent, trademark, and copyright, are in their concern for piracy similarly directed at ethical as well as economic objectives. Yet while the *Kewanee* opinion referred to the state law's primarily economic motive for analogical purposes, the measure of the state law it ultimately took was not of the law's economic objective but of its economic effects, regardless of motive.

This point, though it may appear obvious, deserves to be underscored. Courts, the Supreme Court included, have been noticeably lax to measure the economic effect of other state laws which, though their objectives are predominantly and sometimes exclusively noneconomic, nonetheless bear significantly on the same national interests in competition endorsed in *Kewanee*. State privacy laws, for example, border conceptually on state common law copyright doctrine.[46] The mandate of privacy rules with respect to a work's dissemination may conceivably contradict the larger policy represented by the federal and state common law copyright rule that a writing, once published, should be subject only to the restrictions on use imposed by the federal copyright act. This is not, of course, to suggest that the legitimacy of state rules whose objectives are primarily not economic ought to be measured in the same fashion as that of state rules whose objectives are economic. Yet, the lawyer's instinctive aversion to comparing apples and oranges—noneconomic goals and economic interests—should not blur the fact that what is properly involved here is a comparison of economic effects and economic interests.

State and local obscenity rules seem even more urgent candidates for measurement against the national economic interests endorsed in *Kewanee*. The patchwork quality of state, and probably local, obscenity standards, though it may erect obstacles to the nationwide dissemination of literature, art, and motion pictures, does not necessarily imply that all production of questionable material will cease. The pornographer's trade can be expected to flourish, at prices, however, that may account for diminished production and distribution economies and increased risks of prosecution. Nor as a matter of economic effect does it seem probable that the flow of interstate commerce will be directly affected, with publishers in the mainstream producing for markets in some states but not others.

---

[46] See Goldstein, *Copyright and the First Amendment*, 70 COLUM. L. REV. 983, 1001–06 (1970).

What seems more likely is that mainstream publishers will, maintaining scale, choose for publication works whose content conforms to the blandest, most inoffensive norm adopted by the legislature in any state. And here the affront to expressed national interests becomes clearer. State and local rules will be used to curtail the dissemination of works whose production the copyright law seeks to encourage. While one of the constitutional guidelines for judging state obscenity rules announced in *Miller v. California*,[47] "whether the work, taken as a whole, lacks serious literary, artistic, political or scientific value," might appear to fit nicely with Congress's power under the copyright-patent clause, "to promote the progress of science and the useful arts," the fit seems academic at best.

The reason that measurement of the sort proposed—of the implications for national economic goals of any state law—has not been undertaken, at least for the exemplary cases just given, is, of course, that the challenge to state privacy and obscenity laws has characteristically been framed in terms of the First Amendment's free speech and press guarantees. Where the state rule in question is invalidated under these guarantees, there is naturally no reason for a court to inquire further whether the state rule similarly contradicts national interests in competition.[48] At the same time, when the state rule survives First Amendment scrutiny, judicial custom has been to treat the matter as at an end. It is in this second class of cases that further, unblinkered inquiry into economic effects, inquiry of the sort pursued in *Kewanee*, may be in order.

The difference between the approaches taken in *Sears* and *Kewanee* points to a larger distinction between the methods of the Warren and Burger Courts in these matters. Only the most superficial comparison would conclude that the distinction lies between the Warren Court's solicitude for the small, independent entrepreneur and its successor's attachment to big business. Sears, Roebuck, whose conduct was excused in *Sears*, hardly qualifies as a budding

---

[47] 413 U.S. 15, 24 (1973).

[48] There is, however, the more troubling question, whether inquiry ought to be pursued on the principle that although one constitutional command invalidates the state law, competitive interests may exonerate it. The questionable constitutional status of the stated national competitive interests concerned may deprive this principle of force and, in any event, in the two examples given, the First Amendment's generally accepted primacy would appear to finesse the questions altogether.

enterprise. In any event, the principle employed cut neutrally across all considerations of size. Nor is the distinction between a bias against and for the patent law and other systems of monopoly subsidy. The Burger Court has been quick, where the occasion required, to curtail the patent interest; in at least one case it overruled precedent to do so.[49] The distinction, rather, lies between the blunt, unexamined thrust of the early opinions and the methodical scrutiny of economic effects subsequently initiated by Justice Harlan in *Lear* and pursued in *Goldstein* and *Kewanee*, a method that marks Justice Harlan's and the Burger Court's signal contribution to decision in the field.

III. CONCLUSION

Kewanee, though subject to criticism for its failure expressly to overrule *Sears* and *Compco* and to expunge their broad preemptive method, is to be welcomed for its careful measurement of the effects of state law on national interests in competition. Yet, the Court's preoccupation with cautious empiricism regrettably shunted an equally sustained effort at explication of governing principles. Where *Sears* and *Compco* were short on facts, *Kewanee* was short on reason. Helpfully exemplifying the method for measuring the degree of fit between state economic mechanisms and competitive interests, *Kewanee* yields no clue as to the Court's willingness to take a position on a cognate matter: accommodation with competitive interests of state regulation of essentially noneconomic interests. Some explicit, principled formulation of the decision's informing logic, requiring the accommodation to competitive interests of state laws, whatever their objective, may be in order, for the guidance of lower courts, the business community and the bar.

---

[49] Blonder-Tongue Laboratories, Inc. v. University of Illinois Foundation, 402 U.S. 313 (1971).